MAKING HYPERMEDIA WORK

A User's Guide to HyTime

MAKING HYPERMEDIA WORK

A User's Guide to HyTime

Steven J. DeRose
Electronic Book Technologies

David G. Durand
Boston University

SPRINGER SCIENCE+BUSINESS MEDIA, LLC

ISBN 978-1-4613-6188-6 ISBN 978-1-4615-2754-1 (eBook)
DOI 10.1007/978-1-4615-2754-1

Library of Congress Cataloging-in-Publication Data

A C.I.P. Catalog record for this book is available from the Library of Congress.

Apple, HyperCard, HyperTalk, Macintosh, QuickDraw, QuickTime, and the Apple logo are trademarks of Apple Computer, Inc.
Author/Editor is a trademark of SoftQuad, Inc.
*Dyna*Text is a trademark of Electronic Book Technologies, Inc.
Internet is a trademark of Digital Equipment Corporation.
NoteCards is a trademark of Xerox.
PostScript is a trademark of Adobe Systems, Inc.
TEX is a trademark of the American Mathematical Society.
The X Window System is a trademark of the Massachusetts Institute of Technology.
UNIX is a trademark of AT&T.
Windows and RTF are trademarks of Microsoft Corporation.
Xanadu is a trademark of Xanadu Operating Company.
Any other trademarks are the property of their respective owners.

Printed on acid-free paper.

Contents

PART III

APPENDIXES

Foreword

HyTime is the first official standard for describing the structure of time-based hypermedia documents. Its marketplace acceptance is yet to come. This book, presenting the first in-depth guide to the HyTime specification, both describes its key features and provides guidelines on how it is used. It has been written by two leading experts in the field who have had significant impact on its development and are experts in SGML, the prior standard that HyTime extends.

HyTime represents a confluence of two technical fields and the socio-politico-economic standards process. The two technical fields, hypertext/hypermedia and document processing based on declarative markup, have been maturing over the last three decades. The first researcher to build a hypertext system, Doug Engelbart, in the late '50's articulated his vision for computer systems that would augment human intellect and in the mid-'60's built NLS (the oNLine System) to realize that vision; this monumental system pioneered, among other features, outline editing, journaling, significant linking facilities, and mouse-based interaction with text and graphics on raster displays. In 1967 Theodor Nelson, coiner of the word *hypertext*, co-designed with me and my students the Hypertext Editing System, the first hypertext system to run on commercial computer and display equipment. These early hypertext systems allowed users not just to create and follow links, but also to do interactive editing and word processing far more sophisticated than was available via the line editors of the day, as well as to specify formatting codes for subsequent batch processing and printout. Linear document production, however, was a byproduct, not the main purpose of these interactive authoring and browsing systems.

The second, much larger community worked on document production with increasingly sophisticated batch formatters. Here the leap forward was to replace procedural format codes and macros with declarative markup codes that separated the identification ("tagging") of document elements from their formatting, generalizing the commonly used format macros. In the 70's this idea was the focus of Charles Goldfarb's GML built at IBM and of Brian Reid's Ph.D. dissertation on Scribe at Carnegie-Mellon University.

While rich in functionality, both hypertext/hypermedia systems and document-production systems have been developed as closed, one-of-a-kind systems that force users to live on technology islands. Ted Nelson realized hypertext technology could make possible a universal, integrated super library or "docuverse;" however because of the lack of interoperability of today's closed systems, we have only "docuchaos." Standards, painful as they are to produce and implement and imperfect as they are by virtue of the politically charged process of compromise, at least have the virtue of being designed for interoperability. As one who has worked over several decades on 3D graphics standards, I am really pleased to see SGML taking off; already entire industry segments such as aerospace, telecommunications, and pharmaceuticals have agreed on DTDs (Document Type Definitions) that embody codes of practice for documentation in their industry, so that documents can be easily transmitted and exchanged, regardless of the systems used to author and present them. The firm hand of the DOD has certainly played a useful role here, through the CALS initiative. On the other side of the spectrum, humanists, in the Text Encoding Initiative, have labored to produce a comprehensive DTD for data interchange in literary research. And most encouraging, vendors of word-processing software such as WordPerfect™ have announced support for SGML and are providing both import to and export from their proprietary formats. The key reason to prefer SGML as the exchange format over industry standards such as PostScript™ and RTF™ is that the latter describe merely formatting, not structures that can be presented on display media in a variety of ways; SGML is more powerful because it retains the vital information that describes the document not as a collection of typeset pages but as hierarchy of multi-media elements.

But the designers of the HyTime standard foresaw that SGML would not be powerful enough to deal with time-based multi/hypermedia "documents," since it lacked support for many aspects of rich hypertext and time-based media. HyTime's hypertext features are sufficiently complete to provide a superset of the features in many hypermedia publishing systems available today, including, for example, Brown's Intermedia system and the World Wide Web. It handles multimedia by providing detailed means for specifying coordinate systems and ranges, without specifying the representation, storage and presentation of the media themselves. It has features for scheduling and synchronizing these media as well, though they will probably not be available in the first

HyTime engines. Thus HyTime will probably first be used primarily to encode hyperdocuments with text, sound, and 2D graphics and images. I hope that HyTime will open new areas of capability in synergy with industry proto-standards such as Apple's QuickTime that address related concerns.

Steve DeRose and Dave Durand are uniquely qualified to write the definitive book on HyTime. They are among the few with extensive experience in both hypermedia (since the late '70's) and in SGML (since the mid-'80's); a combination of expertise in both these areas still remarkably rare. Steve and Dave have published papers on SGML and mark-up theory. Steve is the chief architect of Electronic Book Technologies' *Dyna*Text system, the first commercially available SGML-based hypermedia publishing system, and wrote the SGML parser for that system. Both have been leaders in designing and documenting the hypertext part of the guidelines for the Text Encoding Initiative, as well as providing technical SGML advice to the project. Most importantly, at the first Hypertext Workshop in 1987 they advanced the first proposal for an SGML-based hypermedia system, and went on to influence the HyTime standard. Steve, for example, was a principal architect for HyQ, the query language of HyTime. Thus they write from deep experience and authority on HyTime, and have created a work that will be a key ingredient in the complex process of putting a standard into successful practice.

Andy van Dam
Providence, RI
January, 1994

Conventions

We use the following conventions to distinguish different types of names and references in this book:

- Terms being introduced and defined for the first time appear in **boldface roman** type. They are also listed in the index, and important ones appear in the glossary.
- Examples are printed in a `fixed-pitch` font and set off by space above and below.
- Examples that show how *not* to do something (counter-examples) also appear in a fixed-pitch font, but in *`italics`* to emphasize that they should not be used.
- SGML element type names, attribute names and values, and other strings that would appear literally in an SGML document are printed in a `fixed-pitch` font. SGML keywords, however, are in regular capital letters following common practice.
- Architectural form names (see section 5.3) appear in **`bold fixed pitch`** type, because they are HyTime constructs that need not appear literally in documents. When an architectural form name serves as an element name, as in many examples, it appears like other element names, not in bold.
- Functions from HyQ and other functional notations are fixed pitch with an initial capital letter and following parentheses, for example, `Select()`.
- References to the HyTime and SGML standards uniformly use "clause" before the clause, sub-clause, sub-sub-clause, annex, and other numbers.
- Cross-references within this book cite chapter and section number, and are preceded by "Section" or "Chapter."

Acknowledgments

We are grateful to many friends and colleagues who have helped us in our quest to make HyTime understandable, accessible, and therefore useful to more of those working with hypertext and electronic documents. Carl Harris, our editor at Kluwer Academic Publishers, was diligent in seeking out reviewers, encouraging us to keep going, and excelled in patience as the book grew longer and later than we anticipated. Very special thanks to Noah Landow for the art that graces the cover.

Our thinking about electronic documents and hypermedia owes much to the very active community studying such matters at Brown University. The Computing in the Humanities Users' Group, especially Geoffrey Bilder, John Lavagnino, Elli Mylonas, Allen Renear, Richard Ristow, and Mackenzie Smith, has for several years provided an ideal forum for discussion. Research groups ranging from the FRESS team, through the Institute for Research in Information and Scholarship, to the current Scholarly Technology Group, have also contributed many insights. The international Text Encoding Initiative has brought much light to the problems we study. Members David Barnard, Lou Burnard, Robin Cover, Ed Fox, Harry Gaylord, Michael Sperberg-McQueen, Syun Tutiya, Eve Wilson and many others deserve our especial thanks.

We also wish to thank Charles F. Goldfarb, the chair of the HyTime committee, and Steve Newcomb, the vice-chair, for creating HyTime and for many stimulating conversations and debates that have sharpened our understanding. Jim Mason, convener of the ISO/IEC Working Group on document description and processing languages under whose auspices HyTime was developed, has been very helpful, even dredging up early committee documents in record time. We also wish to thank Neill Kipp, Vicki Newcomb, Victor Riley, and all others from the HyTime committee.

Several reviewers gave extensive comments on manuscripts of this book. Most notable among them were David Barnard, whose recommendations on organization and clarity of presentation were very helpful, Yuri Rubinsky, who carefully reviewed two successive versions and provided much helpful critique, and Geoffrey Bilder and John Lavagnino, who each suggested many valuable improvements. Syd Bauman, Michael Bieber, Harvey Bingham, Laurie DeRose, Richard Furuta, Bob Glushko, Debbie LaPeyre, Michael Sperberg-McQueen, Hal Thompson, and Andries van Dam also provided helpful suggestions. Katrina Avery copy-edited the entire book with her well-known thoroughness and insight. We hope that our later modifications have maintained her standards.

Sharon Adler, Anders Berglund, Len Bullard, Dorothy Gross, Steve Newcomb, Chris Nuzum, Tom Reed, Eleanor Selfridge-Field, and others provided helpful comments on particular parts of the book. Robin Cover supplied important information and references, as did Jon Bosak, Paul Kahn, Tim Oren, Darrell Raymond, Brian Reid, Victor Riley, and others. Many of the students in our SGML and HyTime courses at the Hypertext '93 conference gave helpful feedback that led to improvements in the text.

The staff of the libraries at Brown University and Boston University, most especially Jenny Lee and Margaret Goostray, deserve special thanks for the extraordinary help they provided in locating examples of early hypertext-like documents and clearing the permissions needed to reproduce them. Their expertise, speed, and friendliness set a worthy example for the field.

We also wish to thank Electronic Book Technologies, its president Lou Reynolds, and the other staff there for many kinds of assistance including time in which to write, access to high-quality printers, and an environment of active investigation into the issues we discuss.

We have striven for accuracy, often consulting many people to find consensus on points not clear from published sources. Nevertheless both errors and differences of interpretation must remain, and these are our own. We welcome all suggestions for improvements from our readers. We can be reached most quickly by electronic mail: `sjd@ebt.com` and `dgd@bu.edu`.

Thanks to Todd and Despina for special typing help, and for keeping us smiling throughout the process. Finally and especially, we thank our wives, Laurie DeRose and Elli Mylonas, for patience and encouragement despite long hours, unpredictable working schedules, and other tribulations of authorship.

Steven J. DeRose, Ph.D., Electronic Book Technologies

David G. Durand, Boston University

March, 1994

Part I:

Introducing HyTime

1

Introduction

As soon as people began to create written works, the need arose to refer to them and to write down those references. Very early, works came to be identified by their author and title. Scholars developed formal ways of referring not only to entire works but to components of them: sometimes by pages, but more often in terms of significant structural portions such as chapters, verses, or lines of poetry. They also created combinations of related documents or editions, with the interrelationships indicated along with annotations, connections to related graphics and so on. Much the same methods have continued to the present day.

Modern libraries have also introduced standard cataloging systems, and publishers have created formal schemes for assigning unique numbers to books and editions. Both facilitate identifying and locating specific documents reliably, although additional methods must often be used to make references to more specific destinations.

Whatever the means of reference, the problem remains: how to retrieve a work once it is identified. Prior to the printing press this could be quite difficult; as the cost of books decreased and print runs increased, access became much simpler. Yet while one need no longer go to Alexandria to find a copy of certain books, one may wait a week to get them on interlibrary loan, or an hour to locate them in a library blocks away, or at best a take a minute to find the book on one's own shelf and flip to the right page.

Hypertext or **hypermedia** is the latest step in the quest to ease access to information in books and other media. It takes advantage of the fact that computers now store and communicate vast amounts of information cheaply. Using hypertext, one can retrieve a specific book, poem, picture, recording, or movie regardless of whether the copy is stored locally or across the world. This is normally accomplished when one notices a special marker, which indicates a hypertext link or **hyperlink**. Choosing a link (perhaps by clicking on it with a mouse), causes the computer to retrieve some other information and display it. Consider a few of the links that would be useful in this very section:

- One should be able to indicate the word "Alexandria" and request a map, historical information and some explanation of why we chose to mention it, instead of some other city. This should be possible whether or not the supplemental information has been specially prepared for linking.
- One should be able to point to the word "hypertext" and request a definition or a list of sources that discuss it further. On finding out that the term hypertext was coined by Theodor Nelson and is discussed in his book *Literary Machines*, one should be able to retrieve information about the book, or even its content, immediately (perhaps in a choice of editions and translations and with its own links to yet other information).
- One should be able to create marginal notes while reading the document, mark places and treat it in other ways much as one would a book.
- Should this document be available in multiple editions or translations, one should be able to coordinate them smoothly, viewing corresponding parts on demand or even simultaneously.

To accomplish such tasks, the computer must have a formal way of referring to things: of giving them unique names by which it can reliably find them. This act of naming and using names for components of information is required for hypertext, and HyTime provides an internationally agreed-upon method for expressing such names in a way that computers can understand and use.

HyTime was developed as a hypermedia representation through the work and cooperation of many people in many countries, in a committee of the International Organization for Standardization chaired by Charles F. Goldfarb. The standard's formal name is: *ISO/IEC 10744:*

Hypermedia/Time-based Structuring Language. It grew out of earlier work on representations for music and structured documents, two quite different endeavors. It provides a standardized way to express structures known through hypertext/hypermedia research over the last 25 years, and through its non-computerized forerunners over a far longer time.

The greatest value of HyTime is that it provides a standard way of representing connections to information, so that they can be created, processed and exchanged. In particular, it deals with structured information and the ability to link to and from specific components of its structure. It can support data is any notation desired, and has very effective constructs to support the basic hierarchical component structure of most documents. It can overlay cross-references and other connections (which can also constitute components of documents) onto any data representation from ASCII email files to complex multimedia data collections.

In this book we begin with the more familiar structures of books, graphics, cross-references, and the like, and detail the HyTime constructs and models used to identify, locate, and link data. With this foundation we go on to introduce some of HyTime's mechanisms for linking multidimensional, multi-media data, and for scheduling it in space and time. However, we spend limited time on these more advanced aspects, instead aiming to help the reader become fluent in HyTime as it applies to the simpler and most widely understood data types. Having mastered this level of HyTime, readers will be ready and able to explore the exciting potential of HyTime for more sophisticated multimedia applications.

Awareness is growing throughout the world that *data outlasts computer programs*, in the same way that an aircraft manual long outlasts any typewriter, word processor, or other tool used to create it. It is best, then, to represent data in ways that are as independent as possible of particular programs or technologies. Only by putting information into simple, well defined, generic representations can one preserve, re-use and connect that information to other information in the future. A standard representation makes it possible for the many people creating information in electronic form to benefit from each other's work, rather than being trapped on "information islands" where they can access only data created using specific programs.

One such representation already exists and is in widespread use: an earlier ISO standard called the Standard Generalized Markup Language, or SGML. This standard is the foundation for HyTime because HyTime uses SGML as the syntax for representing links (more about this later). SGML is a very general method that is widely used for representing document structures for word processing, information retrieval, document interchange and online delivery. Using the same representation for linking information is quite convenient.

International standards, like the inch, the volt, or musical pitch, are not owned by any company. They avoid prejudice toward particular programs or styles of interface, in favor of describing fundamental structures needed in any such programs, irrespective of how they may be implemented at a particular time.

One important application of both SGML and HyTime is as a *lingua franca: a* common language into which you can translate hypertexts in order to get them from one application program to another. For example, one of the authors wrote a short HyperCard™ program that can convert any HyperCard stack into SGML (such structures consist of stacks, backgrounds, cards, fields, buttons, links and various kinds of data content and scripts), while the other has done so for FRESS, an early mainframe hypertext system developed at Brown University. Others have written similar converters for other hypertext systems (for instance, see Bornstein and Riley 1990).

Meetings of the HyTime committee were open: all contributions were welcomed and considered. If a need was shown, every effort was made to find a way to meet it in the spirit of developing as useful a standard as possible. Moreover, the committee members (who included potential users, hardware and software vendors and researchers) spent many late nights trying to find solutions that would cover not only current, specific problems, but learning what more general principles the problems reflect and handling those as well.

Nelson has envisioned and described a world in which all information could be interchanged, communicated, annotated and viewed without the painful barriers of incompatibility we experience today. Although that utopia has not arrived, one can begin to see it in the distance as more people, companies and entire fields of inquiry begin to use generic computer representations instead of proprietary ones.

1.1 Purpose and scope of this book

This book discusses how the HyTime standard can be applied to real-world problems of navigating from here to there in collections of documents. The HyTime standard itself provides enabling methods and templates for various information structures such as links and various kinds of location indicators. A **HyTime application** specifies how a group applies those templates to their particular requirements. This involves choosing which HyTime structures are needed, setting up conventions for how they are to be used and setting up management and processes for creation, conversion and update of hypermedia documents. A **HyTime engine** is the last ingredient: actually using an application typically involves choosing software to support one's use of HyTime and customizing it as needed. This may be as simple as setting up hypertextual style sheets that determine how links and other things look and act. More specialized applications may require full-scale design and programming.

Like the HyTime standard, this book takes terms such as "document" and "hypertext" in their broad sense: they include everything from a one page memo to a collection of interrelated video and sound productions, and much more. What HyTime provides is a way of referring to any part of such a work from any part of another. Because works vary greatly in their structure, HyTime provides a wide variety of general reference mechanisms. We devote more time to those that have proven to be the more familiar and most widely useful, and provide guidelines and suggestions for using the standard wisely and effectively.

HyTime is a large and complex standard, and takes time to learn. Some users will need only the overview we provide in the first part. Authors and publishers creating HyTime documents will need to go further. HyTime has a definite point of view on information structures and from that perspective many of its features are integrated and even obvious, even though in isolation they may seem opaque. Throughout this book we will try to help you develop the ability to think in HyTime. The basic ideas involved are few — but their combinations and potential uses are unlimited. As you become familiar with the general approach and viewpoint HyTime takes, that familiarity will make the details of HyTime syntax and semantics easier to learn: they will fit together into a coherent whole.

We draw many examples from actual data, some of it current and some of it created long ago. SGML and HyTime are successful as a modern representation for the hypertextual aspects of centuries-old print works, for documents created with some of the earliest hypertext systems (from the late 1960s), and for documents created using cutting edge technology in fields from English literature to military weapons systems and computer software documentation. That SGML has already worked so widely and well is an indication of how well the approach taken by SGML and HyTime can elegantly solve an enormous range of problems.

We draw our examples more heavily from media such as text, structured documents, and still graphics than from sound, motion video, and other newer technologies. The most important reason for this is that such examples permit briefer and simpler explanations, and are accessible to a greater share of readers. Our emphasis should not be taken as detracting from the importance of the wider range of media. Full-motion video, interactive animation, and other technologies are already very important and we believe they are sure to become more so. We also believe that after mastering the level of HyTime we present here the reader will be fluent enough to apply HyTime in these additional domains. Most HyTime principles apply equally in all media: coordinates, measurement in space and time, and models of linking work in much the same way regardless of the number of dimensions involved.

1.2 What is HyTime for?

HyTime is intended to represent interconnections within and between components of information in computer-processable form. It accordingly provides a generic way of saving data as well as information about its associated links and correspondences so that a HyTime compatible system can use it easily. HyTime is capable of storing references to other data formats (such as multimedia or other specialized application data), and specifying intended placements of the data in place and time. Because of this, data can be stored in the most convenient representation for display, editing, or use by other applications. HyTime's SGML-based representations will be most useful for some purposes; for others specialized representations for graphics or the like will be most useful and HyTime will be used to represent the linkage and structure of externally stored information.

Most current applications follow the interchange paradigm and convert information between HyTime and a proprietary internal format. There is nothing wrong with this so long as they keep enough information to get equivalent HyTime back out later. As happened with SGML, systems may be developed that use HyTime as their native language. Systems can use HyTime to integrate the full range of work one does with hypertexts, from creation, review, and revision through publication, distribution, and reader-level actions such as annotation and commentary.

A full-featured integrated HyTime environment would include tools for creating, editing, managing, and delivering hypermedia documents. We sketch how one might fit together in Section 5.5.

In such a HyTime environment, authors can create data in whatever media and representations they choose and bring them together to form complete documents and presentations via an authoring interface. They can create hypertextual connections between and within components of their documents, which are stored in the structure and link database. When it is time to publish, the data can be assembled and optimized to build a distributable document, which readers then view and perhaps annotate, much as they would a book. Even the details of timing, relative placement, and compounding of data can be specified.

1.3 What can HyTime do?

Because you can interconnect data of all kinds with HyTime, you can use it as a key component in almost any kind of interface for displaying, processing and navigating through information. Much of that information may be in SGML, but it need not be. Whether or not your data or documents are in SGML, you can use HyTime for a variety of purposes:

- Creating hypertext links from and to points, components, regions, or spans within and among SGML documents and associated multimedia information. Such applications are relatively simple and a good place to start. We will discuss them and give many examples throughout this book.
- Building systems to help in production and review of new documents by letting editors attach sticky notes, recommend structural changes, make new hypertext connections, track workflow and amend the document as they develop a final version.
- Viewing existing books in electronic form, with added capabilities such as making marginal notes, recording the path the reader has followed, doing full text search and information filtering, along with instant access to figures, cross-references and attachments.
- Managing documents that are studied and discussed in fine detail, such as Biblical, Classical, legal, or medical texts. Such documents may exist in many editions or translations, as well as variant manuscript or print versions, which can be viewed in parallel, compared, and searched as needed.
- Providing a framework for smoothly coordinating sequences and combinations of various media: slides, audio, video and even computer-specific media such as computer animation or expert systems for diagnosis and repair. (See Feiner, Nagy and van Dam 1981, Feiner 1988).
- Tracking events such update and display operations to build systems to record responsibility for changes or enforce varying levels of security access to data.

You can accomplish all these things even with data on CD-ROM or other read only media, because HyTime supports links stored separately from the data linked. This allows hypertext links both into and out of data that cannot be modified.

1.4 How to use this book

HyTime builds upon other standards and conventions. Part I of this book, "Introducing HyTime," presents valuable background information on how this all fits together and will be useful to all kinds of readers. Managers and administrators can read it to get an overview of SGML and HyTime concepts and some examples of how HyTime can be applied to document systems of various kinds.

Designers of HyTime applications will need to continue into Part II to learn the details of how HyTime works for basic hypermedia applications that link together structured documents and multimedia data. Part II goes through the syntax and interpretation of HyTime constructs in detail, but only for the most widely needed parts. Some HyTime application designers, as well as any implementers of HyTime software, will need to go on to Part III, which addresses the next level of HyTime complexity and introduces many (though not all) of the more rarefied aspects of the standard. A few portions of Part III may be useful to less advanced users with specialized needs; other sections refer the reader there when appropriate. There are some specialized aspects of HyTime that this book merely mentions, or does not discuss at all; few users will need these. Users who have unmet needs after reading this book and HyTime implementors will need to use the HyTime standard itself, but will find that the introduction presented here will make the standard more accessible.

Part I discusses basic concepts of hypertext/hypermedia and explains what HyTime is about and what it can help you accomplish. Chapter 3 reviews briefly some crucial SGML concepts. SGML is an important prerequisite for understanding HyTime. You should not skip this unless you are very sure of your SGML fluency, both in terms of its general approach and its syntax. HyTime uses SGML syntax to encode its structures (remember, only HyTime linking information needs to be encoded with SGML; the data being linked can be in any format desired). One excellent book to help you get started in SGML is van Herwijnen 1994. There is also an electronic version of the book's first edition published with Electronic Book Technologies' *Dyna*Text software as the *SGML Tutorial* (van Herwijnen 1993).

Chapter 4 illustrates the basic terminology and structure of HyTime through a series of simple examples. It also describes the "architectural form" notion, which is crucial to understanding how HyTime defines elements and attributes. Chapter 5 then goes into more detail on how HyTime fits together and gives more detail on some important concepts, including the concept of "modules," the major divisions of the HyTime standard.

An extended example of how HyTime can be applied to existing markup schemes is given in Chapter 10 of Part II, which discusses making World Wide Web data HyTime compatible. It can be read without going through the rest of Part II, although some terms and concepts may not be clear at that point. Managers or users who want to get a feel for how HyTime works in practice may wish to turn to Chapter 10 early, and then go back to the rest of Part II to fill in the details.

Part II describes the portions of HyTime of widest general applicability and importance. Among these are the Location address and Hyperlinks modules, that provide the tools for creating links. We also include here HyQ, HyTime's mechanism for query and search, which we consider one of the most useful and flexible parts of HyTime. We also discuss how to take existing documents and modify them for use with HyTime, and provide an extended example.

Part III covers most of the remaining parts of HyTime, including more advanced features of the modules already discussed and additional modules that we expect will be needed by fewer of HyTime's users. The chapters in Part III are mostly independent, and can be read in any order once Part II has been understood. Users who need to explore the fine details of the standard can obtain it as ISO standard 10744. In the US it is available from:

American National Standards Institute
11 West 42nd Street, 13th floor
New York, NY 10036 USA
Phone 212-642-4900, fax 212-302-1286

Several appendixes follow the main text. Appendix A presents the "HyTime meta-DTD," which is HyTime's way of defining the structures and information it uses to represent hyperdocuments. The meta-DTD forms the basis for actual SGML Document Type Declarations for HyTime hyperdocuments. Appendix B provides a set of formal names that we believe readers will find useful for dealing with many modern graphic formats. Appendix C provides an index to HyTime constructs, with cross-references to where they are discussed in the HyTime standard itself.

After the appendixes we include a Glossary of useful definitions, a Bibliography and an extensive subject and term Index, including references to the explanations of each HyTime construct.

2

Hypermedia Concepts

2.1 Introduction

This chapter describes the basic concepts and issues of hypermedia and hypertext as well as examining some of the industry and technical forces that make HyTime a powerful and promising solution to some real problems in hypermedia interchange. We begin with a historical example that introduces the basic points as well as stressing that the notions of hypertext are not really new: the basic problems it addresses have been with us almost since the beginning of writing. It is rather the technology for solving these problems that has changed.

A brief note on terminology is in order. We use the term "hypertext" in its original sense (in which all forms of media are included) and interchangeably with the term "hypermedia." While we occasionally also use "hypermedia" to emphasize the relevance of multimedia, our use of the term "hypertext" does not exclude other media. Similarly, we use the term *document* in a generic way to refer to any integrated piece of information. We introduce many notions in this chapter; some of them will be redefined later in special senses as HyTime technical terms.

We believe that hypermedia systems can structure data to take advantage of the wide range of experience gained by years of book production, as well as take advantage of the many possibilities introduced by computer technology. Ironically, some of the design issues were more thoroughly addressed in the earliest experimental systems than in many of today's products. We see HyTime's flexibility and scope as a real advantage here since its approach is not targeted to one application but can address a very wide range of possible solutions.

We hope also to impart some balance to the "hype" in "hypertext." While hypertext systems are already having significant effects in simplifying the mechanical chores involved in reading, writing and research, hypertext is a technology for writing and display — not a magic ingredient that will automatically improve information delivery. Powerful hypertext systems are *at least* as dependent as books on good writing and organization. We believe that online document design demands even greater skill and art than for paper.

2.2 Print examples of hyperdocuments

The kinds of interconnection that modern hypermedia automates are not new. They have been present in paper publications for millennia, and many have continued to the present in almost identical forms. Figures 2.1 and 2.2 show pages 31 and 93 of a 1647 edition of *Clement, the blessed Paul's fellow-labourer in the gospel, his first epistle to the Corinthians.* The book contains an additional document:*Certaine annotations upon Clement*, a commentary heavily interlinked with the first. With the kind permission of the Boston University Library we have reproduced here one page from each of these parts, Figure 2.1 being from Clement's work, and 2.2 being from the commentary.

One of the more surprising things about this document is how similar many of its conventions are to those of modern books, manuals, and other documents. We can easily identify in these and other pages of the document very modern-sounding structural components, that can be represented without difficulty in SGML:

- The title of the book is prominently displayed; the book is divided into smaller sections as well, whose titles are also emphasized by large type, centering, and font changes, though not so strongly as the book title. The current chapter is reinforced by running heads on every page.
- Paragraphs are apparent by their indentation.

- Quotations are indicated in a more unusual way to the contemporary eye, by the use of an italic font.
- Words with particular significance, such as the names of other authors, appear in italics.

Many of the other structures indicated, however, reflect hypertextual connections of various kinds. The margins of the pages in both the sections of text and commentary contain Roman numerals indicating points of correspondence between the texts.

These marginal numbers also match superscript markers in the text, and appear to indicate page numbers from a prior edition. They serve as a scanning aid to help readers quickly reach a desired reference point, while the superscripts in the text mark the exact location of the earlier edition's page breaks.

Link XLVI, for instance, connects a discussion of Clement's phrase "our High Priest and Ruler" to the phrase itself. Given that the reader cannot conveniently read both pages at one, there is what hypertext researchers call a "transclusion," where content is not only referenced but copied into the referencing context (in this case, the commentary).

Other pages show similar treatments for features of Clement's manuscript, even linking a lacuna (a place where the original text has been lost) indicated by a long row of asterisks, to a commentary on that lacuna. That part of the commentary has its own link in turn: a cross-reference to the notes of a previous edition. The author then suggests possible completions of the missing text based on other Greek authors of Clement's time.

Scripture passages are often cited in the margin using the standard chapter/verse ID system. In the commentary, citations of quoted text (some of which are in Greek) are connected to the prose by superscript symbols or letters. For instance, a comment in the work regarding a Dr. Homes is linked via a small superscript "m" to a marginal note with the citation of his work by title and page range.

Also present, but easily overlooked because we take them for granted, are many conventional markers providing anchor points by which other documents can refer to specific parts of this one. The page numbers obviously serve this function, as well as facilitating locating a document portion once it has been referenced.

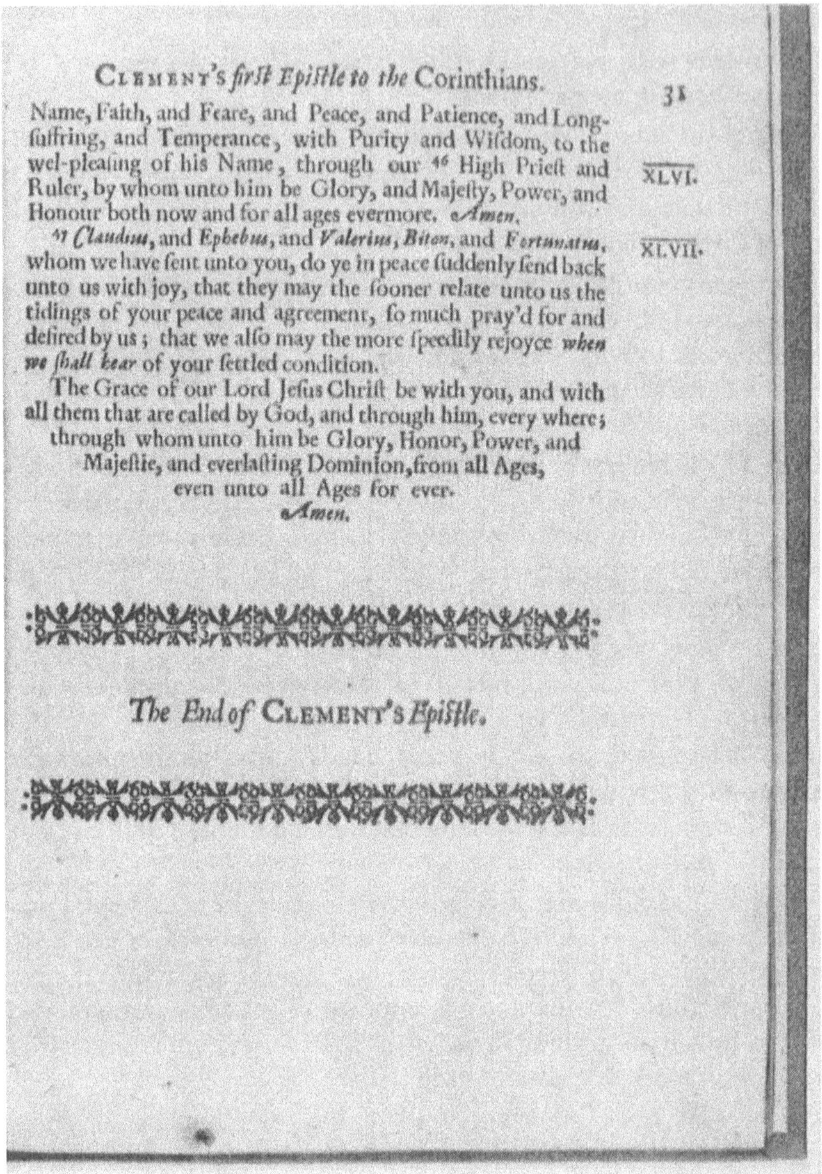

CLEMENT's *first Epistle to the* Corinthians. 31

Name, Faith, and Feare, and Peace, and Patience, and Long-
suffring, and Temperance, with Purity and Wisdom, to the
wel-pleasing of his Name, through our [46] High Priest and XLVI.
Ruler, by whom unto him be Glory, and Majesty, Power, and
Honour both now and for all ages evermore. *Amen.*

[47] *Claudius*, and *Ephebus*, and *Valerius*, *Biton*, and *Fortunatus*, XLVII.
whom we have sent unto you, do ye in peace suddenly send back
unto us with joy, that they may the sooner relate unto us the
tidings of your peace and agreement, so much pray'd for and
desired by us; that we also may the more speedily rejoyce *when
we shall hear* of your settled condition.

The Grace of our Lord Jesus Christ be with you, and with
all them that are called by God, and through him, every where;
through whom unto him be Glory, Honor, Power, and
Majestie, and everlasting Dominion, from all Ages,
even unto all Ages for ever.
Amen.

The End of CLEMENT's *Epistle.*

Figure 2.1: Clement's Epistle

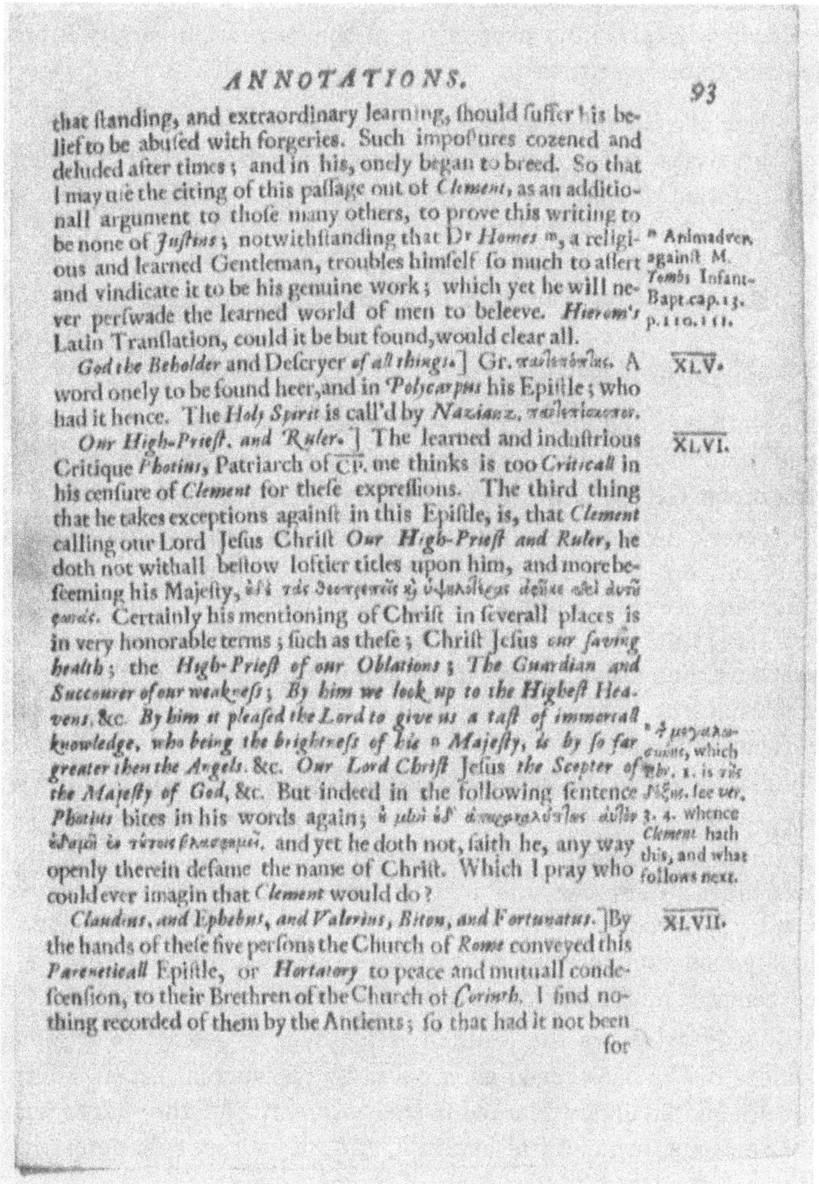

ANNOTATIONS. 93

that ſtanding, and extraordinary learning, ſhould ſuffer his belief to be abuſed with forgeries. Such impoſtures cozened and deluded after times; and in his, onely began to breed. So that I may uſe the citing of this paſſage out of *Clement*, as an additionall argument to thoſe many others, to prove this writing to be none of *Juſtins*; notwithſtanding that Dr *Homes* m, a religious and learned Gentleman, troubles himſelf ſo much to aſſert and vindicate it to be his genuine work; which yet he will never perſwade the learned world of men to beleeve. *Hierom's* Latin Tranſlation, could it be but found, would clear all.

m Animadver. againſt M. *Tombs* Infant-Bapt. cap. 13. p. 110. 111.

XLV. *God the Beholder* and Deſcryer *of all things.*] Gr. [illegible]. A word onely to be found heer, and in *Polycarpus* his Epiſtle; who had it hence. The *Holy Spirit* is call'd by *Nazianz.* [illegible].

XLVI. *Our High-Prieſt, and Ruler.*] The learned and induſtrious Critique *Photius*, Patriarch of CP. me thinks is too *Criticall* in his cenſure of *Clement* for theſe expreſſions. The third thing that he takes exceptions againſt in this Epiſtle, is, that *Clement* calling our Lord Jeſus Chriſt *Our High-Prieſt and Ruler*, he doth not withall beſtow loftier titles upon him, and more beſeeming his Majeſty, [illegible]. Certainly his mentioning of Chriſt in ſeverall places is in very honorable terms; ſuch as theſe; Chriſt Jeſus *our ſaving health*; the *High-Prieſt of our Oblations*; *The Guardian and Succourer of our weakneſs*; *By him we look up to the Higheſt Heavens*, &c. *By him it pleaſed the Lord to give us a taſt of immortall knowledge, who being the brightneſs of his* n *Majeſty, is by ſo far greater then the Angels.* &c. *Our Lord Chriſt* Jeſus *the Scepter of the Majeſty of God*, &c. But indeed in the following ſentence *Photius* bites in his words again; [illegible] and yet he doth not, ſaith he, any way openly therein defame the name of Chriſt. Which I pray who could ever imagin that *Clement* would do?

n [illegible], which *Heb.* 1. is [illegible], ſee ver. 3. 4. whence *Clement* hath this, and what follows next.

XLVII. *Claudius, and Ephebus, and Valerius, Biton, and Fortunatus.*] By the hands of theſe five perſons the Church of *Rome* conveyed this *Pareneticall* Epiſtle, or *Hortatory* to peace and mutuall condeſcenſion, to their Brethren of the Church of *Corinth.* I find nothing recorded of them by the Antients; ſo that had it not been

for

Courtesy: Special Collections, Boston University Library

Figure 2.2 Certaine Annotations

Our second example is from an early geometry book, published in 1661, reproduced with the kind permission of the Brown University Library. The rather imposing title is:

> Euclid's Elements of geometry. In XV. books: with a supplement of divers propositions and corollaries. To which is added, a treatise of regular solids, by Campane and Flussas. Likewise Euclid's data: and Marinus his preface thereunto annexed. Also a treatise of the divisions of superficies, ascribed to Machomet Bagdedine, but published by Commandine, at the request of John Dee of London; whose preface to the said treatise declares it to be the worke of Euclide, the author of these Elements.

The work was "Published by the care and industry of John Leeke and George Serle, students in the mathematicks. London: Printed, by R. & W. Leybourn, for George Sawbridge... 1661."

This work uses many of the same linking and structure conventions as Clement, but is most remarkable for its inclusion of 3-dimensional displays that serve as primitive scientific visualization tools. Figure 2.3 is a page from this work discussing the nature of pyramids with different polygons as their bases. The original publication includes fold-out paper figures that the reader can assemble to make the 3d shapes being discussed: "I have here set two sundry Pyramids which will appeare bodilike, if ye erecte the papers wherin are drawen the triangular side of eche Pyramis...."

In addition to various inline and marginal topic headings, the book has in-text cross-references and a very large collection of references to particular lettered locations on the geometric models. Page, section, and other division numbers permit accurate reference, so that readers can follow complex mathematical arguments.

Also of interest are the frequent references to geometric arguments elsewhere in the book, used as support for the current proof. Alternate proofs are quoted and attributed to their originators. Other pages include figure captions, ornamental capitals, and, of course, side-notes tied to locations in the text by asterisks or other markers.

Many other examples anticipating hypertext linking, indexing, and graphics can be found. Their authors had many of the same goals and methods as today, however limited their technology. Despite the obvious differences, we find a striking similarity of structure and basic techniques along the continuum connecting these early works with the most modern hypertexts.

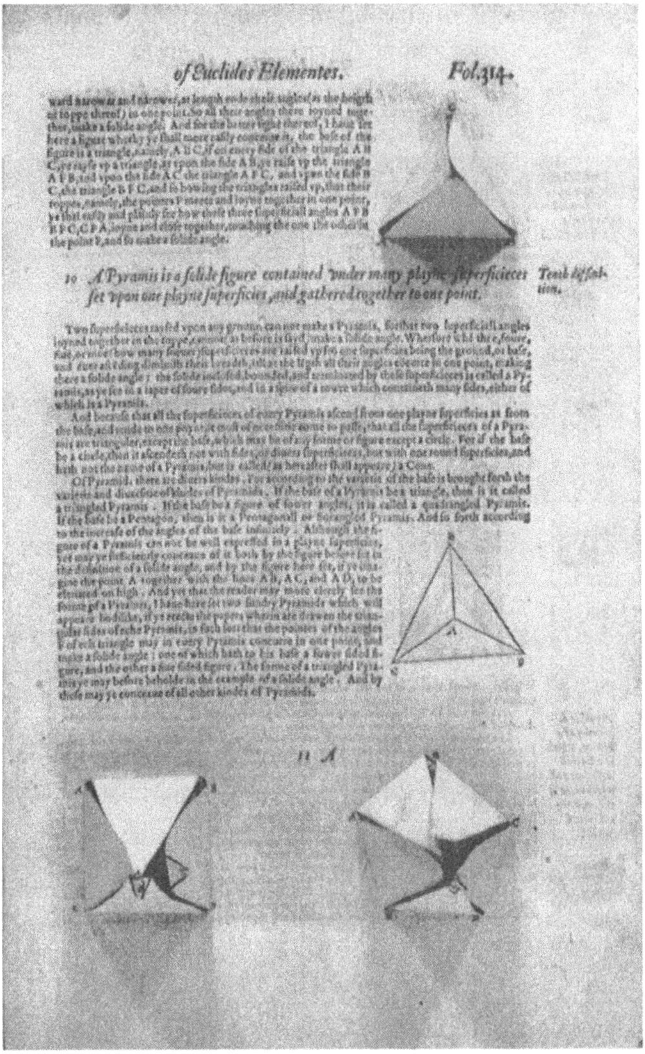

of Euclides Elementes. Fol.314.

10 A Pyramis is a solide figure contained under many playne superficieces set upon one playne superficies, and gathered together to one point.

Figure 2.3: Euclid's Elementes

Figure 2.4 below shows a modern online computer software manual (reproduced with the generous permission of Novell). The basic document structure is indicated by the typography, just as it was nearly 350 years earlier. Many structures, including paragraphs, sections of various levels, lists and so on, are the same. More interestingly, links are present serving most of the same purposes.

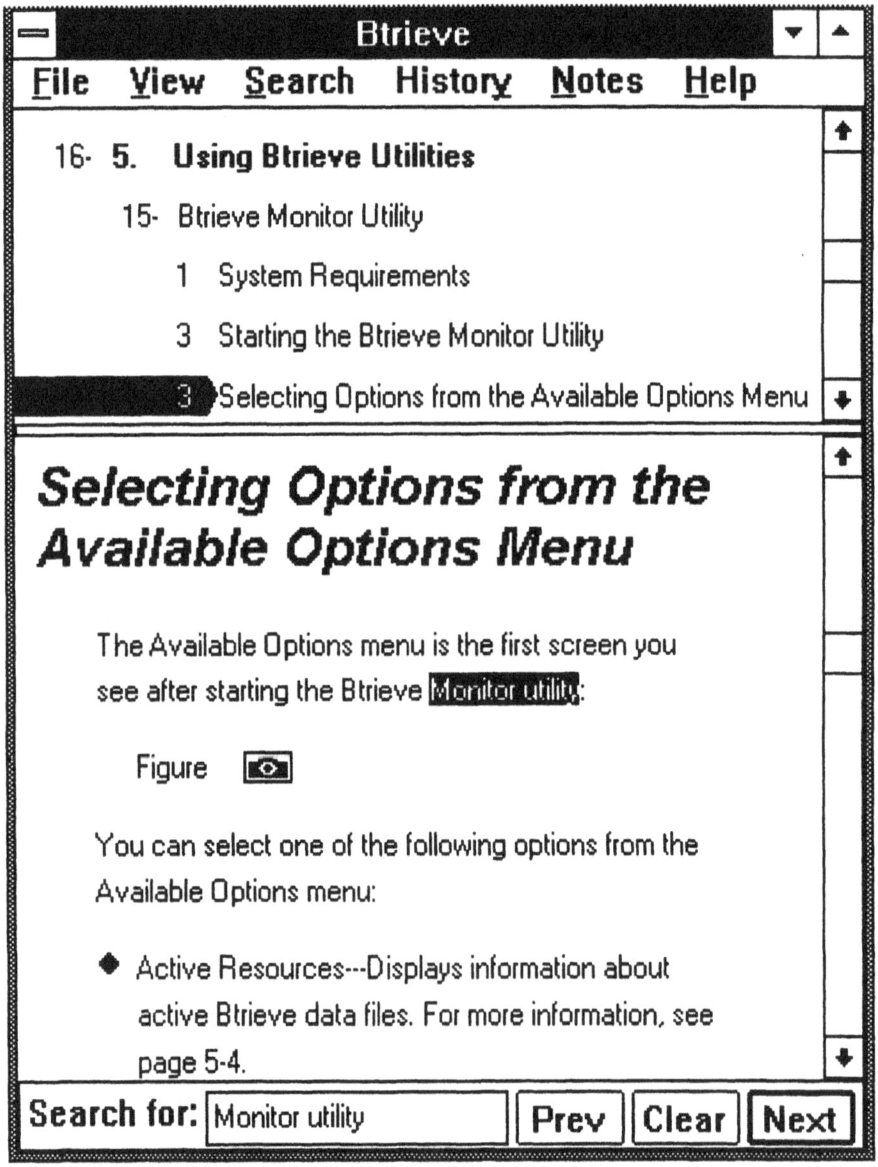

Figure 2.4 A modern structured hyperdocument

In this modern example there are cross-references to graphics, to specific locations in other documents, and words that can be clicked to access glossaries or supplemental information by search. Figures can also be accessed by clicking on references to them. Section numbers ease access as they always have, and some cross-references use them directly.

Marginal displays such as Biblical references and subject headings are seldom used now except in critical commentaries; instead, cross-references are usually placed inline ("see section 12"). They may also be put in footnotes and connected to places in the document by number, a technique used at least as long ago as in Jan Amos Comenius' encyclopedia, published around 1650.

The modern manual of Figure 2.4 exists in a very similar form on paper, but now benefits from automating both formatting and navigation through the use of hypertext software. The problems of referring and connecting to precise editions and locations within documents are not new, nor are the basic approaches to their solution. However, the computer can retrieve the destination of a reference so quickly and easily that it can make an enormous improvement in usability.

2.3 Documents and links

Analysis of printed documents (most especially reference documents) shows that a strikingly large number of different kinds of organizational devices are involved. The crafts of the book designer and typesetter are devoted to clarifying visually both the variety and the interrelations of the many kinds of information on a page.

Documents have two kinds of structure that vary in relative importance but are almost always present in some form:

- An organization (whether simple or complex) of the document's content. For example, technical manuals typically have a deeply hierarchical structure of sections and subsections, while newspapers have a much flatter structure with many loosely related stories and little nesting.
- An overlaid structure of cross-references that interconnects portions of the content and also connects the document to other portions of itself and other documents.

These two kinds of structure are as fundamental to paper documents as to hyperdocuments. The difference between these structures is sometimes obscured in hypertexts by the fact that a program provides both a document structure and a linking structure in a single package. HyTime itself describes just the overlay of link structures, but due to its building on the foundation of SGML it has access to an especially rich document structure.

2.3.1 Document structures

Many issues arise in the choice of fundamental document structures. While link structures can be separated from the underlying media almost entirely, document structures cannot because they are fundamentally involved with content. In this section we indicate some structures entailed by other media. We also note that the organization of video and audio will be augmented over the next few decades, as the flexibility of random access to these media is exploited more fully. The basic structures are streams, hierarchies, the composite of these two, and cards. We discuss the first three structures below and the last in Section 2.3.4, after the discussion of links on which it depends.

Document structures should not be confused with linking structure. Hypertext links function as connections that cross whatever structure documents and data have. For example, links in a hierarchical document reach across the hierarchy, just as links in a card based system can reach across cards.

Streams

A **stream** is a linear sequence of data. Streams are a fundamental part of all text structures, since texts require that a sequence of words be presented to a reader. Streams nearly always include some non-word components such as punctuation and spaces. A stream may also be interrupted by embedded markers, but those markers indicate *events* (such as starting a new line or including a figure) rather than *scopes* (such as whole paragraphs or other components).

In a stream there is no principled distinction between selecting a unit such as a paragraph or a list, and selecting a random fragment of information between any two points. This provides flexibility in cutting and pasting, at the cost of sometimes odd consequences when editing. For example, something formatted as a particular kind of component may change due to minor or seemingly unrelated edits. This is because there is no actual component to which the appearance is attached; instead, the appearance follows from the sequence of preceding formatting signals.

Editors using steam models have difficulty supporting larger units. For example, a list is not a whole object but a sequence of items. This makes dynamic renumbering during edits difficult; with embedded lists it becomes virtually impossible.

This document model is the basis of most word processors. It has the advantage of simplicity, but in many contexts that simplicity has proved limiting. Streams are the only document structure currently available for video, audio, and other time based media. For such media, the individual items in the stream are video frames, sound samples, and the like; one cannot refer to bounded objects, such as a wheel in a picture of a car.

Hierarchies

In the hierarchical model of document structures, objects such as paragraphs, lists and chapters can actually exist. They can contain other objects, such as graphics, other sections, hypertext links, and so on. At the lowest level are small streams that contain the actual words or multimedia objects of the document. Some of the advantages of using hierarchical documents are shown by the simple example below; see DeRose, Durand, Mylonas and Renear 1990 for a fuller discussion.

Many documents contain paragraphs interrupted by a picture (as above), or by a list of points indicated with bullets or other markers. When the paragraph resumes, convention dictates that no indentation should appear (because the text following the list is a continuation of the paragraph). This is easy to arrange with a hierarchical document structure: the paragraph can contain text, followed by a bulleted list, followed by more text. On the other hand, a stream structured file cannot have containers, so must have two sorts of paragraph *separators*: one indicating that the text following is a paragraph, and one indicating it is a paragraph continuation.

Editors supporting hierarchical structures can provide tools and techniques to operate directly on document components of all kinds. Because the system has explicit knowledge of larger units such as lists, sections, and other aggregate components, it can provide useful operations on them such as automatic selection, validation and component-level editing.

Composites

It is possible to create a system that combines hierarchies and streams, although this has not been common (FRESS was such a system). A composite system provides editing and other operations that can operate on arbitrary spans and scopes, as well as on hierarchical units as such. It can then express formatting or other processing using either paradigm: a paragraph, for example, can either be treated as a point event that causes a new line, or as a container of a given type, whose type then determines the processing to be applied within its scope.

2.3.2 Link structures

At first glance, the notion of a **link** seems monolithic. It is a cross-reference embedded in a document that leads either to another document or to another place in the same document. While some systems have adopted this simple model, it is less than satisfactory even for conventional paper documents. A bibliographic citation, for instance, has several components:

- The citation itself is a marker that tells the reader that other relevant information exists.
- The reference associated with this marker shows where the actual information can be found.
- The referenced information should exist somewhere for the reference to be useful.

The citation and the bibliographic entry are both explicit constructs, while the referenced information is implicit. A cross-reference asserts the mutual relevance of the citing and cited regions. In the case of the source of a bibliographic link, the relevant scope of the citing discussion is often implicit in the phrases introducing the reference. A sentence such as "Smith (1997) gives a clear discussion of the theory that underlies this chapter" makes explicit the relevant scope within the citing document. Bibliographic entries also indicate the appropriate portion of the work cited by reference to pages, chapters, figure numbers, or other specifications.

Parts of a hypertext link

Hypertext systems need exactly the same notions. The linked regions of documents are called **anchors.** An anchor could be a point in an image or text stream, a subcomponent such as a list, a video frame, a visual object in an animation, or any other piece of data.

A reference to an anchor is called a **locator**, and is any structure that, like a bibliographic reference, specifies how to find the anchor. It might also provide information about how the anchor is to be treated, for example imposing special formatting.

A **link** is a collection of locators, and expresses their connection. Within the link, each locator serves as one **linkend**. Each linkend of a particular link might have a comment to indicate its relevance, or other information useful for processing. A kind of link or an individual instance might specify information about the connection, such as the number of linkends, the particular kind of relationship between them, or whether the link can be traversed in one direction or both. A link may also assign **anchor roles** to each of its ends, the most common being *source* and *destination*.

Kinds of locations

Systems vary greatly in the **granularity** of the anchors they support. Some provide links only to anchors that are of one size and type: entire documents, pages, whole paragraphs, etc. A more flexible approach supports **fine-grained anchors** that can address portions of documents of any size, large or small. One special type of anchor deserves mention since it is not uncommon in hypertext systems: the **point anchor**. Sometimes a locator can be thought of as specifying not a piece of a document, but only a location. Point anchors usually occupy the space between characters in a text, a coordinate in a graphical document, or a point in time in a document like a video or piece of music. They can be thought of as milestones in a stream structure.

The granularity supported by a hypertext system for anchors has a powerful effect on its capabilities, but the way in which locators are represented is also important. Locators vary widely; some are low level system dependent constructs like internal file offsets, while others are public names registered with a central authority. Some locators may be implicit, for example, links whose own location is one of their anchors. Locators that correspond to queries or network requests for remote retrieval services are also becoming important on the global networks. HyTime locators are flexible enough to handle all these cases and can even be extended as new types of locator are invented.

2.3.3 Link types

Links have many different varieties depending on what they connect, and why and where they are encoded. Analysis of existing documents shows that some links point out references, some indicate where to find prerequisite knowledge for a portion of a document, some connect a document to readers' comments, and others are part of the document's organization.

A hypertext system that tries to reflect this variety will need to store additional information with each link to enable it to determine the link types. Computerization of links offers a host of additional opportunities for link management. For instance, keywords can make possible the guided selection of useful links, as well as permitting access to author information that allows proper attribution of comments and links, security attributes that control access, and a host of other useful information. Such possibilities add power not available in print.

Link directionality is an important characteristic that creates several varieties of computer-supported link: can a link be traversed from any of its anchors, or is there a privileged source anchor which is the only one from which the link can be activated? For a link to be truly bidirectional it must be possible to traverse it beginning at the end (or ends) other than the source. The ability to "Go back" after traversing a link from the source does not make the link bidirectional. Likewise, a system in which the user achieves bidirectionality only by manually creating two separate one-directional links has not really supported it.

Paper based links can be followed only from one anchor, but computer-implemented links have the potential to be followed in both directions. Supporting bidirectional links involves some extra work on the part of an implementation, however, since it must maintain up to date information about both ends of the link and their relationship, even if the documents involved can change.

2.3.4 The card debate

The card model of documents is common in the hypermedia community, and has been widely popularized by Apple Computer's HyperCard™ and similar systems. This model blurs the separation of link and document structures that we have described above. Each document in a card-style (or "chunky") hypertext system is divided into distinct **nodes** or **cards** that usually contain a small number of data items. Cards have a fixed size that is generally coupled to the screen size, so that one card corresponds to one screenful of information. If scrollable text or large figures are allowed at all, they are not well integrated with linking.

Links allow card-to-card access via link markers called **buttons** that are represented by graphic icons or specially formatted text. The built-in link facilities of card-based systems distinguish between source anchors and destination anchors: source anchors are buttons and destination anchors are whole cards. Because sources and destinations differ in granularity, this model only handles one-directional links. Since a card is a relatively small chunk of information, the loss of context caused by not being able to link to destinations with other granularities is acceptable.

This model is attractive to system implementers because a card's correspondence to a single screen display allows a relatively simple interface style. Since cards controlling the layout of an entire screen enable details of presentation to be specified precisely, they are also attractive to document designers.

The chief limitation of the card approach is that not all writing can be reduced to small nuggets strung together in different orders. Most preexisting documents are not amenable to this treatment without heavy editing, and some simply don't fit at all. Another problem is that link granularity is fixed; when only a portion of a card is relevant to a link, it can be difficult for readers to find the relevant information and determine the purpose of the link. Also, locators that specify screen locations rather than locations in the data itself are common in card-based systems, but are a liability when fonts, screen sizes, zooming, or other formatting details cause data to move. These can cause reader disorientation.

It should be noted that this debate is fundamental in the hypertext community, with the opposing sides being dubbed the "card sharks" and the "holy scrollers." The authors are holy scrollers, and strongly concur with Frank Halasz's comment in his keynote address at the first hypertext conference: "The simple node and link model is just not rich and complete enough to support the information representation, management, and presentation tasks required by many applications" (Halasz 1987). HyTime, however, is ecumenical, and provides facilities that are equally applicable to both approaches.

2.4 Open systems

Distinct from the technical and structural issues discussed so far is the issue of open systems. Manufacturers of computing equipment and software have a vested interest in closed, incompatible systems: within the limits set by customers' tolerance, incompatibility seems good for vendors, because it helps lock in the installed base.

Of course, in opposition to this are the interests of the customers themselves. The more easily they can move data, the more likely they are to get the best price on systems with the best technology. Even customers satisfied with single-vendor solutions are well served by open systems, since the working lifetime of computer software is generally much shorter than that of many documents. Military and aerospace systems, for instance, actually begin their useful lives years after the initial manuals are written, and then have lifetimes that are generally measured in decades. The continuing pressure of data conversion is creating momentum for open standards that do not depend on the goodwill or financial health of a single vendor, no matter how powerful.

The analysis above is simplified, but the momentum towards open standards for data representation is a reality. SGML now fills the need for an open document representation format. One of the most important facts about SGML is that it expresses a model of document structure that is powerful and abstract enough to avoid superficial incompatibilities while also providing a firm foundation for representing not only document structure, but also the web of interconnections overlying that structure. Much of this advantage stems from SGML's use of descriptive markup methodology, which we discuss next.

2.4.1 Descriptive markup

The hierarchical model of document structures discussed above still lacks a critical notion: the concept of **descriptive markup** (also known as **content markup**). The basic idea is very simple: a document is described in terms of its structural components rather than in terms of its presentation on a single medium, such as print form or electronic delivery. The components reflect meaningful categories, analogous to "classes" as used in object-oriented design. For example, authors indicate that portions of documents constitute items, lists, chapters, quotations, tasks, or other relevant units. They indicate this directly, rather than specifying processing instructions, that produce an effect, that may indicate the component type when later read.

Particular processing methods such as formatting or retrieval are specified elsewhere, usually via a separate **style sheet** mechanism. The style sheet specifies appropriate processing for each kind of data object. Most word processors give style sheets only a subordinate role, and so do not use them to full advantage. They may support styles only for some kinds of formatting and at one level of granularity (such as paragraph), and not handle larger and smaller text objects, graphical data, and so on. These are not limitations of descriptive markup methodology, but of software that only partially supports it.

The fundamental technique for processing descriptive markup is what computer scientists call "late binding." The decisions about how to process a document are made at the time of processing, rather than when the document is encoded. This is true whether the processing desired is formatting, information retrieval, hypertext delivery, or anything else. It has several powerful advantages:

- *Ease of authoring*. Authors realize their intent to create a new paragraph, quotation, or other component before they think about how to format it, or how to get their program to accomplish the formatting. They can even choose to leave final formatting details and graphical design plans to someone else.
- *Formatting independence*. Reformatting a document is a matter of setting the parameters of a process that renders that document. Changes to the document itself are replaced by changes to style sheets applied to the document.
- *Flexibility*. Reusing a document for an unanticipated purpose is easy, because there is no need to remove old processing information and add new. This also protects the document from being inadvertently corrupted during such changes.

- *Dynamically reconfigurable document views.* The same data is often most meaningful when viewed so as to highlight points of interest. Outline processors, for instance, do this very well. With descriptive markup any number of different viewing specifications and styles can be applied as needed.

The SGML standard has had an enormous effect by promoting this idea and making it possible to apply descriptive markup in a standardized way. Documents can now be routinely published on paper, in Braille and pressed onto a CD-ROM from the same starting point — an SGML coded document.

SGML has two quite different advantages in terms of independence and portability. First is a technical and intellectual advantage it gains because it uses descriptive markup: SGML data is easier to reuse for new purposes, because the intellectual effort involved in identifying components of a document is not lost after formatting and publication, but serve the creator of an automated search facility for the document as well.

The second advantage is a practical one particular to SGML itself: it provides vendor independence, since the SGML standard is fixed and not controlled by any one group. Changing from one SGML-based system to another, while not always trivial, does not involve data conversion or loss. Since the data is the most important part of most document systems, this is a powerful advantage.

Descriptive markup and linking

Many pitfalls come from basing a system on formatting, rather than on descriptive markup structures. One is a common problem found with early versions of HyperCard. The standard "make button" command in HyperCard was based on graphical position on a card. Thus, to attach a link to text one would ensure the text could not be scrolled, find the desired source anchor on the screen, and place a button at that location. Later, if the text moved due to reformatting the button remained at the same rectangle on the screen (thus falling over a different part of the text). This confusion between the *spatial location* of data and its *logical location* led to a few embarrassing failures, where all links would break if the reader installed different fonts or happened to prefer larger type. HyperCard programmers learned to implement more sophisticated text links programmatically. The addition of "grouped text" in later versions of HyperCard has partially addressed this problem.

More recent systems have made the same confusion, particularly with respect to how they let readers attach annotations (sometimes called **sticky notes**) to documents. Many systems attach them by spatial location within a screen or page, which of course fails in many situations. In contrast, descriptive markup not only abstracts away from tenuous details of formatting and layout, but also provides a structure of natural reference points that can be exploited for linking.

2.4.2 Some key systems

Here we provide some historical context by describing instantiations of the concepts described above in various implementations. Since the problems that hypertext and document-handling systems attempt to solve are so universal, solutions have been independently developed more than once. The range of disciplines and groups concerned, throughout industry and academia, makes the compilation of a definitive history extremely difficult. We concentrate on the earliest systems built in the computer science community; despite being less-known, many of them explored a wider range of issues simultaneously than more recent systems. We thus give less treatment to industrial and commercial research work that was not widely published and do not attempt here to assign credit for the origination of ideas, but merely to illustrate the concepts described above with good examples.

One of the dimensions on which systems can be compared is the sorts of tasks they are intended to allow. A hypertext system might be useful for a wide range of activities, among them

- using hypertext in the traditional authoring of a single document
- creating a linked document intended to be read as a hypertext
- reading a document with links
- reading and annotating or linking a document

The primary distinction is between reading and authoring, but some "authoring-style" activities, like annotation or the addition of new links, are also reasonable for readers. Readers may even want to annotate or link data objects stored on read-only media like CD-ROM, and this has definite design implications. The research systems discussed here included both authoring and browsing functionality. It is only recently, with the ubiquity of personal computers and the introduction of media like CD-ROM, that such browsing and publishing systems have become widely available.

The first wave

One of the earliest mentions of the notion that technology was going to revolutionize the management of information was by Vannevar Bush in a prophetic article, *Atlantic Monthly* "As We May Think" (Bush 1945). This article describes an imagined device, the "Memex," for the hypertext-style associative organization of documents and images in terms of the microfilm-based technology of the time. Goldberg 1932 discussed similar technology, but not in such hypertextual terms.

The Memex proposal differed in an important way from the hypermedia systems of today in emphasizing trails more than point-to-point links. Trigg 1991 comments that "Memex links do not primarily embody local relationships between nodes, but function as part of a coherent sequential context under continual development, the *trail*" (see Nyce and Kahn 1991, pp. 60-61).

Although Bush is the earliest author to have described what would become hypertext in a recognizable way, Ted Nelson and Douglas Engelbart deserve the major credit for shaping the modern notion with its emphasis on links. Nelson coined the word "hypertext" and has been an indefatigable proponent of the notion, when it has been both in and out of fashion. He was the first to stress the importance of parallel scrolling texts. His proposed Xanadu system (see Nelson 1987b), while never released, remains one of the most ambitious designs for shared hypertext publishing and editing.

The earliest computer assisted hypertext systems were Engelbart's **NLS**, the "oNLine System," developed starting in the mid-1960s at Stanford Research Institute and **HES**, the "Hypertext Editing System," developed at Brown University starting in 1967 by a group led by Andries van Dam. Both provided online authoring, reading, annotation, and communication environments for working with large document collections. Ted Nelson made major contributions to the design of HES, and comments that "To the best of my knowledge most of the present generation of word-processing programs derived from the Brown [HES] System — but lost the hypertext" (Nelson 1987a, p. DM28).

The same two groups later developed greatly enhanced systems, respectively renamed **Augment** and **FRESS** (File Retrieval and Editing SyStem).

NLS and Augment were used in research environments where project staff communicated, designed, documented, and wrote papers online (van Dam and Rice 1971b, p. 110). Real-time collaborative authoring, publication reference, and linking were all available. The NLS system was strictly hierarchical in the manner of an outline processor and had complex configurable views of documents, created with a custom programming facility. It had point source anchors that could lead to "statement" nodes in the document structure. It pioneered the use of read-only journal files in which significant document versions could be stored for future reference and provide a stable basis for links. For more information see Engelbart 1963, Engelbart and English 1968, and Engelbart et al. 1973. Many relevant papers are reprinted in Greif 1988.

HES and FRESS were used in educational and industrial environments (see Carmody et al. 1969). HES, a simpler system than NLS, was based on the stream model of documents, with links that could connect arbitrary portions of documents and integrated graphics. Its first major application was a patent database with text, graphics, and links. The emphasis on graphical data in HES was an innovation that the technology of the time could barely support for single users.

After learning of NLS in 1968, van Dam's team built FRESS to combine the best features of NLS and HES: hierarchies as well as links superimposed on arbitrary streams. FRESS is discussed in van Dam and Rice 1971b, Prusky 1978, Catano 1979, Meyrowitz and van Dam 1982, Yankelovich et al. 1985, and Feiner 1990. FRESS documents were usually structured in hierarchies, but users could create non-hierarchical documents as well. Links were truly bidirectional and had arbitrarily-sized anchors that could be placed anywhere. Navigational tools such as a link index, structural overview and NLS-like outliner made access easy and flexible.

Descriptive markup was available via macros and redefinable style specifications for component types, as well as changeable **viewspecs** as in NLS, to enable customizing views at any time. All links and structures could have **attributes** (attached keywords with values) that could be used to control visibility and formatting style for parts of the document. FRESS was the first editing system to permit editing operations and anchors to apply to document portions without regard to granularity; most early document systems operated almost exclusively on limited-size lines. Like HES, FRESS had integral support for graphics and for sophisticated print formatting.

FRESS's first major use was in teaching an English poetry course. Students did all of their course reading and writing online. The hypertext environment was called a **web** (Catano 1979), a term still in use today. Students could read, link, and comment on poems, and interact with the instructor and each other. Attributes enabled FRESS to track student activities, so that students who had progressed to the next lesson could read other students' commentary from previous lessons.

Researchers at Carnegie-Mellon University developed ZOG beginning in 1972 (Akscyn 1987), making it the first card-based hypertext system. It had screen-sized frames with no scrolling. Links led from text items to entire frames. ZOG was set aside until 1975 due to hardware limitations, then rekindled and released in 1980. ZOG was succeeded by KMS and inspired many other systems such as Apple Computer's HyperCard.

While all of these systems share the ability to create links between locations in data, only card-based systems impose a requirement to divide data into small chunks. We consider the essence of hypertext to be the common ground of linking. Many popular press articles, and some serious ones, suggest that the essence of hypertext lies in dividing up information; we disagree, and feel that the long history of document structures and cross-references makes such a claim unsound.

Standardization

The most significant standard in document processing was SGML, developed by an ISO committee led by Charles F. Goldfarb based on the **GML** document preparation system he developed at IBM in the early 1970s. This system was the first to provide privileged features for descriptive markup. The idea was independently invented by Brian Reid for his **Scribe** document preparation system, discussed in his dissertation at Carnegie-Mellon. For a history of the standardization of descriptive markup systems through SGML see Goldfarb 1990, pp. 567-570. Reid 1981 also presents a history of word processing and descriptive markup, as do Meyrowitz and van Dam 1982, André, Furuta, and Quint 1989, Kernighan 1990 and Furuta 1991.

The HyTime standard has its origins in the description of musical scores and performance data and the Standard Music Description Language or SMDL project. Since music has the same aspects of cross-reference and interrelation of structure as documents, the basic structures of hypertext were present in some form from its beginning. The terminology and a number of concepts were modified as a result of input from the hypermedia community and the resulting standard is general enough to address the needs of both communities. Like SGML, this standard was developed by an inclusive committee, and like SGML it was developed under the leadership (temporal and technical) of Charles F. Goldfarb, chair of the committee, along with Steven Newcomb as vice-chair. Goldfarb and Newcomb are currently writing a history of HyTime; information may be obtained from the SGML SIGHyper user's group.

One of HyTime's more significant contributions is to provide a standard syntax for expressing locations in various kinds of data. It provides a wide variety of locators, including references to formal names, special addressing methods for trees, lists, character strings, and coordinate spaces. This last method extends the usual spatial addressing of graphical data to account for selecting points and ranges in time as well, and so facilitates integration of motion video and other time-based media. We discuss these and other methods for specifying the locations of anchors in data, in Chapter 8.

3

Overview of SGML

This chapter gives a very brief review of SGML, giving some of the basics and philosophy of SGML for those who are evaluating HyTime but do not expect to encode documents or write software themselves. This very basic background is sufficient to carry a reader through the first part of this book. We also explore some details of SGML syntax that may not be very familiar even to SGML experts but are especially important when using HyTime. If you are not already familiar with SGML and intend to read the entire book, you will need to supplement this chapter with additional reading and practice. The bibliography lists several appropriate books; van Herwijnen 1994 is a popular and accessible introduction. Goldfarb 1990 is a detailed presentation of every feature of SGML, which incorporates the entire text of the standard.

3.1 What is SGML, really?

SGML is short for Standard Generalized Markup Language, as defined by ISO Standard 8879, published in 1986. It provides a flexible and portable way of representing documents on computers. Because the core of SGML is elegant and simple, it has quickly become the most widely used method of representing and interchanging structured documents. SGML has found a level of generality that lets users tailor it to a wide variety of applications while still being able to use a single, simple representation for them.

SGML has been adopted by industry-standard bodies in every major field, first by those with the largest and most complex documents, then rapidly spreading to those with more everyday applications. SGML's applications range from aircraft repair manuals to collections of poetry and other literature.

The foundation of SGML, and to our thinking the primary reason it has gained such wide acceptance, is very simple: It lets you describe document structure directly, rather than describing something temporary, like formatting, that *depends on* the structure. Simply put, SGML lets you tell the truth about your documents.

This fundamental fact is reflected by five key characteristics that form the basis of its wide acceptance:

- **Descriptive markup**: An SGML document consists of objects of various classes (chapters, titles, references, repair procedures, graphic objects, etc.), not sequences of formatting instructions. These objects are called **elements**, and each one has a generic **element type**. SGML marks the boundaries of elements using start- and end-**tags**. For example, a quotation could be stored as:

  ```
  <quotation>Full speed ahead</quotation>
  ```

  By labeling elements *themselves* rather than saying what to do with them, SGML avoids locking information into one program or even one purpose. Processing for various purposes is specified separately, often by style sheets or similar mechanisms.
- **Hierarchical structure**: Elements can contain one another in a hierarchy (a chapter can contain a title and several sections which in turn contain other elements). Therefore one can create, manipulate and manage not only "chapter titles," as in word processors, but also chapters as complete units. Hierarchies are also called "trees" because they branch repeatedly, and every sub-branch comes from only one "parent" branch. For example, a chapter might be stored as:

  ```
  <chapter><title>Getting Started</title>
  <section><title>Overview of SGML</title>
  <p>SGML is...</p>
  ...
  </section></chapter>
  ```

As NLS/Augment and FRESS demonstrated in the 1960s, a tree is a significantly different and more powerful model than a the flat list or partially hierarchical structures used in many word processor and database products.

- **Flexibility**: SGML does not dictate what types of components may appear in a document or how they relate. Instead it gives the user a way to declare those components and how they are related. It also gives a way to check that particular documents have them. Thus individuals or groups can define types appropriate for their kinds of documents.

  Nevertheless, a single SGML implementation can work with all of these. There is no need for new software for each new set of element types.
- **Formal specification**: The specific elements contained in an SGML document are declared before the document begins in the **DTD**, or Document Type Declaration. After reading a DTD, software can check SGML documents and detect many kinds of errors. Such programs are called **validating parsers**. Of course they cannot detect all errors. If you create a poem and tell the computer it is just a plain paragraph (or a repair procedure!), no program will tell you it's poetry.
- **Human-readable representation**: Finally, SGML provides a plain-text format for all this information. This means that one can read and write SGML documents not only with sophisticated SGML-aware tools, but even with no tools beyond any computer's everyday text handling commands (such as "type" or "edit"). One can even read many SGML files without knowing SGML; it isn't hard to figure out, for instance, that this represents an emphasized word:

```
<emph>very</emph>
```

Such simple yet formal representations, based on embedded tags, have another important advantage: they are machine-independent. The internal file formats most programs use seldom survive transfer across wide-area networks, or from one make of computer to another, or across national borders. SGML does.

This kind of representation is a vast improvement over representations such as Adobe's PostScript or Microsoft's RTF (valuable though they are for their primary purposes). It is an even more striking improvement over the proprietary binary representations which programs typically use for optimizing internal operations. A discussion of the advantages of descriptive markup can be found in Coombs, Renear and DeRose 1987.

Notice that in describing SGML's key characteristics we have said little about specific kinds of processing (such as formatting or retrieval), or about specific interfaces. By leaving these issues undefined (while ensuring that the structural information needed to determine them *is* defined), SGML encourages building systems that use the best processing and interface technologies available in any situation.

We have also said very little about syntax. SGML provides a way to define languages for embedding tags within documents, with a wide variety of options. This is very important because only after agreeing about syntax can programs exchange data. However, the greatest value of SGML stems from its use of descriptive markup methodology. The syntax could have been standardized in a number of other ways without diminishing that value.

SGML documents can be created, edited and otherwise processed with generic editors or with WYSIWYG editors that look just like typical word processors. Cooperating authors often use different methods and programs on the same documents. In the same way, the result of authoring can be processed unchanged for many different purposes, such as local printing, high-quality typesetting, display in Braille, information retrieval, linguistic analysis, or hypertext browsing.

In technical terms, SGML defines a meta-language somewhat like BNF, which can be used to define particular languages for marking up documents to indicate their hierarchical component structure. It provides an entity mechanism which is similar to macro or inclusion directives and also supports non-SGML data formats. It provides a typed element structure that expresses the document's part hierarchy via a labeled bracketing, and named attributes attached to components on the basis of their type. And all this is done with a plain text syntax.

There is a great deal of useful information available about structured documents in general, and SGML in particular. The reference works by Cover listed in the Bibliography provide access to such information.

3.1.1 Formatting and structure

Strong separation of formatting from structure is a hallmark of good SGML use. Just using the standard cannot, however, ensure such good practice. It is possible, even easy, to use "legal" SGML syntax with tags that represent only formatting information, but doing this does not get the benefits SGML can provide. For example, it is easy to make a set of SGML element types that looks like raw troff or Script with the delimiters changed. A block quote might then be tagged as follows (like other negative examples, this is italicized to emphasize that it is bad practice):

```
<sk><ds><in l="+10" r="-10">The quotation...
<sk><il l="+10">The following paragraph...
```

Even worse, one can merely put "`<doc>...</doc>`" around a document in any other representation and call it SGML:

```
<doc>
.sk;.ds;.in +10 -10;
The quotation...
.sk;.il +10;
The following paragraph...
<doc>
```

Given corresponding DTDs, both these approaches yield perfectly legal, syntactically correct SGML for which a validating SGML parser would report no errors. On occasion the authors have seen "SGML-conforming" documents in styles closely resembling both of these. However, neither of these documents is SGML in a very useful sense — the information is no more portable or communicative than if it were not using SGML. SGML syntax has been used as a veneer over non-descriptive, non-hierarchical markup, whose meaning is not accessible to the SGML processor for validation or use.

The following SGML coding is clearer, more concise, easier to maintain, more efficient and more useful for a wide range of purposes:

```
<quo>The quotation...</quo>
<p>The following paragraph...</p>
```

3.2 Parts of an SGML document

An SGML document is divided in three parts:

- An **SGML declaration** gives general information about SGML syntax options. It says what character set is used, how long element type names can be, what **delimiter strings** (such as "<" and "</") separate tags from content, what optional SGML features are used, and so on.

  Many SGML parsers allow the declaration to be omitted. Then standard default settings are used, called the **reference concrete syntax**. We assume these settings without further comment throughout this book, except that element and other names may exceed the default eight-character limit.

- A **Document Type Declaration** or **DTD** says what element types and other components are permitted in the document, using detailed **markup declarations**. The declarations also say which element types can contain which others. For example, footnotes or cross-reference markers might not be allowed to contain chapters.
- A **document instance** includes the content of a document as well as the tags and other markup that indicate where elements of each type start and end. A document instance can be stored in more than one file. Methods for including other data by reference are described below.

3.3 SGML basics

In the following section we give a brief review of key points in how documents are tagged using SGML and how tagging schemes are declared in DTDs. This clarifies the issues and opportunities afforded by SGML markup systems, but does not provide all the information required to create SGML markup schemes and documents. We then show the complete SGML markup for a short example document.

3.3.1 Parts of a document instance

An SGML document instance includes content and structure, such as graphics, video, text, indications of structural components, and links. It has four major kinds of objects, each of which is declared in the DTD and may be used in the document instance.

Elements divide the document into logical or meaningful components. They are marked by tags at start and end and have an **element type** that indicates their role, such as "`chapter`," "`part-number`," or "`task`." **Attributes** may be specified for elements and give information about a particular instance of the element type such as a security level or a unique identifier. **Data content**, typically the information to be read or viewed, may occur within elements. Finally, there may be **entity references**, which are **resolved** by the SGML parser and replaced by their values: either externally stored information or strings defined in the DTD. The contents of entities can even be data in non-SGML representations.

While other SGML constructs like **marked sections** can also occur, they have no special treatment in HyTime beyond their normal SGML meaning, and will not be discussed further.

3.3.2 Elements

Elements represent chapters, links, footnotes, graphic references, and so on. As described previously, the beginning and end of each element are marked by **tags**, that explicitly state what element type is starting or ending. By default the tags are enclosed between less-than and greater-than signs or "angle brackets:"

```
<para>This is a paragraph</para>
```

The names of elements, which identify their element type, are known as **generic identifiers** (commonly abbreviated GIs) or as tag names. SGML tag names normally disregard upper/lower case distinctions. By default, tag names can contain letters, digits, periods and hyphens.

The names can be anything the DTD writer chooses. Of course, mnemonic ones are better: `<quote>` is superior to `<q>`, which is in turn superior to `<tag37>`. With modern editing software, these can all be entered with equal ease via a single menu selection or command key, so keeping names short to save typing is false economy.

Although our examples show the actual file representation of SGML, remember that this need not be what users see. Any SGML editing software can hide all this, just as word processors hide their arcane proprietary formats. It is an advantage, however, that one *can* edit SGML with any text editor; this is not possible with proprietary word-processor formats.

The GI as major class identifier

For most SGML applications, the generic identifier tells what an element is and thus what kind of processing is appropriate. This reflects the fundamental descriptive markup approach: name things by what they are and expect the computer to use that name. Deciding *how* such names are to be used can remain separate. Some consequences of this object-oriented approach are:

- Processing programs can usually decide what to do with an element merely by looking at its GI.
- Where finer distinctions must be made, processors generally look at the GI first, and then use other information associated with the GI, such as attributes or position in the hierarchy.
- Users can rely on the GI to find out what an element is: what useful unit it expresses ("chapter"), what its content must be ("a title and some sections"), what attributes it may or must have ("the chapter number"), and so on.

- Other terms the user may have for elements can be derived directly from the GI (an interface may display "Block quotation" instead of "bq" in a menu, but this requires only a simple list of synonyms).

The example below shows two different ways of tagging a list:

```
<ordered.list>
    <item>Hot dog</item>
    <item>Chili</item>
</ordered.list>

<list type=ordered>
    <item>Hot dog</item>
    <item>Chili</item>
</list>
```

A formatter or other processor could be set up to do the same things for both of these tagging approaches. Both are natural and both make use of the GI to specify the **major class identifier** of the element. In the second example, the element name is not sufficient to process a `list` correctly; the `type` attribute is also needed. The processing of `items` in both examples also depends on more than just the GI, since items may be handled differently depending on what sort of list contains them.

In SGML, the GI is typically the main (but not the only) determinant of how the system should process each element. For this reason GIs are the central focus of DTDs. This is why a DTD is sometimes called a "tag set," even though a DTD provides other critical information in addition to the set of tags).

The GI determines processing not directly, but indirectly. For example, all `list` elements are likely to be treated similarly, whether the current application is intended to format them, or search them, or whatever.

3.3.3 Element declarations

Each element type in a DTD is declared with certain rules that determine what subelements it can contain, what order they occur in, how many can occur, whether and where content can occur, and so on. There are many reasons such control can be useful. In many applications, a house markup style allows consistent formatting and uniform tools to be used throughout an organization. In scholarly applications, where the markup chosen for an ancient manuscript may represent a partial analysis of the document's structure, seeing whether the markup and the content match is a useful check on whether the structure has been properly understood.

A simple element declaration for a glossary entry element might look like this, and would appear in the Document Type Declaration:

```
<!ELEMENT        entry         - - (word, defn)>
```

This declaration includes a parenthesized **content model** that requires every `entry` element to contain exactly two subelements, a `word` and then a `defn`. A complete DTD would also declare other elements to hold `entry` elements and would declare `word` and `defn`. The two hyphens are used with SGML's optional minimization features to specify that neither an `entry`'s start-tag nor its end-tag may be omitted.

The definitions for `glossary` (consisting of a list of one or more `entry` elements) and for `word` and `defn` (consisting of strings of characters) could be:

```
<!ELEMENT        glossary      - - (entry)+>
<!ELEMENT        word          O O (#PCDATA)>
<!ELEMENT        defn          - O (#PCDATA)>
```

This defines both `word` and `defn` to contain "parsed character data." This is fancy terminology for plain text. Since the characters that start a tag (like "<") might occur in such text, SGML provides mechanisms to include them without confusion.

The `word` element has an "O" (capital letter O, not zero) in both of its minimization specifications, indicating that it is permissible to omit either the start-tag, end-tag, or both in certain circumstances. A `defn` element may only have its end-tag omitted. Section 3.5.1 discusses minimization.

The `glossary` element itself is declared to contain one or more `entry` elements. The "+" means that the preceding item can be repeated one or more times. Other operators allow optional elements, choices between elements, and elements that can be arbitrarily re-ordered.

Content models may contain sub-models separated by **connectors** which specify what elements are required by a content model:

,	The SEQ connector separates sub-models that must appear in sequence.
|	The OR connector separates sub-models either of which can appear (but not both).
&	The AND connector separates sub-models that must all appear, but can occur in any order.

Content models may contain **occurrence indicators** that indicate how many times a sub-model must occur when it appears. These indicators follow the sub-model to which they apply:

?	The "optional" occurrence indicator specifies that the sub-model is optional.
+	The "required and repeatable" occurrence indicator specifies that one or more instances of the sub-model may occur.
*	The "optional and repeatable" occurrence indicator specifies that zero or more instances of the sub-model may occur.

Instead of a parenthesized content model, a declaration may also use a special keyword:

CDATA	means that delimiters inside the element will be treated as literal data. The most useful application of this is in an element such as `<sgml-example>`, in which "<" will frequently occur. No subelements can occur inside one of these. An end-tag will still be recognized, however, as it is needed to end the CDATA element.
RCDATA	is like CDATA, but permits entity references to be resolved within the element.
EMPTY	means that the element is a point event and cannot contain any text or other elements.
ANY	means the element can contain any mixture of text and other elements declared in the DTD.

3.3.4 Attributes

Simple attributes

An instance of an element may have associated information in the form of attributes. Thus, a footnote may have a reference code, a paragraph may have a security level, or a list may specify whether its items should be shown with automatic numbering, with bullet characters in front, or plain. Attributes appear only within start-tags, at the start of the elements to which they apply:

```
<list type="bulleted">
    <item>...</item>
    ...
</list>
```

Attribute declarations

The attributes permitted for an element type are declared all at once in the DTD using an **attribute list declaration**. Each attribute has a name by which it is referenced, a type that determines the sort of value it can have (SGML identifier, number, etc.), and a default value to be used if the attribute is not specified. A declaration for two attributes that can apply to elements of type `list` might look like this:

```
<!-- Declare two attributes for 'list' element -->
<!ATTLIST       list
    author      CDATA           #IMPLIED
    type        (bulleted | numbered)
                                "bulleted">
```

After a comment, this declares that each `list` element has two attributes. One, called `author`, has a string as value. The keyword #IMPLIED specifies that `author` is optional for `list` element instances. The other attribute, called `type`, can have either the value "`bulleted`" or the value "`numbered`"; it defaults to "`bulleted`" if a value is not specified.

Attribute types

An attribute's type is known in the SGML standard as its **declared value**. Attribute types constrain the range of permitted values to be numbers, a single word, a unique identifier for the element, and so on. Alternatively, an attribute can be constrained to one of an enumerated list of specific values, each of which must be a single name token. The HyTime standard greatly extends the ways to constrain attribute values, most notably with the `lextype` feature (see Section 11.3).

The declared value types known to SGML are ENTITY, IDREF, NAME, NMTOKEN, NUMBER, NUTOKEN (all with corresponding plurals), as well as CDATA, ID and NOTATION. The most important for HyTime are: ID, IDREF, ENTITY and NOTATION.

Attribute defaults

Each attribute must specify what happens if no value is given on the start-tag for its element type. The declaration can specify a default value (as for the `type` attribute above), or some special keywords can be used:

#IMPLIED'	means it is optional but has no default
#REQUIRED	means omitting it is an error
#CURRENT	means the value is the same as last time
#CONREF	is a special case. If a #CONREF attribute has a value, then the element must be EMPTY
#FIXED	means only one value given in the DTD is permitted

HyTime uses the last of these extensively, for reasons we will discuss later. Attributes that have the same value on every occurrence of the element can be useful; if that value is declared as the #FIXED default value, specifying any other value causes a validating SGML parser to report a syntax error. For example, this declaration forbids setting any value for `secure` other than `top`:

```
<!ATTLIST     query
    secure    NAME        #FIXED "top">
```

You can also forego validation and merely declare the desired value as a default, or even have no default at all. However, in those cases the SGML parser cannot verify that the desired value is always used, and errors will surely arise.

IDs and IDREFs

Two types of SGML attributes are especially important for HyTime: ID and IDREF. These permit the attachment of unique identifiers to elements and reference to them from other elements. There may be at most one attribute with declared value ID for a given element type, and its instances must have these properties:

- Any value specified for the attribute must be a valid SGML name: that is, a name start character (normally a letter) followed by any number of name characters (letters, digits, hyphen and period), up to some maximum length.
- The values of all ID attributes in a single document must be distinct (IDs that differ only in case count as equal, such as "chap1" and "CHAP1").

Attributes with declared value IDREF (short for "ID reference") need not each have distinct value, but each such value must match the value of *some* ID attribute elsewhere in the same document.

Because all IDs must be distinct they provide a natural way to refer to a particular element — a way that a validating SGML parser can check. IDs and IDREFs are used very heavily in HyTime for this reason, as they have been for linking in SGML documents preceding HyTime. Here are some examples of declaring ID and IDREF attributes for particular elements:

```
<!-- Declare chapter element with mandatory ID -->
<!ELEMENT     chapter     - - (ct, p+)>
<!ATTLIST     chapter
    id        ID          #REQUIRED>

<!-- Paragraph element has optional ID attribute -->
<!ELEMENT     p           - - (#PCDATA)>
<!ATTLIST     p
    id        ID          #IMPLIED>
```

```
<!-- Cross-reference element has mandatory 'target'
     attribute to point to any element with an ID -->
<!ELEMENT       xref          - - (#PCDATA)>
<!ATTLIST       xref
    target      IDREF         #REQUIRED>
```

Given these declarations, `chapter` elements *must* have distinct, unique identifier attributes and `p` elements *may* have them. Each `xref` element *must* have a `target` attribute that points to an elements by identifier. An example using this tagging scheme is:

```
<xref target="chap1">See also Chapter 1</xref>
...
<chapter id=chap1>
    ...
    <p id=main.point>...</p>
</chap>
```

ID values must be distinct regardless of the element type on which they occur and regardless of the attribute name. Therefore if the following element occurred in the same document as the example above, it would be in error because the ID attribute value "`chap1`" would occur on two different elements and thus not be distinct.

```
<p id=chap1>
```

It is a near universal convention among SGML users that all attributes of declared value ID in any given DTD should have the same name. A less strong convention is that IDs should always be named "`id`". While following these conventions is not necessary, it is especially good practice in HyTime DTDs because there tend to be a lot of IDs around.

Entity and notation attributes

An attribute with declared value ENTITY must have as its value the name of an entity defined in the DTD. Such attributes are generally used to refer to an external entity containing non-SGML data. For discussion of external entities, see Sections 3.3.5 and 3.6.

An attribute with declared value NOTATION must have a declared NOTATION name as its value. It constitutes a claim that the element's content can be interpreted as being in that data representation. Since the element is parsed normally that content must also conform to SGML. For example, if the data content notation happens to use strings that could appear to be tags, they must be recoded using one of SGML's alternative techniques.

3.3.5 Entities and notations

An entity is a normally case-sensitive name given to some piece of data for later reference. The entity itself may be something as simple as an abbreviation for a literal string, or may represent an external data object, such as a file of SGML or non-SGML data. The former are called **internal entities**, the latter **external entities**.

Entities can be used to avoid redundant copies of data and to help organize the parts of documents into files or other storage units. They are important in HyTime for referring to locations outside a single document. This reference is accomplished by naming the entity that contains the location (such as a video sequence) and then perhaps giving a more specific place within the entity (such as a range of frames). A declaration for a non-SGML entity also states what representation the entity is in, to enable proper processing of the data.

Internal entity declarations, placed in the DTD, merely give the entity name and a quoted string that represents the value or **replacement text** as a literal string which is substituted for each reference to the entity in the document:

```
<!ENTITY        safety
    "Ensure that red 'armed' light is not flashing.">
```

An entity reference in the document normally consists of an ampersand, the entity name and a semicolon, as in the example below:

```
<procedure>
    <step>After opening the box, do the following
       safety checks: &safety;</step>
    <step>Replace the entire unit.</step>
</procedure>
```

The effect of this is to include the text "`ensure that the red 'armed' light is not flashing.`" in the document in place of the entity reference "`&safety;`".

Parameter entities

Some entities are intended to contain information that should be substituted within the DTD rather than the document. These are called **parameter entities** and they are syntactically separate from other entities. Names of parameter entities and ordinary entities cannot conflict because they are separately defined. A parameter entity is declared like any other internal entity with the addition of a special signal, the character "`%`" following the keyword ENTITY, for example:

```
<!ENTITY        % para-stuff "p | fn | bq">
```

This entity is called `para-stuff` and can be referenced later in the DTD with the string “`%para-stuff;`”. The following two declarations, for example, would have the same effect:

```
<!ELEMENT       text          - - (%para-stuff;)>

<!ELEMENT       text          - - (p | fn | bq)>
```

External entities

External entities typically correspond to individual computer files, though this need not be true; for them the keyword PUBLIC or SYSTEM appears, followed by quoted identifiers that enable an SGML parser to locate the data that the entity represents (for further details on PUBLIC entities see Section 3.6):

```
<!ENTITY        chap1         SYSTEM
    "/u/sjd/hytime/chap1.sgm">
```

Entities with special parsing constraints

Several other keywords can appear with an entity's value specification to specify how it is to be parsed. Three are particularly important in relation to HyTime. They are used for “data entities” whose replacement text is not to be parsed by the SGML parser. Their meanings are:

CDATA — The replacement text is content in the same character set as the rest of the SGML document, but may contain SGML delimiter strings (such as “<”) as literal data without their being parsed as markup by the SGML processor.

SDATA — The replacement text is specific character data that is by definition system-dependent and should be redefined for each system; this is commonly used for special characters that are not shared among the character sets of various computer systems.

NDATA — The replacement text is in some format or **data content notation** other than SGML and should be passed for processing to some other program that knows that notation. The particular notation should be named after the word NDATA.

When a data content notation is used, there must be a **notation declaration** that relates a notation name to a reference describing that data format. We include some useful notation declarations in Appendix B; they may be used in conjunction with HyTime systems.

Here are some examples of these entity types:

```
<!-- Specify CDATA so journal title is not taken
     as a tag instead of literal characters -->
<!ENTITY        tag.letter  CDATA
    "<TAG>: The SGML newsletter">

<!-- Declare needed Hebrew letter -->
<!ENTITY        aleph       SDATA
    "font(Hebrew) charset(ISO8859-8) codepoint(224)">

<!-- Declare graphic notation and entity using it -->
<!NOTATION      TIFF        PUBLIC
    "+//ISBN 0-7923-9432-1::Graphic Notation//NOTATION
    Aldus/Microsoft
    Tagged Interchange File Format//EN">

<!ENTITY        wheel       SYSTEM
    "fig29.tif" NDATA TIFF>
```

The value for `aleph` would vary from system to system. The `wheel` entity is declared to be in the TIFF notation, which allows the external graphics data to be directed to an appropriate processing program.

3.3.6 The SGML declaration

The optional features, character set used and any syntactic changes to SGML are described in an **SGML declaration**. Documents that use no optional features and the default settings are called **minimal SGML documents** because only the minimal subset of SGML is used. Sometimes the terms "normalized documents" or "canonical documents" are used to mean the same thing. **Basic SGML documents** are those that use only certain optional features, and are quite common. There is seldom a reason to change SGML delimiters, but the default limits on lengths of tag names and other strings, controlled by the **quantity set**, are often increased. Our examples assume increased maximum possible lengths of tag names and attribute values (the NAMELEN and LITLEN quantities). Most products support this, and we use longer names without further comment.

The SGML declaration must often be read by both the person and the computer receiving an SGML document. It determines whether the document uses the same character set as the local system, and what stresses it may put on the processor (such as extremely long tag names or deeply nested document structures). The SGML declaration also states the version of the SGML standard it expects; this should read "ISO 8879:1986," although some older declarations have "ISO 8879-1986". HyTime places no special requirements on the SGML declaration except that it requires setting the FORMAL option to YES and adding the word "`HyTime`" in the APPINFO parameter.

3.4 A sample SGML document

This section presents a small sample document, along with a complete SGML DTD and document instance, showing each of the items described above (the headings separating the three major parts would not be part of the document). We skip the SGML Declaration here, but a sample is available in Section 3.5.1.

Following is a formatted version of the sample document we will be using in this section:

January 27, 1993

Dear Jean Luc,

How are you doing?
Isn't it *about time* you visited?

See you soon,

Genise

Figure 3.1: Formatted sample document

3.4.1 The document type declaration

The DTD contains declarations for all the kinds of units that will occur in the document. The DTD, for example, declares various elements, attributes and entities that can be used to encode documents such as the one above. The declarations are enclosed in a **DOCTYPE declaration**, within a **declaration subset** enclosed within square brackets.

```
<!DOCTYPE      letter [

<!-- declare root element type for document -->
<!ELEMENT      letter       - - (date, greeting,
                                  body, closing, sig)>
<!ATTLIST      letter
    filecode    NUMBER       #REQUIRED
    secret     (yes|no)      "no">

<!ELEMENT      body         - - (para)*>
<!ELEMENT      (date, greeting, closing, sig)
                            - - (#PCDATA)>
<!ELEMENT      para         - - (#PCDATA|emph)*>
<!ELEMENT      emph         - - (#PCDATA)>

<!-- Provide a handy, replaceable greeting -->
<!ENTITY       salute        "Dear">
]>
```

3.4.2 The document instance

With this DTD, the document instance below is a valid SGML encoding. The indentation is added for clarity to show the hierarchical structure; it would probably not appear in the document.

```
<letter filecode="93020401">
    <date>January 27, 1993</date>
    <greeting>&salute; Jean Luc,</greeting>
    <body>
       <para>How are you doing?</para>
       <para>Isn't it
          <emph>about time</emph>
          you visited?
       </para>
    </body>
    <closing>See you soon,</closing>
    <sig>Genise</sig>
</letter>
```

3.4.3 A non-SGML equivalent

Lest one think this representation is unduly complicated, we show below how one popular WYSIWYG word processing system encodes the same document. This puts the comparison on the same terms as above: we are showing what's underneath the interface (which one should avoid seeing in practice, but determines what you can ultimately do with your data). In this case, it directly represents instructions for formatting the document in a certain way. It is obviously much less readable than the SGML representation above.

```
\widowctrl\fracwidth \sectd \sbknone\linemod0
\linex0\cols1\endnhere \pard\plain \s1\li360
\sl280\tx720\tx1080\tx1440\tx1800\tx2160 \f22
{\v 93020401}\par \pard
\s1\qr\li360\sl280\tx720\tx1080\tx1440\tx1800\tx2160
January 27, 1993\par\pard
\s1\li360\sb1440\sa240\sl280\tx720\tx1080
\tx1440\tx1800\tx2160
Dear Jean Luc,\par\pard\s1
\li360\sl280\tx720\tx1080\tx1440\tx1800\tx2160
How are you doing?\par Isn\rquote t it
{\i about time} you visited?\par\pard\s1
\li360\sb240\sl280\tx720\tx1080\tx1440\tx1800\tx2160
See you soon,\par\pard \s1\li360\sb1440\sl280
\tx720\tx1080\tx1440\tx1800\tx2160
Genise\par \pard\plain \f20\fs28 \par
```

Most users do not see all these backslashes in their word processor; likewise, most users of an SGML editor need not see angle brackets. Even so, the SGML representation is both cleaner and shorter; most importantly, the information it contains is more generally useful. Both user interface and data representation are very important; there is no need to accept good interfaces on bad data representations, or bad interfaces on good ones. Only a system that does both things well is adequate.

3.4.4 A graphical interface

As we have said, this SGML file can be edited with a pleasant, WYSIWYG interface. SoftQuad Inc. (based in Toronto) has kindly given us permission to show their **Author/Editor** product below, which is one of several available SGML editing environments. Figure 3.2 shows a formatted view with tag display suppressed (although the bottom window tells the user the context of the cursor), while Figure 3.3 shows the same document viewed with the "Show Tags" option. This view is particularly useful for editing the document structure in detail.

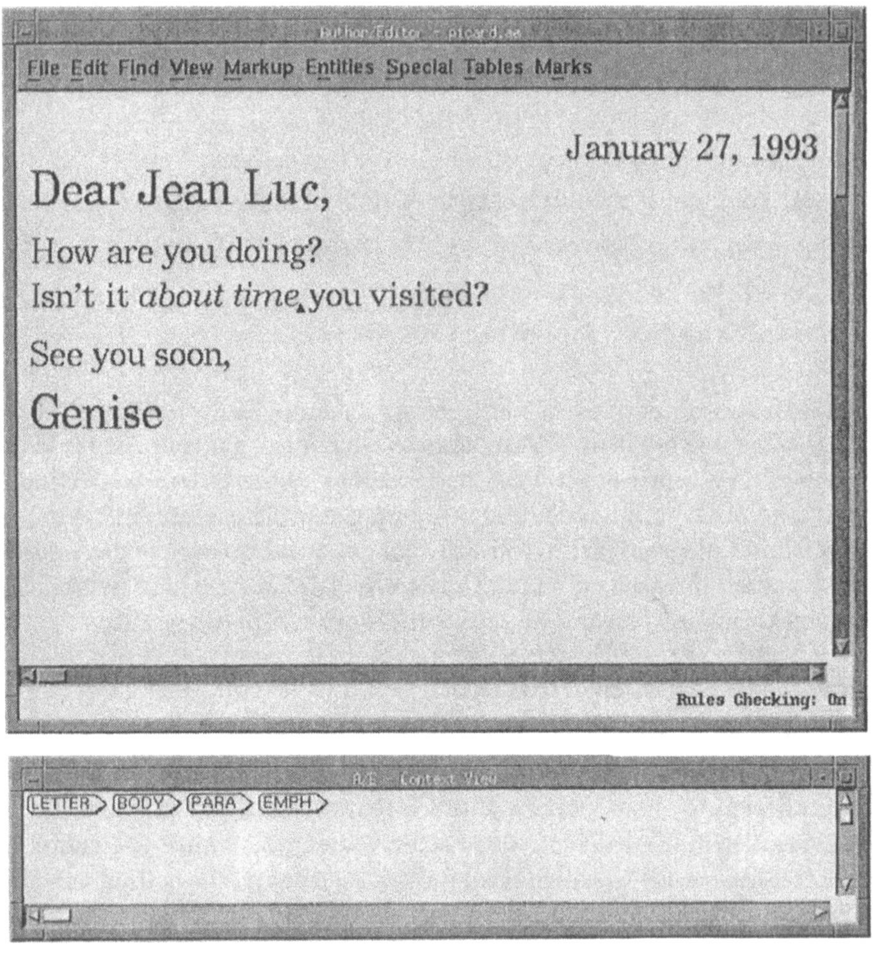

Figure 3.2: An SGML editor, markup hidden

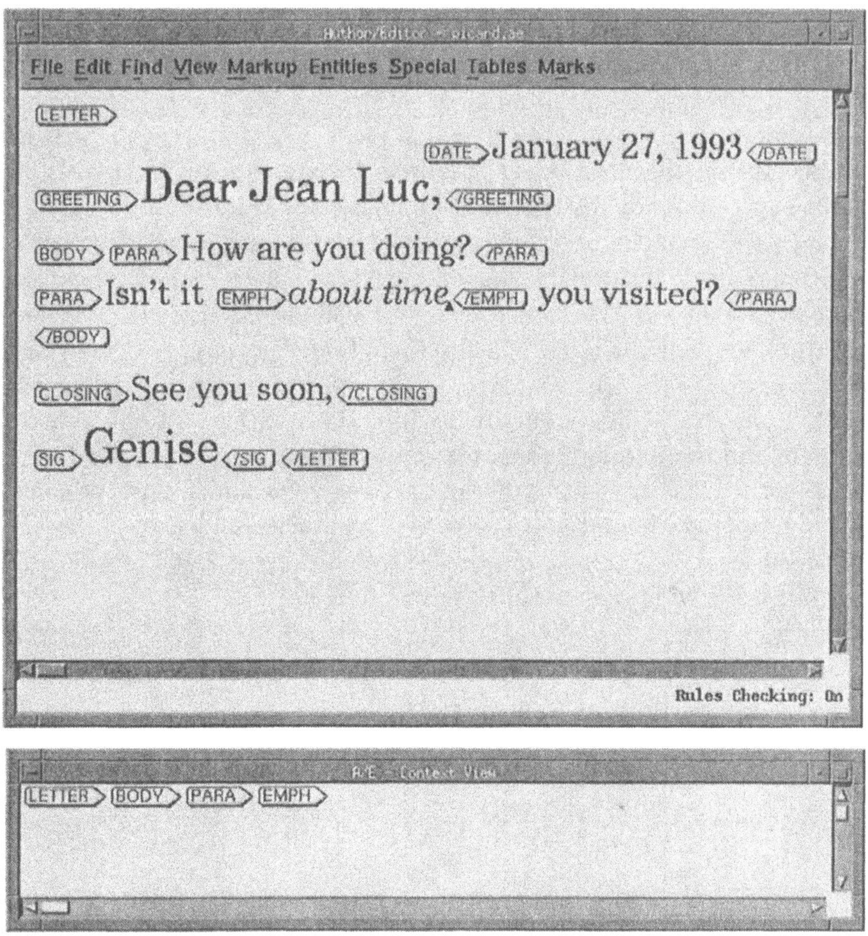

Figure 3.3: An SGML editor, markup displayed

3.4.5 Hypertext interface to SGML

SGML provides several intrinsic features that are used to represent hypertext. First is the document structure itself, which is a necessary means of navigation and orientation in hypertext documents. Hypertext systems lacking support for component structure within documents usually encounter the "lost in hyperspace" problem. Second, SGML provides ID and ID reference mechanisms that provide fine-grained connections between components of documents, providing excellent precision and robustness for hypertext links. These capabilities are exploited and extended by HyTime.

One software system that supports SGML hyperdocuments is *Dyna*Text™, from Electronic Book Technologies in Rhode Island. This system takes SGML documents including their multimedia data entities in various notations, and builds distributable hyperdocuments. Even very large documents can then be rapidly browsed, searched and annotated online. It can apply any number of different style sheets on demand. These determine the format, inclusion and interpretation of text elements, multimedia data and hyperlinks throughout documents. Links can be expressed in SGML terms via names such as IDREFs, coordinates such as paths in trees, and semantic descriptions such as queries, as well as through integration with external programs. These same fundamental methods are used by HyTime as well, as discussed below.

Figure 3.4 shows a picture of the *Dyna*Text user interface, viewing a portion of an SGML hyperdocument. The table of contents is derived directly from the SGML structure, while the numbers in the table of contents and the highlighted words in the main text indicate the results of a search. Icons or "hot text" can serve as hyperlinks, such as to the graphic shown. Readers can attach bookmarks and annotations to document locations, and there are also tools for keeps track of where the user has been, what annotations exist, and so on.

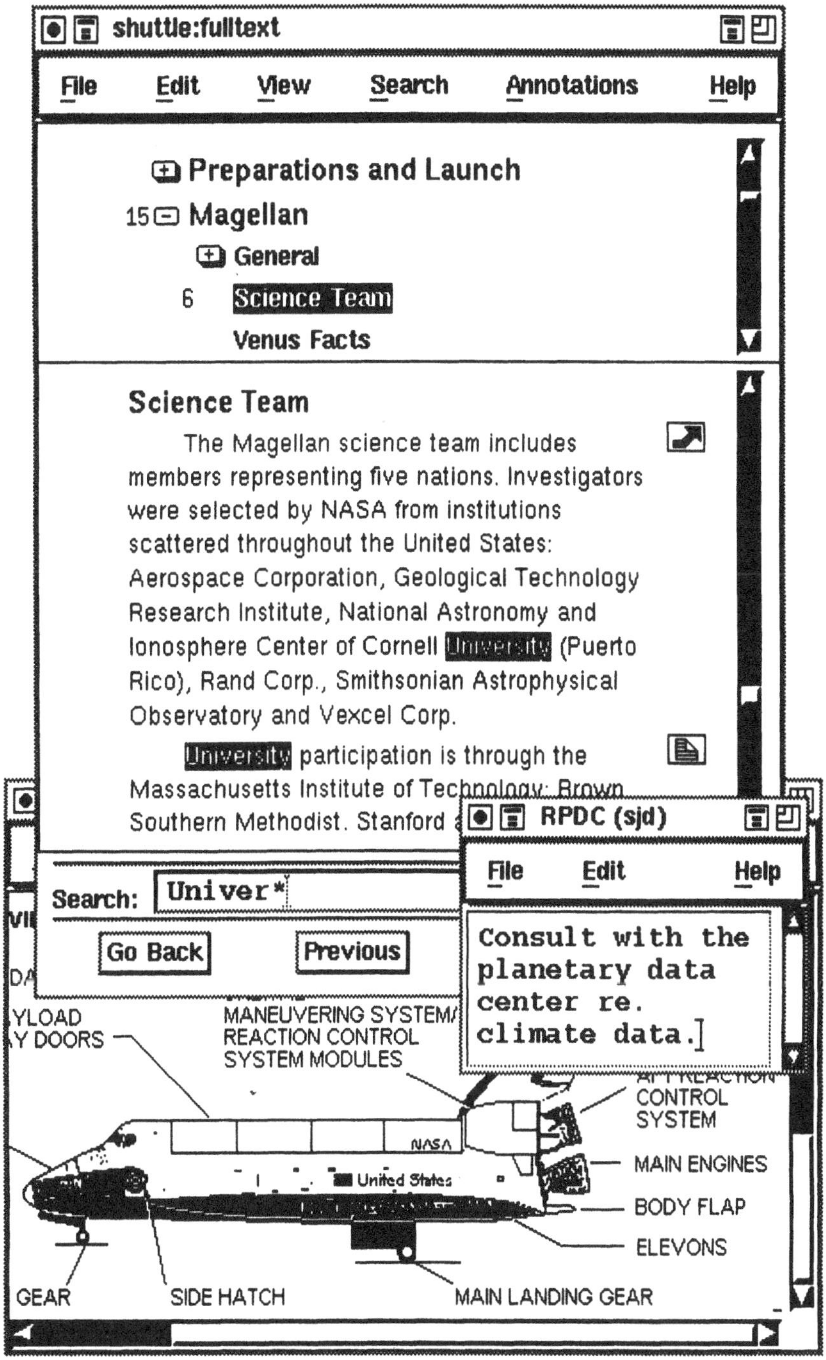

Figure 3.4: An SGML hypermedia viewer

3.5 Optional SGML features

This section discusses SGML's **optional features**, highlighting how they relate to HyTime. For a fuller discussion of SGML features see van Herwijnen 1994. Many of SGML's optional features provide more compact ways of keying markup should that be necessary. The same abbreviation methods may reduce visual distraction if one reads or edits SGML with non-SGML-aware text editors. Other features involve the interactions between documents and various DTDs, and the way in which entities are formally named.

For example, the markup in the following string may be a bit imposing to type or read as-is, and so one might use minimization instead:

```
<quote type=long>...</quote>
```

Current software typically shields the user from such details by providing graphical interfaces for data entry, editing, and display. One might pick an "Insert quotation" menu item (or press control-q) and be done; for display, one might choose to see no tags, but only quotation marks, a formatting distinction, or some other graphical indication of the element's presence. Regardless of such syntactic and interface variations, the fundamental notion of descriptive markup remains essential.

3.5.1 Minimization features

The first of SGML's **markup minimization features** is quite simple. **SHORTTAG** provides ways to make start and end-tags shorter although it never permits omitting them completely. It has several aspects:

- Leaving out quotes around attribute values so long as they contain only name characters (normally letters, digits, hyphen and period):

  ```
  <list type=numbered>
  ```

- Leaving out attributes that have default values. For example, given this declaration:

  ```
  <!ATTLIST  list
     type     (numbered | bulleted | plain)
                                    "plain"
     startnum                number    1>
  ```

  the following `list` start-tags are both valid and equivalent, because the SGML parser will fill in default values:

  ```
  <list startnum=1 type=plain>...</list>
  <list>...</list>
  ```

- Leaving out the tag name from start and end-tags when it can be inferred from context. We forego using this for start-tags, though we occasionally use it for end-tags, as shown here:

```
<list>
   <item>Item 1</>
   <item>Item 2</>
</>
```

- Substituting "`/`" for "`>`" on a start-tag to declare that the next freestanding "`/`" in the document will be treated as the corresponding end-tag:

```
<list/
   <item/Item 1/
   <item/Item 2/
/
```

   This feature is rarely used and should be treated with care. In the example below, the user forgot to quote the `ln` attribute intended to have value `42/a`, and the slash character ends the attribute value. "`a>`" is therefore treated as part of the literal text content of the `l` element:

```
<l ln=42/a>Ode to Spot</l>
```

OMITTAG saves keying tags entirely when the DTD permits them to be inferred. For example, if `lists` are declared to *require* at least one `item`, then the start-tag for the first `item` element can be omitted. In the same way, if `item` elements are *required* never to directly contain other `item` elements, the end-tags for most or all of them can be omitted:

```
<list>
    Item 1
    <item>Item 2
</list>
```

A third feature is called **SHORTREF**. It lets you define **maps**, which are lists of synonyms for markup. For example, you could declare "`|`" to be an synonym for "`<column>`" and then enter a table as shown below (this example also assumes OMITTAG):

```
<table>
    <row>| China    | 1400 million
    <row>| India    | 800 million
    <row>| USA      | 250 million
    <row>| France   | 50 million
    <row>| Canada   | 25 million
</table>
```

We do not use SHORTREF in this book.

3.5.2 Other SGML features

While the remaining SGML features add capability, they are less commonly used. Three features are together known as **LINK**. This provides a possible way of associating processing information with elements in an SGML document. We do not use it in this book. Note that the LINK feature is unrelated to hypertext linking. When we use the word "link" without qualification we mean hypertext links.

The SGML **SUBDOC** feature lets an entire document embed within another as a single element, even if the two use completely different DTDs. **CONCUR** permits two or more completely separate markup structures (defined by separate DTDs) for the same document.

The final SGML feature is required by HyTime, and extremely useful. **FORMAL** requires that public names for documents and entities be in a special form known to SGML. A public name is a publicly registered reference, that does not depend on any particular computer implementation as a filename or network address does (Section 3.6 discusses registered public identifiers).

An entity declaration for an external entity can supply two kinds of identifiers: PUBLIC and SYSTEM (see clause 10 of the SGML standard). In SGML, these identifiers can be in any form at all, so long as

- they are quoted (using either single or double quotes in the reference concrete syntax)
- they contain only "minimum data characters:" letters, digits, white-space and "special" characters, namely `()+,-./:=?`

Any leading or trailing white-space characters in these identifiers are ignored and any multiple internal white-space characters are treated as a single space. This is done in the same way as for SGML attribute values (except those of type ENTITY, ENTITIES and CDATA, which are not so normalized).

When the FORMAL feature is not used SGML permits "informal" public identifiers of any form:

```
<!ENTITY        book1       PUBLIC
    "IEEE 1003.1">
<!ENTITY        fig3        PUBLIC
    "/u/lfd/figurea.tiff">
<!ENTITY        poem        PUBLIC
    "Elli's favorite poem">
```

However, there is a **formal public identifier** (FPI) syntax, which provides internal structure to the identifiers and allows the registration of unique, persistent names for data objects. We describe it in the next section.

3.6 Formal public identifiers

HyTime requires the FORMAL feature so that links to external data objects may be more easily resolvable. Formal public identifiers, or FPIs, have a useful internal structure. When this feature is used, an SGML parser will check that all public identifiers conform to the proper syntax. ISO Standard 9070 describes this syntax and the registration procedures to be used to make an identifier publicly accessible.

One simple way to create a registered FPI is to use an International Standard Book Number, or ISBN, using the registration authority established by the publishing industry. For example, the FPI for this book is:

```
+//ISBN 0-7923-9432-1//TEXT
Making Hypermedia Work//EN
```

An entity representing the book could thus be declared and used in a HyTime **nameloc** to link to the book. A **treeloc** or other locator mechanism would be added in order to link to any component of the book.

```
<!ENTITY          book1          PUBLIC
      "+//ISBN 0-7923-9432-1//TEXT
      Making Hypermedia Work//EN">
```

A formal public identifier has several parts, separated by pairs of slash characters. The double slash sequence may not occur except where specified by the FPI syntax. The parts are shown in Table 3.1.

A HyTime system reports an error should a non-formal public identifier be encountered. In addition to such reporting, however, a practical system will attempt to interpret an informal identifier and continue processing without incident, rather than merely terminating.

ISO registration of public identifiers is not available as of this writing, so the potential of public identifiers has not been fully exploited. However, an International Standard Book Number (ISBN) *can* be used to create a proper public FPI, so that anyone wishing to create formally registered identifiers need merely obtain an ISBN publisher number and can construct a properly registered owner name.

Note that the "owner name" portion of an FPI does not specify the owner of the data object the FPI points to. Rather (see the Introduction and clause 3.10 of ISO 9070), it "identifies the originator of the public identifier...," and thus "The owner of a public identifier is not necessarily the owner of the object that it identifies."

Part	Function
+//	The **owner prefix**, one of: `+//` An owner formally registered under the rules of ISO 9070 `-//` Any unregistered owner prefix (other) Must be an ISO publication number, such as "ISO 8879:1986"
ISBN 0-7923-9432-1	The **owner name**
//	Separator.
TEXT	The **public text class**, usually one of these values: `TEXT` An SGML document or portion `DOCUMENT` A complete SGML document `NONSGML` Data not in SGML (the declaration should include an NDATA specification to describe the data format) `NOTATION` A definition for a notation (as opposed to data expressed in the notation) Other values are mainly for entities peculiar to SGML, such as DTDs, notation specifications, etc.
	An optional "`-//`" to indicate that the replacement text is unavailable for some reason (not used in this example)
Making...	The **description** or name by which a human can locate the entity
//	Separator
EN	The **language** in which the data is encoded ("EN" means English). This should be a language code according to ISO 639. Applications are free to use other codes if no ISO code applies. In accordance with the ISO 9070 recommendations for the situation when no language code is available, we suggest the use of the value XX for computer languages and natural languages without a code.
	An optional description of the display device for which the entity is set up, in case there are versions for different devices (not used in this example)

Table 3.1: Parts of a formal public identifier

When creating a formal public identifier, an organization takes on the responsibility to ensure that any changes in the content of the entity are properly reflected in the name, etc.

To create a registered public identifier, the owner name must be registered according to ISO 9070. To make this process of name assignment easier, owner names can be divided into parts by occurrences of the marker "::". The first field of the name must specify the issuing authority for the name, and the remaining parts can give any additional information needed to identify the object. To create a public owner name from an ISBN, put the string "`ISBN`" followed by the ISBN publisher or book number designating the issuer or a published reference.

Appendix B declares several FPIs for common graphical notations as well as a public FPI to name the collection of notation declarations. These are not only useful in their own right but as examples of FPIs.

4

HyTime Quick Start

This chapter introduces the basic concepts and structures of HyTime through a series of examples. The examples do not include all the required declarations and setup, but working through them will give you a feeling for how HyTime approaches hypertext/hypermedia linking, and what constructs and terminology you should keep in mind throughout the following chapters.

We will begin with the simplest class of HyTime link, a **`clink`**, and show a number of ways to use it to point to data objects of various kinds, such as SGML elements, graphical data in various notations, and so on. We also show how to use coordinates to refer to places in space and time and how to associate objects with each other. Finally, we discuss how HyTime element types are created in SGML using the notion of **architectural forms**.

4.1 Clink, the basic point-to-point link

The **`clink`** is the simplest form of link in HyTime, is also one of the most useful and exactly corresponds to the kind of linking that has been used in SGML since its inception. An element with an SGML attribute of type IDREF occurs at the link's origin or source, and serves as a link to the element with the corresponding ID, commonly called the destination or target. In a typical interface a reader could click on the displayed content of the **clink** in order to follow the link and access the destination's content.

The name **clink** stands for "contextual link," because its instances must occur in context. That is, the markup representing the link itself is located at its source end, as shown here:

```
<p>before holding a garden party,
    <clink linkend=sec30>install the lawn</clink>
</p>
```

The link origin is embedded within a paragraph. The content of the link element, "install the lawn", is special because it is not only displayable text, but also an **anchor**, a portion of the document to which a link is attached. With a **clink**, the attachment is obvious: the link element itself is one end of the link, namely its source anchor.

The `linkend` attribute specifies the other **linkend** of the link, which points to an element somewhere that has ID `sec30`. The destination itself is the other anchor:

```
<chap><ct>Lawn replacement</ct>
    ...
    <sec id=sec30>
       <st>Installation Procedure</st>
       <p>Place sod green side up</p>
       ...
    </sec>
    ...
</chap>
```

The entire `sec` element is the destination anchor for the `clink`. A HyTime system notices the presence of the **clink** and can, when requested, use it to locate the destination. An interface might highlight the source anchor and scroll to the destination anchor if the user clicks on the source anchor. We describe **clink** further as part of the Hyperlinks module of HyTime in Chapter 7.

SGML systems have been using elements like **clink** for years as one way of encoding hypertext links in SGML; only the element and attribute names have differed (and we see below that these do not matter to HyTime).

4.2 Linking to destinations without IDs

All linking in HyTime eventually boils down to an ID: the linkend attribute of a **clink**, for example, must always be a valid IDREF. However, it need not point directly to the destination. The example below is also correct: the first clink points to an element of a second class, a nameloc, which in turn locates the same section element shown above. The nameloc places the IDREF inside an embedded nmlist element, as we discuss later.

```
<clink linkend=link2>
...
<nameloc id=link2>
    <nmlist nametype=element>sec30</nmlist>
</nameloc>
```

Why is such indirection useful? Not every data object has an ID. In particular, inter-document linking is sometimes handled most easily via indirection. Some SGML documents put IDs only on selected elements, such as chapters and sections. Non-SGML data cannot have SGML IDs and may not have any unique IDs at all: a portion of a fax image or video frame, for instance, typically has no ID. Even data formats with distinct objects may not have unique identifiers for them; for example, not all engineering software provides other applications with unique identifiers for individual components.

Because of this, HyTime provides many ways to refer to things lacking IDs. These methods work by declaring a special kind of element, a **locator**, appropriate to each kind of location in data (the term "locator" subsumes several HyTime architectural forms). Instances of that element can point where needed, and those instances can have their own IDs. This done, a clink can point to the data by pointing to the locator.

With this technique, a HyTime link can also point to non-SGML data such as a graphical image. Given an SGML entity named figure3 that stands for a graphical image, you can link to it as shown below (the clink can occur before or after the nameloc):

```
<nameloc id=fig3ptr nametype=entity>
    <nmlist>figure3</nmlist>
</nameloc>

<clink linkend=fig3ptr>See also figure 3.</clink>
```

Again, this is very like the way SGML handles such pointing. The difference here is that the entity's name appears in the content of the nmlist element, rather than as the value of a reserved attribute (which would be more typical in SGML). Thus SGML itself cannot validate that "`figure3`" is in fact an entity name; if it is to be done, such validation must be part of the HyTime system.

4.3 HyTime locators

The methods just shown permit pointing to any entire data object in any format desired: a sound file, a CAD drawing, a movie, or another SGML document. However, most useful links point to a specific portion of a data object. HyTime provides other locator types for specifying components of a data object (they are described more completely in Chapter 8, which describes the HyTime Location address module).

One of the handiest of these locators applies to SGML trees and is called **`treeloc`**. It provides a way to step down through successive levels until a particular element is reached. For example, in a document whose top is a `book` element we might wish to find a paragraph that is

- in the (first and only) `book` element
- in the `body` (not the `front-matter`)
- in the fourth `chap` (not any of the first three)
- in the second `sec` (not the `chap-title` or the first `sec`)
- the first `para` (not the `sec-title`)

If we assume there are no IDs on the `para` element of interest, then there is certainly no way to point a **`clink`** directly at the destination. Instead, one can create a **`treeloc`** that lists which child to take at every step down through the tree.

```
<treeloc id=my-ptr>
    <marklist>1 2 4 3 2</marklist>
</treeloc>
```

The `marklist` serves as a container for the numbers. Also note that the fourth step specifies child number 3, not 2, to take into account the chapter title preceding the sections. The last step likewise accounts for the `sec-title` preceding the desired `para`.

Given the `treeloc` just shown, a **`clink`** can point at the real destination indirectly, by pointing at a **`treeloc`**:

```
<clink linkend=my-ptr>
    See other explanatory paragraph.</clink>
```

Such pointing exploits the essential structure provided by descriptive markup methodology and expressed by SGML syntax. We give a more detailed example and an illustration of this concept in Section 8.4.2.

4.3.1 Location ladders

HyTime also provides a way to combine such pointers explicitly and produce **location ladders** in which each step locates some object relative to another place called the **location source**. This is conceptually similar to the way reference footnotes work on paper: an indicator in the main text points to an entry in the bibliography, which in turn points to the actual source document.

To use this indirect linking method in HyTime, we could split the `treeloc` into two parts:

```
<treeloc id=part1>
    <marklist>1 2 4</marklist>
</treeloc>
<treeloc id=part2 locsrc=part1>
    <marklist>1 3 1</marklist>
</treeloc>

<clink linkend=part2>See other explanatory
paragraph.</clink>
```

The `clink` points to the second `treeloc`, which specifies a path to be followed *relative to* its location source, which the `locsrc` attribute defines to be the first `treeloc`. The second `marklist` adds an initial "1" because **`treeloc`** counts the root of its location source as one step. This example locates the same place as the previous one.

The last example is too simple to be especially useful, since it is easier to keep its two parts together. Location ladders are most useful when the parts are different classes of locators, as in the following inter-document location ladder that finds the three words "In the beginning" from the start of the first `verse` of the first `chapter` of the first `book` of the Bible:

```
<nameloc id=part1 nametype=entity>
    <nmlist>King-James-Bible</nmlist>
</nameloc>

<treeloc id=part2 locsrc=part1>
    <marklist>1 1 1</marklist>
</treeloc>

<dataloc id=part3 locsrc=part2 quantum=word>
    <dimlist>1 3</dimlist>
</dataloc>

<clink linkend=part3>As Danker notes, this
phrase...</clink>
```

In this example the `clink` points first to a `dataloc` with ID `part3`, that picks out words 1 to 3 of the `dataloc` element's location source. That location source is defined by the element with ID `part2`, which is a `treeloc` element. The `treeloc` in turn is interpreted relative to the `nameloc` with ID `part1`, which refers to an entity named `King-James-Bible`. This entity would be found as specified in its entity declaration, via a PUBLIC or SYSTEM identifier. Limits can be imposed on the length of such ladders using the `reflevel` attribute discussed in Section 14.8.

4.4 Graphic locations and geometry

HyTime provides a special class of locator that can be used for picking out components of multimedia data objects. This is **fcsloc**, short for Finite Coordinate Space Location. An **fcsloc** picks out an area of space with a starting position and length along one or more coordinate axes. These axes may represent any number of things, such as:

- height and width within a video frame area
- position in space
- position in time
- physical quantities such as voltage
- abstract units not corresponding to any physical quantity

Measurement along axes requires declaring the name, length and unit of measurement for each axis. For example, to pick out ranges of time in a video via a range of frames one must specify axes and scales for the data. We discuss defining such axes in Chapter 13. With this done and the video itself declared as an entity in a particular non-SGML notation, one can use **fcsloc** to locate specific parts of it for linking.

Assuming the example axes are ordered { horizontal, vertical, time } and count upwards and to the right, a particular video entity could be declared as:

```
<!NOTATION      NTSC          PUBLIC
     ...>
<!ENTITY        MPandHG       SYSTEM
     "python.ntsc"            NDATA       NTSC>
```

The following location ladder specifies a destination that is a squat rectangle in the lower-left corner of that video entity, lasting from frame 2000 to 2099 of the video:

```
<nameloc id=video-ptr nametype=entity>
    <nmlist>MPandHG</nmlist>
</nameloc>

<fcsloc id=rabbit locsrc=video-ptr impfcs=vid-coord>
    <dimspec>1 100</dimspec>
    <dimspec>1 20</dimspec>
    <dimspec>2000 100</dimspec>
</fcsloc>
```

The `impfcs` attribute specifies the measurement system used to address the video. The `dimspec` elements in the `fcsloc` element hold the coordinates of the referenced region. For further information on **fcsloc** see Section 8.4.5 and Chapter 13.

This accomplished, one can create a `clink` element whose destination anchor is that time-indexed rectangle:

```
<p>Sir Robin discovered rabbits can be dangerous,
    as shown here: <clink linkend=rabbit>
</p>
```

Units of measurement can be generic or can be defined in terms of real physical units such as seconds and meters. All HyTime arithmetic uses the following numerical model:

- All quantities are positive integers.
- All coordinate spaces and all **fcsloc**-selected regions are rectangular, but may have any number of dimensions.
- Multiple units may be used for a single dimension (such as length), but must have a common denominator to which HyTime scales all measurements.
- There is a limit on the size of the scaled values, by default 2**32 (slightly over four billion).

For graphical representations with more complex coordinate systems or pointing requirements than **fcsloc** can easily accommodate, it is wisest to define a special locator syntax and use it; HyTime recommends this practice by saying that "Normally, such an object would be addressed by a notation-specific location address (notloc)." We show ways to do this in Chapter 12, Extending HyTime.

4.5 Linking by searching

Sometimes the destination of a hypermedia link is most easily characterized not by a unique name or a unique way of navigating there, but by some fact about the destination. This is sometimes called **intensional**

linking, because such a link specifies a function that finds the destination, rather than the destination itself.

For example, it is both convenient and clear to say that a link goes to the section called "Habañero precautions" rather than to "Section 27.3", or "ID sec.Hab.pre" or some such. HyTime accommodates such cases by providing a way to declare that the destination of some link is whatever a given query finds.

HyTime provides a query language called HyQ especially suited for finding things in hierarchical structures such as SGML documents. Note that HyQ is a query *specification* language: it is not particularly attractive for users to read or write, because it is meant to be used as a foundation on which to build various interfaces. We discuss HyQ in Chapter 9 and the HyLex pattern matching syntax in Chapter 11. As an example, however, to specify that the destination of a link is the element (or elements) that has element type `title` and contains the string "Habañero precautions", you could give this HyQ expression:

```
<HyQ qdomain=my.cooking.manual>
    Select(DOMTREE
          And(Eq(Proploc(CAND GI) "TITLE")
                He(Dataloc(CAND 1 -1)
                   "Habañero precautions")))
</HyQ>
```

In effect, this examines every component in the document tree specified as `my.cooking.manual` and tests each one to see if it has GI equal to `title` and if its data content holds the string "`Habañero precautions`". All components satisfying both criteria become results.

You can include queries using other query languages if your HyTime engine supports them as extensions. However, very few pre-SGML query languages are adept at handling hierarchical structures and so a careful evaluation must be made.

4.6 More complex link structures

The **`clink`** must reside at one of its ends and point to the other. However, there are cases demanding other structures. For example one may want to add links in a document one cannot change. The document may reside on a CD-ROM or other unchangeable storage device, or may simply be owned by someone else. In some cases both ends of a link might be in such documents, as with critical commentary on how two published documents relate.

For such cases HyTime provides an **out of line** link, which need not reside at any of its endpoints. The architectural form for this is **ilink**, for "independent link." An **ilink** element takes a `linkends` attribute, which may specify any number of IDREF values. Like the single IDREF of **clink**, each one on an **ilink** is a linkend, and points to an anchor. The IDREFs may use all mechanisms of the Location address module for indirectly specifying locations. An **ilink** could use two separate location ladders to connect related parts of two books:

```
<nameloc id=kjv nametype=entity>
    <nmlist>King-James-Bible</nmlist>
</nameloc>
<treeloc id=kjv1 locsrc=kjv>
    <marklist>1 1 1</marklist>
</treeloc>

<nameloc id=pl nametype=entity>
    <nmlist>Paradise-Lost</nmlist>
</nameloc>
<treeloc id=pl1 locsrc=pl>
    <marklist>20 3 10</marklist>
</treeloc>

<ilink linkends="kjv1 pl1"></ilink>
```

The location of an **ilink** is not one of its linkends.

The ability to keep links completely separate from the documents containing their endpoints was introduced by the InterMedia system. It is very important, not only for the case of read-only documents, but also to provide a way to organize and differentiate the many links that may be added to important documents. By using this methodology one can create multiple independent **webs**, each including a collection of links developed for a particular purpose.

An **ilink** can have more than two ends. There are situations where this can be useful, such as editorial review, where one might link parts of two editions or two related documents, and comment on the relationship. Other ends might recommend an editorial change, identify the reviewer, and so on. Each element type that is to represent an **ilink** must declare how many ends it takes and assign a named **anchor role** or purpose to each one.

4.7 HyTime and SGML element types

The reader may have noticed that we have shown examples of links of different sorts: some were cross-references leading to supplemental or explanatory information, while others led to commentary or criticism. It is common to express differences in link types by defining more than one SGML element type to represent links, such as `xref` and `commentary-ref`, even though the operational treatment and syntax of these elements may be identical.

For this and other reasons HyTime does not define actual SGML element types at all. Instead, it provides a template for what an SGML element type must be like to be usable as a HyTime element (such as **`clink`**). Thus, application designers can declare any number of elements needed, all of which a HyTime system can recognize and treat properly as subclasses of **`clink`**. HyTime's templates are called **architectural forms**, and **`clink`** is thus an architectural form name (in this book architectural form names appear in boldface monospace type). We discuss the nature and definition of architectural forms in detail in Chapter 5.

A HyTime system must be able to recognize an element as conforming to the **`clink`** architectural form, regardless of its element type name. To make this possible some signal must be provided. The signal is an attribute whose name is `HyTime` and whose value is `clink`:

```
<xref HyTime=clink linkend=sec30>
```

Although this special attribute must always be present for HyTime to recognize the element, it can normally be left implicit. Probably the most familiar way to do this is to specify a default value in the DTD:

```
<!ELEMENT       xref        - - (#PCDATA)>
<!ATTLIST       xref
    HyTime      NAME        "clink"
    linkend     IDREF       #REQUIRED>
```

This works fine, and permits omitting the attribute from start-tags if the SGML SHORTTAG feature is used. We can do even better, however. In typical uses this attribute should never vary: every instance of the `xref` element type will be a **`clink`**. SGML syntax provides ways to ensure this. The clearest way is to insert the keyword #FIXED in the attribute declaration; this causes the SGML parser to report an error if any other value is ever specified for the attribute:

```
<!ELEMENT       xref          - - (#PCDATA)>
<!ATTLIST       xref
    HyTime      NAME          #FIXED "clink"
    linkend     IDREF         #REQUIRED>
```

The HyTime standard uses this method widely in its example declarations. The second way is a minor variation on it. If you declare only one permissible value for an attribute and also make it the default, then any other value would be reported as an error:

```
<!ELEMENT       xref          - - (#PCDATA)>
<!ATTLIST       xref
    HyTime      (clink)       "clink"
    linkend     IDREF         #REQUIRED>
```

You can declare any number of SGML element types that conform to a single architectural form. The following declaration is not in conflict with the previous ones in any way, but merely makes another subclass of **clink** element:

```
<!ELEMENT       comm-ref      - - ANY>
<!ATTLIST       comm-ref
    HyTime      NAME          #FIXED "clink"
    linkend     IDREF         #REQUIRED>
```

These elements both "conform to the **clink** architectural form:" that is, they have a `HyTime` attribute that claims they are **clinks** and they fulfill the requirements to make that claim true (such as having a `linkend` attribute). They have different content models, but those models are both within the limits of variation permitted by HyTime's definition for **clink**. An application may do different processing specific to each subclass of **clink**, in addition to implementing HyTime's inherent semantics for the **clink** class.

Architectural form names need never appear as element type names in your HyTime documents. In fact, they will not appear unless you happen to give your elements the same names as HyTime architectural form names. Unless doing so would mask an important distinction in a document, using such names is good practice.

4.7.1 The structure of a HyTime document

Due to its reliance on attributes to control processing HyTime makes almost no demands that are not directly related to using HyTime facilities. There are a few such demands however, and one is that a HyTime document must identify itself as a HyTime document. There are a number of special declarations that must be included which we discuss later (see Section 5.6), but there is one that is part of the structure of the document, as opposed to a declaration that describes facts about the document. This is the **HyDoc** architectural form.

Each HyTime document is required to have the top-level element be a **HyDoc.** The HyDoc element does not have restrictions on its tag name or content model, but does identify its content as subject to HyTime processing.

5

The Structure of HyTime

This chapter provides an overview of the organization of HyTime and the conventions used to describe and define it. It explores the notion of "architectural forms" used in the definition of HyTime and SGML issues related to using HyTime productively. It also explains the HyTime model of hyperdocument and the major pieces of a complete HyTime software system and how they fit together. Finally, it describes HyTime's method of declaring that an SGML document is a HyTime document and which optional features are used in a document.

5.1 Basic HyTime concepts

A HyTime **hyperdocument** can be a single SGML document that happens to use HyTime constructs such as cross-references between sections. Or, it can be a complex collection of documents and other information units in a wide variety of media and formats, that are interconnected by hypertext links. Some components of a HyTime hyperdocument may be SGML, some may be sound files, graphics, video sequences, or something else. Existing SGML documents can often be made HyTime conforming without changing content or markup at all, merely by altering markup declarations in their DTDs.

The set of links, or **web**, that connects a hyperdocument can be immense. In networked systems the total scope is often difficult to specify since it includes documents from sites all over the globe. From a HyTime perspective, however, the total scope is not an issue. HyTime defines methods for connecting documents to create a hyperdocument, and one needs some document from which to start processing. Beyond that, an application can manage the size of a web however it chooses.

The HyTime starting document is the **hub document** and it determines the *potential* scope of a hyperdocument. A hub document is simply a HyTime-conforming SGML document from which processing can begin. In some applications, typically isolated single-author hyperdocuments, there is only one possible hub document. In large-scale networked applications, however, where hypertext links tie together many people's work, there may be many reasonable starting points and thus many potential hub documents. Any one of these can become a hub document by being designated one to a HyTime processor (no special markup identifies a document as a hub). A hub document *must* be encoded using SGML and HyTime; no other portion of the hyperdocument is similarly restricted.

HyTime defines the term hyperdocument as a set of documents that

- can be reached from your chosen hub document
- is of interest for some reason

A hyperdocument might be a collection of information assembled for publication as a unit or for transport across a network. It could include many kinds of data objects, such as structure and unstructured text, still and motion graphics, interactive animations, sound, and so on.

In general, is not necessary to follow every reference to the very end. Therefore a HyTime hyperdocument is open — a hyperdocument need not include all of the information that can be reached from the hub document. The full set may include millions of documents that are only distantly related to your hub document. The set of documents you care about at a given moment constitutes a legitimate hyperdocument, no matter what its size may be.

Two examples of the far-reaching interconnections that can be created are wide-area bulletin board systems such a as Usenet News and the World Wide Web. Usenet news is a forum for thousands of ongoing discussions called news groups. Users write **postings** that are available to everyone who subscribes to that particular discussion, and the readers then send responses which are in turn forwarded to everyone. A Netnews posting generally includes automatically and manually generated references (links) to the postings to which it responds.

The World Wide Web (WWW) is a public domain hypertext browsing system and protocol that has become very popular on the Internet network. It allows text documents to be linked to other whole texts and graphics, using a simple SGML-inspired linking protocol (in Section 10.2 we will discuss how WWW markup can be made HyTime compliant). Since new WWW sites frequently link to existing sites as well as providing their own information, the set of document links is in constant flux, even without interactive editing.

5.2 Architectural forms

Architectural forms are a definition and implementation technique used to integrate HyTime into SGML applications. Understanding the use of architectural forms is necessary to understanding how HyTime works. This integration technique avoids the need for all HyTime applications to use a single mandatory DTD or fixed set of element declarations. Architectural forms permit DTD writers to use their own element type names for HyTime structures. Not only is the architectural form notion fundamental to HyTime, it is a new and useful SGML coding technique that can, if used wisely, ease the standardization of tagging practices by steering a route between the Scylla of excessive rigidity and the Charybdis of excessive freedom that threaten such standards when they must serve large, disparate groups of users.

For example, the **clink** architectural form represents a simple cross-reference. It needs particular attributes and restrictions on its content model, and so has declarations for these things, but the architectural form does not specify an element type name (GI)) that you must use. In fact, there may be several elements with different names that are all subclasses of **clink**s and will function as such in a HyTime system.

5.2.1 Why use architectural forms?

HyTime could follow the standard SGML pattern and define a specific set of elements, each with a GI, a content model and some attributes. Users of HyTime would then add the definitions to their DTDs and use the elements in their documents. HyTime processors would watch for elements with those particular GIs and process them in accordance with HyTime's definitions. HyTime would, in that case, be a DTD or a DTD fragment.

The "HyTime DTD" solution, however, would have had several deficiencies, and the HyTime committee rejected it. Users need to have special tag names for a variety of reasons:

- Names are language-specific: `link` means little to non-English speakers. In languages that use non-roman writing systems this kind of problem is even more severe.
- Users prefer different terms even within a single language. Hypermedia experts may prefer `link`, while humanities scholars may prefer `reference` and an individual user might prefer `hook` or something else. A standard that forces people to change long-established terminology is unlikely to be used.
- Sometimes it is necessary to make finer distinctions among elements than can be anticipated in advance. Some applications may need 30 different kinds of links, each requiring slightly different processing. Thus it is useful to be able to assign more than one GI to a single conceptual type: to create subclasses. Adding a `type` attribute works, but does not permit subclasses to declare additional attributes or subelements, especially if the subclasses have radically differing structures that must be verified.
- A desired element name may already be used in a DTD, and so cannot be used again without duplication or conflict.

The first two problems could be addressed by requiring that user software be able to substitute localized synonyms for element names whenever they are displayed. However, the last two problems are not so easily solved without additional notions. A standard intended for widespread use thus cannot conveniently enforce particular tag names.

5.2.2 How architectural forms work

An architectural form is a name for a class of element, but is not the SGML GI. A HyTime engine thus needs a different signal to decide how to process an element. To recognize HyTime elements a HyTime engine looks in one place: the value of the `HyTime` attribute.

For example, you can create an element `mylink`, and if it matches HyTime's **`clink`** architectural form, you merely add an attribute `HyTime=clink`. This done, a HyTime engine can identify the element as one of its own and process it correctly:

```
<!ELEMENT      mylink      - - (p)*>
<!ATTLIST      mylink
    linkend    CDATA       #REQUIRED
    HyTime     NAME        "clink">
```

HyTime thus separates the *abstract type* of element from the *concrete type* that SGML knows as the GI. The true abstract type (or major class) of any element that HyTime must deal with must therefore appear in an attribute called the **HyTime architectural form attribute**. The permissible values for the `HyTime` attribute are defined by the HyTime standard and cannot be extended.

In the terminology of object-oriented programming, HyTime provides a set of base classes, all of which are virtual. A particular DTD declares SGML element types that are subclasses of those. Only one level of subclassing is provided. The subclasses can add their own class and instance variables, in the guise of fixed and unfixed SGML attributes. Methods are the domain of particular applications, and are typically defined using style sheets or programs.

Normally, all instances of a given element type throughout a document conform to the same architectural form. Therefore, the `HyTime` attribute normally has the same value on every instance of a given element type. This can be enforced by using the keyword #FIXED on the `HyTime` attribute's declaration:

```
<!ATTLIST       mylink
    linkend     CDATA          #REQUIRED
    HyTime      NAME           #FIXED "clink">
```

If your application has several distinct uses for a HyTime construct, you can declare multiple element types all of which take the same architectural form attribute value. For example:

```
<!ELEMENT       reference      - O (...)>
<!ELEMENT       footnote       - O (...)>
<!ELEMENT       glossterm      - O (...)>
<!ATTLIST       (reference | footnote | glossterm)
    linkend     CDATA          #REQUIRED
    HyTime      NAME           #FIXED "clink">
```

All these elements are treated as **`clink`** elements by a HyTime processor. HyTime makes its definitions in terms of architectural forms. Thus, whenever you see HyTime refer to a **`clink`**, remember that it need not be called `clink` in your DTD: the place to look is the `HyTime` attribute, not the GI. In this book most example elements have the same name as the architectural form the element represents to simplify explanations.

5.2.3 Architectural form conformance issues

A `HyTime` attribute for an element is a claim that the element represents and conforms to the specified HyTime architectural form. Like most claims, this may be true or false. Consider the following typical declaration for a `list` element type:

```
<!ELEMENT      list          - O (item+)>
<!ATTLIST      list
    type       (num | bull | plain)   "plain">
```

It should be clear that adding an attribute `HyTime=clink` to this declaration doesn't make the `list` into a sensible subclass of **`clink`**. When a HyTime processor sees the attribute and tries to treat a `list` element as a HyTime **`clink`**, it will fail. One reason is that the `linkend` attribute required on a **`clink`** is not there.

Although any element that exactly matches the meta-content model and attribute declarations conforms, HyTime also permits such elements to vary their content models and attribute lists within certain limits. Such variations are generally useful in two cases:

- when an element is just like the form except that it needs extra attributes or subelements. For example, in an application intended for military or other secure use, every link might require a "security-clearance" attribute that says who may traverse it.
- when an element is just like the form except that it does not need optional attributes or subelements the form permits. For example, the **`clink`** architectural form permits but does not require an `ID` attribute, which we omitted from the example element declarations above.

Because HyTime elements can differ in content model and attributes from an architectural form, the declarations of architectural forms are not SGML declarations as defined by the SGML standard. Technically speaking they are **meta-declarations**, intended to communicate to humans what actual declarations are allowed. Their content models are properly called **meta-content models**. We leave implicit the distinctions between declarations and meta-declarations and those between content models and meta-content models wherever possible without confusion. This is similar to the HyTime standard's practice of using almost exactly the same syntax for architectural forms as SGML uses for element definitions.

Note that HyTime does not enforce any restrictions on the DTD of a HyTime document. The HyTime standard requires only that the elements of the document *instance* that have HyTime attributes must satisfy the meta-DTD of the element. Non-conforming content models in the DTD are fine as long as only conforming document instances are presented to HyTime. However, even though it is not a requirement of HyTime that the DTD *enforce* HyTime's structure, it is prudent practice to write such DTDs. An overly permissive DTD invites errors.

5.2.4 Attributes on architectural forms

An element that instantiates an architectural form must provide all the attributes and subelements the form requires. It can in general have any extra attributes desired; this is one way to reflect application variations in a single architectural form.

As an example, you might create two link element types: one exactly like the **clink** architectural form and one that adds a `security-level` or `edited-by` attribute needed in your specific application. HyTime defines no processing for such attributes, so they do not affect how a HyTime engine treats the element. An application, however, might use them to affect processing, say by hiding all elements with a `security-level` over a certain value.

Attributes that HyTime does not require need not even be defined in the DTD (in which case they will never occur). In HyTime meta-declarations, required HyTime attributes have a default value prescription of #REQUIRED, as here (from clause 6.7.2):

```
<!attlist      qpn
     HyTime    NAME        qpn
     id        ID          #REQUIRED>
```

Sometimes the expectation that an attribute is to be #FIXED is strengthened to a requirement by adding the notation `#FIXED in-dtd':` to the attribute meta-declaration. For example, the meta-declaration below (from clause 9.2.1) declares that the `anchrole` attribute of an **ilink** must have the same value on all instances of each subclass of the architectural form **ilink**:

```
<!attlist      ilink
     HyTime    NAME        ilink
     id        ID          #IMPLIED
     anchrole  CDATA       #FIXED in-DTD
     ...
>
```

5.2.5 Meta-content-models

Most HyTime architectural forms for elements specify a concrete meta-content model, similar to an element declaration in an actual SGML DTD. However, names in the meta-content model are architectural form names, not element names.

As a simplified example of architectural forms, we will consider a form for lists, whose meta-declaration is shown below. The **list** form is not part of HyTime's architecture; we will call the example architecture "my-arch" instead. My-arch processors detect elements of interest to them by looking for a `my-arch` attribute rather than a `HyTime` attribute. Two meta-declarations in this my-arch architecture would then be:

```
<!element      list         - O (item+)>
<!element      item         - O (#PCDATA)>
```

That is, any element conforming to the **list** architectural form consists of one or more **item** elements, which in turn have only text content.

Both **list** and **item** are architectural form names. An application of the my-arch architecture would declare actual SGML element types that conform to these forms; they may have any names, so long as they specify the `my-arch` architectural form attribute:

```
<!-- Define a repair-list as a kind of list that
      must consist of at least one step
-->
<!ELEMENT      repair       - O (step+)>
<!ATTLIST      repair
    my-arch    NAME         #FIXED "list">

<!ELEMENT      step         - O (#PCDATA)>
<!ATTLIST      step
    my-arch    NAME         #FIXED "item">
```

Because instances of element type `step` conform to architectural form **item**, the content shown here conforms not only to the SGML content models just shown but to the meta-content model for **list** above:

```
<repair>
    <step>Remove case</step>
    <step>Replace logic board</step>
    <step>Reassemble case</step>
</repair>
```

It is also legitimate to have multiple elements conforming to a single architectural form, and all of them can satisfy meta-content model requirements interchangeably. For example, one can add another subclass of **list**, called a test procedure or `testproc`, that must contain a series of instances of another kind of **item**, called `test`:

```
<!-- Define test-procedure, another kind of list -->
<!ELEMENT      testproc      - O (test+)>
<!ATTLIST      testproc
    my-arch    NAME          #FIXED "list">

<!ELEMENT      test          - O (#PCDATA)>
<!ATTLIST      test
    my-arch    NAME          #FIXED "item">
...

<testproc>
    <test>Turn on computer</test>
    <test>Watch for smoke</test>
</testproc>
```

Because the examples just shown are actual element declarations, not meta-declarations, it would not be correct to put `test` elements within a `repair` element or `step` elements with a `testproc`. This would be a syntax error in SGML, encountered before the data ever reached a my-arch processor.

If desired, we could modify the SGML content model for the `testproc` element so that it allowed both `test` and `step` elements as children:

```
<!ELEMENT      testproc      - O (test|step)+>
```

No elements have been added whose architectural forms are not permitted by the **list** meta-model; we have merely taken into account more than one element type of the same form. This change in the actual element declaration would make the following `testproc` element valid in SGML and conformant to the my-arch architectural forms:

```
<testproc>
    <step>Remove case</step>
    <test>Turn on computer</step>
    <test>Watch for smoke</step>
    <step>Replace logic board</step>
    <test>Reassemble case</test>
</testproc>
```

We have illustrated how to map between architectural form names (which occur in meta-content models) and element names (which occur in actual content models). This can be done even when there are several elements of a given form. However, even more variation is permitted in constructing content models that conform to a meta-content model, as we see below.

5.2.6 Modifying meta-content models

You need not make an actual content model by merely substituting element names for architectural form names. When creating element types that conform to an architectural form, you can change the model to make the content models *more restrictive* than the meta-content model. For example, each of the element declarations below has a content model more restrictive than **list**'s meta-content model above, since any structure that passes one of them also passes the meta-content model above:

```
<!ELEMENT       mylist        - O (step+)>
<!ELEMENT       biglist       - O (step, step, step*)>
<!ELEMENT       list.1        - O (step)>

<!ATTLIST       (mylist | biglist | list.1)
    my-arch     NAME          #FIXED "list">
```

It should be clear that absolutely any element instance that conforms to any of these elements' content models also conforms to the meta-content model for **list**. These actual models are all more restrictive than the meta-content model. If this is not clear, review the details of SGML content models.

All such changes are permitted in HyTime. The rule is:

> An element instance conforms to an architectural form if and only if it could be parsed without error under the form's meta-model after renaming all elements to the architectural form that they satisfy. The SGML parser will ensure that it parses under its own actual model.

HyTime allows a great deal of flexibility, since it permits *any content model at all* for an element conforming to an architectural form, as long as each *instance* of the element conforms.

Because conforming to an architectural form is determined for each element instance rather than for the content model, the following element declaration for a subclass of **list** is also legal:

```
<!ELEMENT       headed-list - O (header?, step+)>
<!ATTLIST       headed-list
    my-arch     NAME          #FIXED "list">
<!ELEMENT       header        - O (#PCDATA)>
<!ELEMENT       step          - O (#PCDATA)>
<!ATTLIST       step
    my-arch     NAME          #FIXED "item">
```

This permits authors to create element instances that conform to the **list** architectural form, but does not prevent authors from creating element instances that do not. A conforming element instance would contain only subelements that in turn conform to the **item** architectural form, so could not contain a `header` element.

Documents that parse according to an SGML DTD that contains these declarations may also conform to the my-arch architecture; but then again, they may not. Such declarations are risky because they allow the creation of correct SGML documents that are not valid HyTime documents. Because these content models only *permit* instances of their elements to conform to HyTime's architectural forms, an SGML authoring or validation system cannot ensure the documents are valid.

The `headed-list` element below is valid in SGML parser under the declarations shown above, but does not conform to **list**:

```
<headed-list>
     <header>Tools needed</header>
     <step>Hammer</step>
     <step>Computer</step>
</headed-list>
```

It fails to be a my-arch **list** because it does not consist only of **item** elements. The easy way to remember the rules about HyTime meta-content models is this: only *instances* of an element can conform to an architectural form. An element type as declared in the DTD may happen to rule out any instances that do not so conform, but that is not required.

Our manufactured example using lists is simpler than some HyTime examples, but precisely the same rules apply. A validating HyTime engine will report an error when it attempts to process a non-conforming element instance, but it is not required to report it before that point.

5.2.7 The limits to variation

An element does not conform to an architectural form if it is merely "conceptually equivalent." That would require near-omniscience on the computer's part to ensure correct processing. Architectural forms are a way to rename element types, or to create subclasses of them. If an element differs more than this, one can speak of an "architectural similarity," but similarity is not conformance. Such a weak relation also compromises the desirable ability to validate documents. If an element has four legs and sharp teeth, calling it a duck still doesn't make it one.

5.2.8 Non-HyTime content

The material in this section reflects a number of changes that are expected to be made in a clarifying amendment to HyTime, but are not yet official. There are also some points of possible ambiguity in the standard as written. We explain these points and discuss which interpretations are likely to be safest. These details are not of primary importance for all HyTime users, so the first-time reader may prefer to skim or postpone reading this section.

HyTime distinguishes between three classes of non-HyTime elements in content models:

- Elements that do not conform to any architectural form (they have no `HyTime` attribute) are called **non-HyTime elements**; they may or may not contain HyTime elements. No HyTime processing is performed for these elements themselves.
- Elements for which no HyTime processing (including attribute processing) should be performed at all, even within any subelements are **suppress HyTime elements**.
- Elements that conform to the **`HyBrid`** architectural form have no special meaning to HyTime (such as serving as locators or links); however, they may use HyTime common attributes. These "HyTime Bridge" elements. may have any content model desired.

%HyBrid content

An element that has no specific HyTime semantics but requires use of some HyTime common attributes can be declared to have architectural form **`HyBrid`**. However, the term "HyBrid" is also used as a content model, that can be applied to define an element that may contain any arrangement of HyTime and non-HyTime subelements. This usage is expressed by use of the `%HyBrid;` parameter entity.

`%HyBrid;` content is used for architectural forms in which HyTime permits non-HyTime subelements to occur. HyTime defines such content via the parameter entity `%HyBrid;` which permits subelements conforming to the **`fcs`**, **`HyBrid`**, and **`sHyTime`** forms (**`fcs`** is not important for understanding `%HyBrid;`. We discuss **`sHyTime`** in the next section):

```
(fcs|HyBrid|sHyTime|#PCDATA)
```

Particular HyTime DTDs may add any other HyTime or non-HyTime element types to this list. The **`HyBrid`** *architectural form* enables using HyTime common attributes on an element type that has no other HyTime semantics; `%HyBrid;` *content* is used for elements that do not conform to any HyTime form, but might contain subelements that do.

The basic point of `%HyBrid;` content is to represent those locations where the application designer is free to insert whatever content makes sense for the application.

Architectural forms with %HyBrid; content fall into several categories:

- Generic containers that can contain just about anything, such as the **HyDoc** form for the HyTime document as a whole, or the **clink** form for hypertext links.
- Containers that encapsulate information a HyTime engine needs only to extract and pass to some non-HyTime processor, such as **activity** or **notloc**, whose content may be in any notation.
- Elements that contain non-HyTime processable descriptions such as the **bibloc** form.

The **HyDoc** form adds a variety of architectural forms as permitted inclusion exception elements to its content (`%HyBrid;`). Since these elements are inclusion exceptions on the top-level element of a HyTime document, they are in fact permitted anywhere in any HyTime document.

One of the proposed changes to the HyTime standard clarifies the role of the **HyBrid** form. A paragraph is to be inserted after note 79 of the standard (in clause 6.4) saying:

> An element of a type for which the HyTime attribute is not defined is a 'non-HyTime element:' It has no HyTime architectural form and does not affect conformance to the HyTime meta-DTD. Both HyTime and non-HyTime elements can occur in its content.

sHyTime content

The **sHyTime** form means "suppress HyTime processing." For such elements and all their contained elements, a HyTime processor ignores all `HyTime` attributes occurring anywhere in their content. **sHyTime** elements may have any content model.

HyTime does not declare any elements that have only **sHyTime** as their content. However, **sHyTime** is part of the expansion of the `%HyBrid;` parameter entity. Since the **HyDoc** content model includes `%HyBrid;` any element in a DTD based on HyTime may use it when HyTime processing should be suppressed.

The first printed edition of HyTime refers to **sHyTime** elements as **nHyTime** elements instead. This nomenclature proved confusing because it conflicted with the term non-HyTime element also used in the standard. The HyTime committee has therefore proposed the change to **sHyTime**.

5.2.9 Architectural forms for attributes

HyTime defines many architectural forms for elements, each with an associated attribute list. It also defines a number of attribute lists that are not associated with particular element forms. The Base module, for example, defines a number of **common attributes** that applications may add to the attribute list of any HyTime-conforming element types. The most important of these is the `id` attribute, whose status as a common attribute means it may be declared and then used for any HyTime element at all.

In addition to the common attributes, the HyTime standard defines a number of sets of attributes each of which can apply to particular element forms. For example, several forms in the Location address module can take the **multloc** attributes; they state this via a comment in the meta-declaration (as shown in Appendix A). The definitions of attribute forms other than common attributes include cross-references to the element forms to which they apply. To use such attribute sets, the actual attributes would have to be declared in the DTD, just like any others.

An attribute architectural form provides one or more attributes, but there is no special flag for detecting them, corresponding to the `HyTime` attribute for element forms. Instead, such attributes are detected by name whenever they occur on HyTime elements. They have no effect if specified on elements that do not specify the `HyTime` attribute.

Common attributes can be applied to non-HyTime elements by making the elements into HyTime elements of form **HyBrid**. The only HyTime processing defined for **HyBrid** elements is the processing of common attributes.

5.3 SGML issues in HyTime

5.3.1 Entities and IDs

HyTime documents use SGML's external entity features to locate data outside the hub document. A simple example of a HyTime reference to another file is the following, which leads to the whole of the document in some system storage area (such as a file) called "`letter1.sgm`":

```
<!ENTITY        letter-sample PUBLIC
    "-//sjd//TEXT Sample letter//EN" "letter1.sgm">
    ...
<nameloc>letter-sample</nameloc>
```

Also notice that the entity has an unregistered public identifier. A system that cannot resolve the system identifier "`letter1.sgm`" could use the public identifier to find the data.

In the case of data in non-SGML formats, entities with special declared notations can also be used. SGML does not define particular notation names, and HyTime defines only a few. In Appendix B we give notation declarations for common graphics file formats. We have also assigned a registered Formal Public Identifier (FPI) for this set of notation declarations so that it can be used by others.

HyTime relies heavily on the ID/IDREF capability of SGML to relate HyTime elements in a document. However, although SGML requires uniqueness of IDs and resolvability of IDREFs *within* a single SGML document, it does not support IDREFs between different documents. Two distinct documents may use identical IDs.

A document cannot use an SGML IDREF to designate an element in another document, since SGML's facilities work only on a single document at a time. The following example is legal SGML only if the linkend attribute is *not* declared to be an IDREF:

```
<xref doc=otherdoc linkend=elsewhere>
```

The `xref` element shown here is semantically similar to HyTime's more complex **nameloc** form (see Chapter 7) which also specifies a non-local ID value and an external entity name in order to locate an element in an external document.

5.3.2 Mixed content

SGML elements can be characterized by whether they may contain only other elements, or may contain text. Many types of elements in typical document types can contain only other elements: typically a chapter can contain only its chapter title and sections; all content is then contained in these elements or their subelements rather than directly in the chapter itself. Elements of this kind are said to have **element content**.

On the other hand, some elements may permit only text content with no embedded subelements or a mixture of text and subelements. Any elements that contain textual data are said to have **mixed content**.

It is accepted practice to use mixed content only when the containing element does not restrict the relative placements of subelements and text. Content models that fit this convention use OR connectors rather than SEQ or AND connectors. For example:

```
<!ELEMENT      p              - -
               (#PCDATA | emph | term | keyword)*>
```

Failing to use this convention can lead to counter-intuitive results when referring to subelements by position, involving the interpretation of white-space. If an element does not have mixed content at all, then white-space between subelements can be entirely ignored.

By definition, untagged text portions in mixed content are not elements. Still, one may wish to refer to them. The HyTime standard calls these portions **pseudo-elements** or **pelements** and discusses them in

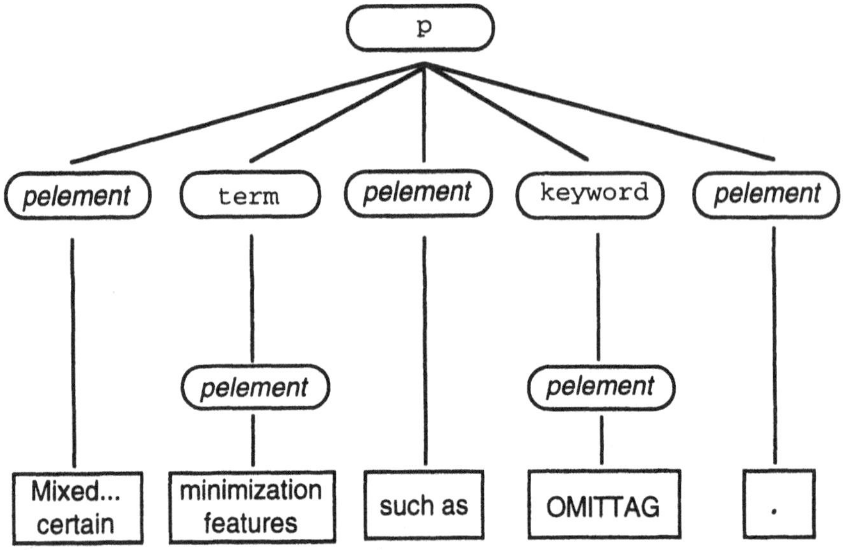

Figure 5.1: Elements vs. pseudo-elements

clause 8.4.2.2. HyTime mechanisms count them just as if they were elements, and one can locate an anchor within them just as one can within a true element.

The paragraph below is an example of mixed content. It has two subelements (one each of types `term` and `keyword`), and three pseudo-elements — don't miss the freestanding period at the end — for a total of five children. Thus, a link to the words "such as" could be accomplished by pointing to child number three of the `p` element, given the tree as shown in Figure 5.1.

```
<p>Mixed content is very common, but can lead to
surprising effects if used in unwise combination with
restrictive content models and certain
<term>minimization features</term> such as
<keyword>OMITTAG</keyword>.</p>
```

5.4 HyTime's hyperdocument model

HyTime treats a hyperdocument as a tree of data items. This tree largely corresponds to the tree that results from parsing an SGML document into elements and pseudo-elements such as described above. HyTime's object structure is similar to the "ESIS" view of an SGML document, which is the information an SGML parser normally communicates to an application program.

The HyTime information structure includes the boundaries and relationships of elements and data content (pseudo-elements). Data entities, entities which are not brought in and parsed by an SGML parser, also constitute nodes in HyTime trees whether they are of type SDATA, NDATA, or CDATA. NDATA entities are especially important because they are the way HyTime refers to non-SGML data such as graphics, video, sound, performance data, and so on. Various HyTime constructs can refer to parts of them for linking, scheduling, and other processing purposes.

The **nodes** of a HyTime tree include elements, pseudo-elements (pelements) and data entities (dataents). HyTime Location module constructs can specify the locations of such nodes.

HyTime also defines a node type that never occurs in document trees but can result from HyTime operations: the **data object** (abbreviated **dataobj**). Clause 8.4.2.2 presents all these types, and defines dataobj as "an object located within data content, a [data] entity, or a property value, addressed by a location address element." That is, any portion of an entity located using HyTime methods. Certain HyTime constructs such as HyQ can create such nodes and then operate on them in various ways.

The nodes of these trees are not, however, all the information available. For example, SGML attributes are not treated as nodes. Instead, they are considered **properties** of the nodes that represent their elements. HyTime defines a wide variety of properties and a few constructs for referring to them. We discuss properties, property names and how properties are located, in Sections 11.7-11.9.

Information not used in HyTime

Aspects of an SGML document that are not part of the ESIS structure are not generally HyTime objects, although certain information is available through various properties. This is true even if the HyTime `unparsed` option is set (although in that case it may be possible to detect the strings that signal the boundaries of non-ESIS components, for example by searching the unparsed data using HyLex). Among the non-ESIS structures are:

- all variations in how markup was typed in (if indeed it *was* typed by hand!): order of attributes, white-space within tags, insignificant record boundaries, and so on

- information that lives only in the DTD (the declared and default values for particular attributes, which elements share the same attribute list declaration for #CURRENT attributes, which elements have declared content EMPTY, etc.)
- USEMAP declarations
- SGML comments
- Marked sections
- Entity boundaries for non-data entities

These objects do not constitute nodes in HyTime trees and therefore cannot be addressed by HyTime locators such as **`nameloc`** and **`treeloc`**. This is not a problem for most applications; indeed it is usually a virtue. An application whose operation depends on particular spacing between attributes, for example, was doomed long before HyTime came along. On the other hand, information such as entity and marked section boundaries is far more generally useful, and an SGML editor in particular may need additional information. Work is underway in the DSSSL (ISO draft standard 10179) committee on how best to represent and access information beyond that of ESIS.

Those familiar with the minutiae of SGML may be wondering whether processing instructions (PIs) and marked sections work the same way as pelement and dataobj nodes. HyTime's addressing mechanisms provide no inherent way to refer to them except by setting the `unparsed` option and searching the unparsed form of an SGML document. Marked section boundaries are not nodes in the trees HyTime uses to represent documents.

5.5 How a HyTime system fits together

The pieces involved in a complete HyTime environment are shown in Figure 5.2. A hyperdocument can include a variety of documents and document components in various media and representations. These are created using tools appropriate to each format and purpose, and are brought together in an authoring interface. The authoring interface manages databases that represent the data objects and their structural relationships. From these databases the author can create published hyperdocuments to deliver to end users. Typically, the delivered documents use a specially optimized database, trading the editing power needed by authors for the speed and responsiveness needed by end users. Although depending on the application end users may not be able to change the published documents, they may well want to navigate and annotate them, and so are provided with a variety of tools for these purposes.

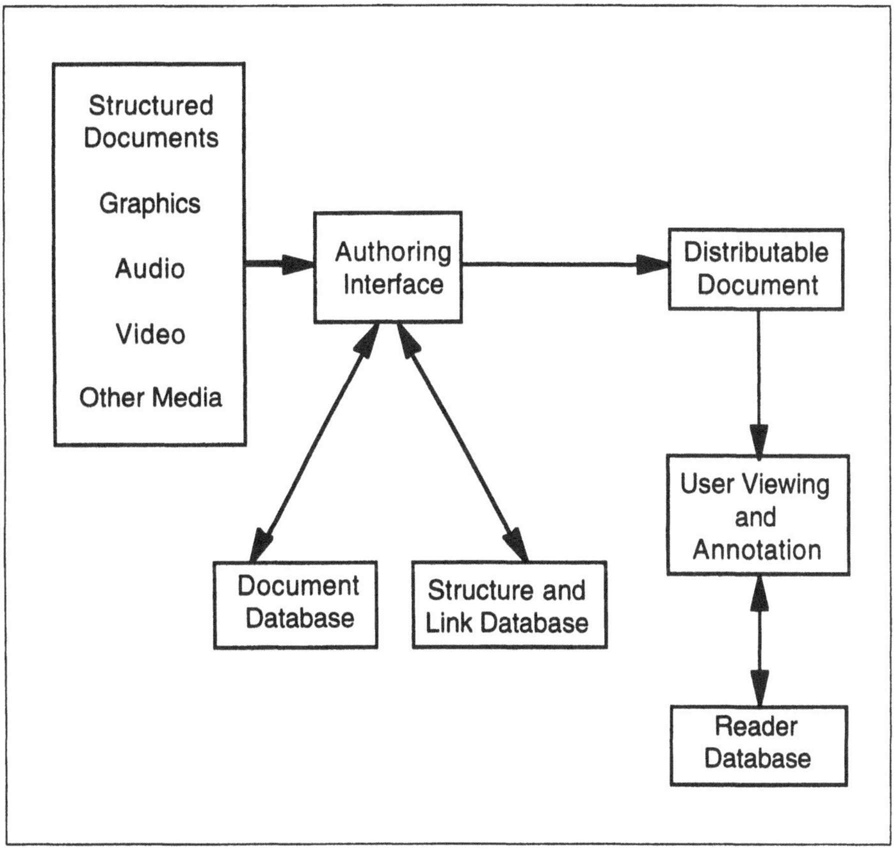

Figure 5.2: HyTime hyperdocument environment

5.5.1 Authoring tools

HyTime authoring involves creating SGML encoding for the links in a hyperdocument, even if much of the other data is kept in non-SGML data formats. Graphical and multimedia data can be prepared using any appropriate tool, since HyTime depends only on the existence of well-defined data formats, not on the details of particular software. While multimedia applications have tended to rely on proprietary data formats, this is quickly changing. Standards such as Apple Computer's QuickTime, and the MPEG and JPEG graphics standards are providing a measure of application independence for multimedia and graphical data.

For publishing, electronic document delivery and other applications that are already SGML-rich, supporting HyTime will be especially easy because SGML processing is already built in. Graphical SGML authoring and document delivery systems are likely to expand their scope quickly to support HyTime, for the same reasons.

5.5.2 HyTime engines

The HyTime standard refers to a **HyTime engine**, which is generic software that can read and process HyTime encoded files. HyTime engines will differ in their efficiency of implementation and the range of external data formats that they can handle. A simple generic HyTime engine would be able to display SGML documents and interpret HyTime's linking and structuring facilities to display textual documents and perhaps illustrations. More complex engines will support the advanced scheduling facilities of HyTime and allow the processing of real-time data like video, sound and MIDI instruments.

Since HyTime is not tied to particular data formats, most HyTime engines will permit extensions for new data formats and access techniques. Like SGML, HyTime opens data to multiple uses by freeing it from a representation that is only suitable for one form of use.

5.5.3 Translators, interpreters and compilers

HyTime engines can be implemented by **translators**, **interpreters** or **compilers**. A translator simply reads HyTime and produces output in another hypertext description format. In general, a translator loses some HyTime-specific information, just as producing a PostScript file from an SGML document loses information. An application to read HyTime documents and create HyperCard stacks from them would be a translator. To edit a translated document, the HyTime source data must be changed and the translation process repeated.

An interpreter operates directly on HyTime encoded data to directly implement the HyTime data model. This is a very flexible, powerful, fully "HyTime-like" implementation strategy. However, due to the amount of data parsing involved, this technique is expected to have efficiency problems; experience will determine whether or not it is practical. Editing is trivial with interpretation, since the HyTime data is directly processed at all times and changes in that data are instantly accessible.

The third implementation method is compilation. Compilation, like translation, involves changing the data format from the raw HyTime data, but a HyTime compiler uses the full HyTime data model directly and thus has an interpreter's fidelity to the nuances of the original document, without incurring an interpreter's overhead of repeated parsing. HyTime compilers can also allow direct editing of the compiled data structure, since it can be reconstructed into an equivalent HyTime encoded document. This technique is used by many SGML editing applications and will probably also be used by HyTime applications.

Even before HyTime engines are commonplace, HyTime will find an important niche as an open, vendor-independent interchange format. Specialized hypermedia or hypertext applications will use translation techniques to export and import HyTime encoded versions of documents to and from proprietary internal formats.

5.6 HyTime declarations

HyTime uses declarations to identify a document as a HyTime document and to specify which particular features, options and limitations apply to it. These declarations can also specify global changes such as renaming the HyTime architectural form attribute (`HyTime`).

5.6.1 HyTime changes to the SGML declaration

A HyTime hub document must identify itself as such. This is accomplished by placing application-specific information in the SGML declaration and HyTime-specific processing instructions in its prolog.

The default SGML declaration for any HyTime document must have the following APPINFO parameter at the end:

```
<!SGML
...
APPINFO "HYTIME"
>
```

The APPINFO string in the SGML declaration can be used to indicate special processing for an SGML file. HyTime uses it to determine if a file uses HyTime encoding. Two additional parameters can also be given here. The first sets the name of the **HyTime prefix** that must appear at the beginning of the SGML processing instructions used to make the HyTime system declaration. These are discussed immediately below. Normally that prefix is `HyTime`, and we have difficulty imagining a good reason to change it; however, changing the APPINFO as follows would set the prefix to be `Myprefix`:

```
APPINFO "HYTIME=Myprefix"
```

The other parameter of APPINFO is a new name for the "HyTime attribute names" common attribute of clause 6.5.1, which we discuss in Section 14.4.6. This attribute, normally called `HyNames`, can be used on any element instance to specify that it uses non-standard names for other HyTime attributes. To change the name of the `HyNames` attribute to `NameChanges` the preceding APPINFO declaration could be amended as follows:

```
APPINFO "HYTIME=Myprefix,NameChanges"
```

These parameters do *not* affect the name of the `HyTime` architectural form attribute that is used to identify elements as conforming to one or another HyTime architectural form. If that attribute is to be renamed, it can be changed by using `HyNames`.

Setting either of these parameters can be confusing; however, in Section 10.3.2 we discuss a plausible use for the `HyNames` attribute in the support of preexisting DTDs.

The APPINFO parameter is the only modification HyTime requires you to make to an SGML declaration, other than ensuring that the FORMAL feature is on. HyTime permits but does not require other SGML features.

5.6.2 HyTime support declarations

The **prolog** of a HyTime hyperdocument must contain the SGML processing instructions, called support declarations, that list the particular HyTime modules and options used in the document.

The prolog (see clause 7.1 of the SGML standard) includes the DTD plus any comments, processing instructions, etc. surrounding it. The HyTime support declarations can appear anywhere in the prolog before the "`<!DOCTYPE`..." declaration, such as at the very beginning.

While HyTime options can be freely combined, several predefined option sets are described in the standard. Clause 12.1.1 defines a **basic hyperlinking HyTime document**. For such documents, the declarations should be as shown here:

```
<?HyTime VERSION "ISO/IEC 10744:1992" HYQCNT=32>
<?HyTime MODULE base
    context desctxt dvlist
    exidrefs HyLex lextype refctl>
<?HyTime MODULE locs multloc HyQ query>
<?HyTime MODULE links>
```

The **VERSION declaration** identifies two things. First, it states which edition of the HyTime standard the document conforms to. At this time there is only one edition and the declaration should appear exactly as shown. If HyTime is amended, however, this declaration will permit HyTime engines to detect whether a document might use newer features or whether special processing is necessary to support obsolete features.

Second, the **HYQCNT option** specifies what range of numbers should be used to calculate dimensions and other quantities while processing this document. The range is specified as the number of bits required to represent the desired range as a positive binary number. For example, a value of 32 for HYQCNT indicates that no such count needed by the document exceeds 2**32 - 1, or 4,294,967,295.

After the version declaration, HyTime **module declarations** indicate that the document uses features from certain HyTime modules, and possibly options of those modules. The full set of options is listed below. It is wise to declare only the options you need, and to stick with the most common and widely used HyTime constructs whenever practical. This maximizes portability by avoiding unnecessary demands on the HyTime processor. Certain core features are much more likely to have widespread support than others (the most obvious and best-supported are simple links to SGML IDs and to entities in other notations).

Of the features included in a basic hyperlinking HyTime document as shown above, some are still rather specialized. The Base module's `context`, `desctxt`, `dvlist`, `HyLex` and `lextype` options are in this category, as is the `multloc` option of the Location address module. Many applications will not need these. On the other hand, the Base module's `lexord` option will likely be commonly used, especially in international contexts.

We discuss the options of each module under the constructs that make use of them; we also list them in the Index.

5.7 The HyTime modules

The HyTime standard is divided into numbered clauses, which in turn contain sub-clauses, sub-sub-clauses, and so on. After the initial introductory clauses, the remaining clauses each present a HyTime "module." Each of them defines a set of constructs useful for certain purposes, and a set of optional features relevant to the module. Generally, we devote a separate chapter to each module:

Base	This module defines concepts such as architectural forms, HyTime module and option declarations and a variety of architectural forms that can be applied to other HyTime elements. Many of these have very specialized applications. The parts that are essential to other modules we cover where they apply; a selection of the rest is discussed in Chapter 14.

Measurement	This module allows for definition and expression of units of measurement in time, space and/or other domains. A small portion of this is used by the Location address module and the Hyperlinks module. We discuss that portion in Chapter 6, and the rest in Chapter 13.
Location address	This module uses measurements, formal names and other techniques to indicate locations within structures such as strings, parsed data, trees, and non-SGML data. It provides the pointing mechanisms used by the Hyperlinks module to create links to locations within data. We discuss this module in Chapter 8.
Hyperlinks	This module facilitates the creation of hypertext links between locations in documents and data of all kinds. It defines two architectural forms: **`clink`** and **`ilink`**. We discuss this module in Chapter 7.
Scheduling	This module provides for events to be specified and scheduled in space and time for presentation or other processing. A component of data can be declared as an event and then placed into space and time relative to other components. The Scheduling model and some applications are described in Chapter 13.
Rendition	This module allows certain presentational aspects of HyTime documents to be described. We give a brief overview of the Rendition module in Chapter 13.

Further details about the modules and their specific options can be found in the chapters listed and in Appendix C.

Part II:

Basic HyTime

6

Basic Measurement

6.1 Introduction to measurement

The Measurement module makes possible the description of the locations and the dimensions (sizes) of HyTime objects. Most forms of HyTime addressing, other than direct references to SGML IDs or entity names, depend on these facilities. For example, as we have seen earlier, the Location address module can select elements out of SGML documents by counting their positions among their sibling elements.

This chapter describes the basic features of HyTime measurement and includes most of the concepts that form the foundation of coordinate addressing. It covers only those HyTime architectural forms and concepts defined in clause 7.1 of the standard. This is all that is required in order to use the Location address module and to handle many forms of hyperlinking. The other, more advanced, measurement features have their primary application in the Scheduling and Rendition modules and are most useful for the description of multimedia documents. We discuss some of them in Chapter 13.

The Measurement module contains features for indicating positional relationships. The meaning of such indications is expressed by those forms that refer to measurements to create anchors, hyperlinks, scheduled multimedia events, and so on.

6.2 Geometric concepts

HyTime's basic measurement concepts are drawn from simple geometry, but with two important differences. First, HyTime measurements are always expressed as integers. Second, all measurements are made within a finite range, with fixed maximum and minimum values.

Underlying the decision to use only rational numbers and integers in HyTime rather than real numbers is a concern for portability. Floating point computation can produce varying results on different machines and lead to subtle difficulties such as rounding errors. The nature of HyTime measurements within a document reflects HyTime's design goal of document representation rather than mathematical modeling.

Each HyTime measurement is associated with an **axis**. In geometry, an axis is a direction along which distances are measured and which allows the location of points by their distance along it. A HyTime axis serves a similar purpose; it defines a range of possible measurements. The coordinates along an axis form its **addressable range**, from a minimum to a maximum positive integer value.

The units of measurement along an axis are called **quanta**. Each quantum represents a discrete position along that axis and has a **coordinate** (which must be a positive number). HyTime constructs refer to positions with such coordinates. For example, you can create a HyTime axis for counting white-space-separated strings in sentences such as this:

```
A toad's eye is the jewel of the animal kingdom.
```

This sentence implies an axis with an addressable range of 10 quanta, with integer coordinates from 1 to 10. Several types of quanta are defined by HyTime, such as tokens, words, characters, nodes in lists and trees, and so on; one could, for example, address parts of a sentence by character instead of word position. These quanta are mainly used with the **`dataloc`** architectural form, which we discuss in Section 8.4.1.

The Measurement module works with the Location address module — HyTime axes can be used to denote token and character positions within data streams, as well as SGML markup elements. All of these predefined axes use arbitrary integer units known as **generic quanta**. The addressable range of these axes is found by counting the quanta of the axis starting from 1. Each use of **`dataloc`** or similar constructs in effect deals with a separate axis (sentences, for example, may differ in length).

HyTime uses the term **dimension** to refer to a range of addresses along a particular axis. The term arises from the frequent use of such ranges in establishing the size of objects along a given axis. Dimensions are, however, used whenever a range of quanta needs to be described.

With the exception of the Scheduling and Rendition modules HyTime requires only generic quanta, unrelated to physical measurement units. Using the advanced measurement facilities allows the definition of custom HyTime axes and their associated measurement systems. We discuss such capabilities in Chapter 13.

6.3 Architectural forms

6.3.1 The marklist architectural form

The element type form **marklist** (clause 7.1.2.2) is used to hold a list of of signed number **markers**. A marker designates a particular location along an axis. An element conforming to the **marklist** architectural form has content consisting of a series of signed numbers or nested **marklist** elements. While each number is a marker, there is no "marker" element form. An example of a **marklist** follows:

```
<marklist>1 2 3 4 -10</marklist>
```

Nested **marklist** elements are allowed but optional, because any nesting is flattened as part of the interpretation of the **marklist**. Because of this rule, the following specification is exactly equivalent to the preceding one:

```
<marklist>1 2<marklist>3 4 -10</marklist></marklist>
```

Marklist elements permit both start-tag and end-tag minimization, so when minimization is enabled and a **marklist** is not optional, no tags need appear for it. Because all coordinates in HyTime are positive, negative markers have special meanings as described in Section 6.3.2.

6.3.2 The dimspec architectural form

The **dimspec** element form (clause 7.1.2) is used to represent a dimension or range of quanta. It must contain a **marklist** with two markers. The first marker represents the left endpoint of the desired range and the second the right endpoint, as an offset from the first. For example, this **dimspec** picks out the fifth through twelfth quanta of an axis, a range that includes a total of eight quanta:

```
<dimspec><marklist>5 8</marklist></dimspec>
```

The left and right endpoints of a **dimspec** can be specified in several different ways. The simplest way is the one just shown: an absolute position and length, from the beginning towards the end of the axis.

Since HyTime axes always use positive coordinates, negative markers have a special interpretation. They indicate positions counting backward relative to an endpoint, rather than positions forward from a starting point. The signs of both markers in a **dimspec** determine how the dimension is addressed. For instance:

```
<dimspec><marklist>1 -1</dimspec>
```

picks out an entire axis: it starts at the first quantum from the left end of the axis and continues on through the first quantum counting back from the right end (that it, the last quantum). The four possible combinations of negative and positive markers have the meanings shown here:

Marker 1	Marker 2	Marker interpretation
positive +n	positive +n	1: position of left quantum; 2: number of quanta in dimension
positive +n	negative −n	1: position of left quantum; 2: position of right quantum measured from the right end of the entire axis
negative −n	positive +n	1: left end of the dimension counting from right end of the axis; 2: number of quanta in dimension
negative −n	negative −n	1: left endpoint of the dimension measured from the right end of the dimension (not the end of the axis); 2: right endpoint of the dimension measured from the right end of the axis

The content of a **dimspec** must be either one or two **marklist** elements, which are interpreted as a single list of markers. The contents of both **marklist** elements taken together should be exactly two markers, interpreted as described above.

For example, in the sentence considered earlier one could address the tokens "eye is the jewel" with several equivalent marker pairs (the numbers above and below this example indicate quantum numbers, counting in both directions).

```
  1   2      3   4  5     6     7  8     9       10
  A toad's  eye is the jewel of the animal kingdom
-10  -9     -8  -7 -6    -5    -4 -3    -2       -1
```

3 4	starts at the third position from the left and continues for four words
3 –5	starts at the third position from the left and continues through the fifth position from the end of the axis
–8 4	starts at the eighth position from the end of the axis and includes four words
–4 –5	starts four words to the left of the second marker's position, which is in turn five words from the right end of the axis

These examples could be tagged in the following ways:

```
<dimspec><marklist>3 4</marklist></dimspec>
<dimspec>3 -5</dimspec>
<dimspec>-8<marklist>4</dimspec>
<dimspec>-4 -5</dimspec>
```

In applications using markup minimization the fully minimized form given in the second and fourth examples is the preferred style. If minimization is not being used, it is simpler to use the markup style with only a single marklist as shown in the first example.

6.3.3 The dimlist architectural form

The **dimlist** architectural form (clause 7.1.2.3) is used when a list of `dimspec` elements is required. It allows a number of shortcuts — the content of a `dimlist` can include any number of

- `dimspec` elements, representing individual dimensions
- text portions, representing markers
- `marklist` elements, whose markers should be paired up
- nested `dimlist` elements, which are flattened in the same manner as nested `marklist` elements

A single `dimlist` might appear in any of these equivalent forms:

```
<dimlist>
    <dimspec>1 2</dimspec>
    <dimspec>5 -3</dimspec>
    <dimspec>9 4</dimspec>
</dimlist>

<dimlist>1 2 5 -3 9 4</dimlist>

<dimlist>1 2<dimspec>5 -3</dimspec>9 4</dimlist>

<dimlist><marklist>1 2 5</marklist>
         <dimlist>-3 9 4</dimlist>
</dimlist>
```

The most generally useful forms of **dimlist** are likely to be the completely explicit form shown first and the simple form shown second. Other forms might be appropriate, for example, in an automatic HyTime generation application in which these constructs reflect the structure of some previously designed software.

The basic measurement constructs form the foundation for advanced measurement and are also used heavily throughout the Location address module discussed in Chapter 8. For example, one can refer to the third through fifth subelements of some element by using an appropriate **dimspec** within certain Location address module constructs.

7

Hyperlinks

7.1 Introduction

The Hyperlinks module ties together locations, which by themselves are simply addresses of data items, and turns them into links, the focus of hypermedia. Links record relations between data objects and form the basis of hypermedia navigation. Linking is intimately related to the details of addressing (see Chapter 8) and the description of multimedia data to be linked (see especially Chapter 13 and Section 12.5).

The Hyperlinks module provides two architectural forms: one for a simple cross-reference link, the **`clink`** (for contextual link), and a second for a generalized link, the **`ilink`** (for independent link). It also provides attributes to describe various kinds of connection that a link can represent, as well as restrictions on the access a link provides.

7.2 Basic Concepts

A **hyperlink** or **link** connects one or more items of information. The full set of possible connections can never be catalogued, since such a catalog would be a complete analysis of human knowledge. Fortunately, however, the full range of semantic information is not needed to implement hypermedia systems. Applications can reflect the semantics they need by creating element types and instances based on HyTime's architectural forms. The SGML generic identifiers (or GIs) of those element types can distinguish appropriate subclasses of links. Because of this usage, the GI of a HyTime hyperlink is known as its **link type**. Applications in which a fixed set of link types is inadequate can define additional attributes to distinguish user-defined link subtypes.

HyTime provides exceptional facilities for capturing general properties of hyperlinks. HyTime can describe the sorts of links that have been implemented in the hypermedia commercial and research communities, and even some that have only been proposed in the research literature. This wide scope comes from the combination of a few general facilities to create particular link types.

Hyperlinks connect data items known as **anchors**. Since HyTime allows bibliographic references and user-defined address notations, an anchor can literally be anything that can be unambiguously located by a human or computer using a formal or informal notation. Most commonly, links provide a navigation metaphor for accessing information, as potential pathways that a user can follow.

Unlike some hypertext implementations, HyTime imposes no restrictions on the size or location of anchors. Systems based on a "card metaphor" are easily represented in HyTime, but a general HyTime engine can handle anchors of any granularity, from very small to very large. If such restrictions are desired, they are the application's responsibility to enforce.

A **linkend** is the part of a link that designates an anchor. The simplest form of a linkend is an IDREF to an SGML element which is the anchor. However, all of the facilities of the Location address module can be used to indicate an anchor and thus anchors need not be single SGML elements, or even SGML data at all. For clarity, we use direct element references in this chapter rather than the facilities of the Location address module described in the next chapter.

7.2.1 Hyperlinks: presentation and content

One of the trickiest conceptual issues in defining link types is how closely they should be coupled to the behavior of a particular application. In some situations, the exact format and behavior of a hyperlink are of great importance. For example in describing a business presentation, the exact appearance of an on-screen button is of great importance. In a technical documentation application, however, links are generally useful for more than one purpose. Cross-references in a document may need to be displayed as buttons in one situation, but also queried like a database to create a visual map of meaningful connections in another.

This tension between different views of a document is very similar to that between formatting information and content information in SGML. The reusability of a document is enhanced if details (like formatting) peculiar to one use of the data are kept separate from the data itself. In hypermedia, however, the line between content and presentation is not yet completely clear and many current systems treat links solely in behavioral way. This leads to the common impression of hypermedia as an interface and display style, rather than a data-structuring technology.

Links directly represent connections. The fact that these connections may be expressed in ways as different as creating a printed index to a book or dynamically flashing related material on a screen during playback is not intrinsic to the link itself.

7.2.2 Types of hyperlink

Since links are in essence a data representation for those aspects of document structure that are not sequential or hierarchical, links can have an extremely wide range of potential application. HyTime divides links into two classes based on their formal properties, but the range of semantic applications includes at least the following:

- Cross references are perhaps the most common sort of hyperlink. They provide an optional reading path by indicating potentially useful information elsewhere.
- Navigational links are cross-references elevated to a central role in document structure. Some systems, like online help files, use links to promote a free-form browsing approach for information access, where explicit links both control and ease access to information.
- Annotation links make assertions or comments on a pre-existing document. Critical to workflow automation and editorial systems, annotation links may also come to have an important application in networked systems, since many online discussions in fact tend to revolve around commentaries or **threads** of discussion based on an initial document.
- Parallel documents are common in scholarly applications, editing and other situations where successive revisions or translations of a document are involved. The correspondence between two texts can be treated as a specialized web, or as a complex multi-ended link. In either case, multiple connections between document portions must be represented.

Revision control systems, where links can be used, for instance, to indicate portions of other documents that should be included as if they occurred locally. Such **transclusions**, to use Ted Nelson's term, can be thought of as another way to deal with those parallel texts that revisions of pre-existing documents.

The HyTime **clink** or contextual link can be used to represent the extremely common cross-reference or navigational link. A **clink** connects the location where the link itself appears to another location. Many hypermedia systems provide only this sort of link. Since such links are stored in the document containing their origin anchor, they cannot be edited when that document is on read-only media or otherwise inaccessible. That such links can have only two ends is also a limitation.

A simple example of a **clink** that refers to a location via an IDREF looks like this:

```
some topics, like <clink linkend=dest1>links</clink>
are complex.
```

For applications that need links connecting more than two locations or stored separately from documents, HyTime provides the **ilink** or independent link. An **ilink** is stored separately from its endpoints and can even be in a separate document from any of its anchors. It can thus be used to annotate read-only media. A simple example of an **ilink** connecting two locations in the same file with it follows:

```
<p id=nels1>Nelson's notion of "deep rock archives"
...
<p id=bush>Vannevar Bush's concern about the
possibility of nuclear war
...
<ilink linkends="nels1 bush">
```

These are the only two architectural forms for links in HyTime. While all links could be represented by **ilinks**, the extra complexity involved in the more general definition can be avoided by those applications whose needs are satisfied by **clink**.

7.2.3 Properties and varieties of anchors

Anchors are arbitrary components or pieces of data stored in any place accessible to an application. This implies that a given anchor may be shared by several links. In some applications, attempting to traverse from such an anchor produces a menu of available links for which the anchor is a linkend; in others, an automatic selection is made on the basis of some application-specific criteria.

Each link specifies an **anchor role** for each linkend; this is an identifier that distinguishes the function of a particular linkend. For example, one type of link may always connect an "origin" to a "destination," while another connects a "target" with a "criticism," and so on. Since an anchor may be used by several links it may have several anchor roles, one in each link of which it is a part. The set of anchor roles for a link is fixed for each link *type*.

Because some linkend properties vary from instance to instance, anchors also have **link end terms**. A link end term holds information about an anchor for the application's use. Like an anchor role, this information can be used in retrieval and in determining the proper rendering of the anchor. However, unlike an anchor role, link end terms are specific to a *particular instance* of a link. Thus link end terms can be used to specify special properties of individual linkends, whether or not they affect the rendering of the anchor. Link end terms can only be used with **`ilinks`**, not with **`clinks`**.

Since the full facilities of the Location address module can be used, an anchor can also be an aggregate. An aggregate anchor is a group of several different items that is treated as a single object for some purposes (see Section 8.7 for a discussion of aggregate locations). An aggregate anchor allows a link to connect some other relevant information to a set of items that are separately stored. For instance in a language education application translated words might be linked. However, a single word in one language may be represented by an idiom of several words in the other language. In the sentence "He threw the bum out" the words "throw" and "out" might be linked as an aggregate to a single word of translation.

Aggregate anchors can also be regarded as locations to be traveled between. For instance, the common hypermedia notion of guided tours or paths (see Zellweger 1989, Mylonas and Heath 1990) could be represented as a link with two anchors. One anchor would be an explanation of the path's content and purpose; the other would be an aggregate link, each of whose members is a stop on that path. HyTime aggregates can be used to represent single entities or to represent sets of locations with particular roles. This is a primary distinction for the notion of aggregate anchor: it may represent a single disjoint entity, or a significant set of discrete entities.

7.2.4 Traversal

In HyTime, one fundamental action on hyperlinks is **HyTime traversal**. This is the action a HyTime application takes to start at an anchor and use information stored in a link to access another anchor of that link.

In the traditional interactive hypertext application, traversal is a user-initiated action that causes the display of some new relevant information. However, link traversal is more general than this, since a traversal may be requested by a program as part of some other processing. For example, a batch document processor might traverse hyperlinks to create appropriate human-readable cross-references in a typeset output document.

Links may also be used to access anchors in ways that are not HyTime traversal, since some uses of links cannot be interpreted as access of information in one anchor starting from another anchor. For instance, an application could take a list of **`ilinks`** and make a table of correspondences with each row representing an **`ilink`**, each column a linkend, and the contents of the cells being the corresponding anchor. The data access performed to create such an overview table could be performed by a HyTime application, using the information represented by HyTime links, but it is *not* considered HyTime traversal.

HyTime has a set of notions that can be used to describe restrictions on HyTime traversal in particular situations. Such restrictions are known as **traversal rules** and they allow a link to specify what forms of HyTime traversal are allowed from any anchor via a link of which it is a linkend.

While these rules can capture some forms of restriction on HyTime traversal, they are ambiguous for anchors that are shared by more than one link. Given this limitation of the notion of HyTime traversal, we recommend that traversal restrictions be handled by each application as a part of the "style" of linking that it allows. This also permits applications to support different kinds of traversal and link processing for different classes of users if desired, such as giving authors global link overview, editing and review tools. Since the HyTime standard explicitly allows non-HyTime traversal, this application-based strategy is permitted under the standard.

7.3 Architectural forms

This section describes the architectural forms provided by the Hyperlinks module.

7.3.1 Contextual links

The **`clink`** architectural form defines the class of contextual links. One endpoint of such a link is the **`clink`** element itself. The other is designated by the `linkend` attribute, which is an IDREF to an anchor or to a location element that indicates the anchor. Its content is `%HyBrid;`

which means that it can contain any information needed by an application. Typically, the content within a `clink` is rendered as the label of a button or a highlighted term that leads to further information when selected by a user. For example:

```
<p>An interesting discussion of punk
rock and surrealism is found in <clink
linkend=Marcus92>Lipstick Traces</clink>
...
```

In this case, the content of the `clink` might be rendered in italics or a special color, to show that it provides a link to other data. Such links are often referred to as **inline** links because they are stored in the document from which they originate, at the location of their origin anchor.

7.3.2 Independent links

The **ilink** architectural form is considerably more complex than the **clink** form because it can describe the relations among several linkends locating anchors with different roles. The basic properties and terminology for **ilink** have already been discussed. Now we will examine the syntactic details.

Basic ilinks

Like **clink**, the meta-content model for **ilink** is `%HyBrid;`. This gives a HyTime application freedom to store any additional information needed by its link model, such as link captions or database keywords, within the link itself.

The roles and number of linkends are defined by the `anchrole` attribute, which indicates the anchor roles of each linkend. The number of distinct anchor roles determines how many linkends the link has. The value is a series of SGML NAMEs. `Anchrole` must be declared #FIXED in the DTD, so that any single **ilink** element type must have a fixed number of endpoints.

The specific linkends of an **ilink** are specified by the `linkends` attribute, which has declared value IDREFS. Each reference corresponds to one of the `anchrole` values; there should be the same number of `anchrole` tokens as `linkend` IDREFS. The sole exception is a proposed change that would permit omitting the first linkend, in which case it would default to being the **ilink** element itself. This would make **clink** be a special case of a two-ended **ilink**.

An example **ilink** element type declaration and instance would look like this:

```
<!ELEMENT      vocab-link   - O EMPTY>
<!ATTLIST      vocab-link
    HyTime     Name         #FIXED ilink
    id         ID           #IMPLIED
    anchrole   CDATA        #FIXED "Spanish English"
    linkends   IDREFS       #REQUIRED>

...
<title id=pkd-s>Tiempo de Marte</title>
...
<title id=pkd-e>Martian Time-slip</title>
....
<ilink linkends="pkd-s pkd-e">
```

This example declares a subclass of **ilink**, called vocab-link, that has two anchor roles, Spanish and English. Then an instance of vocab-link is used to link two titles for a translated book.

If a link has information about linkends that changes from link to link (unlike the #FIXED anchrole), then that information can be stored as link end terms using the endterms attribute. This attribute has a declared value of IDREFS. The elements it refers to can have any type (the meta-content model is %HyBrid;) depending on the needs of the application.

Aggregate traversal

An **ilink** can define special meanings for linkends each of which points to multiple locations, but only if such aggregates are expressed by elements that set aggloc=agglink (see Section 8.7 for discussion of aggregate and multiple locations).

For a linkend to be permitted to be an aggregate, the anchrole for that linkend must be followed by the special token #AGG. Because of this, anchrole's declared value of NAMES in the standard must be corrected to CDATA. The #AGG token permits, but does not require, linkends for the anchor role whose name it follows to point to aggregates.

The interpretation of multiple locations for each linkend is then determined by the value of the aggtrav attribute. This attribute has a declared value of NAMES and its value must be a list that meets the conditions below. This attribute is *not* #FIXED and so may be different on each individual link, unlike anchrole.

- It must have either one value for each linkend, or a single value that applies to all linkends.
- Each item must have one of the three values agg, mem or cor.

The default value for aggtrav is agg, which means that any aggregate locations are treated as referring to the aggregates themselves, not to their collective members. That is, the destination of the link is the element that sets `aggloc=agglink`, not the collection of elements or other data that element points to.

The value `mem` specifies that the aggregate location should be fully resolved and that the members of the aggregate are the (possibly discontiguous) anchor for the corresponding linkend.

The value `cor` specifies that the elements of the aggregates are treated as a table of correspondences. All linkends on a link that specify `cor` for aggregate traversal must have the same number of members. Each member of such an aggregate is associated with the members at the corresponding position of any other such aggregates. Traversing one of these aggregate members resolves to the corresponding member of another linkend. This feature is called **correspondent traversal**. It can be used, for example, to interconnect the corresponding parts of different revisions, translations or editions of a document.

As a simple example of correspondent traversal, one can connect certain corresponding parts of the Synoptic Gospels in this way (assuming for brevity that every `verse` element has its canonical reference as its ID):

```
<nameloc aggloc=agglink id=h.matthew>
    <nmlist nametype=element>
       MT13.1 MT13.2 MT13.3 MT13.4 MT13.5
       MT13.6 MT13.7 MT13.8 MT13.9
</nmlist></nameloc>
<nameloc aggloc=agglink id=h.mark>
    <nmlist nametype=element>
       MK04.1 MK04.1 MK04.2 MK04.4 MK04.5
       MK04.6 MK04.7 MK04.8 MK04.9
</nmlist></nameloc>
<nameloc aggloc=agglink id=h.luke>
    <nmlist nametype=element>
       LK08.4 LK08.4 LK08.5 LK08.5 LK08.6
       LK08.6 LK08.7 LK08.8 LK08.8
</nmlist></nameloc>
...
<harmony hytime=ilink anchrole="matthew mark luke"
    linkends="h.matthew h.mark h.luke" aggtrav=cor>
    Encodes the correspondence of some verses.
</harmony>
```

This example neglects correspondences that apply only to parts of verses, because of the simplifying use of only verse-level IDs. For example, verses 8 and 9 of Matthew 13 correspond to parts of the longer

Luke 8:9. Features of the Location address module can be used to encode more detailed correspondences at any level desired.

7.4 Hyperlinks and webs

The term **web** has been used in several senses in the past. We use it to denote a meaningful explicit collection of links. Usually they are **ilinks** so that the links in a web need not be stored inside the document(s) they link. They may be placed within documents that contain content and anchors or they may be placed in a separate document (like a link database). HyTime does not have any architectural form to correspond to a web, but webs are easy to represent by an element type that can contain many **ilinks**:

```
<!ELEMENT       web             - - (ilink)*>
```

7.4.1 Inline and out-of-line links

Storing links inline has some advantages for a system implementer:

- Since the links are stored directly with the data, it is easy to keep link anchors in place as the data is edited.
- A single file often suffices to hold an entire document.
- Having link information in the same place as the anchors often simplifies implementation.

There are also some problems with inline links:

- They require that editing software be intelligent enough to deal with the link anchors in the data.
- If there are many links to data by groups of users with widely differing needs, each user pays a price in terms of time and space for storing and processing other users' links.
- Users asking to look at the set of links originating at any given place may be overwhelmed by the range of choices, many of them irrelevant to their needs. This problem worsens for popular, highly linked documents.
- The reusability of documents may be compromised by large numbers of links relating to other uses of the document. The documents must be copied and the extraneous links removed, which then means that updates to one may need to be propagated manually to the other.

Storing links and anchors separately avoids the problems above. Even the disorientation problem can be ameliorated, because users need only see those webs needed for their task. This notion of separately stored webs was one of the key contributions of the Intermedia system (Meyrowitz 1986, Garret, Smith and Meyrowitz 1986). There is, however, a price to be paid for avoiding these problems:

- Even a simple hyperdocument requires two parts: the data it contains and a web that connects that data.
- Updating a document may affect any or all of the webs that link it, so that documents must contain enough information (like SGML IDs) to make anchors persist despite the editing.
- Users need to think about what webs they need for a task, since they do not get automatic access to all links in the system.

It is clear that neither of these strategies is optimal for all systems. Separate link storage is pointless overkill in a hypertext help system for a word-processor. On the other hand, internal link storage as a sole linking mechanism is inadequate for managing large evolving multi-user hyperdocuments.

7.4.2 Query links

One form of link that has been attracting some attention recently is a **query link**, or intensional link (see DeRose 1989). These are links that allow hypertext navigation through legacy databases or other large data collections. They differ from the classical link in that they specify one or sometimes all linkends as *queries*, to be evaluated at the time the link is traversed. Expressing all linkends of a link in this way can only be done with **`ilink`**, since the anchors are determined by the results of a query (for more information on queries in HyTime, see Chapter 9). Such links have been proposed as a method of integrating databases with hypertext, as well as a way to guarantee that link endpoints are always "up-to-date" by recalculating them every time the link is followed. For instance, a "weather" linkend might query an online server and produce the latest predictions. HyTime's query language, called HyQ, can be used in building such links. We discuss it in Chapter 9.

8

Locating Data Objects

8.1 Introduction

This chapter describes HyTime's Location address module, which provides HyTime's way of referring to specific data objects and portions or locations within them. While links represent the relations between locations, the flexibility of addressing locations is a major factor in how effective a hypermedia system can be. HyTime's addressing mechanisms are extremely general. This chapter discusses HyTime locators in detail, providing the information needed to apply them in practice.

This chapter is relatively long and is organized into 7 major sections, with the bulk of the chapter contained in Section 8.4 and Section 8.5. The sub-topics in these two sections are fairly independent so that reading them completely is not initially required.

8.2 Naming, counting and querying

The HyTime Location address module (clause 8) provides three ways of locating data objects, or parts of them. These correspond directly to methods people use every day:

naming — A name space location address describes a thing by its formal name, which must be unique in the applicable context: for example, an SGML entity name or ID.

counting — A coordinate location address describes a thing by its position along a list of things: "the third item in this list."

querying — A semantic location address describes objects by some characteristic property they have: "the first element with a `type` attribute whose value is 12."

Formally, all these methods can be reduced to the last one: names can be considered properties of objects, as can positions. Nevertheless, the distinction is a useful one in practice, and one that HyTime uses. HyTime architectural forms in the Location address module allow you to exercise each of these natural methods in a wide variety of contexts. For example, named locations include special forms for names that are IDs and for names that are entities.

Element type forms distinguish kinds of locations and specify subelements and/or attributes for whatever information the particular method needs. For example, counting along a list of items can only be done if two things are known: the list itself and the position(s) desired.

For contexts not yet imagined or not yet amenable to computer processing, a few "escape hatches" are provided that let you express references in any way you like:

- "the third book on cooking that the reference librarian recommends"
- "Milton's allusions to the Bible"
- "the 45th object in file X as determined by company Z's proprietary application"

This capability is important for future expansion and completeness, but using it can compromise portability. HyTime's generic methods should always be used unless there is very good reason to the contrary. In the last example, HyTime might be able tell you the name of the destination file and the name of the company that knows how to interpret it, but it could not itself interpret the link if company Z holds the file format as a trade secret or has failed to explain it to the rest of the world.

8.2.1 Locator types

HyTime expresses each of these fundamental addressing types by one or more architectural forms that represent **location address elements** (introduced in clause 8.1). For brevity, we also call architectural forms that fall into this category **locators**. We describe all locators except the optional and complex **pathloc**.

We discuss the types of locators in turn, grouped by the three fundamental kinds of pointing they express, and describe how to combine them to create link pointers to any kind of data. These are the tools you need to understand and use the Hyperlinks module fully. To use any locator as one end of a hypertext link, it is sufficient to give it an ID and then list that ID as a linkend on an element that conforms to one of the architectural forms for links described in Chapter 7.

8.3 Named location addresses

This section describes HyTime's methods for accessing items that are labeled by names. These facilities are based on SGML's built-in naming facilities for entities and for elements, as discussed in Chapter 3.

The first kind of name is for an entity, which gets its name within a given document by being declared. After the declaration below, `book5` is known as the name of an external entity; the SGML entity manager can, when needed, access it via the system identifier `tennyson.sgm`:

```
<!ENTITY        book5         SYSTEM
    "tennyson.sgm">
```

The second kind of name is the SGML ID. Like entity names, IDs must be unique in a given document but have no restrictions across documents. IDs are separate from entity names: the declaration above would not preclude having an element with ID `book5` in the same document.

8.3.1 Named elements and entities

HyTime provides a way of linking to anything that can be named as an entity or via an ID. The architectural form used to accomplish this is called **nameloc**. It is a locator whose content consists of one or more **nmlist** elements, each of which contains one or more entity names or IDs. You cannot (without guaranteeing that no entity and ID have the same name) combine both entity names and IDs in a single **nmlist** — that is one reason that a **nameloc** can contain more than one **nmlist**.

Consider the simplest case first: referring to an element in the same document, which already has its own ID attribute. This can be done merely by using the ID on the HyTime element that needs a locator (such as a **clink**). It can also be accomplished by a **nameloc** like the following, assuming the ID in question is `chap10`:

```
<nameloc id=mypointer>
    <nmlist nametype=element>
       chap10
    </nmlist>
</nameloc>
```

This `nameloc` is a locator that points to the element with ID `chap10` in the same document. A **`nmlist`** is simply a container for the name or names being referenced. We discuss the details below, but note especially that the locator *itself* has an ID: `mypointer`. Any link or locator that points to that ID actually points to the `nameloc`'s destination (see Section 8.3.2).

Almost the same structure can be used to point to the entire `book5` entity declared in an example above:

```
<nameloc id=mypointer>
    <nmlist nametype=entity>
       book5
    </nmlist>
</nameloc>
```

The `nametype` attribute is required and must have the value `entity` or `element` to specify the interpretation of the names in the `nmlist`.

Note that although HyTime interprets `book5` in this context as an entity name, SGML does not. Thus if the entity were not declared, HyTime could detect an error but an SGML parser could not.

Entity references in SGML and HyTime

The syntax HyTime uses to refer to entities is somewhat more complex than in SGML. An SGML document can refer to an entity directly, by placing a delimited entity reference anywhere; but doing that as shown here would have a different meaning than that needed in HyTime:

```
<p>This is also discussed in &book5;</p>
```

An entity reference causes the entire content of the `book5` entity to be retrieved while parsing the paragraph. How the entity is treated then depends on the type of the `book5` entity. An entity declared with SGML's SUBDOC keyword can have a DTD different from that of the document that referred to it and can be parsed just as if it had no relationship to the referring document — for example, it may reuse ID attribute values without conflict. A notation data entity, declared NDATA, is not parsed at all. If no special type is specified, an entity is parsed and treated as if had appeared inline. In that case, the example would be valid only if the `book5` entity contained elements that are valid within `p` elements.

None of these produces the effect one wants for a hypertext link: a link refers to data somewhere else and should provide access to that data whenever needed; but a link does not in general copy data from place to place. Imagine the effect if every printed book included a full copy of every article listed in its bibliography!

The HyTime usage also differs from another SGML usage for entity names. SGML can mention an entity without referring to it by putting an entity name (not an entity reference) in an attribute value whose declared value is required to be an entity name:

```
<!ELEMENT       docref       - O EMPTY>
<!ATTLIST       docref
    docname     ENTITY       #REQUIRED>
...
<!ENTITY        book5        SYSTEM
    "book5.sgm" NDATA SGML>
...
<docref docname=book5>
```

An ENTITY attribute may only name a data or sudocument entity. Since SUBDOC is not appropriate here, an NDATA specification is required. Naming an entity via an attribute does not cause an SGML parser to retrieve and access the content of the `book5` entity (doing so would give the `docname` attribute an incredibly long value). The parser merely reports the entity reference, and the application can use the information to retrieve it on demand. Many applications before HyTime have used this mechanism for encoding inter-book links. A HyTime **nameloc** is similar because it does not cause entities to be retrieved or parsed, leaving this to be done on demand (perhaps when the user clicks on some icon).

8.3.2 Indirect references

We just showed a direct pointer from an element of form **nameloc** to a destination. However, it can happen that the destination is itself a HyTime locator element that points somewhere else. In that case the destination is not the locator itself, but whatever it points to. For example, one **nameloc** element can point to another and thus only indirectly to its destination, as shown here:

```
<p id=p1>...</p>
<p id=p2>...</p>
<p id=p3>...</p>
<p id=p4>...</p>
<p id=p5>...</p>
```

```
<nameloc id=middle-para>
    <nmlist nametype=element>p3
    </nmlist>
</nameloc>
<nameloc id=even-paras>
    <nmlist nametype=element>p2 p4
    </nmlist>
</nameloc>
<nameloc id=odd-paras>
    <nmlist nametype=element>p1 middle-para p5
    </nmlist>
</nameloc>
<nameloc id=all-paras>
    <nmlist nametype=element>
       even-paras odd-paras
    </nmlist>
</nameloc>
```

These `nameloc` elements point to their destinations with various degrees of indirect reference:

- The one with ID `middle-para` has a direct pointer to the third paragraph via its ID.
- The one with ID `even-paras` also points directly, but points to two paragraphs, not just one.
- The one with ID `odd-paras` points to a total of three paragraphs: `p1` and `p5` directly, and `p3` indirectly, by pointing to the `nameloc` with ID `middle-para`.
- The one with ID `all-paras` points even more indirectly, by pointing to `even-paras` and `odd-paras`. Thus it reaches `p3` in three levels and the other paragraphs in two.

A HyTime engine follows all such indirect references out as far as it can, stopping when any of the following happens:

- The element found is not a HyTime locator.
- The HyTime engine has reached an optional limit on the number of levels of indirect references to be followed. This value can be specified via the `reflevel` attribute on the **`nmlist`**.

8.3.3 Free-standing object names

The `obnames` attribute of the **`nmlist`** form provides another way to control the interpretation of name list references. If it has the value `obnames` (rather than `nobnames`, as specified in the previous examples) then it causes any element content that is the same as an ID to be interpreted as a reference and to be followed by HyTime. Consider the following paragraph and reference:

```
<chapter id=c4>
    ...
    <p>
       <note id=note1>c4 </note>is an explosive.
    </p>
    ...
</chapter>
...
<nameloc id=nameloc1>
    <nmlist nametype=element obnames=obnames>
       note1
    </nmlist>
</nameloc>
```

This nmlist appears to point to the note element. However, since the content of that note is "c4", which is a list of valid IDs from the same document, HyTime will further resolve this reference and the reference will be to the chapter, rather than the note.

The HyTime standard lists the obnames attribute as required for all elements conforming to the **nmlist** form. However, the HyTime committee has proposed a change to provide nobnames as the default value. This attribute will probably always be set to nobnames in your application, in which case you can declare it with nobnames as its default or #FIXED value.

8.3.4 Other options for NAMELOC

Several other attributes can be used in more complex situations.

The docorsub attribute

A docorsub attribute may be added to a **nmlist** if the names to be used in the content are known not in the **nmlist**'s own document but in some other document. In such a case docorsub would name the entity containing the document in which those names *are* known. If docorsub is never specified, names are assumed to be defined in the document containing the **nmlist**. When referring across documents, the documents involved should all have the same SGML declarations (see Section 8.4.1 for a discussion of how to change this using the anysgml option).

Once docorsub is specified in a document HyTime uses a default scheme (clause 8.3.2.2), with the effect that the docorsub attribute is treated much as if it had a default value of #CURRENT rather than #IMPLIED. That is, its value is the value specified for it on the nearest preceding element of the same type. For example, if these two nmlists occur in a document called book7 in the order shown below, then the first one refers to an element with ID note1 in book7 and the other two both refer to some other element that happens to have the same ID, but is in document book5:

```
<nameloc id=first>
    <nmlist nametype=element>
       note1
    </nmlist>
</nameloc>
<nameloc id=second>
    <nmlist nametype=element docorsub=book5>
       note1
    </nmlist>
</nameloc>
<nameloc id=third>
    <nmlist nametype=element>
       note1
    </nmlist>
</nameloc>
```

The HyTime standard does not clarify the defaulting behavior for the case where the DTD defines more than one element type conforming to the **nmlist** form. Our recommendation is to specify docorsub always or never in a given document, not sometimes. Not only are there some ambiguities about the default mechanism, but using it imposes requirements for care in the placement of **nmlists**: Adding a link to a hyperdocument could cause links whose nmlists come later in the file to refer to places they did not refer to before.

The dtdorlpd attribute

The dtdorlpd attribute specifies which of several alternative DTDs or Link Process Definitions (LPDs) should be used to parse the target document. This specification is only meaningful if the CONCUR or LINK features of SGML are used.

8.3.5 Combining locators into location ladders

Just as in everyday language, it is necessary to combine addressing methods to give a brief and clear description of a destination. “Go left on Main Street and it’s the third green house on the right” combines all three kinds of address: a name (“Main Street”), a selection based on a property (“green”), and a numbered location (“third”). In HyTime such combinations can be accomplished by chaining locators to form **location**

ladders. The simplest example of the concept is a link to an identified element in a different document:

- a `nameloc` that points to the document entity is not enough because it has no way to specify the target element's ID
- a `nameloc` with just the ID is not enough, because it has no way to specify the document in which to find the ID

For such cases HyTime provides a way to connect locators end to end. This is accomplished by making one locator specify that it is to be interpreted *relative to* another one. We have already seen one special way to do this with the `docorsub` attribute. For example, consider a pointer from one document to an element with ID `sec1` in another document kept in a system file called `chapter3.sgm`:

```
<!ENTITY        otherdoc    SYSTEM
    "chapter3.sgm" NDATA SGML>

<nameloc id=mypointer>
    <nmlist nametype=element docorsub=otherdoc>
       sec1
    </nmlist>
</nameloc>
```

The `docorsub` attribute, as we saw before, specifies an entity name defined in the document where it occurs. The content of the `nmlist` gives the ID reference(s) to be interpreted; the destination of this hypertext link is the element that has `sec1` as its ID in the `otherdoc` entity.

This example needs only one extra qualification beyond the ID used, and so can be handled by the built-in `docorsub` attribute of **nameloc.** However, in many cases longer chains of locators are needed, so various types of location specifications can be attached end-to-end to make location ladders, in which the last step leads to the result.

As a simple example, one can specify a location within the `sec1` element just described by using two locators joined into a location ladder (see Section 8.4.2 for more on **treeloc**):

```
<!ENTITY        otherdoc    SYSTEM
    "chapter3.sgm" NDATA SGML>
```

```
<treeloc id=treeptr locsrc=entptr> 1 3 </treeloc>
<nameloc id=entptr docorsub=otherdoc>
    <nmlist nametype=element> sec1 </nmlist>
</nameloc>
```

The `nameloc` is called the **location source** for the `treeloc`. It is referred to by ID, from the `locsrc` attribute of the other element. The `locsrc` attribute is an IDREF which means that the locator element on which it appears must be interpreted relative to the element to which it refers. In this case, the selection specified by the `treeloc` is interpreted in the context of the entity and element specified by the `nameloc`.

This is a typical use of location ladders: a linkend states the most specific part of a destination's reference and uses a more general reference as the location source. A program or human interprets a location ladder by following it out to find its end and then working back to derive more and more specific locations until the goal specified by the pointer is achieved.

In this case the process is as follows (it is carried out, for example, when the user traverses a link with `treeptr` as a linkend):

- Resolve `treeptr` to the `treeloc`.
- Find the `locsrc` attribute and resolve it to the `nameloc`.
- Interpret the `nameloc` to locate the `otherdoc` entity.
- Locate the element there with ID `sec1`.
- Interpret the `treeloc` to locate the third child of that element.
- The resulting element (or pseudoelement) is the destination.

Location ladders can be as long as necessary. The ladder just described could, for example, have additional steps to find parts of the element just described, elements referred to by IDREFs in its content, or whatever. The typical sequence is:

- Use a `nameloc` to select a complete data object, or an element with an ID within a complete data object.
- Use one or more coordinate location methods such as a `treeloc` (described in Section 8.4.2) to narrow the reference to a specific element within the identified object.
- If necessary, use a `dataloc` to select a particular range of text or other data in the element.

8.4 Coordinate location addresses

Coordinate locations are those HyTime locators that refer to parts of data objects by counting. In principle, all pointing could be accomplished merely by listing positions in a file: "bytes 2000-3000 and 271828" (see Section 8.4.1), but such numbers are completely unintuitive and bear no obvious relationship to how data objects are structured. For example, in an SGML document the third chapter may (or may not) occupy a single range of bytes in one entity, but the location of that range in a file is irrelevant and certainly less clear than a description such as "chapter 3".

Because *representations* of data objects vary greatly and change frequently, and because they not semantic, HyTime provides a variety of location mechanisms appropriate to particular *kinds* of data objects.

Attributes for coordinate location forms

The coordinate location forms can take an extra attribute for certain special cases. It is called `overrun` and determines the outcome if given dimensions specify nonexistent offsets into the axes used (see clause 7.1.2.1). The default value is `error`, which causes an error to be reported. The other possible values are as follow:

`wrap`	indicates that the values should wrap around as if the ends of the axis were adjacent
`trunc`	indicates that the dimension should get as much as is available, without reporting any error
`ignore`	indicates that the entire dimension should be treated "as though it had not been specified. In some circumstances, an error could result"

8.4.1 Addressing parsed linear data with dataloc

One of the simplest location methods uses the **dataloc** architectural form to refer to characters or word tokens within a piece of data by number. Many hypertext links or other references to data use **dataloc**, most often as a final step. For example, one can locate an SGML element by its ID using **nameloc** and then locate a particular portion of its content, such as the fourth word, using **dataloc**.

Dataloc divides information content into components (called **quanta**) according one of several predefined rules, and then counts the quanta. **Dataloc** specifies the kind of quantum to count with the `quantum` attribute.

Dataloc provides quantum types for counting not only the characters of a piece of data, but also words, numbers and other useful kinds of tokens. There must therefore be a method for dividing up the data: one cannot simply apply a scale factor as one could for continuous physical quanta such as meters and inches. **Dataloc**'s method for most quantum types is to divide all possible distinct characters into two classes: token and separator. Every character of the data is considered either part of a token or part of a separator; each contiguous sequence of token characters counts as a quantum. The resulting quanta are counted and become an addressable HyTime axis. The possible quantum types are listed here, and then described:

Type	**Description of token characters**
`str`	each character is a quantum and a token character
`norm`	all but white-space (SGML's RS, RE, SEPCHAR and SPACE characters)
`word`	All SGML "name" characters
`name`	SGML name tokens
`sint`	signed integers: digits, the plus sign and the minus sign
`date`	dates in the form: yyyy-mm-dd
`time`	Coordinated Universal Time: hh:mm:ss.decimal
`utc`	date plus time: yyyy-mm-dd hh:mm:ss.decimal

The str quantum

For the `str` (short for "string") quantum type, each character (not necessarily each eight-bit byte) of the data is a quantum. If no value is specified for the `quantum` attribute `str` is the default. You can use **dataloc** with `str` quanta to specify direct locations in data objects such as disk files:

```
<dataloc id=myloc quantum=str>
    16180338
</dataloc>
```

This can be useful, but for many data representations such numbers are unwieldy. Unintuitive enough with text, for graphics and other media they are completely nonsensical. It is usually far better to use structures suited to the task (such as **fcsloc** or a notation-specific **notloc**, discussed in Sections 8.4.5 and 8.5.3).

Similar offsets could be applied to SGML documents but would be similarly noxious (not to mention unworkable if the location's boundaries cross entities). HyTime adds to the reasons for avoiding both raw numeric pointers and asynchronous element structures by providing better location methods for almost all situations, especially those involving SGML documents.

The norm quantum

With norm all characters except for SGML's white-space characters count as token characters. The SGML white-space characters RS, RE, SEPCHAR and SPACE are all separator characters. By default these are the everyday ISO 646 line feed, carriage return, tab and space characters. With norm quanta the following example has four tokens:

```
Love's labours    lost, alas--alack!
------ ------     ----- ------------
   1      2         3        4
```

Notice that under the rules for norm quanta, punctuation marks are nothing special: they are just part of tokens. This is why the first and last tokens are not divided at the apostrophe and hyphens. Note also that the extra spaces after the word "labours" have no effect on the tokenization. If the example occurred within a paragraph:

```
<p id=shake>Love's labours lost, alas--alack!</p>
```

the dataloc shown below could address the five character long token "lost,":

```
<dataloc quantum=norm locsrc=shake>
    <dimlist>3 1</dimlist>
</dataloc>
```

This selects a range of one quantum starting at the third quantum of the locsrc.

The word quantum

With this quantum, tokens consist of strings of SGML "name" characters. By default in SGML, the name characters are the unaccented Latin letters in upper and lower case, the digits, hyphen and period. Therefore all other characters (including punctuation marks other than hyphen and period) count as separators. This includes apostrophe and so, as noted in the standard, the following contains five word quanta:

```
Charles' and Linda's Abyssinians
-------  --- ----- - -----------
    1     2    3   4      5
```

A dataloc can be used just as before; assuming this example is the content of an element with ID cats, choosing tokens four through five (two tokens starting with token four) will yield "s Abyssinians":

```
<dataloc quantum=word locsrc=cats>
    <dimlist>4 2</>
</dataloc>
```

The name quantum

This quantum is almost the same as the `word` quantum, except that an additional condition is imposed on the strings of token characters. This condition is that each possible token must also be a valid SGML name. So not every space-separated string counts as a quantum:

```
The 1 el lama, he's a priest
---   -- ----  -- - - ------
 1    2    3   4  5 6   7
```

This reflects the rules for SGML names, which state that they cannot begin with a digit. Therefore the candidate name-character string "`1`" is not recognized by HyTime as a token. All the remaining quantum types use similar sorts of syntactic restriction.

Tokens are first constructed by converting any characters that are not legal for that quantum type into spaces; anything not broken by a space is then a candidate token. Finally, the syntax of the resulting tokens is checked and illegal ones are removed. According to the HyTime standard (clause 8.4.1), a token is "constructed by filtering the bit combinations." In the case of quantum types other than `str` (which uses no filtering), filtering is defined in this way:

> ...the addressable range is viewed as a token list by converting all bit combinations that are not allowed in a token into SPACE characters. The range is then normalized by stripping leading and trailing spaces and replacing sequences of spaces by a single space.

This rule (which is very similar to SGML's rules for normalizing attribute values), is used to generate the token list. However, no other rules are explicitly given in the standard for filtering tokens. The existence of the last step can be deduced from the fact that without such a step (already implied by the additional restrictions on token strings) there would be no difference between the `name` and `norm` quantum types.

The sint quantum

This quantum type is convenient for managing lists of signed integers. Permissible token characters are the digits, the plus sign and the minus sign. `Sint` picks numbers out regardless of intervening character text. This works because any other text characters are not permissible token characters: they are separators, which in effect disappear before counting quanta. Thus, in the following string only the integers 1 and 2 are tokens, and a `dataloc` using `sint` quanta can address only those two tokens:

```
The 1 el lama, he's a priest
the 2 el llama, he's a beast
```

The example below illustrates two important special cases: First, because the quantum type is for signed integers, not for real numbers, "39.95" constitutes two tokens. Second, because the definition does not include comma, "1,999" also constitutes two quanta. In some countries the characters for decimal point and thousands-separator vary, but the same rules apply.

```
At -10%, they are $39.95 each, for $1,999.
   ---             -- --          - ---
    1               2  3          4  5
```

Because the notions of "plus sign" and "hyphen" are not defined by SGML each HyTime engine must decide what characters have these meanings in the input character set. The negative sign for integers in particular may be seen represented not only by hyphen, but by many distinct dash characters of differing widths.

As with `name`, tokens must be legal `sint` tokens. None of these strings, for example, are countable tokens of quantum type `sint`:

```
+++
14++
--
```

The date quantum

This type permits digits and hyphens and counts calendar dates in ISO 2014/R form. This form is always ten characters long, consisting of a four-digit year, a hyphen, a two-digit month, another hyphen and then a two-digit day. Many SGML DTDs require that all dates be coded in this way to facilitate later processing. For example, the Text Encoding Initiative guidelines permit marking any part of a text as a date, but the ISO equivalent form normally goes on an attribute:

```
<date value='1993-02-23'>
    Feb. twenty-third, 1993</date>
```

The time quantum

`Time` quanta are parallel to `date` quanta. They use Coordinated Universal Time: two digits each for hours, minutes and seconds (all separated by colons), optionally followed by a decimal point and an arbitrary number of digits representing fractional seconds, as shown here:

```
<time utc='23:59:59.999'>almost midnight</time>
```

The UTC quantum

`UTC` simply combines `date` followed by `time`. They must be separated by characters not permitted in either:

```
<timeline>
    1993-02-23 23:59:59.999
    1066-01-01 12:00:00
    2001-04-02 10:30:00
</timeline>
```

Multiple location sources

It is possible to specify a location source for a `dataloc` that includes more then one location; this requires using the `multloc` option discussed in Section 8.7. In such a case, it matters whether the multiple locations are viewed as a single stream or as independent objects. HyTime provides the `catsrc` and `catres` attributes to distinguish these cases. For example, one might refer to a location source consisting of two `p` elements as shown below:

```
<p id=p1>But that's a priceless Steinway</p>
<p id=p2>Not anymore.</p>
...
<dataloc quantum=word locsrc="p1 p2">1 2</dataloc>
```

This `dataloc` refers to the first two words of its location source. By default, it will apply to each location source separately, in this case finding "`But that`" and "`Not anymore`". This corresponds to the default attribute setting of `catsrc=nocatsrc`. If you set `catsrc=catsrc`, however, the data content of the `p` elements will be concatenated directly end-to-end before counting tokens. The result will then be the single string "`But that`".

The `catres` attribute, on the other hand, determines whether the results found are concatenated. Its default value is `nocatres`. If the source was concatenated as just described, then `catres=catres` has no effect; but if not, then the multiple found portions will be joined into a single location as the final result, in this case "`But thatNot anymore`".

The HyTime committee has proposed adding two more attribute values for the **dataloc** form: specifying `catsrc=catsrcsp` would cause the source concatenation to insert a single space character between the components of the multiple location source; `catres=catressp` could then cause these spaces to be retained in the concatenated result.

The anysgml option

In order for HyTime to work with multiple SGML declarations the `anysgml` option must be enabled. Otherwise, linking to SGML documents with different declarations is not allowed by the standard. This is especially important since the SGML declaration determines character sets, delimiters and other syntactic features.

For instance, in Europe many documents' SGML declarations add letters with accents to the set of SGML name characters, in order to use them in SGML generic identifiers. If this is done, then the text below has six `norm` quanta as shown; if not, the "`í`" and "`ñ`" characters are separators, and so the same text has eight tokens:

```
Vamos a San Fermín, en España.
----- - --- ------  -- ------
  1   2  3    4      5   6
```

The ability to change the set of SGML NAME characters raises an important question of interpretation for `word` and some other quantum types. Two SGML documents are involved in any `dataloc`:

- the HyTime document that contains the `dataloc` itself
- the document containing the data being counted.

These may be the same document, but they do not have to be; the second might not even be in SGML. However, if the second is a distinct SGML document, its SGML declaration may define different white-space or name characters.

This potential conflict requires knowing which declaration **`dataloc`** uses. When linking from an English document using SGML's reference concrete syntax with a **`dataloc`** to part of the Spanish string just shown (which occurs in a document that includes "`í`" and "`ñ`" as SGML NAME characters), HyTime will apply the Spanish document's SGML declaration to the destination and will produce six tokens. If HyTime applied the English document's SGML declaration, then the tokens would differ because the accented vowels are not NAME characters there:

```
Vamos a San Fermín, en España.
----- - --- ---- -  -- ---- -
  1   2  3   4  5   6    7  8
```

Where possible, it is good practice to avoid such differences by using the same SGML declaration for all SGML documents that are part of a hyperdocument. However, one cannot prohibit users from creating hypertext links with anchors in documents they do not control, and so the `anysgml` option is likely to be necessary in many applications.

8.4.2 Multi-step tree navigation with treeloc

The **treeloc** form (clause 8.4.2.4) provides a convenient way to choose a single node from a tree. **Treeloc** can address any kind of tree, not just SGML documents. But because a HyTime hub document is an SGML document and because SGML is so widely used, many HyTime users will have SGML documents around. For those users and their SGML documents, **treeloc** is one of the most important constructs in HyTime.

Treeloc is quite simple if you picture a tree whose root is the location source. Consider the example in Figure 8.1. **Treeloc** selects a node from such a tree by specifying how to get to it, step by step, from the root. For example, to get from the root to the `item` element containing "`Human-readable representation`", step down the tree by choosing:

- the root of the tree,
- the second subelement or "child" of the root (the `body`),
- the first child of that node (`chapter` 1),
- the second child of that node (`section` 1),
- the fourth child of that node (the unordered `list`),
- the fifth child of that node (the desired `item`).

This is exactly what **treeloc** does; the list of numbers needed is included in an element of form **marklist**:

```
<treeloc locsrc=P1>
    <marklist>1 2 1 2 4 5</marklist>
</treeloc>
```

It should be clear that any node in a tree can be reached from the root by a unique list of **treeloc** values, and that any such list of values specifies a unique node. Because the element structures of SGML documents are trees, **treeloc** can be used to refer to any element of an SGML document. We recommend this as the clearest, simplest, most easily processed and most intuitive location method for single elements in trees. The only better identifier for an element is an ID attribute (which is, unfortunately, not always available).

If multiple locations are used (we discuss them in Section 8.7.1), you can specify the `treecom` attribute to determine whether the several components of the location source should be considered independent trees. The default value is `ntreecom`, which means that the `treeloc` applies in turn to each component of the location source; the result is then a multiple location with as many components as the location source. The alternative value is `treecom`, which means that the components are treated as if they were siblings. This is the main case in which the first marker in a `treeloc` would not be 1, because the first marker could be used to pick out particular components of the location source.

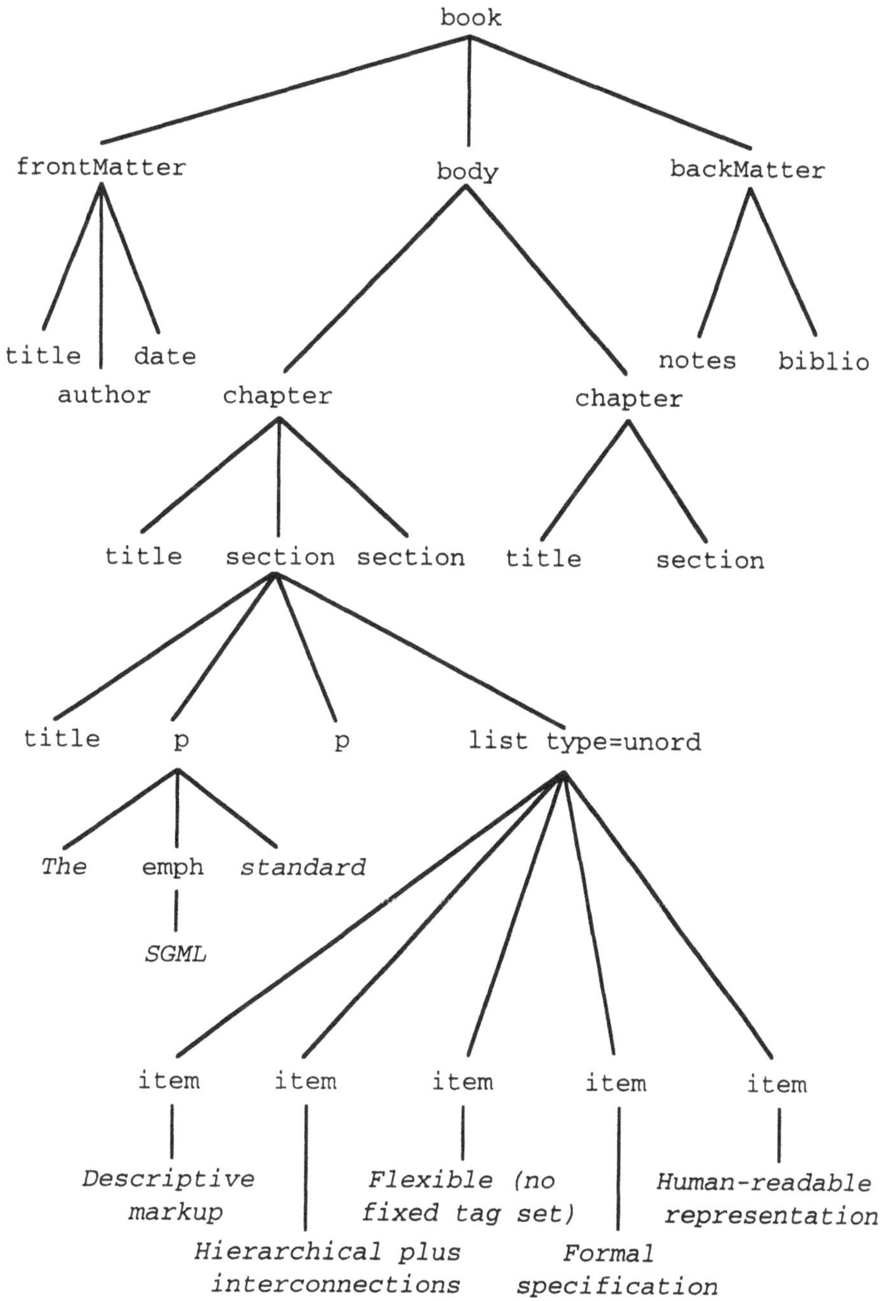

Figure 8.1: Example document tree

Pseudo-elements: addressing text

Treeloc provides a simple and clear way of making links. In one case the meaning of **treeloc** may be less than intuitive, however. Many SGML DTDs define elements that can directly contain a mixture of both text and subelements. For example, a paragraph element type `p` might permit both character content and subelements for emphasis, as follows:

```
<!ELEMENT       p              - - (#PCDATA | emph)*>
```

The following paragraph (from a comment by Brian Kernighan) is valid under the declaration above and is said to have **mixed content**:

```
<p>The trouble with WYSIWYG is that what you see
is <emph>all</emph> you get.</p>
```

Notice that this paragraph has one child that is an element: the `emph`. However, it also contains two components of text data, one on either side of the `emph` subelement. The question that arises with **treeloc** is how to number the children of such a `p` element. The HyTime term **pseudo-element** or **pelement** refers to character data portions that are not SGML elements but form structural units in the element tree. **Treeloc** counts pseudo-elements just as if they were full-fledged elements. Hence the `p` shown above has three children:

1 `The trouble with WYSIWYG is that what you see is`

2 (the element of type `emph`)

3 `you get.`

Properly, the `emph` child is the only one that is an element and has an element type (or GI). The others are commonly called **PCDATA portions.** With mixed content, it is important to count carefully — ideally, all such counting is done by machine. Consider the following paragraph, with record breaks shown by line breaks:

```
<p>
<e2>This</e2>
<e1>is</e1>
the important sentence.
</p>
```

There appear to be three children of the `p`: two subelements and one pseudo-element after them. However, there are really four children under SGML rules and a `treeloc` specification must allow for this. An SGML application program never sees the record separator immediately after `<p>`, as it gets its information after parsing (called the "ESIS" information). However, the record separator after `</e2>` is the second one within the `p` element and hence may be a significant literal character that an SGML parser will pass to an application (depending on the DTD). Because #PCDATA is a part of the content model for `p`, there is a pseudo-element between the two emphasis elements, whose content is a single record separator:

```
1   <E2>This</E2>
2
3   <E1>is</E1>
4   the important sentence.
```

SGML's rules about record separators are not widely understood, and so DTD designers strive for designs where such understanding is not necessary. Avoiding mixed content models in which PCDATA is not allowed everywhere, avoiding minimization when such models must be used and being careful with HyTime constructs that count children in mixed content all help to avoid problems.

8.4.3 Single-step tree navigation with relloc

Although the most common way of navigating through a tree is to step down through it in the manner of **`treeloc`**, it is useful to be able to step upwards through a given node's ancestors, or left and right through its siblings. The **`relloc`** architectural form (clause 8.4.2.7) provides these capabilities.

`Relloc` has four sub-types, one for each direction. The intended direction is specified via its `relation` attribute. **`Relloc`** also takes a single **`dimspec`** in its content to indicate what nodes to choose in the given direction — note that this is different from the **`marklist`** used by the **`treeloc`** form described above. The `relation` attribute must have one of these values (examples below omit ID attributes for brevity):

`anc`
: Counts down from the root to the parent of the location source. The root is the first quantum of the axis and the parent is the last. So, for example, to select the node's immediate parent one can use:

```
<relloc relation=anc>-1 1</relloc>
```

More than one ancestor can be selected at once. For example, the root and its immediate child on the path to the location source can be addressed with:

```
<relloc relation=anc>1 2</relloc>
```

`esib`
: Counts among the elder (or left) siblings of the location source. Thus, the leftmost sibling of the location source is the first position. This can be addressed with:

```
<relloc relation=esib>1 1</relloc>
```

The last sibling of the location source that precedes it is the last position. This can be addressed with:

```
<relloc relation=esib>-1 1</relloc>
```

`ysib` Counts among the younger (or right) siblings of the location source. Thus, the first right sibling of the location source is the first position and the last sibling is the last. The sibling following a node can be addressed with:

```
<relloc relation=ysib>1 1</relloc>
```

while the last child of a node's parent is

```
<relloc relation=ysib>-1 1</relloc>
```

`parent` This is shorthand for the nearest ancestor. When this relation is used, the **dimspec** is not needed and must be empty:

```
<relloc relation=parent></relloc>
```

`children` This returns all the direct children (subelements) of the location source. The **dimspec** is not needed and must be empty:

```
<relloc relation=children></relloc>
```

The variations on the **relloc** form provide a nice example of how the flexibility of architectural forms can lead to compact markup. One can define an element type corresponding to each subclass of **relloc.** This can make the markup more compact and allows SGML validation to prevent errors. For example, the following declarations could be used:

```
<!ELEMENT     anc          - - (dimspec)>
<!ATTLIST     anc
    HyTime    CDATA        #FIXED "relloc"
    id        ID           #REQUIRED
    relation  NAME         #FIXED "anc">

<!ELEMENT     children     - O EMPTY>
<!ATTLIST     children
    HyTime    CDATA        #FIXED "relloc"
    id        ID           #REQUIRED
    relation  NAME         #FIXED "children">
```

This means that it is impossible to specify a `dimspec` when using the `children` element type. It also makes the `dimspec` required for the `ancestor` element and makes the relevant SGML document instance smaller and clearer.

8.4.4 Single-layer lists with listloc

The **listloc** or list location address is the simplest node location form. Given a list of nodes, it allows you to select from those nodes by position in the list. The content of an element conforming to the **listloc** form is a **dimlist** which ultimately resolves to a list of marker pairs. Each marker pair specifies a subset of the initial list and the subsets are joined end to end to make the final resulting node list.

The following example selects the first ten nodes of a list, omits the second ten, selects the third ten, and so on as far as numbers are listed:

```
<listloc id=mylist>
    <dimlist>
       <dimspec>
          <marklist>
             1 10 21 10 41 10
             61 10 81 10 101 10</>
       </dimspec>
    <dimlist>
</listloc>
```

The markers could be grouped into **marklist** elements in many other ways with no change in meaning.

8.4.5 Graphical and temporal data with fcsloc

The coordinate location address, or **fcsloc** is used to refer to locations in views of images or other multimedia and graphical objects. Such objects range from a one-dimensional timeline with years as its units, to a holographic movie where any object exists at a position in three-dimensional space and also at positions during the time the movie runs. **Fcsloc** can address positions in any number of dimensions.

Unlike the other locators we discuss in this chapter, **fcsloc** is defined not in the Location address module but in clause 10.7 of the Scheduling module. Using it requires setting the `coordloc` option of the Location address module. A simple example of **fcsloc** is in Section 4.4.

Consider a timeline for a movie. Most current video technologies represent motion via a series of still pictures, shown at various frame rates. For a frame rate of 30 per second one might treat a two-hour movie as a series of 2*60*60*30 or 216,000 frames and refer to them by number. If Act I, Scene 4 starts ten minutes in and lasts for five minutes, one way HyTime could refer to it is by frame numbers (10*60*30 = 18000):

```
<fcsloc locsrc=movie1 impfcs=video-fcs>
    <dimspec>18000 9000</dimspec>
</fcsloc>
```

The domain and units of reference to be used for the view of the data are defined by a finite coordinate space, which for the moment we assume matches the coordinate space of the data itself. The `fcsloc` points to the "imposed fcs" using an IDREF on the `impfcs` attribute. Exact frame rates such as for NTSC video can be accommodated by measuring in more precise units such as milliseconds. Precise frame reference are needed for video editing or detailed work; for general use it might be more appropriate to round off to the nearest second, at least in the user interface.

Fcsloc can be used to pick a spatial as well as temporal area to view. The coordinate space imposed by a view need not match that of the data object. Consider a movie with pixel resolution of 1000 by 1000 pixels and a time span of 2 hours. **Fcsloc** can impose a view independent of this, say 100 by 100 by 100 units in size. Assume that both the data's and the view's FCS assign coordinates from left to right, then from top to bottom, then from beginning to end.

When viewed through an **fcsloc**, the dimensions of the located data are pro-rated to the axis lengths of the imposed `fcs`. In this case, that means that one can link to spatial and temporal portions of the data by giving the desired percentages to be shown. To pick out the left lower quarter of each frame for the last quarter of the movie's running time, specify dimensions of (1 50), (51 50), (76 25). This would be encoded as:

```
<fcsloc locsrc=movie1 impfcs=cropped-video>
    <extlist>
       <dimspec> 1 50</dimspec>
       <dimspec>51 50</dimspec>
       <dimspec>76 25</dimspec>
    </extlist>
</fcsloc>
```

The imposed FCS can use different axis lengths than the data's FCS, but the view's particular measurement units and domains are ignored. It is imposed purely on a pro-rata basis for each axis.

As with all HyTime axes, spatial and temporal locations for **fcsloc** describe positions via integers (see Section 6.2); negative values specify locations counted backward from the end of an axis. Special adjustments are therefore required to use the traditional Cartesian graph space.

The easiest way to convert coordinate systems is to decide what level of precision is required and then scale all coordinates so the smallest possible coordinate is 1. For instance, measure in millimeters instead of meters, or seconds instead of hours:

1.618 meters is represented as 1618 millimeters

0.1 hours is represented as 360 seconds

Negative numbers are also commonly used by graphical programs and their interfaces. In the Macintosh™ toolbox, for example, objects are assigned positions in an x,y plane where both x and y run from –32767 to +32767. This range can be translated by adding 32768 to all values:

–32767 is represented by 1

0 is represented by 32768

32767 is represented by 65535

Such conversions can and in many cases should be completely hidden from the end user of a HyTime system. When dealing with standard notations that use pre-defined coordinate domains, it may be more convenient to use `notloc` than `fcsloc`, using a pointing mechanism tailored for the specific data representation. We describe this process in Chapter 12, and coordinate systems, units of measurement and related topics in Chapter 13.

8.5 Semantic locations

The third and final category of HyTime locator methods includes semantic locations, which find their destination by specifying:

- a context to search
- one or more criteria the desired data object must satisfy

The object (or in some cases objects) fitting the criteria and found in the context forms the destination.

8.5.1 Finding the values of properties with proploc

Most representations have ways to associate properties with instances of data objects and/or portions of them; SGML attributes and GIs are examples. The `proploc` architectural form provides a way to find the value of any property of an object given the object and the property's name.

Here are some instances in which the notion of properties and `proploc` are useful:

- In object-oriented databases, instances of a given class may have named "instance variables" that give instance-specific information about the data object.
- In LISP and other programming languages, "association lists" can be attached to various data structures so as to encode any properties desired.

- In SGML, "attributes" can be attached to any element and are typically used to include information *about* the particular occurrence of the element (as opposed to information about the element type in general).

In all these cases **proploc** is the appropriate HyTime tool for referring to the value of a property. The `locsrc` attribute for the **proploc** specifies the object whose property is of interest; the content of the **proploc** is a "qualified property name" as discussed in Section 11.7.5. For example, to refer to the value of the `security` attribute of the element with ID `para239`, this locator would suffice:

```
<proploc locsrc=para239>attval[security]</proploc>
```

We give many more examples of properties and property locations in Chapter 11 on lexical types and properties and in Chapter 9 on the HyTime query language.

Proploc has some optional attributes as well. The `joint` attribute applies only when the location source is a multiple location, consisting of several components as we discuss in Section 8.7.1. This attribute takes the value `joint` or `several`, and indicates respectively that the property is one that applies to the location as a whole, or to each component in turn. `Joint` is the default.

The `apropsrc` attribute determines whether the property may be sought in an alternate location as well as the location source, as we discuss in Section 11.7.2. This is most commonly used to permit finding attributes of an SGML element even when pointing at pseudo-elements within it. The default value is `solesrc`, meaning that no alternate property sources are checked; the alternative is `apropsrc`.

The final attribute of **proploc** is `notprop`. It specifies what should happen if the requested property cannot be found. The default value is `ignore`, meaning that "the proploc will be treated as though it had not been referenced" (with whatever effect that may have on the containing structure); the alternatives are `error`, which indicates that an error should be reported to the user, and `empty`, which treats the reference as if the property found "an empty data object" as value. The behavior of an ignored or empty reference is undefined, except that a note indicates that the reference is held not to exist for `ignore` and to exist for `empty`. Questions remain as to whether HyQ functions would treat such results as being contained by, less than, unequal to, or otherwise related to other data objects.

8.5.2 Queries to find locations

For clarity of exposition we describe querying here under semantic locations even though it is described under its own heading (in clause 8.7) in the HyTime standard. The HyTime architectural forms **nmquery** and **mrkquery** are used when a location is to be identified as the result of a process defined by a query language. These elements have a `%HyBrid;` content model, since the form of the query can be arbitrary.

The queries we discuss in this book use the HyQ query language. This optional feature of HyTime defines a query language for SGML documents with powerful retrieval structures that also includes all of the facilities of the Location address module. The HyQ language itself is discussed in detail in Chapter 9

The attribute list form **query** defines two attributes, `qdomain` and `qcontext`, which specify how the query is to be interpreted. The `qdomain` attribute specifies the data source to be queried, while the `qcontext` attribute allows the specification of any context required to interpret the query. The `qcontext` might include syntactic details like an SGML parsing context or semantic details like macro definitions that must be in effect for the query to be interpreted. HyQ does not require `qcontext`.

The other important attribute used with **nmquery** and **mrkquery** is the HyTime global attribute `notation`, which is used to indicate the data content notation used to express the query. For HyQ the value of the notation attribute must be `HyQ`.

The following is an example of a `nmquery`:

```
<nmquery qdomain=book3 notation="MyQ">
    find all top-secret elements
</nmquery>
```

8.5.3 Non-HyTime location methods with notloc

The designers of HyTime were aware that as technology advances new methods of reference will become important. For example, new representations of data frequently emerge; many ways of representing full-motion video sequences already exist, and new ones are introduced surprisingly often. Some new representations or new media provide their own specialized reference methods. The HyTime **notloc** architectural form provides a way to accommodate such methods. There are three major situations where **notloc** is appropriate:

- HyTime may lack a specific pointing method appropriate to a particular kind of data, and hence require extension

- a particular data representation may have a standard location address method, which should be used for compatibility
- a particular user community may have a standard practice for specifying locations, which should be used in order to be compatible with that community's needs and expectations

In these cases **notloc** is very important and can help bring the benefits of HyTime's standardization and portability to a wider range of applications than might otherwise be possible. Its form is very simple: an SGML element that conforms to the **notloc** architectural form, whose content may be anything at all, as specified by `%HyBrid;` in the architectural form's meta-content model (see Section 5.2.8 for a discussion of `%HyBrid;`). All these are valid:

```
<notloc>123456789-a</notloc>

<notloc>OLE -559038737</notloc>

<notloc place="<ct> containing 'Intro'">   </notloc>
```

Since **notloc** addresses "a portion of data whose interpretation is subject to the rules of a data content notation," interpreters are needed both for that data notation and the **notloc** pointing syntax. These interpreters could be part of the same software, and could also be integrated directly into a HyTime implementation.

One restriction is that **notloc** cannot be used to specify the location source of another locator unless the `notsrc` option is specified. That is, another locator's `locsrc` attribute cannot normally point to a **notloc**.

In general a **notloc** ought to provide certain minimum information:

- the data object
- the notation the data object is in
- the desired portion of the data object

The most natural way to specify a data object in HyTime is via a declared entity. The simplest syntax is to put an attribute of declared value `entity` on the **notloc** element.

Note 221 in the HyTime standard reminds us that HyTime does not require that addressed data be an entity. While a **notloc** content could have some other way of locating the data object to be addressed, a generic HyTime engine could not find the object without special knowledge. For portability, it is better to ensure that every data object referred to by a **notloc** uses an entity declaration to locate the referenced object.

There are various ways to determine the notation for a data object. A data entity whose declaration specifies its notation needs no further specification on the **notloc**. For example:

```
<!NOTATION   TIFF  PUBLIC
    "+//ISBN 0-7923-9432-1::Graphic Notation//NOTATION
    Aldus/Microsoft
    Tagged Interchange File Format//EN">
<!ENTITY  figure3  SYSTEM
    "fig3.tif" NDATA tiff>
<notloc object=figure3>
```

Alternatively, an element type conforming to the **notloc** form can be defined for each notation used. This is useful because an application can then determine from the GI of each **notloc** how to process each location specification using each notation's favored location method.

A **notloc** commonly uses attributes and/or content to specify what piece of the data object is desired. Because the **notloc** architectural form can have either HyTime content or non-HyTime content or both, the location specification can be of almost any form, typically something like:

```
<!ELEMENT       notloc       - - (#PCDATA)>
<!ATTLIST       notloc
    HyTime      NAME         #FIXED "notloc"
    object      ENTITY       #REQUIRED
    ntn         NAME         #IMPLIED
    -- any other application-specific attributes -->
```

A **notloc** usually fully defines a location and has no need of a location source such as used by many other location forms. Thus, there is no `locsrc` attribute on the **notloc** form. There is, however, provision for the **query** attributes, `qdomain` and `qcontext`. A **notloc** may use these to indicate its domain when appropriate, or it may define other attributes, subelements, or content as required for that purpose.

The `ntn` attribute shown can be used to specify the notation in which the locator itself is specified (as opposed to the notation the referenced data is in). This is especially useful when **notloc** is used to integrate other standard locator methods into HyTime, a practice recommended, for example, in the SIGHyper user's group newsletter (October 1991).

The danger of non-standard notlocs

Notice that in the discussion above standardization still figures prominently. **Notloc** provides a crucial way to extend HyTime in order to handle the full range of possible locations. However, if it is used for no nobler purpose than enabling a closed architecture product to print "HyTime compatible" in its advertisements, then **notloc** will do far more harm than good. While such a vendor could simply use their internal identifiers, place "`<notloc>... </notloc>`" around them and declare themselves HyTime conformant, their customers would gain no advantages from this HyTime conformance. **`Notloc`** is portable only when the notation used is published and can be interpreted by everyone — otherwise a HyTime engine cannot interpret the **`notloc`**. A generic HyTime engine would detect the **`notloc`** and perhaps be able to identify it as applying to a certain named notation, e.g.:

```
-//ACME products//NOTATION
Coyote pointer form 37 (patent pending)//EN
```

But what happens then? At best, the engine can pass information to another proprietary program. That may suffice for some purposes, but if that program is not available, the link is uninterpretable (read: useless).

Better uses of notloc

When a reference method with an established user community has important properties not provided by existing HyTime location methods, then it is time to think about using **`notloc`**. We already know of a few such cases:

- The DSSSL (Document Style and Semantics Specification Language) draft international standard, nearing completion, has very refined methods for characterizing and selecting data in SGML documents. Many of these are conceptually similar to HyTime methods.
- The Text Encoding Initiative began several years ago to develop SGML representations for reference methods commonly used in the arts, humanities and social sciences, some of which originated centuries ago. Established practices in this large user community precede and sometimes differ from HyTime's methods; like DSSSL, they apply especially to a certain range of applications, but are carefully optimized for those applications. We discuss this reference method in Section 12.7.
- Some operating systems are beginning to provide built-in support for giving data objects permanent names by which other data can link to them. Should these methods be widely accepted and applied, it will behoove HyTime implementers to support them and **`notloc`** is the logical way to do this.

8.5.4 Non-automated references with bibloc

The **`notloc`** extension method is intended for location methods that can be readily processed by computer. There also exist references that only humans are expected to interpret, and **bibloc** is the locator to use for these. When converting a pre-existing paper document to electronic form, one may wish to mark bibliographical references as links. It is useful to mark up such references as links even though only humans are likely to interpret them in the near future.

There may also be links that cannot be mechanically followed:

```
<bibloc>Milton's allusions to the Bible</bibloc>
<bibloc>Herodotus' unfulfilled promises</bibloc>
<bibloc>All of Danielle Steele's writings</bibloc>
```

People may differ about just what these links point to; in the last example the link's end-set changes over time. All these cases are appropriate applications of **bibloc**.

8.6 Creating robust pointers

The only built-in, fully *validated* pointing mechanism that SGML itself provides is the ID/IDREF mechanism. This is not to say other pointing mechanisms cannot be used; nevertheless, we consider an ID to be the best way to refer to an element whenever possible because:

- An SGML parser automatically checks that all ID attributes in a document are unique and that every IDREF points to an ID; this checking can catch many user errors.
- Programs typically do not modify IDs unless the user specifically requests it; therefore IDs are usually stable through time as a document is edited or revised.
- Common editing operations do not invalidate IDs, and so elements can be located in later editions of a document. This is very important, for example for software's ability to reattach information such as marginal notes.
- Authoring programs can easily manage deletions so as to avoid reusing IDs so that even over very long time periods links will not take readers to the *wrong* place: at worst, the system detects that the ID is missing, rather than taking the user silently to the wrong information.
- HyTime works in large part by converting other kinds of pointers to IDs and IDREFs; this becomes trivial when the intended destination data already has an ID.

Given such advantages, one might expect software systems or industry groups to require an ID on every SGML element in every document. This would have many benefits, especially for editors and for the users of hypertext documents and documents that change frequently. With IDs on all elements, use of HyTime is dramatically simplified. However, there are a few reasons that most documents do not use IDs quite everywhere:

- Generating unique mnemonic IDs is hard, especially in very large projects. Computers can easily create unique IDs, but they are unlikely to be meaningful to anyone.
- Each ID takes some space and users of small systems or software that loads entire documents into memory at once may run into practical limits.
- For validation the parser must keep a list of all defined IDs (otherwise, of course, it could not know that a new ID duplicates one it already saw). This can slow down a parser even on a big machine and may exceed the capacity of a small one.

The best compromise is to put IDs on all major structural elements (such as chapters, sections, poems, lists, etc.) and then use HyTime methods such as **treeloc** for precise references within those elements.

Such pointers typically involve a location ladder with a **nameloc** and a **treeloc**. The **nameloc** points to the nearest ancestor having an SGML ID, and the **treeloc** walks down the tree with the **nameloc** element as location source. Such links are easy to generate automatically. For example, if the first section in Figure 8.1 had `ID=sec1` then one could specify the location of the last `item` with the location ladder below:

```
<treeloc ID=t1 locsrc=idptr>
    <marklist>4 5</marklist>
</treeloc>
...
<nameloc ID=idptr>
    <nmlist nametype=element>
       sec1
    </nmlist>
</nameloc>
```

This convention has many benefits, but one stands out above all: reorganizing the document anywhere outside of the ancestor that has the ID has no effect on the link. Specifically, the link is not broken and so readers of the document will have fewer problems. The ancestor can also be moved without breaking the link.

Of course, **treeloc** does not protect links against every kind of document editing. Specifically, changes *within* the identified elements can still cause problems. If, for instance, you insert an extra `section`, the child-numbers of following siblings change and if a **treeloc** uses them, it points to a different node. The link may even point to no node at all, if there are not enough children at some point along the path.

There is no ultimate solution to this problem in the general case, unless the software used to do all edits keeps track of every change as it happens. Thus, without a very advanced integrated authoring environment, a document can be edited enough that a link will fail. However, you can build relatively robust links by maximizing use of IDs and then using simple methods such as **`treeloc`** for navigating within small regions selected by ID.

8.7 Aggregates and spans

So far we have discussed how to locate single information units within data objects, such as a region in a graphic, a set of frames in a video, or a structural element at any level in a document. One must also sometimes create a link to several units at once, or to a contiguous range of items. **Aggregate locations** are sets of items that an application wishes to treat as a single entity for some purpose. **Spans** are contiguous ranges of items that are linearly arranged.

Both spans and aggregate locations are treated by HyTime as forms of **multiple location**. Aggregate locations obviously fit this model, but spans do also, since a single span is bounded by two locations, and may be composed of several sequentially ordered items. We discuss generalized aggregates first and then the special notations provided for the common special case of spans.

8.7.1 Multiple locations

Many of the locator elements described in this chapter can point to multiple locations at once, though we have ignored this fact until now. For example, a `nameloc` can specify any number of named locations merely by listing all their names together:

```
<nameloc id=reflist.indexing>
    <nmlist nametype=element>
       index.1 index.5 index.8 index.20
    </nmlist>
</nameloc>
```

Here we assume that the names listed are IDs of elements marking the locations where indexing is discussed in the document, such as:

```
<p><indexentry id=index.5>Indexing</> is an art,
as one can clearly see by comparing
the automated page-number lists so
common today to the carefully crafted
navigation tools sometimes found.</p>
```

The various parts of the location are called **members** or **components** of the multiple location.

The multloc attributes

Aggregate and span locations are only legal if HyTime's `multloc` option is set. Whenever a locator specifies a multiple location, it may also use the **multloc** attributes, which are defined in clause 8.2.2 of the Location address module. While the option and the attribute form have the same name, the **multloc** attributes are not required just because the `multloc` option is enabled.

There are three **multloc** attributes, `ordering`, `set` and `aggloc`. They apply to any of the locator element forms except **bibloc**. Since a HyTime engine can't interpret a **bibloc** automatically, it does not care whether it is multiple.

The `ordering` attribute tells the application whether or not the order of the components in the multiple location is significant. This attribute can have two values: `ordered` and `noorder`. The default for this attribute is `noorder`; you can set `ordered` by coding the attribute on locator element instances or by setting a different default in the DTD. This attribute has no effect on HyTime processing but may be crucial for certain applications to work properly.

The `set` attribute tells HyTime to discard duplicates generated by the locator. The possible values for `set` are `set` and the default value `notset`. Thus, if a name is listed more than once in a **nameloc** and the element has a `set` attribute whose value is `set`, then the extra instances are ignored.

For example, an application might use a multiple location to represent a path or trail through a document, giving the users Next and Previous buttons to navigate along the trail. Using `set=set` would guarantee that users would not visit the same place twice when following a path, because when the list of places is first evaluated, duplicates are discarded.

The `aggloc` attribute is used to define whether or not a multiple location is to be treated as an aggregate. Its value must be `aggloc`, `nagg`, or `agglink`. The values respectively specify that a multiple location is to be treated as a single location that happens to have multiple components (an aggregate), as a list of separate component locations, or as an implicit hypertext link among its components. The default value is `nagg`, so that multiple locations are not treated as aggregates by default.

This distinction is most significant when a multiple location is specified as one end of a link. As described in Section 7.3.2, some link-ends are best thought of as groups of items. For instance, a single two ended link could use two `nagg` multiple locations with the same number of components to connect corresponding portions of two documents.

The `agglink` value provides a way to associate the components of a multiple location just as if they were the various ends of a link, without encoding a link element. Thus, an element conforming to a locator form that locates multiple places and sets `aggloc=agglink`, is defined to function "like a hyperlink" connecting its location of definition and each of its components.

The `agglink` value has an important application in supporting inline links (like **`clink`**) where the location is given by a special locator syntax that appears on an attribute. The `aggloc` attribute can be used to turn a `notloc` into a link. For an example of this see Section 10.3.2. For a discussion of TEI extended pointers and how they can be supported with this technique, see Section 12.7.

Other attributes relevant to multiple locations

HyTime defines several attributes for other architectural forms, that are used only or mainly when the forms must deal with multiple locations. We discuss these under the forms to which they apply. For example, under **`dataloc`** (in Section 8.4.1) we discuss the `catsrc` and `catres` attributes, which deal with how characters and tokens are counted when the **`dataloc`**'s location source is a multiple location.

8.7.2 Span locations

A span location is one that arbitrarily overlaps the structure of the data object to which it applies. HyTime defines spans specifically for SGML, where the simplest example is a contiguous character data portion that crosses element boundaries, such as the string "`loveSONG`" here:

```
<poem>...
<l>Under the tree where she dropped her glove; </l>
<l>Fell in a swoon then fell in love</l>
</poem>
<poem>
<head>SONG</head>
...</poem>
```

Spans in HyTime are a special interpretation of a multiple location. Referring to them requires the spanloc option. It enables the two **spanloc** attributes, spanloc and limsort, which can apply to the **nameloc**, **dataloc**, **treeloc**, **listloc** and **relloc** forms. All of these forms also accept the **multloc** attributes discussed above, in fact, the multloc option is required to use spans.

The spanloc attribute can have the values nspan, spanloc and spanlink. The default value is nspan, which means that the location element does not indicate a span. The value spanloc indicates that the multiple location is to be interpreted as a span. The value spanlink is similar to the agglink value of the multloc attribute; we do not discuss it further.

Any multiple location that has exactly two components can represent the span between those two components. For example, to encode the span above one can introduce empty elements at the intended ends of the anchor, and then point to them from a nameloc:

```
<poem>...
<l>Under the tree where she dropped her glove; </l>
<l>Fell in a swoon then fell in
<anchor id=span-start-1>love</l>
</poem>
<poem>
<head>SONG<anchor id=span-end-1></head>
...</poem>

<nameloc id=nl-1 spanloc=spanloc>
    <nmlist nametype=element>
       span-start-1 span-end-1</nmlist>
</nameloc>
```

This done, any link that gives nl-1 as one of its linkends designates an anchor consisting of everything from the first point to the second (inclusive). Of course, one can also point to the same locations without inserting anchor or similar elements; any of the Location address module's locator methods can be used to indicate the endpoints.

The HyTime standard states that spans include the element structure information that exists between the ends, so HyTime engines that support the spanloc option must provide for representing unbalanced or **asynchronous** markup as part of the span:

```
love</l>
</poem>
<poem>
<head>SONG
```

Since this information is not a sensible tree, it would be folly to use it as the location source for a locator like **treeloc**.

The second **spanloc** attribute is called `limsort` and has two possible values: `limsort` and `nlimsort`. The HyTime standard says that `limsort` "specifies whether span limits are sorted," and comments it in the architectural form definition: "Are limits sorted with span start first?" This seems to offer two possible interpretations:

- `limsort` specifies whether span limits are *already* sorted in the specification as received by HyTime, and it is an error if they turn out not to be in order
- `limsort` specifies whether span limits are *to be* sorted by the HyTime engine, and hence no ordering errors can arise

Given this ambiguity we recommend use of `limsort=nlimsort`.

8.7.3 Overlapping locations

Because locations can be specified by many locators, there is nothing preventing the creation of overlapping links. For example, one can link specific groups of words using **dataloc** even when the anchors specified overlap, as in this sentence where two reviewers have created annotations suggesting alternate corrections:

```
<p id=pt73>
    The mouse the cat the dog chased ate died.
</p>

<dataloc id=d1 locsrc=pt73 quantum=word>3 5</dataloc>
<comment id=c1>Move to separate sentence.</comment>
<ilink linkends="d1 c1">

<dataloc id=d2 locsrc=pt73 quantum=word>1 4</dataloc>
<comment id=c2>What happened to the mouse?</comment>
<ilink linkends="d2 c2">
```

The first **dataloc** points to the words "`the cat the dog chased`", while the second points to the words "`The mouse the cat`". These anchors overlap, in that they both contain "`the cat`." Such situations arise frequently in any text important enough to have many links.

Links from overlapping anchors can only be created using **ilink**, not **clink**. This is because **clink** origins are expressed directly as part of the document structure, which is a tree. Syntax such as shown below is not well-formed in SGML, because it does not form a tree. However, **ilink** can create overlapping links with no problem, as shown above.

```
<p id=pt73>
    <clink2>The mouse <clink1>the cat</clink2>
    the dog chased</clink1> ate died.
</p>
```

9

The HyTime Query Language

9.1 Purpose and basic capabilities

HyQ, the HyTime **query language**, provides the answer to situations where you need to specify hyperlinks to locations that may change over time or where a compact notation is preferable to a long location ladder. HyQ queries are similar to database queries, except that they have special facilities for dealing effectively with hierarchical structures like SGML documents, something that is not practical in the relational database model.

HyQ provides a low-overhead way to find parts of documents and is described in clause A.3 of the HyTime standard. Its principles should already be familiar since they build upon HyTime's Location address module. Like the Location address module, HyQ includes tools for locating data in non-SGML documents and data objects as well as powerful methods for locating data in SGML documents.

HyQ can also be used as a searching tool for users who must locate specific parts of documents on the basis of their content. This capability is vital in systems for working with large documents; if you have a 30,000-page aircraft maintenance manual or a collection of all the Greek or English literature from a certain century, searching is important indeed.

Although HyQ provides capabilities for doing such direct searching, it is not intended as a user interface. The exact form of HyQ queries is not one that untrained users would want to type. It is quite easy, however, to build friendly user-interfaces for specifying queries combined with a small program to turn the query into HyQ for processing. This is exactly like the situation with SGML itself: most users don't want to type (or even see) explicit tags, but they can still create SGML with whatever kind of interface they prefer (mouse, control keys, buttons, voice-recognition systems, and so on).

9.2 An example

What does a HyQ query look like? The first HyQ example in the HyTime standard "locates all 'equation' elements in a document." A non-graphical interface might express this query as:

```
in mydoc, find <equation>
```

where the angle brackets specify that instances of "equation" must be found that constitute an SGML element type, not simply a word in the document's text content. A graphical interface could provide a forms-based interface to construct queries.

Either a text or graphical interface could use HyQ for processing. The resulting HyQ equivalent is more imposing when typed literally, but is only a little more complex conceptually:

```
<HyQ qdomain=mydoc>
    Select(DOMTREE Eq(Proploc(CAND GI) "EQUATION"))
</HyQ>
```

This query works by selecting some nodes out of the entire tree headed by an element with ID `mydoc`. The nodes selected from these candidates are those on which a certain property can be located with a given value: namely, their `GI` property must be equal to `EQUATION`. We now describe this process in much more detail.

A HyQ query is a single element with a `qdomain` attribute that points (using IDREFS) to one or more data objects to be searched. In this example, `mydoc` must be an ID on some element in the same document, and that element is the starting point for the query. Of course, if that element is itself a HyTime locator, it may be resolved further. The elements or other objects to which qdomain points are called **nodes** and the qdomain is consequently a **node list**.

The query itself appears in the content of the HyQ element. The query language is **functional**, meaning that it consists of many small tools that can be combined in the manner used for functions in simple algebra and computer languages. Functional languages are best understood by reading the innermost parentheses first and working outward. HyQ provides a set of functions or **operators** that for the most part manipulate three kinds of data:

- nodes or node lists
- data values such as strings and numbers
- truth values (TRUE or FALSE)

The example applies three such tools to nodes in its query domain:

Proploc()	checks a node for the property named GI and returns the property's value, in the same manner as the **proploc** architectural form from the Location address module, discussed in Section 8.5.1
Eq()	tests whether that property value is equal to the literal string "EQUATION"
Select()	chooses certain nodes out of the domain, on the basis of whether they satisfy the test

The Select() function takes two parameters: a node list and an assertion. The node list DOMTREE, shown here, expands each data object in the query domain and treats it as a larger node list, containing all the individual subelements within it down to the leaves. For example, if the document contained the following element as the query domain:

```
<task id=mydoc>
    <step>Place duck on scale</step>
    <step>Place witch on scale</step>
    <step>Remove the supports</step>
    <step>See if they
       <emph>truly</emph> balance</step>
</task>
```

then DOMTREE would cause the Select() to test 12 different nodes (six elements and six pseudo-elements), not just the task. With DOMROOT, however, only the task itself is a potential candidate for matching. In either case each node selected is tried in turn and the Proploc() refers to it as the current CAND or candidate. Proploc() corresponds to the **proploc** location form (see Section 8.5.1 and clause 8.5.1). The instance in the example above tests the candidate node for the property named GI.

This built-in HyTime property (see Section 11.7 on properties and clause A.2.1.2) holds the element type name of each SGML element.

The `Eq()` function then compares the GI of the candidate against the literal string "`EQUATION`". Thus the end result of this example query is a node list containing only those nodes from the original domain having the GI `EQUATION`. We show the GI in upper case on the assumption that SGML's default behavior applies, ignoring case of such names. If this is false or uncertain for the data being queried, one must use techniques we describe in Section 9.4.2 to ensure appropriate methods of comparison.

9.3 HyQ syntax

In describing HyQ's syntax we use the following conventions to distinguish kinds of tokens and their uses:

- Function names are in initial capitals with following parentheses, as was also done in examples above: `Select()`.
- Function parameter names are in lower case: `nodelist`.
- Literal reserved words that can appear as parameters are in all capital letters: CAND.
- Question mark, asterisk and plus sign are never literal; they appear at the end of parameter names to indicate whether they are optional, optional and repeatable, or required and repeatable, respectively (this usage is already familiar to users of regular expressions or SGML DTDs).

The following conventional parameter names indicate what kind of data is expected:

`node` — The parameter must be a node; this can be any of:

- a single- or double-quoted literal string
- the reserved name CAND
- a reference to a parameter of a containing `Query()` or `Useq()`, such as `%1`, `%2`,... `%999`
- a function that returns a node (either `Oo()` or `Count()`)

`nodelist` — The parameter must be a node list; this is not a syntactic grouping of the nodes just defined; rather, a nodelist can be either of:

- a function that returns a node list
- the reserved name DOMROOT or DOMTREE

`anynodes` — The parameter can be a node or a node list.

`assert` The parameter must be a truth value; this can be any of:

- a function that returns a truth value
- the reserved names TRUE and FALSE
- a nodelist (non-empty ones are equivalent to TRUE)

`int` The parameter must be a integer; it may be signed but cannot be zero (except where otherwise specified below).

literal A literal data string, quoted by either double- or single-quotes (SGML LIT or LITA delimiters).

9.3.1 Creating a HyQ query

HyQ queries do not depend on their own unique architectural form in the same way as the HyTime facilities discussed so far. HyQ is a notation defined by HyTime to allow the expression of queries. To be used with HyTime, it must be declared in the `notation` attribute of an element conforming to either the **nmquery** or **mrkquery** architectural forms.

The HyTime standard also defines such an element type called HyQ; the relevant parts of its declaration are shown below (see Appendix A for the full declaration):

```
<!NOTATION     HyQ           PUBLIC
    "+//ISO/IEC 10744:1992//NOTATION
    HyTime Query Notation//EN">
<!ELEMENT      HyQ           - - (#PCDATA)>
<!ATTLIST      HyQ
    HyTime     NAME          #FIXED "nmquery"
    notation   NAME          #FIXED "HyQ"
    fn         NAME          #IMPLIED
    qdomain    IDREF         #IMPLIED>
```

9.4 The HyQ functions

Since HyQ is a functional language, its semantics are defined by a set of independent definitions of individual functions (also known, in the standard. as "operators") along with a few facilities (such as CAND) for relating functions that are not syntactically adjacent. These functions fit into groups, each of which provides facilities for a particular sort of problem (such as dealing with logical relations). We organize the discussion of HyQ functions by these groups, since each group often has syntactic similarities as well as semantic ones.

9.4.1 Selecting nodes

HyQ functions are generally concerned with finding **nodelists**, sets of items in a query domain that satisfy particular properties. Since we describe the application of HyQ to **nmquery** elements, these nodelists are lists of elements or pseudo-elements. These elements must be accessed starting from the `qdomain` of the query, and HyQ uses the reserved words `DOMTREE` and `DOMROOT` to designate two different ways of accessing the query domain.

`DOMTREE` specifies that the items in the query domain include the root of the tree as well as each of the tree's direct and indirect subelements (an "expanded node list," see clause A.3.1 and clause 8.4.2.1). For example a query like the following:

```
<HyQ qdomain=book1>DOMTREE</HyQ>
```

would select every element contained in the element with ID book1, including itself. Such a query is not very useful in itself but `DOMTREE` forms the usual starting point for more precise queries.

`DOMROOT` indicates that the specified query domain itself is the entire domain of the query and no subelements need be considered. This is useful mainly when the query domain is specified as more than one IDREF, in which case the query applies directly to the elements listed in the query domain and only to those elements. This allows dynamic selection from a pre-determined list of possibilities to be expressed.

The Select function

`Select()` is probably the most basic function in HyQ. It has the same purpose as the Select function in traditional query languages: it picks out of a node list just those nodes that have some property. It never adds any new items; the node list resulting from a `Select()` must be identical to or a subset of the node list given to it. The effect of `Select()` is as if it looks at every node in a node list one at a time, discarding all those for which the assertion specified by the second parameter is false. For a proper definition of how HyQ defines truth and falsehood, see Section 9.4.2 on comparison and logic functions. The syntax for `Select()` is:

```
Select(nodelist assertion)
```

Within a `Select()` a special name is defined: `CAND` is the current node being tested. Almost all occurrences of `Select()` use `CAND` because testing it is the most convenient way to state conditions required for selection, as in the example used earlier:

```
Select(DOMTREE Eq(Proploc(CAND GI) "EQUATION"))
```

You can also use a `Select()` within another `Select()`. For example, one way to find all `section` elements that directly or indirectly contain `footnote` elements is to find all nodes that simultaneously fulfill two conditions:

- they have GI `SECTION`
- they contain ("dominate") at least one node with GI `FOOTNOTE`

This can be expressed with a pair of `Select()` functions, one inside the other:

```
<HyQ qdomain=mydoc>
    Select(DOMTREE
          and(Eq(Proploc(CAND GI) "SECTION")
             Select(DOMTREE
                   Eq(Proploc(CAND GI) "FOOTNOTE"))
          )
    )
</HyQ>
```

Note that the keyword `CAND` occurs twice. The first occurrence is completely outside of the inner `Select()` and so can refer only to the node being tested in the outer `Select()`. However, the second `CAND` is inside both `Select()` functions. In such cases, `CAND` always refers to the node being tested by the innermost, that is the nearest, containing `Select()`. Also note that the GI is in upper case, because `Eq()` defaults to case-sensitive comparison while SGML normally ignores case distinctions, returning tag names in capital letters.

9.4.2 Comparison and logic functions

The truth values of HyQ are represented by the reserved words `TRUE` and `FALSE`. A nodelist, however, can also be interpreted as a truth value on the basis of its contents. An empty nodelist represents `FALSE`, while a nodelist containing any nodes at all counts as `TRUE`. This makes it particularly easy to write conditions checking if an element with a certain property exists simply by using the list of elements with that property as a boolean value.

Comparison function syntax

The comparison functions produce `TRUE` or `FALSE` results based on their parameters and are often used to check the value of properties. They all take the same list of possible parameters:

`quantum` Specifies a quantum type as defined for the **dataloc** architectural form (see Section 8.4.1 and clause 8.4.1). If omitted, plain string comparison is used.

`Oo(lexord)` Specifies a lexical ordering definition to be applied to data being compared. Lexical ordering is discussed in clause 6.5.2.2 and in Section 14.4.4. This parameter is crucial when testing SGML-related properties such as `GI`.

`nodes` Specifies any number of nodes and/or node lists, which are concatenated to form a single list before its members are compared. You cannot, for example, use the comparison functions to compare two node lists to each other, as aggregates.

Thus, the syntax of all the comparison functions is:

```
function-name(quantum? Oo(lexord)? anynodes)
```

Quantum type in comparisons

All comparisons "are done in a way appropriate to the quantum." The default quantum type is the same as the default value of the **dataloc** form's `quantum` attribute: `STR`. This means that the nodes are compared strictly as strings, on the basis of alphabetical order (more precisely, character set order). The example below therefore yields `TRUE`:

```
Lt("a" "b" "see")
```

Numerical comparison is quite different; for example, "9" is numerically less than "10" even though the first character of "9" is not less then the first character of "10." For numerical comparison specify quantum type `SINT as shown here:`

```
Lt(SINT "3" "21" "144")
```

Without `SINT` this comparison would yield false, because `3` as a string comes after `21` in alphabetical order — in comparing the characters of the string left to right, `3` is compared to `2` and is found greater; there is no need to look further.

Appropriate quantum types must be specified for comparisons involving date and time tokens, normalized text, or anything other than raw string comparison. To compare quanta not supported by **dataloc**, such as real or other non-integer numbers, you must use an external assertion handler. Such a handler can be accessed through the `Ah()` function described below.

Lexical ordering in comparisons

Strings are compared with regard to case. This can be changed by choosing one of the quantum types that inherently ignores case, such as

NAME, though this will also result in normalization of spacing and other effects; or as described next. The following, for example, yields TRUE:

```
Eq(NAME "a" "A")
```

This distinction is important. For example, property values that correspond to SGML syntactic tokens such as tag names will be returned in upper case if the document being searched uses the reference concrete syntax. With the default quantum type STR, comparison is case-sensitive: "a" does not equal "A". Therefore, a literal to be compared with a tag name must be in upper case as we have shown in examples above.

Rather than requiring all literals to be upper case, one can specify a lexical ordering that will be applied before the comparison is done. This can be done using an IDREF that points to a **lexord** element, as discussed in Section 14.7. This is done as follows:

```
Lt(Oo(mycasetable) "apples" "Oranges")
```

One may wish to express a query that will work whether the document being searched ignores or regards case of element type names. In that case neither STR comparison nor any specific case translation will necessarily be correct. One can, however, use the reserved word #SGMLCASE, which indicates that the SGML case-translation rules apply:

```
Lt(Oo(#SGMLCASE) "a" "B")
```

Throughout this chapter we omit this parameter for brevity, although in most situations it should be specified when applying comparison functions to tag names and other SGML names.

N-way comparisons

Unlike some other languages, HyQ does not limit its comparison functions to two operands. In effect, comparison of more than two operands is treated as a series of pairwise steps, first comparing operand 1 to operand 2, then 2 to 3, 3 to 4, and so on. All these comparisons must be TRUE for the comparison as a whole to be TRUE. HyTime also permits these functions to have a single parameter, but does not state clearly what the result is in such cases.

For the negated comparisons Ne() and Ns(), the test is done without the negation and then the result is negated at the end: Ne("1" "2" "1") is TRUE even though the first and third operands are equal, because it is merely the negation of Eq("1" "2" "1").

As an example, given three nodes treated as signed integers the Lt() (less-than) comparison below yields TRUE (a literal can be treated as a node and used in comparisons):

```
Lt(SINT "3" "21" "144")
```

However, the following comparison yields `FALSE` because 144 is not less than 21, even though 3 is less than both 144 and 21:

```
Lt(SINT "3" "144" "21")
```

HyQ comparison functions

The individual HyQ comparison functions are listed below. They are categorized into comparisons of value, of size and of containment. Along with each function there appears an example that will cause it to return the value `TRUE`.

Numeric/string comparison functions

Name	Tests whether	True example
`Eq()`	All operands are equal	`Eq(SINT "3" "3")`
`Ne()`	Not all operands are equal	`Ne(SINT "0" "3")`
`Lt()`	Less than	`Lt(SINT "1" "2")`
`Le()`	Less than or equal to	`Le(SINT "1" "2")`
`Gt()`	Greater than	`Gt(STR "Z" "Yak")`
`Ge()`	Greater than or equal to	`Ge(SINT "99" "99")`

Node list size comparison functions

Name	Tests whether	True example
`Ss()`	"Same size" function: each operand has the same number of quanta of the specified type. Node lists are concatenated in the same manner as done by **`dataloc`** and the quantum count is the total for the entire nodelist	`Ss("Dog" "Cat")`
`Ns()`	The operands do not all have the same number of quanta of the specified type	`Ns(WORD "a c" "abc")`
`St()`	Each operand has a smaller number of quanta than the next	`St("abc" "defg" "hijkl")`
`Se()`	Each operand has a smaller number of quanta than the next, or the same number	`Se("abc" "def" "hijkl")`
`Bt()`	Each operand has a greater number of quanta than the next	`Bt("001" "9")`
`Be()`	Each operand has a greater number of quanta than the next, or the same number	`Be("Allen" "David" "Steve" "Elli")`

Containment comparison functions

Name	Tests whether	True example
`Ho()`	Each operand "holds" the next: that is, the next is a substring of it but does not exhaust it	`Ho("Hypermedia" "media")`
`He()`	Each operand "holds" the next or is equal to it: that is, the next is a substring of it and may exhaust it	`He("HyTime" "HyTime")`
`Ih()`	Each operand "is held by" the next: that is, it is a substring of the next, but does not exhaust it	`Ih("a" "mayhem")`
`Ie()`	Each operand "is held by" or equal to the next: that is, it is a substring of the next, or may exhaust it	`Ie("node" "node")`

The Ordered function

The `Ordered()` function tests whether the nodes in its node list occur in the node list in the same order that they occur in a single context (typically, this means in a single element of a document — see below). The syntax of the function is:

```
Ordered(nodelist flag?)
```

For example, if a document contains this paragraph:

```
<p id=MND>This man's speech is like a tangled chain:
    Nothing impaired, but all disordered</p>
```

then one can make a node list containing the four underlined chunks of this paragraph in this way (remembering that under the **dataloc** form's rules for word quanta, the apostrophe is a word separator and so the "s" following it is a word token):

```
<HyQ qdomain=MND>
    Query(Create(
        Dataloc(DOMROOT WORD  1  1)
        Dataloc(DOMROOT WORD  4  2)
        Dataloc(DOMROOT STR  27  2)
        Dataloc(DOMROOT STR  45 14)
    ))
</HyQ>
```

This query produces a node list containing four text content nodes: "`This`" "`speech is`" "`a `" "`thing impaired`".

If this node list is passed to `Ordered()`, the result is `TRUE` because two conditions are fulfilled: First, these four data nodes have a common "alternate property source" or "apropsrc," namely the paragraph (as discussed in Section 11.7.2, text data in an SGML document has its immediately containing element as its apropsrc). Second, they occur within that apropsrc in the same order that they occur in the node list.

The `flag` parameter is optional and can be set to either `OVERLAP` or `NOVERLAP`; no default value is specified. `NOVERLAP` means that "each node ends before next begins" — they need not be butted end-to-end with no gaps. `OVERLAP` still requires the nodes' starting points to be in order, but their scopes may overlap. The previous example would yield the value `TRUE` with either `NOVERLAP` or `OVERLAP`, but this example would be `TRUE` only if `OVERLAP` is specified, as shown:

```
<HyQ qdomain=MND>
    Ordered(
       Query(Create(
          Dataloc(DOMROOT WORD  1  5)
          Dataloc(DOMROOT WORD  2  1)
          Dataloc(DOMROOT STR  10  -1)
       OVERLAP))
    )
</HyQ>
```

Boolean functions

HyQ provides the usual boolean functions `And()`, `Or()` and `Not()`. As we have noted, any nodelist can be treated as a boolean value: the value is held to be `TRUE` if the nodelist is not empty.

The logical function `And()` has the following syntax:

```
And(assertion1, assertion2,...)
```

`And()` takes any number of assertions and returns the value `TRUE` if and only if *all* of those assertions are `TRUE`.

The logical function `Or()` has the following syntax:

```
Or(assertion1, assertion2,...)
```

`Or()` takes any number of assertions and returns the value `TRUE` if and only if *at least one* of those assertions is `TRUE`.

The logical function `Not()` has the following syntax:

```
Not(assertion)
```

Not() merely inverts an assertion. If the assertion given to it is TRUE, Not() returns FALSE, and vice versa.

The Forall function

The Forall() function applies a given query to each node in its node list in turn. It returns TRUE if and only if all such applications return non-empty node lists. That is, it requires that the query find something for every node in the node list passed.

```
Forall(nodelist query)
```

The query parameter is required and must consist of either a Query() or Useq() function. The query will typically need to refer to the current node, much as is done with CAND inside a Select(). However, Forall() does not use CAND itself and so does not interfere with the current meaning of CAND when it is part of a Select() or vice versa.

The Useq() and Query() functions have a qdomain parameter that is optional. When either of these functions is used inside Forall() this parameter will normally be omitted. Its default value is the node currently being tested by Forall() function. That is, the query that is the second parameter of Forall() is interpreted once for each node in the Forall() function's node list, using that node as the qdomain.

Forall() is useful if you want to determine whether something is true of every node in a node list obtained from another source. For example, if you select all poem elements with a given value for the author attribute, you may wish to see whether all of them also have the attribute rhymed=true. Assuming you have all of the poet's work in your collection and that it is marked up correctly this query would let you discover whether the poet in question always used rhyme, or varied:

```
Forall(
    Select(DOMTREE
       And(Eq(Proploc(CAND GI) "POEM"))
           Eq(Proploc(CAND attval[AUTHOR]) "Nash"))
    Query(Select(
          Eq(Proploc(CAND attval[RHYMED]) "TRUE")))
)
```

The node list of the Forall() is defined by a familiar Select(), which locates all poem elements with author=Nash. For each of these nodes another query is then executed, which uses that node as its domain and tests whether the value of the rhymed attribute is true. Only if this holds for every node does the Forall() return TRUE.

This example is not surrounded by HyQ start- and end-tags, because Forall() by itself does not constitute a complete query — the top level of a HyQ query must evaluate to a node list, which `Forall()` does not. However, a `Forall()` can be embedded in a more complex query anywhere an assertion can go. A HyQ-supporting application could also provide its users with a way to evaluate such expressions and simply learn whether they are `TRUE` or `FALSE`. This would be useful in certain applications, and is legal HyTime; the application just may not call such services HyQ queries.

One special case arises with `Forall()` if the node list is empty. If there are no poems by Nash, is it `TRUE` or `FALSE` to say that all poems by Nash are rhymed? HyTime does not state the result in such a case. We recommend that unless an amendment to HyTime should declare otherwise, `Forall()` implementations return `TRUE` if the node list is empty, in keeping with the meaning of "for all" in formal logic.

The Query function

`Query()` packages a HyQ query as a function rather than a HyQ element. It is used to embed one query within another, and allows values to be passed into the embedded query using HyQ's argument forms. It returns a nodelist and can appear wherever a nodelist can. The syntax of `Query()` is:

```
Query(nodelist)
Query(nodelist anynodes*)
Query(nodelist qdomain anynodes*)
```

`Query()` takes three possible parameters, which can occur in the combinations shown above:

- The query body itself, which can be any expression that returns a node list.
- The qdomain, which also can be any expression that returns a nodelist.
- A parameter list, which can be any number of individual nodes or nodelists (see below).

The `Query()` function evaluates the query body with respect to the query domain (just as a `HyQ` element evaluates its content with respect to its `qdomain` attribute). The nodelists that are passed as arguments to `Query()` are stored in HyQ argument variables. These begin with a `%` and are numbered in the order they appear in the query. The first argument thus is stored in `%1`, the second in `%2`, and so forth. `Query()` returns the node list that results from evaluating the query.

The next example shows a more complex and more useful application:

> In a repair manual, find all `part-needed` elements, whose IDs are also cross-listed as `item` attributes.

The difficulty here is how to refer to the CANDs of two Select() functions at the same time. In this example, the method is to make the outer CAND an argument to an embedded Query. In that embedded Query() it then has the argument name %1.

The second Select() occurs within the embedded Query() and therefore uses its query domain, which will consist of all elements in the tree because the Query() specified DOMROOT as the query domain. The inner Select() can access both its own CAND and the Query() function's %1 argument (which is the CAND of the outer select):

```
<HyQ qdomain=my.repair.manual>
    Select(DOMTREE
        And(Eq(Proploc(CAND GI) "PART-NEEDED")
            Query(
                Select(DOMTREE
                    Eq(Proploc(CAND attval[ITEM])
                        Proploc(%1 ID)))
            )
            DOMROOT
            CAND
        )
    )
</HyQ>
```

Note the use of a qualified property name to pick out the item attribute in particular from among the inner CAND's attributes. We discuss property names in Section 11.7.5.

In the first published edition of the HyTime standard, arguments to Query() can only be nodes, not nodelists. The HyTime committee has proposed correcting this limitation. The args passed to Query() and Useq() are changed from node*, to (node | nodelist)*. The only limitation is that for both Query() and Useq(), if the first parameter *is* a nodelist as opposed to just a syntactic node, then the query domain must be explicitly specified (otherwise you couldn't tell if the first node list was the qdomain or the first arg!).

9.4.3 Location functions

Each function described in this section corresponds directly to an architectural form of the same name, defined in the Location address module. They share the characteristics and requirements of those architectural forms; for example, if the form requires that a particular HyTime option be in effect, then the corresponding function has the same requirement.

The first parameter is always a node list that serves as the location source (`locsrc`) for the function. Because this node list can be a complex one constructed using other HyQ functions, the functions here have no need for parameters corresponding to `multloc` or `spanloc` attributes of their related element forms (except in special cases discussed below).

The other parameters depend on the particular architectural form. Normally there is one parameter corresponding to the content and one corresponding to each relevant attribute. We defined the parameter types `node`, `nodelist` and `anynodes` earlier. The other parameters used by these functions correspond to attributes defined for the forms (and have the same default values). They are discussed with the relevant architectural forms in Chapter 8.

The Dataloc function

The `Dataloc()` function corresponds to the **dataloc** architectural form (clause 8.4.1) discussed in Section 8.4.1. It addresses parts of atomic data, such as character strings parsed into individual characters, words, SGML names, dates, etc. Its syntax is:

```
Dataloc(nodelist quantum? catsrc?
        catres? mkpair* overrun?)
```

For example, to select the fourth through seventh words (that is, `WORD` quanta) of some paragraph with ID `t27.2`, `Dataloc()` could be used in this way:

```
<HyQ qdomain=t27.2>
    Query(Dataloc(DOMROOT WORD 4 4))
</HyQ>
```

The Treeloc function

The `Treeloc()` function corresponds to the **treeloc** architectural form (clause 8.4.2.4) discussed in Section 8.4.2. It is used to step down through a tree to reach some direct or indirect subelement of the location source. Its syntax is:

```
Treeloc(nodelist snzi* overrun? set? treecom?)
```

The `snzi` parameter represents the **marklist** that the **treeloc** form uses to specify the path to its destination. The example below picks out the last `item` from the tree discussed in Section 8.4.2, assuming the first chapter is given ID `chap1`:

```
<HyQ qdomain=chap1>
    Treeloc(DOMROOT 1 2 4 5)
</HyQ>
```

The Relloc function

The `Relloc()` function corresponds to the **relloc** architectural form (clause 8.4.2.7) discussed in Section 8.4.3. It locates nodes that are related by tree structure to a known node, for example as ancestors or siblings. Its syntax is:

```
Relloc(nodelist anynode relation?
       mkpair* overrun? set?)
```

The `anynode` parameter serves as the `root` attribute. The example below finds the parent of the `item` element found by the example of `Treeloc()` above:

```
<HyQ qdomain=chap1>
    Relloc(Treeloc(DOMROOT 1 2 4 5) DOMROOT ANC -1 1)
</HyQ>
```

The Listloc function

The `Listloc()` function corresponds to the **listloc** architectural form (clause 8.4.2.6) discussed here in Section 8.4.4. It picks out particular nodes from a node list by their numeric positions, counting across the node list from 1 to the end. Its syntax is:

```
Listloc(nodelist mkpair* overrun? set?)
```

The example below picks out the 3rd through the 50th `section` elements within the element with ID `chap1`. The `TRUNC` value of the `overrun` parameter (see Section 8.4) indicates that it should not be considered an error if too few `section` elements are available.

```
<HyQ qdomain=chap1>
    Listloc(
       Select(DOMTREE
          Eq(Proploc(CAND GI) "SECTION"))
    3 48 TRUNC)
</HyQ>
```

The Proploc function

The `Proploc()` function, which corresponds to the **proploc** architectural form discussed in Section 8.5.1, returns the value of one of a node's properties, given that property's name. It is most commonly used when locating an SGML attribute or retrieving such an attribute in the process of interpreting some other link or reference. Its syntax is:

```
Proploc(anynodes qpn joint? apropsrc? notprop?)
```

There are many examples of `Proploc()` throughout this chapter. The most common case uses only the `qpn` (qualified property name) parameter and specifies either `GI`, or `attval` and an SGML attribute name. The other parameters treat more unusual cases and are discussed with the **proploc** form. The following example using the `apropsrc` parameter would select *both* the elements with SGML GI `P`, and all their contained PCDATA pseudo-elements:

```
<HyQ qdomain=chap1>
    Select(DOMTREE
       Eq(Proploc(CAND GI APROPSRC) "P")
    )
</HyQ>
```

The Oo function

The "object-of" or `Oo()` function is a way to refer to the destination of a location ladder. `Oo()` returns a node list (typically containing a single node) and thus can be used anywhere node lists can appear. Its syntax is:

```
Oo(idref)
```

For example, given the IDs of several relevant `speech` elements from a collection of government records, say `sp.1` through `sp.4`, you can make them into a node list and select directly out of it list in this way:

```
<HyQ qdomain=book23>
    Select(
       Create(Oo(SP.1) Oo(SP.2) Oo(SP.3) Oo(SP.4))
       Eq(Proploc(CAND attval[SPEAKER]) "O'Neill"))
</HyQ>
```

The `Create()` function used here groups the IDs to make a node list; it is discussed in Section 9.4.4.

Such IDREFS need not appear literally; they could instead be the result of other HyQ functions. If the desired IDREF values appear as the value of an attribute of another known element, `Proploc()` can be used to get them and the result can be the domain of a `Select()`:

```
<xref id=mylist targets="SP.1 SP.2 SP.3 SP.4">

<HyQ qdomain=book23>
    Select(
       Oo(Proploc(Oo(mylist) attval[TARGETS]))
       Eq(Proploc(CAND attval[SPEAKER]) "O'Neill"))
</HyQ>
```

9.4.4 Node list operations for set processing

The Create function

The `Create()` function groups a list of nodes and/or node lists into a single node list that can then be used as a parameter for another function. Its syntax is:

```
Create(anynodes)
```

The following example combines the results of several other functions into a single nodelist:

```
<HyQ qdomain=Nova-express>
    Create(Oo(ID.1) Oo(ID.2)
       Select(DOMTREE Eq(Proploc(CAND GI) "P")))
</HyQ>
```

The name of this function can be omitted without changing the meaning. Thus the following form is equivalent to the preceding:

```
(Oo(ID.1)
 Oo(ID.2)
 Select(DOMTREE Eq(Proploc(CAND GI) "P")))
```

The Union function

Although HyQ node lists are ordered lists and not unordered sets, HyQ provides the most common set operations. `Union()` creates a node list that contains all the nodes in any of the node lists provided as parameters, one copy of each. The syntax is:

```
Union(nodelist+)
```

For example, applying `Union()` to two node lists, the first containing all `footnote` elements and the second containing all `citation` elements, yields all of both. Likewise, applying `Union()` to the list of all `footnote` elements and the list of all elements having attribute `type=reference` yields all elements that fit either property. An element can only appear once in the result, even if it occurs in both lists as would the following:

```
<footnote type=reference>...</footnote>
```

Because all node lists are ordered (unlike sets in general), the question arises of what order the resulting node list has. The answer in HyTime (clause A.3.1) is that

> Node lists are inherently ordered... and their ordering is preserved by HyQ. HyQ operators that create node lists determine

> their ordering by preserving the order of their operands (and of the nodes within the operands) and the order in which objects occur in the domain....

This nicely covers most cases, but may be ambiguous in some situations. For example, consider a query with several subparts:

- One part locates chapters 1, 3, 5, 7 and 9 of the book that is the query domain.
- Another part locates chapters 2, 4, 6, 8 and 10 of the same book.
- A final part uses the `Union()` function on these two node lists.

Preserving the order of `Union()`'s operands yields a node list of chapters in the order 1 3 5 7 9 2 4 6 8 10, while preserving the order in which these objects occur in the domain yields 1 2 3 4 5 6 7 8 9 10.

When a query domain includes nodes from several different documents or entities this problem does not arise, since nodes in different documents or entities have no inherent relative ordering. There is no domain order that holds between nodes from different documents.

The Inter function

`Inter()` provides set-intersection capability: the resulting node list contains one copy of any node that occurs in *all* the node lists provided as parameters. The order of the result is determined using the same rules just discussed for `Union()`. The syntax is:

```
Inter(nodelist+)
```

For example, if one intersects three node lists respectively containing

- all `task` elements
- all elements with attribute `skill=novice`
- all elements containing a `tool-list` containing "`hammer`"

The resulting node list includes a much more restricted set of nodes: only those elements that simultaneously fulfill all three conditions and therefore appear in all three lists.

There is a close relationship between the `Inter()` and `And()` functions. The following two queries produce the same result: the first selects nodes by requiring that they satisfy several conditions together:

```
<HyQ qdomain=repair-manual>
    Select(DOMTREE
       and(Eq(Proploc(CAND GI) "TASK")
           Eq(Proploc(CAND attval[SKILL]) "NOVICE")
           Select(DOMTREE
              and(Eq(Proploc(CAND GI) "TOOL-LIST")
                  He(Dataloc(CAND 1 -1) "hammer")
                 )
           )
       )
    )
</HyQ>
```

The second query achieves the same result by retrieving the sets of nodes that satisfy each criterion individually and then intersecting them:

```
<HyQ qdomain=repair-manual>
    Intersect(
       Select(DOMTREE Eq(Proploc(CAND GI) "TASK"))
       Select(DOMTREE
          Eq(Proploc(CAND attval[SKILL]) "NOVICE"))
       Select(DOMTREE
          and(Eq(Proploc(CAND GI) "TOOL-LIST")
              He(Dataloc(CAND 1 -1) "hammer"))
       )
    )
</HyQ>
```

HyQ imposes no requirement on how to express queries when such alternatives are available: you can use whichever form you prefer. In practice, end users will probably see neither of these forms, but will have a graphical query interface. A HyQ processing program can also choose to execute both these queries in a variety of ways to achieve the best possible performance.

The Diff function

`Diff()` creates a node list by subtracting its second parameter from its first. That is, its result includes all nodes appearing in the first node list but not the second. The syntax is:

```
Diff(nodelist, nodelist)
```

Only two node list parameters may be used. For example, the difference of the following two node lists is just `{ c e }`:

```
{ a b c d e }
{ a b d }
```

The first printing of the HyTime standard combines `Diff()` with `Sdiff()`, described next. It incorrectly says that `Diff()` can take any number of parameters, interpreted pairwise; that definition yields a list containing all nodes appearing in an *odd* number of the nodelist parameters.

`Diff()` as corrected works as shown below to retrieve all `poem` elements that lack attribute `form=haiku`:

```
<HyQ qdomain=repair-manual>
    Diff(
       Select(DOMTREE
              Eq(Proploc(CAND GI) "POEM"))
       Select(DOMTREE
              Eq(Proploc(CAND attval[FORM]) "HAIKU"))
    )
</HyQ>
```

The Sdiff function

`Sdiff()` creates a node list by finding the symmetric set difference between its parameters (compare `Diff()`, above). Its result includes all nodes that occur in exactly one of the nodelist parameters. The syntax is:

```
Sdiff(nodelist+)
```

For example, `Sdiff()` applied to the following nodelists would return the result nodelist `{ a b f g }`:

```
{ a b c d }
{ c d e f }
{ e g }
```

The Count function

`Count()` is a simple but useful utility that returns a number indicating the size of the data in a node list (the node list should contain only data nodes, not nodes such as SGML elements). The syntax is:

```
Count(nodelist quantum?)
```

The size is counted in units specified by the quantum parameter, which defaults to `STR` (to count characters). If there is more than one data node in the node list, the returned size is the size of their data.

For example, to find all paragraphs with more that 100 words, the following query could be used:

```
<HyQ qdomain=book1>
    Select(DOMTREE
          And(
             Eq(Proploc(CAND GI) "P")
             Gt(Count(CAND WORD) 100)
          )
    )
</HyQ>
```

9.4.5 String and pattern matching functions

The Match function

The `Match()` function searches all text in the node or node list that is its first parameter to find all occurrences of data matching the second parameter. This is somewhat like the `Select()` function except that it operates at the level of text data, rather than at the level of nodes. Its syntax is:

```
Match(anynode (hylex|qltn|literal)
      Oo(lexord)? boundary? int? int?)
```

The second parameter must be either a HyLex expression (see Section 11.5), a qualified lexical type name (see Section 11.4.1), or a quoted literal. For example, to find all occurrences of the literal string "`Eve`" in a certain document `Match()` could be used thus:

```
<!ENTITY       kjv          SYSTEM
    "bible.sgm">

<nameloc id=bible>
    <nmlist nametype=entity>
       kjv
    </nmlist>
</nameloc>
...
<HyQ qdomain=bible>
    Match(DOMROOT "Eve")
</HyQ>
```

This is straightforward; other parameters handle special cases. To find the same string without regard to case distinctions, you can use the built-in lexical ordering definition named `#SGMLCASE` or define one that converts lower to upper case, or that also converts accented vowels to unaccented ones (see Section 14.7 for more on lexical orderings). You then specify such a **lexord** element's ID using the `Oo()` function:

```
<HyQ qdomain=bible>
    Match(DOMROOT "Eve" Oo(casetable))
</HyQ>
```

Unlike the **dataloc** form and associated function, `Match()` does not offer a choice of quantum type. It normally requires that all matches be word quanta, that is, surrounded by end-of-text or non-SGML-name characters. Thus the example above would find the 4 occurrences of the word "`Eve`" in the King James translation of the Bible, but would not find the three-letter sequence "`Eve`" where it is part of another word such as "`ever`" or "`evening`" or "`seven`."

The `boundary` parameter originates from HyLex (see clause A.1.1.5 and Section 11.5), but has a different default, namely `ISCIEC`. This means that by default, a hit found by `Match()` need not exhaust the content of the location source. To change this, alternative values can be used:

`SODEOD`	(Start Of Data, End Of Data) means the match must be the entire domain searched.
`SODIEC`	(Start Of Data, Ignored Ending Characters) means the match must start at the beginning of the domain, but that extra characters are permitted between the end of the match and the end of the domain.
`ISCEOD`	(Ignored Starting Characters, End of Data) means that characters may be skipped at the start of the domain, but the match must extend to the end of the domain.
`ISCIEC`	(Ignored Starting Characters, Ignored Ending Characters) means the match may constitute any subportion of the domain.

The optional integer parameters at the end are known as a `hitrange`. For each input node, `Match()` finds how many matches occur; if that number is not in the range that these parameters specify, the hits for that input node are discarded instead of being returned as part of the result. The first number is the minimum number of hits a node must have to qualify; the second is the maximum (if omitted, there is no maximum limit). Both numbers must be positive if specified at all.

These `hitrange` parameters provide a way, for example, to find all string matches that occur within elements having more than two string matches, while discarding more isolated occurrences:

```
<HyQ qdomain=bible>
    Match(DOMTREE "Eve" Oo(casetable) 3)
</HyQ>
```

Likewise, they can be used to find all nodes in which a string occurs at most three times:

```
<HyQ qdomain=bible>
    Match(DOMTREE "Eve" Oo(casetable) 1 3)
</HyQ>
```

or occurs exactly twice:

```
<HyQ qdomain=bible>
    Match(DOMTREE "Eve" Oo(casetable) 2 2)
</HyQ>
```

Because these expressions search in the DOMTREE domain rather than the DOMROOT domain shown above, every element in the document tree is checked. Assuming that every verse of this text is its own SGML element, then verses with the required numbers of hits are returned, as are any higher level elements that, taken as wholes, match the request.

A match is constrained to lie within a single word quantum unless the `bigmatch` HyTime option is selected. The HyTime standard documents this in clause A.3.2, under `Match()`.

The HyLex function

The `HyLex()` function can be used only in the second parameter of `Match()`, as an alternative to a qualified lexical type name or a literal. It allows you to use the HyTime lexical expression facility discussed in Section 11.5 to characterize the text pattern `Match()` is to find. The syntax is:

```
HyLex((hylex-expression) norm? Oo(lexord)?)
```

The first parameter is any expression in HyLex. The `norm` parameter indicates whether the model and the data searched for it are to be normalized like SGML attribute values. The `Oo(lexord)` parameter can indicate a lexical ordering definition for the model and the searched data. Such a lexical model could be used to fold case, remove accents, or perform other preprocessing.

9.4.6 Variables and assignments

The Assign function

This function makes an assignment to a temporary variable that is valid within the query body where it is created. This could be the `HyQ` element's content or the first parameter of a `Query()` or `Useq()` function. The syntax is:

```
Assign(name nodelist)
```

The variable is valid for any queries inside the one where it is created, but not in queries further out; it is not a global variable. `Assign()` does not contain an expression to be evaluated after the given assignment, so the references must occur elsewhere in the containing query body. This means one must make assumptions about the order in which parts of the query body are interpreted to ensure that assignments occur before references to the names they assign to. If an assigned name is used as part of the nodelist of another `Assign()`, the order of the assignments matters. The HyTime committee has proposed a clarification that parameters should be evaluated from left to right.

When assignments are needed, it is almost always clearest to use `Query()`. This allows any number of simultaneous "assignments" via its argument list. Since the arguments must be evaluated before the body of the nested query, no ambiguity exists.

The Nlref function

`Nlref()` treats the `name` parameter as a variable and returns the node list that was assigned to be its value. This is the way to use a variable that was set via the `Assign()` function just described. The syntax is:

```
Nlref(name)
```

9.4.7 HyQ macro support

HyQ provides support for macros by allowing the definition of queries that can be invoked later. A HyQ macro is any HyQ query with a value for its `fn` attribute. This attribute specifies a "function name" for the query, under which it can be invoked in other queries.

While any HyQ query can be made into a macro by giving it an `fn` attribute, most such queries will also use "argument references" to specify parameters that can be replaced by arguments passed when the macro is invoked. For example, to make a reusable query called `hasgi` that can find all elements of some given element type:

```
<HyQ fn=hasgi>
      Select(DOMTREE
            Eq(Proploc(CAND GI) %1))
</HyQ>
```

This query should look familiar except that we have replaced a literal value for the desired GI with an argument reference: `%1`. The query has no specific meaning until `%1` has a value. Argument variables from `%1` to `%999` are available, as discussed with the `Query()` function in Section 9.4.2.

The Useq function

The `Useq()` function is the way to use a HyQ macro in a query. Such an "indirect query" invokes a query defined by name elsewhere, by naming it as the first parameter of the `Useq()` function and passing it any number of `nodes` and/or nodelists as arguments. The named `HyQ` element serves as the query body; an indirect query is otherwise interpreted in the same way as a direct query. Its syntax includes the following three forms:

```
Useq(fn)
Useq(fn anynodes*)
Useq(fn qdomain anynodes*)
```

To use the `hasgi` query defined above, apply the `Useq()` function and specify the desired GI as an argument:

```
<HyQ>
    Useq(hasgi DOMTREE "PARTNUM")
</HyQ>
```

9.4.8 Integrating external queries

HyQ specifies a method for the results of non-HyQ operations to be used in HyQ queries. This mechanism essentially provides a place for HyTime engines to integrate extensions that may be needed for a specific application.

The Ah function

The assertion handler function `Ah()` provides a way to extend HyQ with externally defined assertions. These are functions, like the comparisons, that take parameters and return a truth value: `TRUE` or `FALSE`. A HyTime application could define special assertions to do things not already provided in HyQ, or even provide users with an entire language for making their own assertions. The syntax of `Ah()` is:

```
Ah(idref nodelist)
```

Specialized extensions are often the most efficient way to accomplish specialized purposes. On the other hand, using them can reduce portability. Therefore, it is good practice to avoid custom assertion handlers whenever you can achieve the required effect without them, or when portability is of special concern. We give an example of defining an assertion handler in Section 12.2.

9.5 HyQ and other query languages

At the time of writing, there is much debate over query languages for documents. There are two main schools of thought, of which HyQ follows the second. The positions, somewhat oversimplified, can be summarized as:

a) A document and likewise any multimedia data object can be adequately represented by catalog-card information such as author, title, etc., followed by a long blob. Search tools need have little or no knowledge of internal structure: the document is to be retrieved and passed to other tools, which may use any markup so long as the search or database tool need not know about it.

b) A document is a highly structured data object, and a search or database tool that is unaware of that structure cannot do much useful work with it. Search tools must have some knowledge of document structure to support real documents effectively.

There are fundamental differences between these positions, with far-reaching consequences. Traditional query languages were designed for model a, perhaps because they were designed before text was widely viewed as something to manage in electronic form. Newer models such as object-oriented databases have much more in common with model b, the model of SGML and HyTime.

Readers who have come this far probably do not consider text to be unstructured. Indeed, the structure of texts is more sophisticated and more complex than database tables and needs more powerful formalisms. We believe these are the reasons that the document-using community has felt compelled to develop new searching tools, such as HyQ, the DSSSL location model, and commercial tools from companies such as Electronic Book Technologies and Open Text.

The "record-oriented" information of traditional databases is intrinsically different from documents (such as books, articles, manuals, and the like):

- Record-oriented information uses the same structures over and over, whereas document structures are far more varied.
- Records are not inherently ordered (although they are often sorted one way or another for ease of access), whereas paragraphs and other textual objects are.

- Most sub-components of records occur once or perhaps a fixed, small number of times, whereas most element types in a book are unpredictably repeatable, without limit.
- Individual data fields are generally very small, whereas books and multimedia data include objects from quotations and emphatic phrases, on up to movies, animations, chapters, repair procedures, and a wide variety of other components.
- Objects in form-like applications seldom contain other objects, whereas documents are deeply nested and recursive structures.

These reasons lead most of us to buy both a spreadsheet and a word processor, rather than trying to create books and letters with a spreadsheet program, or manage a personnel database with a word processor.

Imagine a document with several levels of sections, lists and other typical markup elements. Say you want to find all `chap` (chapter) elements that contain `fn` (footnote) elements using a relational representation of the document hierarchy. A relational query (expressed in SQL) would start out like this:

```
SELECT element FROM e-table
WHERE (type=chap AND element IN
          (SELECT parent FROM e-table
             WHERE type=fn))
```

This looks fine, but it finds only cases in which the `footnote` is *directly* inside the `chapter`. If the footnote is within an embedded `p`, `section`, or anything else, it is ignored. One can get the `footnote` elements that are "grandchildren" and combine them via OR:

```
SELECT element FROM e-table
WHERE (type=CHAP AND element IN
          (SELECT parent FROM e-table
             WHERE type=FN))
    OR
       (type=chap AND element IN
          (SELECT parent FROM e-table
             WHERE element IN
                (SELECT parent FROM e-table
                   WHERE type=FN)))
```

This of course leaves out the next level of descendants. One could repeat this process, adding a longer expression each time, for any fixed number levels as needed at the cost of an extremely long, repetitive and inefficient query.

HyQ's solution is better; the language includes an inherent distinction between direct and indirect containment and it includes primitives for dealing with hierarchical structures:

```
<HyQ qdomain=mydoc>
    Select(
       DOMTREE
       And(
          Eq(Proploc(CAND GI) "SECTION")
          Select(
             DOMTREE
             Eq(Proploc(CAND GI) "FOOTNOTE")
          )
       )
    )
</HyQ>
```

We discuss the misapplication of record structured databases to textual data because it is easy to assume that all "databases" are the same and that record-based models must be good enough for text. As we have shown, while such models *can* be used they are limiting. The new wine of structured hyperdocuments does not belong in the old wineskins of relational databases and SQL.

10

Modifying a DTD for HyTime

10.1 Introduction

HyTime's use of architectural forms and of SGML's intrinsic ID/IDREF pointing mechanism make it possible to convert many existing SGML hyperdocuments to use HyTime syntax easily. In some cases the hyperdocuments themselves need not change at all because modifications to the DTD will suffice to add the appropriate HyTime attribute values to the existing elements in the document.

This chapter shows you how to take an existing DTD and either make DTD changes so it can work with HyTime, or make document modifications to enable HyTime linking with as little disruption of the DTD as possible. We show this with an extended example using the simple HTML DTD used with the World Wide Web system available on Internet, describing the individual steps of a conversion effort in more detail. We close the chapter with some guidelines for effective use of HyTime.

10.2 HTML and the World Wide Web

HTML, short for HyperText Markup Language, is a simple DTD used by the World Wide Web system. WWW is a hypertext system that runs on computers connected to the Internet, for which a variety of browsers exist. When a reader clicks on a link the browser requests the target document from some computer on the network which transfers it back to be viewed. WWW supports a number of data formats (like graphics or sound) much as SGML does, by permitting users to declare the format of data objects so they can be passed to viewing programs that know those formats. The most common data formats encountered in the Web are HTML and a few raster graphic formats like JPEG and GIF (see Appendix B for a description of common graphics formats).

A key technology used in the implementation of the Web is a **Uniform Resource Locator** or **URL**. URLs are defined by the IETF Draft *Uniform Resource Locators* by Tim Berners-Lee (edition dated July 14, 1993). A URL is a simple specification of a machine on the Internet, a protocol to use to retrieve data, and a name for the piece of data to be retrieved. This location mechanism is extremely easy to implement, as it is built on well-established techniques in use on the Internet.

The URL approach has some robustness problems, however. Referring to data by a *location* rather than by a *name* is fraught with peril. There is an ongoing effort to formalize **Uniform Resource Names** (**URN**s) and to coordinate them with ISO formal public identifiers and ISBNs. We consider URNs essential to the long-term success of systems like WWW. The problems with URLs include:

- If a destination file is renamed or moved to another directory, all links to it break.
- If a destination file is moved to another computer, or the computer gets a new Internet address, all links to it break.
- If the destination computer is down, links cannot be followed.

These problems all remain even if the exact same document resides on the reader's local file server or hard disk. URLs cannot take advantage of the fact that copies of a data object may exist. A target document must be transferred from its own server every time it is accessed.

10.2.1 The HTML tagset

The HTML DTD (the edition we have is dated July 13, 1993) defines a set of tags that supports document structures such as lists and emphasis. It provides a relatively presentation-oriented model for small documents with limited internal structure. A newer and more ambitious version called HTML+ is under development, but is still in draft as of this writing. The full DTD is available on the Internet, documented in Berners-Lee and Connolly, *Hypertext Markup Language*, an IETF draft document.

The text-markup tags defined in HTML are mainly point tags, that is, tags with a content model of EMPTY. This means that HTML uses what we called the stream model of text and markup in Chapter 2. The targets of links are usually whole documents (links to internal anchors are of limited capability and not in common use). HTML+ is expected to change some of this — in particular, the paragraph, chapter and list item tags will become container tags yielding a more hierarchical document model.

Despite the existence of the HTML DTD, current WWW software is not based on an SGML parser. To create SGML documents that will work with the WWW software some restrictions must be observed. HTML uses none of SGML's optional features except FORMAL. It uses the reference character set and SGML's reference concrete syntax. Documents may not have marked sections. It uses the quantity set of the reference concrete syntax, except for the following settings (that can be set in the SGML declaration): NAMELEN 34, TAGLVL 100, LITLEN 1024, GRPGTCNT 150, and GRPCNT 64.

Three elements embody the hypermedia facilities of HTML:

`a`
: A non-empty tag that surrounds a link anchor in the document. The URL of the link destination is stored as an attribute of the element. This is the key hypertextual element in the HTML DTD.

`img`
: An empty element that marks (but does not contain) any kind of graphic image and takes a `src` attribute that may be a URL. Many browsers will resolve that reference and insert the graphic inline. The image data is not present inline nor is it referenced via an SGML entity.

`link`
: The `link` tag can appear in the header of an HTML document to indicate another document that may be relevant to the documents containing it. This provides a node-to-node linking facility.

10.2.2 The HTML link target notation

The a element represents a hypertext link origin, and is named a for "anchor." It is similar to HyTime's **`clink`** architectural form, though **`clink`** is not an anchor in HyTime terminology. The a element may occur most places and contains text to be highlighted by a web browser as a link source. An a element must directly specify the destination to be accessed when the user activates the link. This is specified by an attribute named href whose value is a URL. Since SGML requires quotes around attribute values (like URLs) that contain the "/" character, a typical link would look like this:

```
For further information, click
<a href="ftp.brown.edu/cis/doc/www/intro.html">
here.</a>
```

Several other attributes are available to give extra information about the link (whether of type link in the document header, or of type a in the body). The declaration of the a element is:

```
<!ELEMENT     a           - - (%text;)>
<!ATTLIST     a
    name      NMTOKEN     #IMPLIED
    href      %URL;       #IMPLIED
    rel       CDATA       #IMPLIED
    rev       CDATA       #IMPLIED
    urn       CDATA       #IMPLIED
    title     CDATA       #IMPLIED
    methods   NAMES       #IMPLIED>
```

The parameter entity %text; allows any of the HTML text-markup and emphasis tags within the link anchor. The href attribute is the locator, and may have a URL as its value (or in HTML+, a URN). Name is an identifier for the link element itself; in HTML+ it will likely be renamed id and be an SGML ID. Rel and rev indicate what kind of relationship holds between the anchors of the link. (HTML+ proposes a particular list). The urn attribute holds the Uniform Resource Name of the destination document. Title should match the content of the title element in the destination document. Methods will likely be deleted in HTML+.

10.2.3 An HTML example

The following example is drawn from the entry "Electricity" in the first edition of the *Encyclopedia Britannica,* published in 1769 and marked up using the HTML tag set. We also show (in Figure 10.1) a screen shot of the document viewed using the Macintosh version of the Mosaic browser developed by NCSA (the National Center for Supercomputing Applications).

```
<html><head><title>Electricity</title>
<base href="cs.zu.edu/electricity.html"></head>
<body>
<h1>Electricity</h1>
<p>The word <dfn>electricity</dfn> signifies, in general, the effects of
a very subtile fluid matter, different in its properties from every other
fluid we are acquainted with. This fluid is capable of uniting with almost
every body, but unites more readily with some particular bodies than
with others: its motion is amazingly quick, is regulated by peculiar laws,
and produces a vast variety of singular phenomena, the principal of
which shall be enumerated in this article.
<p>As we are entirely ignorant of the nature of the electrical fluid, it is
impossible to define it but by its principal properities: that of repelling
and attracting light bodies, is one of the most remarkable. The ancients
were only acquainted with this property in amber. William Gilbert, a
native of Colchester, and physician at London, in his treatise <cite>De
Magnete,</cite> in the year 1600, was the first person who discovered,
that sulphur, wax, resinous substances, glass, and precious stones, when
dried and rubbed a little, were endowed with the same property of at-
tracting and repelling straws and other light substances. Sir Francis
Bacon, in his <cite>physiological remains,</cite> gives a catalogue of
electrical bodies. Sir Isaac Newton, in 1675, was the first who discovered
that excited glass attracted light bodies. See also
<a href="cs.zu.edu/pub/astro.html"> Astronomy</a>
<p>After Gilbert, Hoyle, and Otto Guericke, Mr Hawkesbee, in his
<cite>Physico-mechanical Experiments,</cite> published in the year
1709, first discovered the electric power of glass, the light proceeding
from it, and the noise occasioned by it, together with a variety of
phaenomena relating to electric attraction and repulsion. The discovery
of a plus and minus electricity was by Dr Watson and Dr Franklin about
the year 1746.
<h2>On experiments</h2>
An iron wire, 12,000 feet in length, was suspended about five feet from
the ground by silk cords; one end of it was connected to the globe of an
electrical machine, and at the other a lead ball was hung in order to per-
ceive when the matter reached it.
<ol>
<li>After five or six turns of the wheel, the matter had passed along the
whole wire, and communicated its virtue to the ball, which instantly at-
tracted and repelled light bodies.
<li>When the wire was cut in several places, the electrical matter
darted through all the interruptions, and appeared in the ball at the
furthest end. A strong blast made by a bellows across one of the
```

interruptions, did not obstruct the passage of the matter; neither did the interposition of a piece of glass, wax, and other non-conductors: but all conductors, as the hand of a man, the point of a sword, and even a moist vapour, obstructed its course towards the ball.
<li>When a man stood on a piece of rosin, and put a point of a sword in one of the interruptions, he was instantly filled with the matter, although neither he nor the sword touched the wire.
<li>The same iron wire suspended by silk cords was extended 6000 feet, (just one half of its length), in a straight line; the other half was turned back in a parallel direction towards the globe, leaving about nine or ten inches of interval between the two halves of the wire: Each extremity of the wire was supported by a dry silk cord about seven or eight feet from the globe, and the lead ball was hung at one of them. An iron chain was then fixed with another silk cord above the globe, in order to receive the matter at one of its extremities; the other end of the chain was fixed to a rod of glass about five feet long, in such a manner that the matter received from the globe might be transmitted at pleasure to the wire, by applying the end of the fixed chain to the glass rod. Matters being thus prepared, the chain was applied to one end of the wire; at the same instant the ball at the other end attracted and repelled bits of gold-leaf.
</ol>
<h2>On materials</h2>
<p>Although globes or cylinders are now of the most extensive use in electrical experiments, glass tubes are still most convenient for several purposes; they should be about three feet long, and as wide as a person can conveniently grasp, (Plate LXXIII. fig. I a.). <img src="cs.zu.edu/pub/lxxiii.gif">
<p>The thickness of the glass is not material; perhaps the thinner they are the better, if they can bear sufficient friction. See the article on <a href="cs.zu.edu/pub/glass.html">Glassblowing</a>.
</body></html>

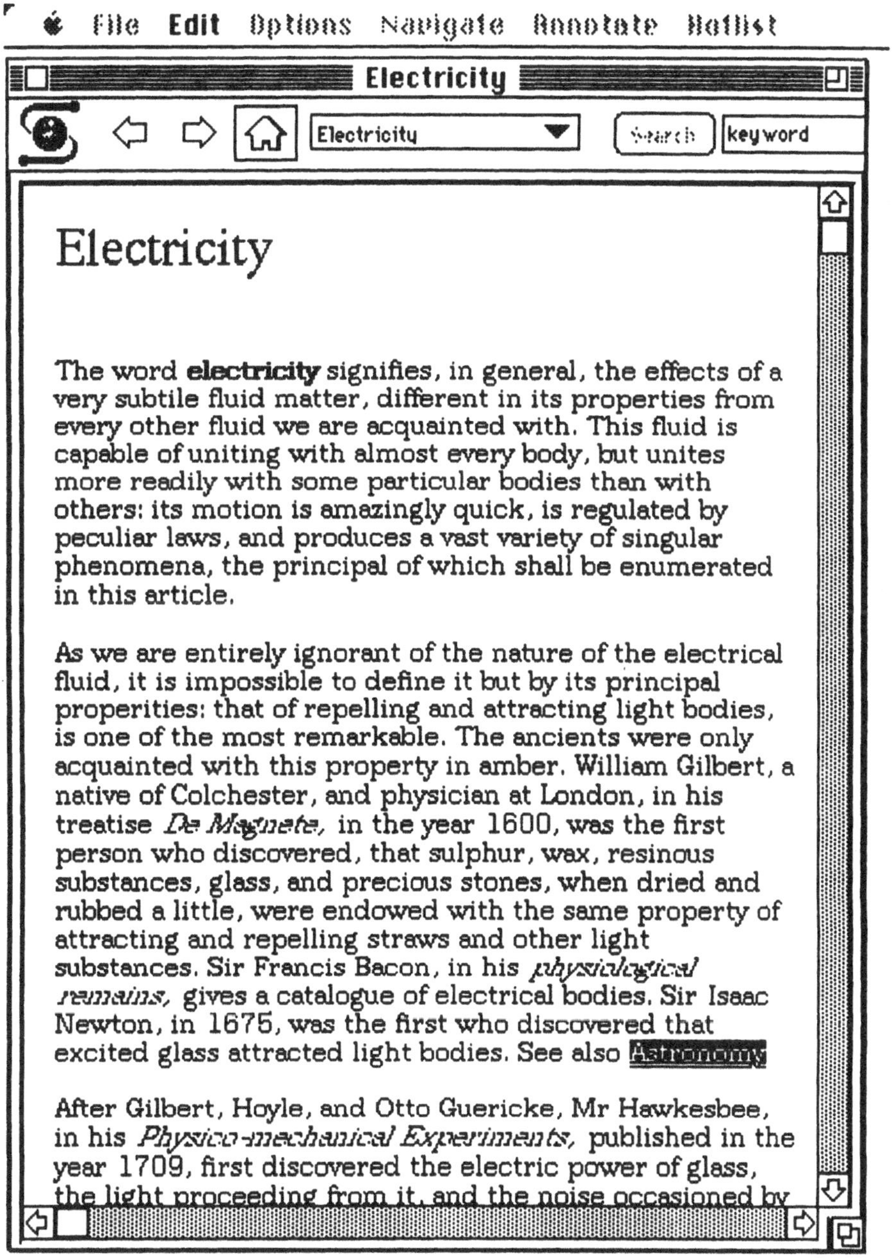

Figure 10.1: Browser view of the sample document

10.3 The DTD conversion

In this section we describe the process of converting a DTD to use HyTime. As we discuss each step, we will show how we chose to handle that step in converting the HTML DTD to work with HyTime. The steps involved are:

- find the link elements
- understand the link semantics
- categorize other elements

Having done these steps, one can write the necessary declarations to create appropriate HyTime-conforming documents.

10.3.1 Find the link elements

For HTML, this step is easy because there are only a few hypertextual element types. We believe the first proposal for a HyTime-compliant version of HTML was by Eliot Kimber. It appeared on the comp.text.sgml forum on May 24, 1993.

In general, one must examine the DTD and decide whether each element serves a hypertextual purpose. Element names like `xref`, `link` or `anchor` are typical giveaways. They usually map to the **`clink`** form. However, subtler questions can arise. For your DTD consider:

- Should artwork, figures, tables and the like be handled as linked objects to be displayed on demand, or as part of the normal text flow? Although they are usually part of the text flow on paper, this may or not be as effective a method online.
- How should footnotes, sidebars and the like be handled? They can be linked whether or not they are collected in one place.
- Should portions of text that are not marked up, but serve as links, be turned into explicit links? For example, phrases such as "see chapter 12" or "see also pp. 20-25" can serve as link origins.
- Should asides in the text, such as reference information for quotations, background information and the like be treated as separate linked text components?
- Should specialized terms connect the reader to a dictionary, glossary or other reference works? For example, definitions, menu items in documentation, foreign words and many other things.
- Should typically hidden markup such as index entries, identification of part numbers and so on do something?

In HTML, the candidate elements are `a`, `link` and `img`. For brevity of exposition we will not treat images as HyTime constructs and so the central task will be to handle the `a` and `link` elements.

10.3.2 Understand the link semantics

The second major step in preparing a DTD for use with HyTime is to determine just how each kind of link is *already* accomplished. Common practices include using SGML IDs and IDREFs, attributes whose values name entities, references to IDs outside the referencing document, and pointers to destinations using special location syntax.

In most of these cases links are marked up at their origin and thus correspond to HyTime's **clink** form. Bidirectional links are sometimes best represented by two unidirectional **clinks**, and sometimes by an **ilink**. It is less usual to find links that are stored separately from any of their endpoints, like HyTime **ilinks**. Although bidirectional links are commonly used in hypertext research systems, only a few SGML based hypertext systems have provided them so far.

ID and IDREF

Most SGML users are already familiar with using IDs and IDREFs to create hypertext links within their documents, and this usage is accommodated easily by HyTime. Scanning the DTD for attribute list declarations with IDREF attributes is a good way to discover such constructs. For example, one commonly finds structures like the ones below in existing SGML DTDs:

```
<p>For more information on walruses,
    <xref rid=chapter7>see Chapter 7.</xref></p>

<p>This is also discussed in <bibref item=oren90>
Oren 1990</bibref></p>
```

To convert such constructs into a HyTime **clink**, usually no document changes are required, but only additional attribute declarations. First, one must add the `HyTime` architectural form attribute to identify the element to HyTime-aware software. Second, one must account for the fact that the **clink** IDREF is called `linkend`, whereas the attribute name already in use will likely be different.

To change the attribute name use the `HyNames` attribute discussed in Section 14.5.1. The `HyNames` attribute is used to rename other HyTime attributes on a given element. Its value is a list of pairs of names: first a HyTime attribute name, second the name that attribute will have on instances of the element. The declaration changes for the first example above would look like this:

```
<!ATTLIST       xref
    ...
    rid         IDREF         #IMPLIED
    HyTime      NAME          #FIXED "clink"
    HyNames     CDATA         #FIXED "linkend href">
```

Because the **clink** architectural form places no restrictions on its content, there is no need to adjust the content model or declared content.

Entities

Another common way documents encode hypertext links is by declaring the target document as an entity and naming the entity:

```
<p>As shown in this portrait:
<graphic entity-name=j.smith></p>
```

In some cases it is not necessary to treat entities mentioned on attributes as links. In order to make this a HyTime link without changing the markup in the document, one could use the methods described below under the heading "locator syntaxes." Alternatively one can break the markup into two elements, a **clink** element and a **nameloc** element to designate the entity (we discuss **nameloc** in Section 8.3.1):

```
<p>As shown in this portrait:
    <clink linkend=graphic29></clink>
    <nameloc id=graphic29><nmlist>j.smith</nameloc>
</p>
```

References to IDs in other documents

Many users have encountered the need to link between documents and have designed conventions for doing so. These conventions are typically like this:

```
<!ATTLIST       xref
    doc         ENTITY        #REQUIRED
    xid         NAME          #REQUIRED
    caption     CDATA         #IMPLIED>
```

`Doc` points to the entity that holds the destination, as in the last section. The `xid` attribute gives an IDREF valid in the destination document. It cannot be declared as type IDREF, because it does not point to an ID in its own document. NAME imposes the same syntactic requirements as IDREF without requiring a matching local ID. The `caption` gives a prose explanation of the link's significance.

The semantics of this construction resemble HyTime's **nameloc** form. An entity is referenced and then an element with a particular ID is selected within the document contained in that entity. Such constructs include in one element the functions of three HyTime architectural forms:

clink A traversable link, pointing to a **nameloc**.

nameloc A container for **nmlist** elements.

nmlist Specifies the destination entity name on the docorsub attribute, and the destination ID within its content.

Thus, rewriting the document itself to use HyTime constructs would replace an original syntax like:

```
<xref doc=book3 xid=sec27 caption="On Ailerons">
    Get a big hammer and read the manual</xref>
```

with HyTime elements like this:

```
<clink linkend=n1>
    Get a big hammer and read the manual
</clink>
...
<nameloc id=n1>
    <nmlist nametype=element docorsub=book3>sec27
</nmlist></nameloc>
```

Locator syntaxes

Many DTDs use special locator syntaxes to link to objects that do not have IDs. We describe the Text Encoding Initiative's extended pointer syntax in Chapter 12 and show examples of the Internet URL syntax in this chapter. The effectiveness of a locator syntax, the amount of data already using it and the degree in which it differs from HyTime constructs are among the factors that need to be weighed in deciding whether it is best to stick with a special locator syntax (with a **notloc** form as described in Section 8.5.2) or to convert the documents to use HyTime locator types.

If the existing locator syntax is to be retained, it must be supported. It is often relatively easy to implement **notloc** semantics in application software, but it does require some extra effort. It is usually easy because one typically defines a **notloc** because a locator syntax is *already* in use. If it is already in use, then it has probably already been implemented and so does not require breaking new ground.

One must next understand how the links themselves use the locator syntax. A simple and widespread method is for the location specification to appear directly on the link element. This resembles SGML references using IDREF attributes. It is also the method used in HTML and other specifications, for instance:

```
<a href="eniac.com/cs101/ir/grader.data">
Watch your error checking.</a>
```

This element serves as a link from its own location to somewhere else and is thus similar to a **clink**. However, special locator syntaxes cannot be placed directly on **clink** elements. A single element cannot be both a **clink** and a **notloc**, and **clink** requires an IDREF indicating the destination or a location ladder to the destination. Only the Location address module provides for locator syntaxes other than IDREFs.

Several ways have been proposed to address this limitation while remaining HyTime conforming. We know of two key ones: One requires changing all the links in the documents. The other changes only the DTD, but depends on a subtle use of the **multloc** attributes to combine the effect of a **clink** and a **notloc** into one element. It is also possible to obtain the desired effect via implementation-specific conventions for non-HyTime traversal from **notloc** elements, but this is less desirable.

Changing all the links in existing documents to use HyTime constructs directly is pretty similar to the cases we have discussed above, except for the use of the **notloc** form instead of the **nameloc** form. Following we show the relevant fragments of the changed DTD and the new markup:

```
<!ATTLIST     a
    HyTime    NAME      #FIXED "clink"
    HyNames   CDATA     #FIXED "linkend href"
    href      IDREF     #IMPLIED>
<!ELEMENT     url       - O EMPTY>
<!ATTLIST     url
    HyTime    NAME      #FIXED "notloc"
    id        ID        #REQUIRED
    href      CDATA     #REQUIRED>

<a href=url.1>Watch your error checking.</a>
<url id=url.1 href="eniac.com/cs101/ir/grader.data">
```

This approach is natural for HyTime, but has disadvantages. The link is no longer a single data object — it requires extra IDs and GIs — and the same document cannot be used in both HTML and HyTime systems. Document conversion may be impractical in certain situations.

There is an alternative method for accommodating extended location syntaxes, in which the existing link element is declared to be of form **notloc** and given **multloc** attributes. Setting the `aggloc` attribute to the value `agglink` specifies that the location pointed to by the element "is an aggregate that can be treated like a hyperlink..." (see clause 8.2.2). The **notloc** holds the locator syntax to be supported, and is defined as addressing the location specified by the locator syntax. These elements are treated by HyTime like a link because of the `aggloc` attribute. This attribute can be fixed in the DTD, in which case no changes are required to the document itself.

If used, HyTime traversal rules in this case "treat the agglink element itself (the aggregate) as both an ilink element and an anchor, and each member location is also an anchor. Bidirectional internal and external traversal is possible between the aggregate and each of the members, between adjacent members, and between the last member and the first." Therefore, a conforming HyTime system provides for traversal when such an element is encountered.

The declaration required to use this method for HTML is shown below. The `multloc` option of the Location address module must be enabled.

```
<!ATTLIST       a
    HyTime      NAME          #FIXED "notloc"
    id          ID            #REQUIRED
    href        CDATA         #IMPLIED
    aggloc      NAME          #FIXED "agglink">
```

One problem remains: HyTime requires an ID attribute on **notloc**, but the HTML 1.0 DTD does not declare it for a. However, current HTML implementations permit it, and the HTML 2.0 DTD has it. Thus a document works in both worlds if it always provides an ID on a. Based on our recollection of the committee's intent and the fact that HyTime does not need the ID in the agglink case, this may be a typographical error, however, no official adjustment has been made.

10.3.3 Categorize other elements

Although the primary elements to be mapped into HyTime equivalents are those that correspond to architectural forms in the Hyperlinks and Location address modules, others will be necessary as well.

HyDoc

The root element of a document containing HyTime constructs must have the architectural form **HyDoc**, so would have the declaration:

```
<ATTLIST        html ...
    HyTime      NAME          #FIXED "HyDoc">
```

sHyTime

Any element within which HyTime elements should *not* be recognized should declare itself to be of architectural form **sHyTime**, as discussed in Section 5.2.8. This might be necessary if documents contain examples that might contain HyTime elements not intended to be processed. Non-HyTime elements (unlike **sHyTime**) have no effect on HyTime processing.

New elements

If the conversion to HyTime introduces new element types they must be added to the DTD. For example, if `xref` is identified as being a **`clink`**, then new elements of forms **`nameloc`** and **`treeloc`** must be declared in the DTD as well as added to the document.

This raises the question of where to place such elements. Since HyTime relates constructs largely by IDs, the placement is an application choice. For practical purposes, however, it is wise to set conventions. The rule of thumb we recommend is to place all location constructs either directly adjacent to the links that use them or in a single element provided for that purpose.

10.4 Evaluating a HyTime product

Know what you need and want before looking at lists of features. A feature list is most useful if you already know what you need, and why. As with most software, some features make a critical difference while other are important only for special needs.

Thus, when evaluating HyTime-aware software it is best to understand the basics of HyTime first. Once you have a pretty good idea of what you do and don't need, the questions you should ask about any HyTime product include:

- Exactly what modules and options does it support, and are they necessary for your application?
- Does it interpret or compile links?
- Does it have strategies for preserving links after editing (this depends on your working environment as well as the system)?
- What media types does it support?
- How big can documents be and how does this affect performance?
- Very important: Can you get the SGML and HyTime structures back out, or can you only import with loss of structure?
- Can it accommodate the links in your existing SGML documents?
- Does it work well with the other pieces you need?

10.4.1 Examining your requirements

HyTime provides an enormous range of features. The challenge, then, is to use HyTime wisely so that the resulting documents are as portable as possible and so that existing documents do not require enormous conversion effort. There is one basic rule: "keep it simple."

Probably every SGML-based system available can deal with a **clink** with a direct IDREF as `linkend`. An SGML parser can validate this all by itself within a single document. Many SGML systems can easily handle analogous inter-document links as well. If you stick with such links, you need nothing beyond your current SGML software. This approach is completely upward-compatible to full HyTime engines.

The second level adds references to needed multimedia data. This can be done using axes and **fcsloc**, or with locators for particular data representations using **notloc** as discussed in Section 125. If your SGML documents use the appropriate ENTITY and NOTATION declarations then the HyTime constructs should not pose much difficulty here.

The third level uses the more flexible capabilities of the Location address module. Of those, we believe you will find **nameloc**, **bibloc** and **proploc** indispensable, and **treeloc**, **relloc** and **dataloc** the next most useful. HyQ is also a particularly important construct, both as a means of expressing locations for hypertext linking and for searching documents for particular data and structures on demand.

This subset of HyTime features can handle a wide range of hypermedia applications. It does not, however, address the scheduling and sequencing of multimedia objects into time and space. Those applications will increase in importance, and HyTime's measurement and scheduling modules provide support for them, as we discuss in Chapter 13.

10.5 Summary

Converting existing SGML data to use HyTime is not necessarily difficult but does require some planning. Identifying document features that should be handled hyertextually is the first stage, and then the next big decision is whether conversion of the markup in the document is possible, or whether the existing markup must be preserved. This will determine what strategy of document and DTD changes will be appropriate to the conversion.

A related task is the selection of the HyTime software to use. This decision may be predetermined by the platform or by other technical considerations, but if this is not the case, the analysis of the needs of the documents themselves should provide the primary guidance about which HyTime software features are important.

Part III: Intermediate HyTime

11

Lexical Types and Properties

11.1 Introduction

This chapter explains HyTime's lexical type features and property mechanism. Lexical types allow the specification and use of relatively complex syntactic structures. These can be used to express queries that search data for a structure matching the restrictions, as well as to constrain attributes to match a particular syntax. This powerful mechanism is discussed in Sections 11.2 through 11.6 of this chapter.

HyTime's property mechanism allows a HyTime document to access information from an SGML parser, or HyTime's semantic constructs. User-defined properties are also possible, providing one method of extending HyTime. Properties are discussed in Sections 11.7 through 11.9.

This chapter contains a relatively large number cross-references between sections, because HyTime properties and lexical types are closely linked. For each property there is an appropriate lexical type, and many lexical types are built using other lexical types that are defined by the properties with which they are associated.

11.2 Introduction to lexical types

HyTime provides facilities for testing strings of character data against expressions, to see if they match certain patterns. The patterns are called **lexical types** and are expressed by **lexical models**. HyTime uses lexical types and models for a variety of purposes. Lexical models provide the ability, via the HyQ `Match()` function, to search data content for strings and string patterns.

HyTime also uses lexical models as a validation aid. The `lextype` common attribute can be added to any HyTime element. It specifies a list of lexical type names, and which attributes or content of the element must conform to those lexical types. Because you can declare any element to be a HyTime element of form **`HyBrid`**, you can apply lexical type checking to your own elements as well as to HyTime ones.

Finally, the HyTime standard uses lexical type names in the text of the standard itself as a way to specify the syntax of various HyTime constructs. These constraints are intended to be implemented by builders of HyTime systems.

A lexical model must either be inherent (that is, built in as a basic part of HyTime), or be defined by an element conforming to the **`lexmodel`** architectural form. Every such model has a **lexical type name**, which must be unique among all instances of the same element type. When a lexical type is to be used, its name is given, possibly along with the element type of the **`lexmodel`**-conforming element that defines it.

The `lextype` attribute is one of the `all-lex` common attributes (see clause 6.5.2) and can therefore appear on any HyTime element. Its purpose is to specify validation requirements for other attributes and/or the content of the element. It contains a list of name pairs in which the first name must be the name of some attribute that can occur on the same element, and the second must be the name of a lexical type defined somewhere in the document.

For example, you can define a lexical type called `digit` and use it to restrict the value of the reading level attribute on all `p` elements to a single digit, or define a lexical type called `security` to restrict another attribute to having the value `public` or `topsecret`. Having defined such types, and declared all needed attributes for the `p` element, you could then do this:

```
<p r-level=1 sec=public HyTime=HyBrid
    lextype="r-level digit sec security">
```

The `lextype` attribute imposes two constraints, one each on the two attributes `r-level` and `sec`. If the same constraints apply to every instance of the `p` element, then it would be convenient to declare the value for `lextype` as a default or #FIXED value in the DTD. This is typically the desired effect.

Given the `lextype` constraints just shown, the following would be a HyTime error (although not an SGML error):

```
<p r-level=12 sec=low>
```

If the attribute is not #FIXED, it is possible to provide a different constraint on different element instances rather than a single constraint in the DTD, so the `p` elements below would be unusual but correct:

```
<p lextype="r-level digit" r-level=3>

<p lextype="r-level security" r-level=topsecret>
```

Lexical type restrictions operate in addition to any effects of the declared value prescription of the SGML ATTLIST declaration. Section 11.4 discusses how to define lexical models.

11.2.1 Qualified name default attributes

The **all-qual** attribute form includes the `qpnpsn` attribute, which can list the property sets to be used within the element, and the `qltnlmgi` attribute, which accomplishes much the same end for lexical type names. We defer discussion of `qpnpsn` until Section 11.7.3 since it relates to properties rather than lexical types.

The qltnlmgi attribute: selecting lexical type sets

Lexical types are divided into sets such that lexical types are members of the same set if they are defined by elements sharing the same GI (*not* the same architectural form; all lexical models are of form **lexmodel**).

The **all-qual** attribute form includes the `qltnlmgi` attribute, which controls the search for named lexical models. This attribute, whose name is fortunately shorter than "qualified lexical type name lexical model generic identifiers," holds a list of element types. When looking up a lexical type specified by `lex` attribute anywhere within the element specifying `qltnlmgi`, the elements of those types are searched in that order.

This is useful if you define so many lexical types that you declare multiple GIs for **lexmodel** to divide them up, and you use the same lexical type names in more than one group. It would also be useful to avoid name conflicts when including packages of lexical types defined by others.

11.3 HyTime lextype type constraints

The HyTime standard uses lexical type constraints widely to specify the permitted range of values for attributes, and sometimes for content. These specifications appear as comments rather than `lextype` attributes in the meta-DTD (see Appendix A).

HyTime uses only a few lexical types for this purpose. Typical types used are (we list the predefined lexical type names in Section 11.6):

- one or more legitimate SGML names such as a NOTATION, GI, or attribute name
- simple syntactic tokens such as words, digits, numbers
- one or more tokens chosen from a list (SGML only validates enumerated token lists from which a single token is used)
- lists of constraint pairs that give attribute or other names, each followed by some constraint indicator (the `lextype` attribute itself has a lexical type of this kind)
- special HyTime syntax, primarily qualified lexical type names and qualified property names

Almost all lexical type constraints imposed by the HyTime standard apply to attributes. A few, however, apply to content, as with the **qltn**, **marklist**, **dimlist**, **nmlist**, **proploc**, **date**, **abstime**, **timeoff**, **juldate** and **extlist** forms.

11.4 Defining lexical models

If the predefined lexical types do not suffice for your needs, you can define new lexical types using elements of the **lexmodel** architectural form (clause 6.5.2.1). Such an element must specify a name for the lexical model it is defining on the `ltn` attribute, and the language used for the definition itself on the `notation` attribute; the content is the definition.

Lexical types can be defined in any definition language, such as LEX, UNIX regular expressions, or the like (though of course your documents are then portable only between systems that support that notation). The HyTime standard's examples of lexical model definitions all use HyTime's own HyLex definition language (see Section 11.5, below).

To define your own lexical model named `dig3` that matches three-digit numbers, you could use the following `HyLex` element, depending on the intrinsic lexical type named `digit`:

```
<HyLex ltn=dig3>(digit, digit, digit)</HyLex>
```

Using a NOTATION called `regex` for UNIX regular expressions, you could express the same lexical model in this way:

```
<expr notation=regex ltn=dig3>[0-9][0-9][0-9]</expr>
```

A more significant example would match real numbers in the exponential notation used by many computer systems, such as "+6.02E+23":

```
<HyLex ltn=realnumber>
    [+-]?, digit+, (".",digit+)?, ("E",[+-]?, digit+)?
</HyLex>
```

The **lexmodel** form permits additional attributes for specialized processing, over and above any you might add for a particular lexical model notation other than HyLex. One is the `lexord` attribute. If present, `lexord` specifies a translation table to be applied before matching data against the lexical model. The attribute value is an IDREF pointing to an element of the **lexord** form, or the reserved word `#SGMLCASE`. Instances of the **lexord** form define translation tables, and are discussed more fully in Section 14.7. This feature can be used to create lexical types that ignore case distinctions, treat accented vowels as equal to their unaccented counterparts, and so on. The value `#SGMLCASE` indicates that SGML's name character translation should be used.

The other extra attribute is `boundary`. For a string to match a lexical model, it normally must match in its entirety; "`a333b`" is not a `dig3` as defined above because, although it contains a `dig3`, it also contains other information at the ends and so is disqualified. This reflects a default setting of `boundary=sodeod` (start-of-domain, end-of-domain). Other values for `boundary` permit you to relax this constraint at either or both ends, or to assert that boundary constraints are encoded in the model itself wherever they apply, and need not be checked otherwise. HyTime's boundary constraints follow:

`sodeod` — The lexical type must match the entire string. This method is used when testing whether something such as an attribute value conforms to a lexical type, as with `lextype`.

`sodiec` — The lexical type must match from the very beginning of the string, but need not go all the way to the end. This and the following methods can be used when searching a range of data for a portion(s) that matches the expression, as with HyQ.

`isceod`	The lexical type need not match starting at the beginning of the string being tested, but must match all the way to the end.
`isciec`	The lexical type matches if it matches anywhere within the string being tested, whether or not there is extra data beyond it at either end.
`inmodel`	The only boundary constraints that must be satisfied are specified within the lexical model itself.

Specifying boundary constraints within a model is similar to UNIX regular expression notation, which uses the "`^`" character to match beginning-of-domain and "`$`" to match end-of-domain. A HyLex lexical model can use the reserved tokens `#SOD` and `#EOD` for the same meanings.

You can also write an expression that matches like `isciec` even though its boundary constraint is `sodeod`, by adding wildcards to account for the "remainders" at each end. For example, you can modify the lexical model "`(digit)`" to match any strings that contain a digit anywhere. This can be done as shown below ("#" is the HyLex wildcard character, which will match any character):

```
(#SOD, #*, digit, #*,#EOD)
```

HyLex also provides shorthand for both ends of this expression: The reserved token `#ISC'` ("ignore starting characters") is equivalent to `(#SOD, #*)`; the reserved token `#IEC'` ("ignore ending characters") is equivalent to `(#*, #EOD)`. Thus the last example is equivalent to:

```
(#ISC, digit, #EOD)
```

11.4.1 Multiple lexical type sets

To define many lexical types, you can divide them into groups by defining multiple element type names (GIs) that all conform to the **lextype** architectural form. In that case, the `lextypgi` attribute may be used to say which GIs are checked to resolve any name conflicts. A lexical type name that is disambiguated in this way is called a **qualified lexical type name**, or **QLTN.**

A special syntax is used for QLTNs: the GI the lexical model belongs to, then a plus sign, then the lexical type name. For example, to specify that you want the `number` lexical type from the `roman` set rather than some other set, you could define and use the property thus:

```
<roman HyTime=lexmodel notation=HyLex ltn=number>
   [ivxlcmIVXLCM]+
</roman>
```

```
<date HyLex=HyBrid lextype="#CONTENT roman+number">
   MCMXCIII
</date>
```

11.5 HyLex

HyLex is a particular notation defined by HyTime for expressing lexical models (see clause A.1). It describes string patterns in much the same way and with much the same function as regular expressions. Syntactically, it has the advantage of being very similar to the notation for SGML content models.

HyLex is an optional feature that can only be used if you set the `HyLex` option of the Base module. Because it is a notation, HyLex requires a NOTATION declaration, which must be added to the DTD of any document using it:

```
<!NOTATION      HyLex         PUBLIC
    "+//ISO/IEC 10744:1992//NOTATION
    HyTime Lexical Model Notation//EN">
```

Specific lexical models expressed in HyLex appear in elements whose element type is also `HyLex` and conform to the **`lexmodel`** architectural form described in the previous section. `HyLex` is not an architectural form in itself. For example, the following lexical model element (from clause A.1.3) creates a lexical type called `frac`, intended to match strings consisting of two natural numbers to be treated as a fraction. The following models assume that the standard HyTime lexical types `number` and `s` have been defined (as described in Section 11.6):

```
<HyLex norm ltn=frac>
   (number, s+, number)
</HyLex>
```

11.5.1 The HyLex language

The content of a HyLex element is a HyLex expression. Attributes give other information about how that expression is to be applied, as discussed in Section 11.5.5. The `ltn` attribute is the lexical type name by which the expression can be referenced.

A HyLex expression consists of literal strings, operators, and references to other HyLex expressions. The example above can be broken down as follows:

Part	Abstract name	Description
(	XGRPO delimiter	Marks the start of a sub-expression
number	reference to another lexical type	Matches a number as declared in clause A.2.1.2.1 "SGML basic constructs" and ultimately defined as in the SGML standard
,	XSEQ delimiter	Indicates that the expressions it separates must both occur, and in the order listed
s	reference to another lexical type	Matches white space as declared in clause A.2.1.1.1 "SGML character classes" and ultimately defined as in the SGML standard
+	XREP delimiter	Indicates that the preceding expression is required and may be repeated any number of times (thus any amount of white space is permitted at this point).
,	(as above)	(as above)
number	(as above)	(as above)
)	GRPC delimiter	Marks the end of a sub-expression.

As should be clear from this example, lexical type names can appear freely in the definition of other lexical types. Literal strings may also be used, and must appear within single or double quotes:

```
<HyLex norm ltn=IDRN>
    (IDREF | "#NULL")
</HyLex>
```

In this example IDREF is another predefined lexical type, and the expression matches anything that is either syntactically an IDREF, or that is the literal string #NULL, such as these strings:

```
chap37
#NULL
```

11.5.2 HyLex delimiters

The complete set of delimiters used in HyLex definitions appears below. Those fluent in SGML will recognize many of SGML's delimiters here, under the same name with "X" prefixed. Although all these delimiters are single characters, as in SGML this is not a requirement and the values can be changed (as described below).

<table>
<tr><th>Role and Value</th><th>Description</th><th>Comments</th></tr>
<tr><td>XESC
\</td><td>Escape</td><td>Causes the next character to be interpreted literally even if it is the start of a HyLex delimiter</td></tr>
<tr><td>XGRPO
(</td><td>Group open</td><td>Marks the start of a HyLex expression or sub-expression</td></tr>
<tr><td>XGRPC
)</td><td>Group close</td><td>Marks the end of a HyLex expression or sub-expression</td></tr>
<tr><td>XLIT
"</td><td>Literal start or end</td><td>Marks the start or end of a literal string. A string started with XLIT is ended by the first unescaped XLIT, but may freely contain XLITA.=</td></tr>
<tr><td>XLITA
'</td><td>Literal start or end (alternative)</td><td>Marks the start or end of a literal string. A string started with XLITA is ended by the first unescaped XLITA, but may freely contain XLIT</td></tr>
<tr><td>XSEQ
,</td><td>Sequence connector</td><td>Indicates the expressions adjacent to it must both occur in the order listed</td></tr>
<tr><td>XOR
|</td><td>Or connector</td><td>Indicates one or the other of the adjacent expressions must occur</td></tr>
<tr><td>XDTGO
[</td><td>Alternative single-character pattern open</td><td>Marks the start of a set of characters, any of which matches the expression at that point (called an alternative single-character pattern or ASCP)</td></tr>
<tr><td>XDTGC
]</td><td>Alternative single-character pattern close</td><td>Marks the end of an ASCP. This delimiter must be escaped using XESC if it is to be listed as data within an ASCP</td></tr>
<tr><td>XOPT
?</td><td>Optional occurrence indicator</td><td>Indicates that the preceding expression may but need not occur</td></tr>
<tr><td>XREP
*</td><td>Required and repeatable</td><td>Indicates that the preceding expression must occur at least once, and may occur any number of times</td></tr>
<tr><td>XOREP
*</td><td>Optional and repeatable</td><td>Indicates that the preceding expression may be omitted, or may occur any number of times</td></tr>
<tr><td>XMINUS
-</td><td>Negation and range</td><td>Meaningful only within an ASCP (see below)</td></tr>
</table>

XRNI \#	Reserved name indicator	As a prefix, indicates that a token is a HyLex reserved name, and not the name of some other lexical model. In isolation, serves as a wildcard that matches any single character

The **alternative single-character pattern** or **ASCP** mentioned above is a list of characters enclosed by square brackets. It is almost identical to the corresponding regular expression usage that matches any of the characters in the group. For example, this pattern matches any single English vowel:

```
[aeiou]
```

If the XMINUS delimiter (a hyphen) occurs immediately after the initial bracket, the pattern instead matches any character *not* in the following list, such that this pattern matches any non-vowel (this function is commonly "^" rather than "-" in other regular expression languages):

```
[-aeiou]
```

A hyphen in the middle of a pattern indicates a match to any character whose numeric code lies between those of the characters on each side. Thus on machine with certain character sets, this expression matches any upper or lower case letter:

```
[A-Za-z]
```

The tokens that these various delimiters connect must each be one of these things:

literal	A quoted string as defined in the SGML standard (the HyTime standard does not clearly state whether one can use XESC to include quote characters within a quoted literal: we believe this should be allowed)
QLTN	A qualified lexical type name that matches a substring which the type would match
QPN	A qualified property name that matches a substring that the property's associated lexical type would match
#	The XRNI delimiter, which matches any single character as a **wildcard**
#T	A reserved name that matches any single token; this can only be used in a normalized lexical model, as defined below

[...]	An alternative single-character pattern (see above)
boundary	A **boundary constraint**, which is one of the following reserved tokens and may not be followed by an occurrence indicator (*, +, or ?):
	`#SOD` matches the start of the string or domain being tested
	`#EOD` matches the end of the string or domain being tested
	`#ISC` matches any pattern at the start of the string or domain being tested
	`#IEC` matches any pattern at the end of the string or domain being tested

11.5.3 HyLex matching rules

Wildcard matching

As in other pattern-matching languages, the existence of repeatable patterns leads to a question: if the pattern can match in more than one way, which one counts? Consider this HyLex expression that finds any sequence of letters and spaces, followed by the string "`the`":

```
([A-Za-z ]*, "the")
```

When this is applied to the string "`these are the ones they wanted`", the resulting match could conceivably be any of these:

```
the
these are the
these are the ones the
```

According to clause A.1.1.7, "HyLex finds the longest match for known sub-models (sequences of literals and ASCPs) and the shortest match for wildcard sequences. A match on an ASCP or literal that follows a wildcard sequence in the model terminates the wildcard sequence." Because the example just shown contains no true wildcards (#), HyLex finds the longest match. However, substituting a true wildcard would lead to getting the shortest match ("`the`"):

```
(#*, "the")
```

Character set mapping

During matches and comparisons HyTime performs a great deal of character set mapping. The order in which it occurs is this:

- The SGML parser parses the document with no knowledge of HyTime semantics, and applies case translation and white-space normalization as defined by the SGML standard.
- If the lexical model is a normalized one, HyTime applies normalization as for **dataloc** with `quantum=norm`.
- If a `lexord` is in effect, HyTime applies it.
- HyTime matches the result of all this against the model.

11.5.4 Issues of interpretation

The same clause that talks about longest and shortest matches for wildcards states that "HyLex uses the SGML rules for recognizing delimiter strings as its rules for matching sub-models." The similarity is that matching is done without overlap. An apparent similarity is that the longest match among alternatives in an OR group is chosen, but this is not identical to SGML, because of constraints against ambiguous content models in SGML and because in HyLex one can OR wildcards, ASCPs, and other things that have differing rules for choosing among alternative possible matches.

HyLex interpretation also differs from SGML delimiter and content model syntax in that SGML contextual and recognition mode constraints do not apply in HyLex (or apply in ways not defined by SGML, such as that the XMINUS delimiter is not recognized outside ASCPs).

A more interesting point in the interpretation of HyLex is that the string syntax for qpns and qltns (defined in clause A.1.3 and discussed in Sections 11.2, 11.7.4 and 11.7.5) can contain both square brackets and the plus sign (or to be precise, the SGML delimiters these characters normally represent). For example, this is a legal qualified property name:

```
HTseml+attval[type]
```

HyTime resolves this potential ambiguity by treating the string as a qualified property name if possible, otherwise as a valid lexical type name. If neither is possible, then the string is treated as a regular pattern.

Clause A.1.1.3 states that the "lexical type names and property names must have been defined prior to use in a HyLex model." HyLex definitions should be grouped together before any references to them.

11.5.5 The HyLex element and its attributes

The `HyLex` element type is a specific element type defined by HyTime and conforming to the **lexmodel** architectural form. Its content is a

HyLex expression as defined above. Several attributes can provide information about how the expression is treated:

```
<!ELEMENT      HyLex          - O (#PCDATA)>
<!ATTLIST      HyLex
    HyTime     NAME           lexmodel
    notation   NAME           #FIXED "HyLex"
    ltn        NAME           #REQUIRED
    boundary   (sodeod|sodiec|isceod|isciec|inmodel)
                              sodeod
    delims     CDATA          #IMPLIED
    qpnpsn     NAMES          #IMPLIED
    qltnlmgi   NAMES          #IMPLIED
    lexord     CDATA          #IMPLIED
    norm       (norm|unorm)   norm
    wildmax    NUMBER         512>
```

The `notation` attribute is a common attribute that identifies the notation used for the query. The HyTime processor uses this to determine that the lexical model requires a HyLex interpreter to apply it. To use HyLex expressions the HyTime engine must include such an interpreter, and the `HyLex` option must be set.

The `ltn` and `boundary` attributes are defined by the **`lexmodel`** form. They provide a name for each lexical model and constraints on the scope of matches.

The `qpnpsn` and `qltnlmgi` attributes are common attributes that constitute the **`all-qual`** attribute form, discussed in Sections 11.7.3 and 11.2.1. They can be used to specify the property set(s) and element types of **`lexmodel`** to be searched for lexical types mentioned within the lexical model.

The `delims` attribute is a common attribute from the **`all-id`** form. It defines delimiter substitutions to be made when interpreting the contained expression, much as an SGML declaration does for SGML documents. In this case it is the HyLex delimiters illustrated above that may be changed. For example, HyLex models normally use parentheses (the `XGRPO` and `XGRPC` delimiters) to mark the boundaries of groups or sub-parts. To use curly-braces instead, specify

```
<HyLex delims="XGRPO { XGRPC }">
```

The syntax within the `delims` attribute consists of any number of pairs, each containing a delimiter name and its new string value. The names and values cannot contain white-space characters, and can only contain single or double quotes if care is taken not to violate the SGML syntax for attribute values. This attribute cannot prevent ambiguity caused by ill-chosen delimiter changes.

The `lexord` attribute of the **lexmodel** form provides a lexicographic ordering definition to apply to strings before matching them against the lexical mode (see Section 14.7). It interacts closely with the `norm` attribute, although `norm` is specific to the `HyLex` element type and not all elements of the **lexmodel** form.

The `norm` attribute, when set, causes the string to be normalized in the manner prescribed for the **dataloc** form when using `quantum=norm` (see Section 8.4.1). That is, leading and trailing white-space characters are deleted, and internal sequences of white-space characters collapse to a single space. The lexical *model* itself is also normalized to the extent that "tokens in the model that represent white space strings" are reduced to a single space.

This is done because a model requiring multiple spaces could never match without such normalization — all the runs of white-space in the string that could have matched the sequence in the model would be gone. However, this can have a subtle side-effect in some cases, because whether a token in a model does in fact "represent white space" may not be determined by the model alone. For example, the second token in this model may or may not match white space (although the third always does):

```
("foo", [ d]?, " ", "bar")
```

We recommend avoiding models that raise this structural problem, much as one avoids ambiguous content models in designing SGML DTDs.

11.6 Accessing public lexical types

HyTime provides many inherent lexical types, whose names can be used in HyTime and user-level constraints. We describe the predefined types in the table below (based on clause A.1.3). To access these lexical types, include the following entity declaration in your DTD and reference the entity in your document to include the HyLex elements:

```
<!ENTITY        lextypes    PUBLIC
    "+//ISO/IEC 10744:1992//TEXT
    Useful HyLex Lexical Types//EN">

...
&lextypes;
```

All of HyTime's inherent properties, listed in Section 11.9, also have associated lexical types. They can be used in the same way, but do not require that declarations be embedded.

The LTN column shows the formal lexical type name, the Definition column gives its formal syntax in HyLex, and the Description explains its use or significance.

LTN	Definition	Description
IDRN	(IDREF | "#NULL")	An SGML ID reference or the literal "#NULL"
NAMES	(NAME, (s+, NAME)*)	SGML NAME list (redundant with like-named property)
GIL	(GI, (s+, GI)*)	List of tag names
IDR2	(IDREF, s+, IDREF)	Pair of ID references
IDR21	(IDR2, (s+, IDR2)*)	At least 2 ID references
ATTORCON	(ATTNAME| "#CONTENT")	Name of an SGML attribute, or literal "#CONTENT" to indicate a reference to an element's content
numl	(number, (s+, number)*)	List of numbers (as defined for an SGML attribute declared value)
frac	(number, s+, number)	Fraction expressed as numerator followed by denominator
fracs	(frac, (s+, frac)*)	List of fractions
snum	([+-]?,number)	Signed number
nzdigit	([1-9])	Non-zero digit
unzi	(nzdigit,digit*)	Unsigned non-zero integer
snzi	([+-]?,unzi)	Signed non-zero integer
word	(nmchar+)	Sequence of SGML NAME characters (normally letters without regard to case, digits, period, and hyphen)
words	(word, (s+, word)*)	A list of word tokens as above
literal	((LIT,#*,LIT) | (LITA,#*,LITA))	SGML literal, enclosed in single or double quotation marks. This is the only lexical type from this list that is unnormalized(see Section 11.5.5).

Qualified lexical type and property name syntax

The following lexical types define the syntax for the qualified lexical type names used to specify lexical types and for the qualified property names used to specify properties. They are usually used for HyTime validation of attribute values that are qualified names.

LTN	Definition
`qltn`	`((LMGI,PLUS)?, LTN)`

`qpn`	`(((PSN,PLUS)?,`
	`(PN,(DSO, (QPN|QLTN|word|literal), DSC)?)),`
	`(NET, ((PSN,PLUS)?,`
	`(PN,(DSO, (QPN|QLTN|word|literal), DSC)?)))*)`

`arg`	`(PERO, nzdigit, (digit, digit?)?)`

These definitions refer to other lexical types, some of which are not defined above. The table below lists these types and gives references for more information on them. They are also examples of the use of SGML properties to express lexical constraints. This type of usage is possible for all HyTime semantic properties (defined in clause A.2).

Lexical type name	Where defined
digit, nmchar	From A.2.1.1.1 properties: SGML character classes. (see Section 11.9.1)
IDREF, NAME, GI, NUMBER, ATTNAME	From A.2.1.2.1 properties: SGML basic constructs. (see Section 11.9.2)
LIT, LITA	From A.2.1.1.2 properties: SGML delimiter role names. (see Section 11.9.3)

11.7 HyTime properties

HyTime gives a long list (clause 6.7.1) of properties: named pieces of information that a HyTime engine associates with data objects. The simplest example is that a HyTime engine gives access to SGML attributes as properties of elements. This section describes how properties are defined and accessed, and discusses the intrinsic properties supplied by HyTime.

11.7.1 Introduction

Properties can be used with the **proploc** architectural form and the corresponding HyQ `Proploc()` function. Each of these gets a property by specifying two things: the object that has the property and the name of the property wanted from that object. The name of the property is a qualified property name. The attributes of the **proploc** form correspond to the parameters of the `Proploc()` function. In this chapter we will describe modifications in terms of the attributes. For more information on the architectural form, see Section 8.5.1 and on the HyQ function, see Section 9.4.3.

For example, given the following `poem` and `proploc` elements, the value of the `proploc` is the string "`rhymed`". Since there may be more than one attribute on an element, the particular one desired is specified in brackets (that is why it is called a "qualified" property name):

```
<poem id=poem-65537 type=rhymed>...</poem>
...
<proploc id=ptr1 locsrc=poem-65537>
   attval[TYPE]
</proploc>
```

11.7.2 Where properties are found

Every property must be a property *of* something, as attributes are properties of elements. If a HyTime construct requests a property that does not exist for the object in it gives as the location source then special handling is required.

The `apropsrc` attribute has two values. If `apropsrc` is set to `apropsrc` a second place called the **alternate property source** is checked (as described below). Otherwise if the default value `solesrc` is set, then no alternate location is checked. If the property is still not found, the `notprop` attribute determines the outcome:

`error`	An error is reported and what happens then is up to the particular implementation.
`empty`	The property is given an empty object as its value.
`ignore`	The property reference is ignored. This is the default value of `notprop`.

There is an ambiguity in the interpretation of the `ignore` value when used with HyQ. It is not clear what a `Select()` should do when its condition tests the value of a nonexistent property that is to be ignored. We recommend that in such cases the element *not* be selected.

Alternate property sources

The alternate property source is a fixed, predefined alternative place to check for properties. For example, while #PCDATA pseudo-elements by definition cannot have attributes, it is often useful to treat them as though they inherited all of their containing element's attributes. Rather than complicate HyQ expressions and **proploc** elements to account for this special case, properties are defined to inherit as follows.

The alternate property source of a data object depends on the kind of data object involved, of which HyTime has four (see clause 8.4.2.2, and Section 5.4):

element	an SGML element
pelement	a CDATA portion in mixed content
dataent	a data entity as defined in SGML
dataobj	any HyTime data object addressed by a Location address element

The default alternate property source of each type is as follows:

element	none
pelement	the immediately containing element
dataent	none
dataobj	"Either the data entity in which it occurs, or the element in whose content or property value it occurs" (clause 8.4.2.2) — plus special cases we won't go into

Under the last definition, an attribute has SGML properties, namely those of the element it occurs on. For example, the GI of an attribute value is the GI of the element on which it occurs.

11.7.3 Qualified name default attributes

The **all-qual** attribute list form includes the `qpnpsn` attribute, which can list the property sets to be used within the element, and the `qltnlmgi` attribute, which accomplishes much the same end for lexical type names. We discuss `qpnpsn` here, and `qltnlmgi` in Section 11.2.1.

The qpnpsn attribute: selecting property name sets

This is required if you omit the property set name (psn) from any property reference. Because each property set is declared as an SGML NOTATION, the `qpnpsn` attribute's value is a list of notation names.

Whenever a qualified property name does not specify a property set name, the HyTime engine looks for the property in each of the property sets listed in the `qpnpsn` attribute. For example if the `psn` attribute were omitted, the qpnpsn attribute would have to be specified (in this case it selects two of HyTime's built-in property sets):

```
<book HyTime=HyDoc qpnpsn="HTsem1 HTsem2">
     ...
     <proploc locsrc=someid>attval["linkend"]</proploc>
     ...
</book>
```

The HyTime standard states that property sets listed on qpnpsn are "used in the element." We interpret this to mean *everywhere* in the element, including all subelements and descendants, and that if more than one containing element specifies the qpnpsn attribute, then the innermost one applies. In the example below, the property sets myProps and HTsem1 are checked, in that order, but HTsem2 is not checked:

```
<book HyTime=HyDoc qpnpsn="HTsem1 HTsem2">
     ...
     <p HyTime=HyBrid qpnpsn="myProps HTsem1">
        <proploc locsrc=someid>
           attval["linkend"]</proploc>
     </p>
     ...
</book>
```

The HyTime standard states that the qpnpsn attribute applies *only* when the psn is omitted. If a **proploc** requests a property and specifies a particular property set in the qualified property name but the property cannot be found, the situation is a failure to find the property and is treated as described in Section 11.7.2.

11.7.4 Properties as lexical types

Every property can also be used as a lexical type under the same name to match things of the kind named. The SGML-related properties of clause A.2.1.1 indicate formal definitions in the SGML standard: GI, for example, represents an SGML generic identifier.

HyTime defines many additional optional properties in clause A.2.1.2. We list these in Section 11.9 (including a few corrections proposed by the HyTime committee since the standard's publication).

11.7.5 Qualified property names

While simple properties can be accessed by a single name, some properties have multiple instances for a given data object, and require a more complex specification. Qualified property names also allow contextual specifications, which cascade, each one applying to the result of the previous specification.

A qualified property name can be specified as a compact **qpn** or as an element structure. Most commonly the string form takes one of the four forms below, where the punctuation is literal, `PN` represents a property name, `PSN` represents a property set name, and `token` represents a specifier (either as a quoted literal string, an unquoted single-word token, a qualified lexical type name, or an embedded qualified property name):

```
PN
PN[token]
PSN+PN
PSN+PN[token]
```

For example, to get at the value of an element's `linkend` attribute you could use this qpn:

```
attval[linkend]
```

or alternatively:

```
attval["linkend"]
```

The `attval` property is part of the `HTseml` property set, which could also be explicitly specified:

```
HTseml+attval["linkend"]
```

The qpn string syntax also permits any number of additional specifications divided by the SGML NET delimiter (which is "/"). For example, if a `linkend` attribute was an IDREF then you could qualify the property further, for example with the `elem` property (see Section 11.9.3). This is an inherent property that indicates the element referred to by an IDREF:

```
attval["linkend"]/elem
```

Interpretation proceeds from left to right like other interpretations in HyTime. Each /-separated step specifies a property of the preceding result object, not the other way around.

A qualified property name can also be expressed using a separate **qpn** element. That element must contain a list of property names (plus an optional specifier for each) exactly corresponding to the steps of a qpn string. The equivalent of the last example is:

```
<qpn id=clink-dest-qpn>
    <pn psn=HTsem1>attval</pn>
    <spec>linkend</spec>
    <pn psn=HTsem2>linkedto</pn>
</qpn>
```

We strongly prefer the qpn string approach over the `qpn` element because it makes all the relevant information available in one place.

The information about the syntax and semantics of qualified property names appears in several sections of the standard. Clause 6.7.2 documents the syntax of the **qpn** architectural form and the semantics of qpns, clause A.1.3 gives the syntax of qpn strings, clause A.21.2.2 defines properties for HyTime constructs, and clause 8.5.1 describes the **proploc** form (also discussed in Section 8.5.1).

11.8 Property definition

Each property is defined or described by some element conforming to the **propdef** form. This form requires the use of the **all-qual** common attribute list form. HyTime's inherent properties use the `HyPD` element, one of the element types that HyTime defines. `HyPD` or other **propdef** subclasses can be used to define new properties if the `xpropdef` option is supported and set. Property definitions are grouped into property sets by sharing a single **property set name**, which is an SGML notation. In this section we discuss `HyPD` as the canonical example of how property definition works. Property definitions are discussed in clause 6.7.1 of the HyTime standard.

11.8.1 The pn and psn attributes

Every property definition must include these attributes to identify the property and the method to get the property (the system must, of course, also support a mechanism for calculating the property):

`pn`	the name of the property being defined
`psn`	the name of the property set it is in (which must be a formal NOTATION declared in the DTD; HyTime's intrinsic properties are in the `SGML` and `HyTime` property sets)

11.8.2 The inherent and lex attributes

The `inherent` attribute of **propdef** indicates where a built-in property is defined. Its value is a notation that defines the properties. If the inherent properties are to be used, the following NOTATION definitions are required and should be included in the DTD:

```
<!NOTATION      SGML          PUBLIC
    "+//ISO 8879:1986//NOTATION
    Standard Generalized Markup Language//EN">

<!NOTATION      HyTime        PUBLIC
    "+//ISO/IEC 10744:1992//NOTATION
    Hypermedia/Time-based Structuring Language//EN">
```

Having defined these notations, the inherent property sets can be used as described in Section 11.9.

All non-inherent properties must specify the `lex` attribute. It gives the name of a lexical type for all values of the property. It is not specified for inherent properties because their lexical types are built in by the implementer of a HyTime engine. When specified, `lex` indicates a qualified property name or a qualified lexical type name. A qpn used as a lexical type indicates the property's associated lexical type.

11.8.3 The dspec attribute for defining specifiers

The **propdef** form also takes the `dspec` attribute. The name `dspec` stands for "definition of specifier for property." As we saw for `attval` (in Section 11.7.5), a specifier distinguishes multiple instances of the same property in the same domain.

These are referred to by bracketed tokens in qpn strings as discussed in Section 11.7.5. The property specifier must conform to the lexical type given by `dspec`. For example, to use an attribute name as a specifier for the `attval` property, it must conform to the syntactic requirements for an SGML attribute name. HyTime's declaration for the `attval` property imposes this constraint as shown here (from clause A.2.1.2.1):

```
<HyPD psn=HTseml inherent=SGML
    pn=attval dspec=ATTNAME>
    attribute value
</HyPD>
```

11.8.4 The deforsyn attribute: synonyms for qpns

If a particular qpn is frequent or particularly complex, it may be useful to define an synonym for it. The `deforsyn` attribute of **propdef** lets you do this: it can have either the default value `def`, to indicate that it is a property definition, or the value `syn`, specifying that it is a synonym. If the value is `syn`, the content of the **propdef** must be a valid qpn. For example, HyTime declares a property `enot` that is a synonym for getting at a notation declared by a given entity:

```
<HyPD psn=HTseml deforsyn=syn pn=enot>
    etype[ENAME]/notation
</HyPD>
```

11.8.5 The qpnpsn and qltnlmgi attributes

The `qpnpsn` and `qltnlmgi` attributes specify where HyTime looks for any lexical types or properties mentioned in the definition. They are permitted on `HyPD` by virtue of being in the **all-qual** common attribute form defined in the Base module. We describe them in detail in Sections 11.7.3 and 11.2.1.

11.8.6 The property definition's content

The content of the HyTime property definition architectural form, **HyPD** element, is `%HyBrid;`. It contains a description of "the constraints that must be satisfied by instances of the property. Any method of description is acceptable to HyTime." The HyTime standard defines inherent properties by prose content of `HyPD` elements, for example:

```
<HyPD psn=IDREFS pn=HTseml inherent=SGML>
   id reference list
</HyPD>
```

To define a new property four key things must be specified:

- *lexical* requirements that determine how references must look (for example, the specifier for `attval` must be an entity name)
- *applicability* requirements that determine when the property applies (for example, `attval` applies only elements)
- *semantic* requirements that determine what the property means and how its value is created in the first place (for example, attributes are strings directly copied from the SGML attributes found when parsing an SGML document)
- *representation* requirements that determine what the property value itself looks like (for example, the returned attribute value is represented as a string without quotation marks that may have surrounded it in the SGML file). This is crucial because HyTime constructs such as **dataloc**, **proploc**, and HyQ can examine or search the returned property value.

The point to remember is that although you can describe a property for anything at all, until it has been implemented in software with your HyTime engine, you cannot be certain what the cost will be to support it.

Also, non-inherent properties will decrease the portability of your documents because other HyTime engines will probably not know about them. It is wisest to stick with the inherent properties as much as possible.

11.9 Inherent property definitions

In this section we present HyTime's inherent properties, as defined in the HyTime standard. We break them down into the same groups the standard uses, and include the necessary declarations for accessing them. For some elements we have added our own explanatory comments.

The inherent HyTime and SGML properties all imply corresponding lexical types that can be used to define more complex lexical types (as done in HyTime itself). They can also, however, be used to obtain information via the **proploc** architectural form and `Proploc()` HyQ function.

To access the HyTime inherent properties, the additional NOTATION declarations shown with each property set below must be included in the SGML DTD. An appropriate value should be set for `qpnpsn` if unqualified property names are to be used. The properties that apply to entire SGML documents (Sections 11.9.1 and 11.9.2 below) use the document root element as the location source. This is especially important if multiple SGML declarations are in use in different documents.

11.9.1 HTlex1: SGML character classes

The SGML character class properties (defined in clause A.2.1.1.1) match the classes defined in the SGML standard (clause 9.2 Figures 1 and 2, clause 7.3, and as listed below); they also have the same meanings. Their normal values are shown here, although these can be changed by modifying the SGML declaration for your document. To access the properties of property set `HTlex1` in a HyTime document, include this notation declaration:

```
<!NOTATION      HTlex1      PUBLIC
     "+//ISO/IEC 10744:1992//NOTATION
     HTlex1::SGML character classes//EN">
```

Abstract syntax character classes

Property	**Lexical syntax**	**Comments**
`digit`	`[0-9]`	The Arabic digits
`lcletter`	`[a-z]`	Lower-case letters
`special`	`'()+,-./:=?`	Special minimum data characters
`ucletter`	`[A-Z]`	Upper-case letters

Concrete syntax character classes

Property	Lexical syntax	Comments
`datachar`	(implicit)	Dedicated data characters
`delmchar`	(implicit)	Delimiter characters
`funchar`	(none defined)	Inert function characters (if defined, added into the fnch property described below)
`lcnmchar`	(hyphen and period)	Lower-case name characters (added to lcletter to make the set permitted within SGML "NAMEs")
`lcnmstrt`	(implicitly lcletter)	Lower-case name start characters (can start element and entity names)
`msichar`	(none defined)	Markup-scan-in characters
`msochar`	(none defined)	Markup-scan-out characters
`msschar`	(none defined)	Markup-scan-suppress characters
`re`	(carriage return — 13 in ISO 646)	SGML record end character
`rs`	(line feed — 10 in ISO 646)	SGML record start character (normally discarded — see SGML clause 7.6.1)
`sepchar`	(tab — 9 in ISO 646)	Separator characters
`space`	(plain space — 32 in ISO 646)	Canonical space character
`ucnmchar`	(hyphen and period)	Upper-case name characters (in addition to the implicit ucletters)
`ucnmstrt`	(none)	Upper-case name start characters (in addition to the implicit ucletters)

Syntactic variables derived from SGML character classes

Property	Lexical syntax	Comments
`s`	`space	re	rs	sepchar`	SGML white-space separators of clause 6.2.1

<table>
<tr><td>fnch</td><td>re | rs | space | sepchar | msochar | msichar | msschar | funchar</td><td>SGML “function” characters of clause 9.2.2 (the base types are listed above)</td></tr>
<tr><td>nmsch</td><td>lcletter | ucletter | lcnmstrt | ucnmstrt</td><td>Full set of SGML “name start characters” (including the implicit ones) of clause 9.2.1</td></tr>
<tr><td>nmchar</td><td>nmsch | digit | lcnmchar | ucnmchar</td><td>Full set of SGML “name characters” of clause 9.2.1</td></tr>
<tr><td>muchar</td><td>nmchar | fnch | delmchar</td><td>SGML markup characters of clause 9.2.1</td></tr>
<tr><td>char</td><td>muchar | datachar</td><td>SGML characters of clause 9.2.1</td></tr>
</table>

11.9.2 HTlex2: SGML delimiter role names

All of the SGML standard's formal delimiter strings are available as properties in property set `HTlex2`, defined in clause A.2.1.1.2. They originate in the SGML standard (Figure 1 of clause 9.6) using the same names as in `HTlex2`. The value of each of these HyTime properties is the literal string assigned to the SGML delimiter, such as “<” for STAGO (start-tag open). To access these properties in your HyTime document, include this declaration in the DTD:

```
<!NOTATION      HTlex2       PUBLIC
    "+//ISO/IEC 10744:1992//NOTATION
    HTlex2::SGML delimiter roles//EN">
```

For brevity, we have not included a table of the delimiter properties here. They can be found in a text on SGML such as van Herwijnen (1994), or in the SGML and HyTime standards themselves.

11.9.3 HTsem1: SGML basic constructs

`HTsem1` defines properties that reflect SGML semantics in clause A.2.1.2.1. They are most useful within lexical models, though they can also be used with **proploc** and HyQ queries. The HyTime standard defines each property name in either all upper-case letters, or all lower-case. This convention is followed here as well and serves as a reminder:

the upper-case properties reflect SGML information for which case distinctions are normally ignored.

These and the following semantic properties provide information about a particular document and context. For example, a string matches the IDREF semantic property only if it can be found on an attribute of type ID in the same document. To access HyTime's SGML semantic properties, include this declaration in your DTD:

```
<!NOTATION      HTseml       PUBLIC
    "+//ISO/IEC 10744:1992//NOTATION
    HTseml::SGML basic constructs//EN">
```

The concrete lexical representations of the SGML semantic constructs defined in this section are not defined by the standard. We assume that the representation of each semantic object will contain all the information that an SGML parser must have about these objects.

Declared value prescriptions of attributes

These properties correspond exactly to the declared value prescriptions available for SGML attributes as defined in the SGML standard (clause 11.3.3). The names are also identical. See the SGML standard or a text on SGML such as van Herwijnen (1994) for further information. For brevity, we have not included a table of them here.

Identifiers of objects or properties

Property	Lexical syntax	Comments
ENAME	entity name	The name of a specified entity
ATTNAME	attribute name	The name of the specified attribute
GI	generic identifier	The element type name of the element specified
CID	ID of current element	The value of the ID attribute, if any (whatever its name)

Properties of a prolog

Property	Lexical syntax
dtd	document type definition
lpd	link process definition
ASSGI	associated element type
ASSNOT	associated notation name
etype[ENAME]	entity type
attdefs[ASSGI]	attribute definition list

attdef[ATTNAME]	attribute definition
ATTDV[ATTNAME]	declared value
ATTDVNMT	name token in ATTDV name token group

Properties of a parsed document instance

Property	Lexical syntax
ent[ENAME]	entity
enotetype[ENAME]/notation	
datatts[ENAME]	data attribute specification
elem[ID]	element
celem	current element
attspecs[ID]	attribute specification list
linkatts[ID]	link attribute specification
linkres[ID]	result element specification
attval[ATTNAME]	attribute value

11.9.4 HTsem2: HyTime constructs

HyTime also defines a number of properties that apply to HyTime data objects of various kinds (clause A.2.1.2.2). No conventions have yet been established for how these are expressed or used. To access them, include the following declaration:

```
<!NOTATION      HTsem2       PUBLIC
    "+//ISO/IEC 10744:1992//NOTATION
    HTsem2::HyTime basic constructs//EN">
```

Identifiers of objects or properties

Property	Lexical syntax	Comments
LTN	lexical type name	
LMGI	lexmodel element type	lextype is GI
PN	property name	
PSN	property set name	The property set the property was found in
spec	specifier of property	The instance-specifier used to access the property
FN	function name	
OCI	object class identifier	

PCOBJ	PTR to current object	
NLNAME	HyQ node list name	
REFTYPE	reference type	The reference type constraint that applies to a given location specification
LEXTYPE	lexical type	The lexical type model that applies to a given location specification

Location addressing properties

Property	Lexical syntax	Comments
`object[PTR]`	object	
`cobj`	current object	
`locsrc`	location source of object	
`cand`	HyQ selector candidate	used within a `Select()` function in HyQ
`DQ`	dataloc data quantum	Meaningful with respect to dataloc element or function
`pelement[PTR]`	pseudo-element	
`dataent`	data entity	
`dataobj[PTR]`	data object	
`elpelem[PTR]`	element or pseudo-element	
`NODETYPE`	node type: (element | pelement | dataent | dataobj)	The type of the indicated node, as a string from the list shown
`docroot`	document root	
`docpos`	pathloc document position	
`docpostl`	treeloc document position	
`datapos`	data position	
`apropsrc`	additional property source	

Hyperlinking properties

Property	Lexical syntax	Comments
`hylink[PTR]`	ilink or clink element	
`anchors`	objects linked by a hylink	
ANCHROLE	anchor roles of anchors of hylink	
`linkedby`	hylinks that link an anchor	
`linkedto`	other anchors of linkedby	
`LINKEDAS`	role of anchor in hylink	Taken from anchrole attribute

11.9.5 HTsem3: unparsed SGML text

These properties, defined in clause A.2.1.2.3, may be used only if the `unparsed` option is available with your HyTime engine. It permits you to access not only the structure of the SGML document (elements, attributes, content, and so on) but also the character stream representation of the document from before it was parsed. In the case where it is needed, include this declaration:

```
<!NOTATION     HTsem3      PUBLIC
    "+//ISO/IEC 10744:1992//NOTATION
    HTsem3::Unparsed SGML text//EN">
```

Property	Lexical syntax	Comments
`unpelem [ID]`	unparsed element (includes tags)	Value may not be parseable once taken out of document context, or if crosses entity boundaries
`unpcontxt`	unparsed content (excludes tags)	No blanks inserted between paragraphs. May be unintuitive if features such as SHORTREF or DATATAG are used
`unpcont [ID]`	unpelem[ID]/ unpcontx	
`tag[GI]`	start-tag	May be empty due to OMITTAG
`unpatt [ATTNAME]`	attribute value specification	May be unintuitive if application must distinguish implied from explicitly null values
`KEYWORD`	keyword parameter	Applies to marked sections; may return parameter entities

12

Extending HyTime

12.1 Introduction

HyTime provides numerous mechanisms to create links to, from, within, and between a wide variety of data and media types. However, new media and new information structures will inevitably be developed in the future. Also, as discussed in relation to the **notloc** architectural form (see Section 8.5.3), particular user communities have standardized on pointing mechanisms optimized for their needs. To address such situations, HyTime provides several extension mechanisms: architectural forms and markup conventions that permit a HyTime application to recognize information that is in some non-HyTime notation, and pass it to an appropriate interpreter for handling.

These extension mechanisms can be extremely useful, but some of them have a drawback: because they use notations that are not part of HyTime, there is no guarantee that all HyTime processing applications are aware of them. This can compromise portability.

Because of these portability concerns, HyTime should be extended with care and forethought. The simplest HyTime extensions do not introduce new notations or syntax, but use HyTime's own methods for defining higher-level combinations of existing tools. Thus they do not have the same potential to compromise document portability as other extensions.

12.2 HyQ extensions

As discussed in Chapter 9, the HyQ query language provides macros, which are reusable abbreviations for more complex queries. They can be used freely without compromising portability, because HyQ macros are an intrinsic part of HyTime.

HyQ also permits an extension that requires application support. HyQ has several built-in Boolean "assertion" functions that test conditions such as the equality of two data items. It is possible to define a custom assertion in addition to these, and to implement it through an application program. This requires programming it and making the program reachable from HyQ via the `Ah()` function.

Using `Ah()` requires that you specify the `uassert` option, which is part of the Location address module. If your application supports this and you do define user assertion handlers, then you can use the `Ah()` function in HyQ to access a handler and get back a true or false result.

For example, to locate `title` elements containing incorrect capitalization in their content, a program to check case could be hooked up through an assertion handler that takes a node and returns true if it contains a spelling error. If this assertion handler is called "`titleCaps`," you can access it as follows within a HyQ expression to get a list of all error-containing elements within a certain domain (in this example, the domain is an element with ID `sec28`):

```
<HyQ qdomain=sec28>
  Select(DOMTREE, Not(Ah(titleCaps, Create(CAND))))
</HyQ>
```

The first parameter to the `Ah()`, in this case `titleCaps`, must be an IDREF and must lead to "an object that implements the assertion" (clause A.3.2.7). The second parameter must be the node list on which the assertion operates (it may take only one, as here). In the example shown, the `Create()` function converts the single node `CAND` into a node list acceptable to the `Ah()` function.

The object that implements the assertion handler must be in a programming or scripting language that can access and understand the node list that the HyTime engine will pass to it. Given that, there are several ways to refer directly to the "implementation object" using an IDREF (the IDREF may also point indirectly with the facilities of the Location address module).

One way to express the implementation object is to place it directly in the document and flag it as being in a special notation. For example, one can define Apple's scripting language from HyperCard™ as a special data content notation, and then create an element type whose purpose is to contain such scripts within SGML documents:

```
<!NOTATION      hypertalk   PUBLIC
    "-//Apple Computer, Inc.//NOTATION
    HyperCard(tm) Scripting language//EN">

<!ELEMENT       script      - - RCDATA>
<!ATTLIST       script
    id          ID          #REQUIRED
    notn        NOTATION (hypertalk)
                            #FIXED hypertalk>
```

Having done this one can put scripts in documents, giving each a unique ID by which to refer to it from `Ah()` functions. The SGML parser and the HyTime engine can then locate the scripts and pass them off to an appropriate interpreter for processing. For example, here is a HyperTalk script that checks whether the text content of a node follows certain simplified rules for capitalization of English titles:

```
<script id=titleCaps>
    function titleCaps nodes
       get " a an the of and to from for "
       put it into common
       put GetContent(nodes) into string
       if islower(char 1 of string) then
          return 0
       end if
       put the number of words of string into n
       repeat with i = 2 to n
          put " " & word i of string & " " into w
          if islower(char 2 of w) then
             if w is not in common then
                return 0
             end if
          else
             if w is in common then
                return 0
             end if
          end if
       end repeat
       return 1
    end titleCaps
```

```
    -- Return 1 if string is capitalized as a title.
    function islower c
       get charToNum(c)
       if it < charToNum("a") then return false
       if it > charToNum("z") then return false
       return true
    end islower
</script>
```

We assume that when this assertion handler is used, the HyTime engine passes the function definition to a HyperTalk interpreter, and calls the HyperTalk function `titleCaps` with a single parameter that identifies the node list; this communication must be accomplished by some arrangement between the HyTime implementation and a HyperTalk interpreter. The `GetContent()` function is an interface back to the HyTime implementation, which gets the data content of a specified node.

When putting non-SGML notations directly in-line in the SGML document, characters such as "<" and "&" may have to be expressed as entities (or otherwise modified) so as not to violate the rules of SGML syntax. In the example above the ampersands are not troublesome, because they are followed by spaces, and SGML will ignore them.

An application-defined assertion handler can be arbitrarily complex and do any specialized processing needed. We anticipate, however, that need for them will be relatively rare. HyQ is general enough to manage a wide range of tasks without application-dependent extensions.

12.3 Lexical types

HyTime provides many built-in lexical types that can be used to locate properties of objects, test strings against syntactic requirements, and so on. HyTime's HyLex language can be used to extend the set of lexical types, and the types so defined can be used for searching, pattern-matching, and so on (see Section 11.5 for more information on HyLex).

It is also possible to forego HyLex entirely and express string patterns using other notations. If you define such notations then you can use them wherever HyLex can be used.

The most likely extension in this area is to support pre-existing pattern-matching syntaxes, such as regular expressions. Many systems use regular expressions heavily for searching, editing, and matching strings.

To use one of these pattern-matching syntaxes with HyTime, you must first give it a name and declare it as an SGML NOTATION. We provide declarations and registered formal public identifiers below for the three most common variants of regular expressions on UNIX and some other systems. Whatever identifiers are used, the notation in which a lexical model is expressed must appear on an attribute of the lexical model element..

```
<!NOTATION      grep         PUBLIC
   "+//ISBN 0-7923-9432-1::Lexical Notation//NOTATION
    Regular expressions::grep//EN">
<!NOTATION      egrep        PUBLIC
   "+//ISBN 0-7923-9432-1::Lexical Notation//NOTATION
    Regular expressions::egrep//EN">
<!NOTATION      fgrep        PUBLIC
   "+//ISBN 0-7923-9432-1::Lexical Notation//NOTATION
    Regular expressions::fgrep//EN">
```

12.4 Properties

The HyTime standard provides many built-in properties that apply to information units such as elements, entities, and so on. Additional properties can be declared in the same way those are defined, using the **propdef** architectural form (see Section 11.8).

For example, some application might need to assign an additional identifier to every SGML element and pseudo-element, separate from the SGML IDs that some elements may have. It could support these with a new property, perhaps called `app-id`.

Providing such new properties requires great care. It can seem like a solution to nearly any imaginable problem, because (as the philosophers tell us) absolutely anything can be expressed as a property of some kind: the property of being the third child of the present king of France; the property of not having been modified since April 2; and so on *ad nauseam*. Unfortunately such solutions tend to work only in the short run. Each new property requires implementation at the level of the HyTime engine itself, and is not portable across different HyTime engines. For these reasons we recommend avoiding custom property definitions whenever possible.

12.5 Specific elements for media links

The HyTime Location address module does not provide specific syntax to accommodate every possible data representation, such as the variety of formats currently used for graphic and multimedia data. However, any such data can be referenced, and special locators can be defined to address parts of such data. Regardless of the notation, the method for including such information objects in an SGML document is the same. First, the object as a whole is accessed; then pointers into it are coded using a custom locator appropriate to the particular data content notation the data object uses. This done, HyTime links can be used to connect up those locations with others anywhere.

12.5.1 Accessing non-SGML entities

To access data in any notation, the required steps are these (we use graphics terminology for simplicity, but the methods apply to all media):

- The notation's name must be declared.
- Each image must be declared as a named SGML external entity with a SYSTEM or PUBLIC identifier and an NDATA specification indicating its notation.
- Each image is then specified at its point(s) of occurrence in the SGML document, either with a direct entity reference or by giving the entity's name on an attribute (the second method is superior, among other reasons because the element can add a variety of other information in additional attributes or content).

An example follows:

```
<!NOTATION      TIFF         PUBLIC
    "+//ISBN 0-7923-9432-1::Graphic Notation//NOTATION
    Aldus/Microsoft
    Tagged Interchange File Format//EN">

<!ELEMENT       figure       - - (head?, caption?)>
<!ATTLIST       figure
    object      ENTITY       #REQUIRED
    links       IDREF        #IMPLIED>
<!ENTITY        ent37        SYSTEM
    "fig1.tif" NDATA TIFF>

<figure object=ent37><head>Figure 1</head></figure>
```

Note especially that the `object` attribute takes as value the name of an entity, not a reference to it (such as `&ent37;`).

12.5.2 Referring into a graphic notation

For graphical notations that do not map conveniently to FCS addresses (see Chapter 13) the **fcsloc** form may not be the best solution. Situations where specialized addressing methods are preferred should be handled with HyTime's **notloc** architectural form, which we discuss more fully in Section 8.5.3.

A **notloc** element must have `id` and `HyTime` attributes. Beyond that, it can have whatever other attributes or content are needed to support the particular kind of pointing needed. As a simple example, an element might be defined to refer to portions of Apple QuickDraw graphics. QuickDraw uses a two-dimensional coordinate area, with each integer axis running from –32767 to +32767. A point is normally described by two integers: the vertical coordinate followed by the horizontal. A rectangle is defined by two such points: one for the top left corner and one for the bottom right, in that order. For example, a small squat rectangle in the lower-right quadrant can be described as { (0,0) (–10,20) }.

The element must also refer to the entity, for which we show an `object` attribute that names the entity. We do not use `qdomain` here, because it is of type IDREFS. Selecting a particular entity by name is part of the meaning of each `rectref` instance. Given that, any number of different syntactic structures can then be used to refer to such rectangles within a given graphical entity. An attractive option is to put each number in a separate attribute with an appropriate name. This is clear; someone receiving the document need waste no time puzzling over which number is which. In the same way, an encoder may specify the attributes in any order desired, and an SGML parser can validate that all four attributes are specified (although it cannot ensure that they are signed numbers):

```
<rectref object=ent37 top=0 left=0
    bottom=-10 right=20>
```

A slight variation would give the four coordinates in a single attribute using a conventional order. This is compact, but gives up SGML validation that there are four numbers, and does not express the required conventional order (thus making it mysterious to later users):

```
<rectref id=g1 object=ent37 rect="0 0 -10 20">
```

A third option is nearly the same but places the numbers in unadorned content. This seems even less clear and is even less receptive to SGML validation:

```
<rectref id=g2 object=ent37>0 0 -10 20</>
```

Finally, any of these cases could have additional syntax or punctuation. This is often a very good solution if a standard notation, familiar to users, is already in use:

```
<rectref id=g4 object=ent37 rect="(0 0) (-10 20)">
```

Although these methods vary in how much validation an SGML system can provide by itself, it is possible to use HyTime lexical types (see Sections 11.2-11.5) in order to get HyTime validation:

```
<rectref id=g5 object=ent37
   top=0 left=0 bottom=-10 right=20
   lextype=
       "top snum left snum bottom snum right snum">
```

The `lextype` attribute indicates constraints on the four attributes, namely that each must match the lexical type named `snum` (which is an inherent type for signed numbers). For the punctuated syntax it is clearer to define appropriate lexical types elsewhere and use them by name. Here we define two such lexical types: `Point-2d` matches a parenthesized pair of numbers, and `Rect-2d` matches two occurrences of `Point-2d`, possibly separated by white-space:

```
<!-- Two-dimensional point, vertical coord first -->

<lexmodel ltn=Point-2d norm=norm>
    ('(',s*,snum,s+,snum,s*,')')
</lexmodel>

<lexmodel ltn=Rect-2d norm=norm>
    (Point-2d,s*,Point-2d)
</lexmodel>
```

The `lextype` attribute can then use these types to constrain the `rect` attribute as shown below. Should the constraint apply to all instances of `rectref`, it can be set as a #FIXED value in the DTD.

```
<rectref id=g6 object=ent37 rect="(0 0) (-10 20)"
    lextype="rect Rect-2d">
```

In the rest of this section we assume the four-attribute syntax shown first. We also assume that lexical type validation is used, although we do not show the `lextype` attribute explicitly.

12.5.3 Building links on top of notloc

Given such a way to point within data, links may be created using HyTime's normal linking tools. Each link includes a pointer to an image portion and a pointer to the data location associated with it (with the **`clink`** form, the latter is implicitly the **`clink`**'s own location).

For example, to create a one-way link from a place in an SGML document to a place in a graphic, insert a **`clink`** in the SGML, which uses a **`notloc`** element of type `rectref`:

```
<p>Tighten the bolt until it snaps,
    then back off 1/4 turn. Note the
    <clink linkend=g1>special wrench
    in figure 37:</clink>
    <rectref id=g1 object=ent37 top=342 left=370
     bottom=300 right=512>
</p>
```

When a HyTime system displays this portion of the hyperdocument, it can either show the graphic inline with the relevant rectangle highlighted in some way chosen by the application, author, or reader, or provide a way to request the graphic when needed, say by changing the style of the text within the `clink` element, or adding a nearby button.

HyTime places one special restriction on the use of **notloc** locators: they cannot serve as location sources for other locators unless the `notsrc` option of the Location address module is set.

12.5.4 Links to more complex regions

It is also useful extension to refer to non-rectangular regions. One approach to representing shapes uses their outline, as in a connect-the-dots game. The user specifies a series of points, and the computer infers a line connecting each to the next and the final point back to the beginning. The area enclosed is the referenced region. Regions can be expressed with a trivial modification of the punctuated syntax of Section 12.5.2 and this is one advantage of that syntax over the one with four attributes:

```
<lexmodel ltn=Region-2d norm=norm>
    (s*, (Point-2d,s*)+)
</lexmodel>
...
<region object=ent37 rect="(0 0) (1 0) (1 1) (0 2)"
   lextype="rect Region-2d">
```

When designing a HyTime application, you can define as many different element types based on **notloc** as needed to support the special media and data notations you are using. It is good to minimize the number of different locator types in order to cut down on overall complexity. Fortunately, a few general pointing types such as the ones just shown for rectangles and regions can handle a wide range of needs and can be applied to a wide range of notations (coordinates, for example, work similarly in many graphic notations). `Notloc`-based element types could also be designed that use the scheduling facilities of HyTime to declare the coordinate system being used.

12.6 A protocol for hot spots on graphs

A common need in documents containing both text and graphics is the graphic **hot spot**: authors may wish to define areas of a graphic to be hypertext links that take the user to some other information. Such links often appear on paper as numbered or lettered "callouts" on the graphics, sometimes with cross-references listed in the caption or nearby in content. Readers may also want to make such links.

Very few of the formats currently used to store graphics provide any way to include hot spot definitions in the graphic files themselves. For this reason an external mechanism such as HyTime's **ilink** is essential: links can then be created without corrupting the graphic data itself. The same mechanism can then apply to all kinds of interconnections regardless of their endpoints' media. You can link a frame sequence from a movie to a paragraph of text, one sound bite to another, etc.

Consider a link from a small square in one corner of a figure entity with ID `fig3`, that leads to this document element:

```
<p id=caption12>Tighten bolt (a) until it breaks.</p>
```

The text end of this relationship can be specified by an ID (indirectly if desired). The graphic end of the link points to a locator element of a type specific to the graphical notation:

```
<rectref id=g1 object=fig3
    top=342 left=370 bottom=300 right=512>
<ilink linkends="caption12 g1" anchrole="ref target">
</ilink>
```

Although an **ilink** can have any content (the meta-content model specifies `%HyBrid;`), HyTime defines no particular meaning for such content. In many cases it makes sense to keep all **ilink** elements empty. Other options include putting all the link's referenced elements within it for neatness, or including some kind of supplemental information such as human-readable comments about the link. Consistency and documentation are the key principles in making any of these approaches useful.

Exactly the same method can be used to interlink portions of two graphics, rather than a graphic and a text element, or to interconnect any two pieces of data in general. A link from a callout in figure 4 to one in figure 3 could be represented as in the example below:

```
<rectref id=g8 object=fig3
    top=342 left=370 bottom=300 right=512>
<rectref id=g9 object=fig4
    top=100 left=100 bottom=0 right=200>
<ilink anchrole="callout callout" linkends="g8 g9">
</ilink>
```

12.6.1 Correspondent callouts

Any number of links can be attached to a graphic in this way, each by a separate instance of an element type based on **ilink**. However, this method cannot express relationships among the callouts of a single graphic, and can be unwieldy if there are many of them.

One way to improve the coding of such relationships is to declare a container to hold the links, whose presence represents the relationship between them. Below, we use a `textcallout` element type that is based on **ilink**. We could also add a `lextype` constraint to ensure that exactly two IDREFS appear on each instance.

```
<!ELEMENT       textcallout - O EMPTY>
<!ATTLIST       textcallout
    HyTime      NAME        #FIXED "ilink"
    linkends    IDREFS      #REQUIRED
    anchrole    NAMES       #FIXED "ref target">

<linkgrp id=fig3.callouts>
   <textcallout linkends="sec1 fig3.callout1">
   <textcallout linkends="sec2 fig3.callout2">
   <textcallout linkends="sec3 fig3.callout3">
   <textcallout linkends="sec4 fig3.callout4">
   ...
</linkgrp
```

A better alternative is to use multiple locations as linkends. Then the entire relationship can be represented by a single link with two linkends: the first a list of the text locations and the second a list of the callout locations. HyTime then parses the two lists and combines them, pairing an element from one list with an element from the other. Each pair then consists of a document location and a location on the graphic. These lists use the `multloc` attributes (see Section 8.7.1), while the link itself specifies `aggtrav=cor` to obtain the pairwise treatment desired:

```
<nameloc id=aggregate1 obnames=nobames
   ordering=ordered set=notset aggloc=nagg>
   sec1
   sec2
   sec3
</nameloc>

<fcsloc id=aggregate2 locsrc=fig3id impfcs=myview
   ordering=ordered set=notset aggloc=nagg>
    <extlist>
         1   1  10  10
       100 100 110 110
       203   1 204  87
    </extlist>
</fcsloc>

<pairwise hytime=ilink anchrole="textlocs callouts"
   aggtrav=cor linkends="aggregate1 aggregate2">
```

This approach has pros and cons. An advantage is that the connection is unified in a single element. A disadvantage is that the individual pairs are invisible: to see which callout goes with which text location, either the computer or a human reader must parse both lists and count tokens. In the `linkgrp` approach the pairs are obvious, and it is far more difficult to damage any pair by editing others (say, by deleting a callout and the wrong text location from the lists). Also, using multiple locations requires the `multloc` option, and so may not be supported in all HyTime engines.

12.7 TEI extended locators

The TEI (Text Encoding Initiative) is a major international effort that has developed guidelines for SGML encoding of documents and other data of scholarly interest. Formal TEI work began in 1987, and the first edition was fully reviewed and published by mid-1990 (Sperberg-McQueen and Burnard 1990). The first major revision is expected to be complete around the time that this book is available. The TEI hypermedia committee developed **extended locators** with many of the same goals in mind as the HyTime Location address module. The emphasis is on reference within SGML documents, although other kinds of references are also supported. TEI extended locators use a syntax that achieves goals particularly relevant to TEI users:

- Locators should directly reflect the canonical and structural reference syntaxes traditionally used by scholars in a variety of humanities fields.

- Locators should be highly readable and therefore compact, uniform, and contiguous (that is, finding an entire locator should not require looking in many different places).
- No long-distance dependencies should need to be worked out in order to interpret a locator.

12.7.1 The structure of TEI extended locators

A TEI extended locator is a single attribute on an SGML element, with internal structure. Detailed definitions of the TEI extended locators are provided in Sperberg-McQueen and Burnard (1990 and forthcoming). The syntax is open for anyone to implement and use, and is likely to become a commonly available option in HyTime and other hypermedia engines. A TEI extended locator can be treated as an instance of HyTime's **notloc** architectural form using the methods in Section 10.3.

Within a TEI extended locator attribute, there may be any number of **location terms**, each serving as the location source for the next. Each serves a specific locator purpose, much like the forms in HyTime's Location address module.

Each location term starts with the name of its **location type**, which specifies what kind of locator should be used for that step of the locator, and usually continues with parenthesized parameters for the location term. For example, this syntax can express the equivalent of the following HyTime location ladder that locates a particular element by its ID using **nameloc**, then steps down to some sub-element using **treeloc**, and finally picks out some characters of the text content using **dataloc**:

```
<nameloc id=n1 nobnames>
   <nmlist>sec3</nmlist>
</nameloc>
...
<treeloc id=t1 locsrc=n1>
   <marklist>4 3 5</marklist>
</treeloc>
...
<dataloc id=d1 locsrc=t1>
   <dimspec>5 3</dimspec>
</dataloc>
...
<clink id=c1 linkend=d1>
   Content of link origin...
</clink>
```

The equivalent TEI extended locator is:

```
<xref target="ID (sec3) TREE (4) (3) (5) STR (5 7)">
   Content of link origin...
</xref>
```

This accomplishes the original goals cleanly and effectively, is easy to implement and also has the advantage (for many applications that don't require the powerful indirection feature of location ladders) that the rungs of the location ladder remain together. Although it is good practice to keep HyTime rungs together as shown above, each could appear anywhere because they are connected only by their IDs.

12.7.2 TEI location terms

TEI extended locators also give direct support for certain pointing mechanisms not provided in HyTime. One of these is traversing down a tree not by absolute child numbers, but by typed child numbers. This is convenient because people tend to number things by type: "section 2" of a chapter is often the third SGML child of the chapter, since there is probably a chapter-title element before the first section. With extended locators one can filter elements by type and attributes to make very intuitive locators (these filters can also use regular expressions as well as string constants; they can be accomplished in HyQ, though with increased complexity):

```
<xref target="TREE (3 chap) (2 sec) (4 para)">

<xref target="TREE (3 POEM TYPE rhymed) (2 LINE)">
```

The complete list of TEI locator types appears below, as of the current revision of the TEI Guidelines (Sperberg-McQueen and Burnard, forthcoming); they combine into location ladders in the order specified in a given locator (links across documents must specify a destination entity on an attribute). The first four location types do not depend on a prior location source, and so make sense only as the first location term in any extended locator:

`here` Takes no parameters; refers to the location of the link origin itself (used for relative addressing).

`root` Takes no parameters; refers to the containing document element.

`id` The parameter is an SGML IDREF whose referent is the resulting location (as with HyTime **nameloc** elements, this is not an IDREF in SGML's view and so can be used with inter-document references).

`ref` — The parameter is a canonical reference (used in many humanities texts; the document's TEI header defines their syntax in a formal way that permits it to be interpreted when used).

`ditto` — Used only in a `to` attribute, indicates the location specified by the `from` attribute (which may then be used as the location source for further terms).

All the next location types take any number of following parameter lists; they apply from left to right. Each parameter list can have up to four arguments: a number *n*, a GI, an attribute name, and an attribute value. Only elements matching all specified GI and/or attribute constraints are counted, and of them, the nth one in sequence is chosen. The element type and attribute constraints can be either constant values or regular expressions.

`child` — Each following parameter list steps down the document tree one level, like a marker in a HyTime **treeloc**.

`descendant` — The parameters step down the document tree as with `child`, but each step can search through not only direct children, but all descendants.

`ancestor` — The parameters step up through the elements containing the location source, using constraints like those for `child`. The sequence counts upward from the parent of the location source towards the document root (this is the opposite of a HyTime **relloc** of type `anc`).

`previous` — The parameters step through preceding siblings of the location source.

`next` — The parameters step through following siblings of the location source.

The remaining location types address portions of data content, much like HyTime's **dataloc** form, and provide extension mechanisms, like HyTime's **notloc** form:

`pattern` — The parameter is a regular expression and the first match within the location source is the resulting location.

`token` — The parameter specifies the start and end of a range of words, counted as for **dataloc** with `quantum=word`, to be selected from among those in the character content `str` The parameter specifies the start and end of a range of characters (not bytes) to be selected from among those in the (parsed) character content.

`space` There may be one or two parameter lists, each containing a vector in a coordinate space with any number of dimensions. If only one parameter is used, the location is a point; if two, the location is a rectangle or rectangular solid.

`foreign` The parameters are in some special notation, presumably to be interpreted by a special application. The first following parameter list by convention contains the name of that notation and the second contains any parameters it requires. This is much like a HyTime **`notloc`**.

`hyq` The parameter contains a HyTime Query language (HyQ) expression.

For further information on TEI extended locators, see Sperberg-McQueen and Burnard (1990 and forthcoming). These sources also include detailed discussions and examples of how locators can be used to encode a wide variety of complex structures in documents, including the equivalent of span locations.

13

Advanced Measurement and Scheduling

13.1 Introduction

This chapter introduces three separate but closely related topics for handling multimedia: the advanced portions of the HyTime Measurement module (clause 7), for representing units and measurements, the Scheduling module (clause 10), for representing the temporal and spatial relations of data in multimedia presentations, and the Rendition module (clause 11) for representing processes that affect the presentation of data.

The complexity of multimedia systems and the lack of widely accepted data models and formats to fill the role that SGML does for text make full coverage of the topics in this chapter impractical in a book of this size. To fully examine the problems of multimedia scheduling would take a separate book in itself. This chapter presents the basic ideas of HyTime scheduling and measurement, and describes some of the most important facilities in detail. We have tried to select essential features that are immediately useful and that provide a basis for understanding HyTime's approach; this has meant omitting many optional features and mentioning some sophisticated facilities only briefly. Use of these advanced facilities will require recourse to the HyTime standard.

Many multimedia scheduling issues are sufficiently complex that there is not even agreement on the fundamental operations. For example, rendition in a fixed period of time may or may not be possible without degradation, depending on the medium, application or even hardware performing the rendition. HyTime can describe degradation strategies with labels, but leaves decisions about how they are executed to the application. Many of the facilities of the Scheduling and Rendition modules are only partially specified in order to allow the needed flexibility.

The facilities discussed in this chapter all require the support of the HyTime Scheduling module, and some of them also require support for the Rendition module.

13.2 Units of measurement

HyTime advanced measurement, like basic measurement, is based on positive integral position values. Unlike word positions in a string or child numbers in a tree, multimedia measurements need to be anchored to real physical units of measurement (such as points in time). To display a video clip, the frame rate is as important as the frames themselves if the display is to be correct. HyTime generalizes scheduling to include positioning in space or along any other set of physical axes, so that any physically defined unit of measurement may be specified.

13.2.1 Measurement domains, units and granules

A **measurement domain** is an abstract structure within which quantified references are meaningful. A measurement domain corresponds to either abstract measurements, such as a number of characters or a number of bits (we have already seen such measurements) or to physical measurements, such as durations of time or distances in space.

Standard measurement units

Each HyTime measurement domain defines a single base unit called an **SMU** (or **standard measurement unit**). Each SMU is defined as an SGML notation, whose formal public identifier identifies the basic unit of measurement in the domain. Appendix B shows definitions (from clause A.5.1) for the Systeme Internationale units which are included in HyTime. The most important of these units for most applications are

SIsecond and SImeter for time and length, but all of the SI base units are included.

While each domain could use only a single unit, measuring the distances between cities in light-years or dating checks in milliseconds since January 1, 1901 would not be convenient. Therefore units may be defined as specified fractions of the SMU. These units are called **granules**. Measurements in HyTime can use any defined granule, a fact particularly important in HyTime because the use of integer coordinates can easily cause measurements to become very large numbers. Unit definitions for a measurement domain are grouped together in an element of the **measure** form, which specifies the SMU for the domain on the `smu` attribute. The granules themselves are specified by **granule** elements with attributes for the granule name (`gn`) and definition (`gd`).

A sample SMU definition and related granule definitions would look like this:

```
<!NOTATION      nybble      PUBLIC
    "-//dgd//NOTATION nybble//EN">

<measure smu=nybble>
    <granule gn=bit            gd="1 4 nybble">
    <granule gn=nybble         gd="1 1 NYBBLE">
    <granule gn=byte           gd="2 1 nybble">
</measure>
```

This defines an SMU called a `nybble`, which old assembly language programmers will recognize as half a byte or four bits. The `measure` element specifies the measurement domain and SMU by reference to an SGML notation, and each of the granules is defined by specifying two numbers (representing the numerator and denominator of a fraction) and another unit which should be multiplied by the fraction to produce the value of a granule. Thus a bit is defined as 1/4 of a nybble, and so forth.

Granule names are case sensitive, since case is significant in the standard metric abbreviations. However, since SMUs are SGML notations, their names are not case-sensitive. The fact that the character cases are different allows the definition of the granule "nybble" as exactly one "NYBBLE."

HyTime also defines three abstract measurement domains (and associated SMUs) that do not relate to physical quantities: the generic (unitless) quantum `gquantum`, plus virtual time and length units `virtime` and `virspace`. These three are used when numbers are purely arbitrary and have no fixed relationship to real-world units. For example, the children of a node in an SGML document tree, the frames of an animation sequence, or the rows of pixels in a graphic image, could be counted in terms of `gquanta`, `virtime` or `virspace`.

HyTime defines granules for the virtual units as follows:

`vtu`	virtual time unit: equal to 1 `virtime` unit
`vsu`	virtual space unit: equal to 1 `virspace` unit
`quantum`	generic `gquantum`
`bit-combination`	`gquantum` for counting characters
`token`	`gquantum` for parsed tokens
`cell`	`gquantum` for table or spreadsheet cells

We do want to note one serious limitation of granule definitions. Since a granule definition must specify a granule in terms of a ratio of the SMU for that domain it is not possible to express granules that are related to a measurement unit by an irrational number. This point may seem arcane, but since the SMU unit for angles is the radian, more convenient units of angle such as the degree cannot be defined accurately. A degree is 2π / 360 radians, which cannot be expressed as a granule.

We suggest the use of a defined notation for the degree, based on an FPI such as this one:

```
<!NOTATION      degree       PUBLIC
    "+//ISBN 0-7923-9432-1::Angle SMU
    Notation//NOTATION Degree 2pi/360 SIradians//EN">
```

A less attractive possibility is to use an explicit rational approximation for π in a granule definition: while this will guarantee identical results on all HyTime systems it will also guarantee inaccuracy on all systems.

13.2.2 Measurement calculations in HyTime

The **HMU**, or **HyTime measurement unit**, is any unit that is used in a HyTime document to specify a position along an axis. An HMU can be a granule or a ratio of a base granule. All HMUs eventually are defined in terms of an SMU.

All internal HyTime calculations are made as integral values. In order to facilitate this each axis of measurement has an associated internal calculation unit: the **MDU** or **measurement domain unit**. All calculations and measurements made by a HyTime engine are performed in the relevant MDU.

No matter how they are specified in HMUs, all measurements that occur in a document must be an integral number of MDUs. This condition is satisfied as long as the MDU is a common denominator (though it need not be the least) of all the measurements in a document. If no MDU is specified for a measurement domain, the base SMU is used. For most applications these default units of time (second) and distance (meter) will be too imprecise.

The docmdu attribute of the **HyDoc** form specifies the MDUs to be used for all measurement domains used in the document. If the units used in a document vary widely, it is possible to override the docmdu setting for particular elements.

If the MDU is not a common denominator of all the measurements you actually use, those measurements are HyTime errors. However, a reasonable HyTime engine will respond intelligently to this problem: that is, it will report the error and perform the needed calculations with the possibility of round-off error, rather than crash and burn.

The increased accuracy of integer arithmetic has a price: the total range of magnitudes is much smaller than that of floating point values. If MDUs must be very small — perhaps because of the need to mix units with awkward ratios in the same measurement domain — then the total range of possible measurements can be quite small. For example, if the MDU for time is microseconds, then an hour is 3,600,000,000 MDUs and a 32-bit counter does not have sufficient range for the full duration of a two and a half hour movie. To address this problem HyTime has a special parameter hyqcnt that is set in the HyTime version declaration. The value of hyqcnt is the number of bits that should be used to represent HyTime integers for calculation. The default value of hyqcnt is 32, but some applications may need to increase this if they need high precision over a large dynamic range.

13.3 Axes and finite coordinate spaces

In Chapter 6 we discussed the HyTime notion of an axis that defines an addressable range of quanta. In order to handle scheduling and alignment of objects, HyTime has adopted a model for space and time that is based on finite axes that each define an addressable range in a given measurement domain. A **finite coordinate space** is a set of such axes. For instance, a simple sound editing program might define a single time axis against which sounds would be scheduled. The following SGML declarations define the time axis of this simple one-dimensional space:

```
<!ELEMENT      time         - O EMPTY>
<!ATTLIST      time
    HyTime     NAME         #FIXED "axis"
    axismeas   CDATA        #FIXED "SISECOND"
    axisdim    CDATA        #FIXED "4000000">
```

The attributes of an **axis** element are #FIXED because each axis is part of the static definition of a coordinate space. This reflects the fact that axes are referenced by their GIs when defining a coordinate space. This means that all axis elements of a given element type are required to be the same, since otherwise there would be no way to resolve conflicts in the properties of individual instances of an axis. Although axis elements are always referred to by GI, and their relevant information is fully expressed in the DTD, we recommend that documents include explicit `axis` elements for clarity.

The `axisdim` attribute specifies the size of the axis in MDUs. We are assuming that the document element (of architectural form **HyDoc**) specifies the time domain's MDU as milliseconds. So this axis can have coordinates in the range of 1 to 4,000,000 milliseconds. The `axismeas` attribute specifies the measurement domain of the axis, and is required.

The following declaration uses this axis to define a one-dimensional space within which we can place schedules representing sequences of events:

```
<!ELEMENT       musicfcs      - - (evsched+)>
<!ATTLIST       musicfcs
    HyTime      NAME          #FIXED "fcs"
    id          ID            #IMPLIED
    fcsmdu      CDATA         #FIXED "SISECOND 1 1000"
    axisdefs    NAMES         #FIXED "time">
```

This declaration defines an element type `musifcs` which conforms to the **fcs** architectural form. Like **axis**, this form has #FIXED values for all its attributes. The `axisdefs` attribute lists the axes that define this space by GI — in this case the single axis `time`. The `fcsmdu` attribute is optional and specifies the default MDUs for the measurement domains of the axes of the **fcs** and the event schedules within the space. If the `fcsmdu` attribute is to be used to override the default MDU for this FCS, the `fcsmdu` option must be specified.

13.3.1 Multiple axes

HyTime is not restricted to one-dimensional axes, but extends its notions of measurement to any number of axes that an application may require. To use multiple axes the HyTime `manyaxes` option must be specified. Simply specifying `manyaxes` allows **fcs** forms to have any number of axes. If a limit to the number of axes is required, the option can also be specified with an explicit limit on the number of axes. For example the (partial) HyTime declaration:

```
<?HyTime sched manyaxes=3>
```

would limit the number of axes in an **fcs** to at most three.

Following is a simple description of a multiple-axis **fcs** that has two spatial dimensions (measured in 72nds of an inch) and a temporal dimension (measured in 60ths of a second). For brevity, granule definitions are not included (the relevant granule definitions appear in clause A.5 of the HyTime standard):

```
<!ELEMENT      x-axis       - O EMPTY>
<!ATTLIST      x-axis
    HyTime     NAME         #FIXED "axis"
    axismeas   CDATA        #FIXED "meter"
    axisdim    CDATA        #FIXED "640">

<!ELEMENT      y-axis       - O EMPTY>
<!ATTLIST      y-axis
    HyTime     NAME         #FIXED "axis"
    axismeas   CDATA        #FIXED "meter"
    axisdim    CDATA        #FIXED "480">

<!ELEMENT      time         - O EMPTY>
<!ATTLIST      time
    HyTime     NAME         #FIXED "axis"
    axismeas   CDATA        #FIXED "second"
    axisdim    CDATA        #FIXED "4000000">
<!ELEMENT      animate-fcs  - - (evsched+)>

<!ATTLIST      animate-fcs
    HyTime     NAME         #FIXED "fcs"
    id         ID           #IMPLIED
    fcsmdu     CDATA        #FIXED
                             "second 1 60 inch 1 72"
    axisdefs   NAMES        #FIXED
                             "x-axis y-axis time">
```

This FCS might be used to record the placement and movements of images on a display device. One new feature in this example is the use of the HMU defaulting rules. Since all the spatial axes of `animate-fcs` are measured to the same resolution, the axes do not specify an `axismdu`. The MDU for the axes then defaults to the MDU of `animate-fcs` for the relevant domain. Also note that an **fcs** element can declare an MDU for each measurement domain used. If an axis requires a different MDU from the default specified on the relevant `fcs` element, then it can override that default by specifying its own `axismdu` attribute.

13.3.2 Mathematical definition of axis and FCS

Mathematically speaking, the notions of axis and FCS are simple. An axis is simply the subset of the integers from 1 to some maximum value and an FCS is simply the Cartesian product of the elements of several axes. These notions correspond to fundamental entities of set theory (although with a more complex notation), and so can be applied to modeling many different situations. For example, we will see in Section 13.5 that FCSs provide a reasonable model for tables.

13.4 Events and extents

An FCS must be able to describe the positions and sizes of objects within the space. The Scheduling module provides the facilities to create **event schedules**, which are fixed assignments of objects to regions of an FCS, each such region defined by fixed ranges along each of the axes. In a normal space with perpendicular axes such regions are generalized rectangles or cubes.

The HyTime model is that at presentation time, data objects are rendered into the real space and/or time corresponding to the FCS into which they are scheduled. An **event** is the association of a data object (whose semantics and rendering are defined by the application) with a particular **extent** within that space. Each extent is defined by a dimension along each of the axes of the space. Remember from the discussion of basic measurement that HyTime uses the term "dimension" in the sense of an engineering drawing, to mean a size along a particular axis. Figure 13.1 shows an extent positioned within an FCS.

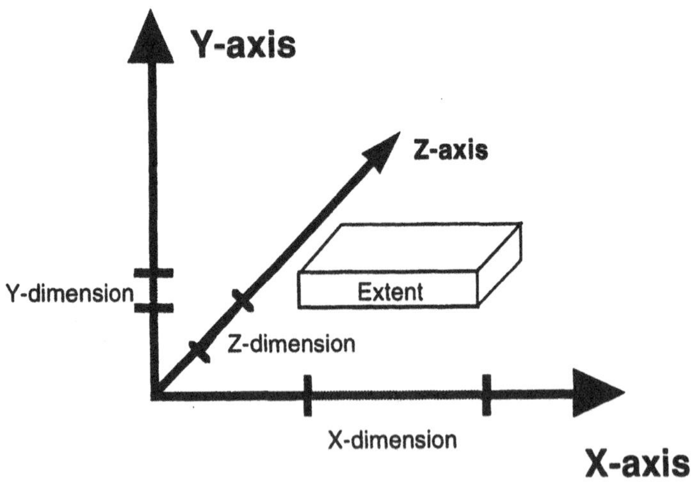

Figure 13.1: An extent within an FCS with three axes

13.4.1 Event schedules

The data objects to be displayed by the rendering of a HyTime schedule can be represented in any way required by the application. An event schedule is represented by an element of the **evsched** architectural form. An **evsched** is a sequence of events, each containing or referencing an object to be rendered.

Many element forms are involved in specifying a complete schedule. The following example is broken into parts followed by their explanations. We declare a single axis FCS for time, with single minute precision and a four hour addressable range:

```
<!ELEMENT      time         - O EMPTY>
<!ATTLIST      time
    HyTime     NAME         #FIXED "axis"
    axismeas   CDATA        #FIXED "SISECOND"
    axisdim    CDATA        #FIXED "240">

<!ELEMENT      musicfcs     - - (evsched+)>
<!ATTLIST      musicfcs
    HyTime     NAME         #FIXED "fcs"
    id         ID           #IMPLIED
    axisdefs   NAMES        #FIXED "time">
```

As we saw before, a finite coordinate space defines the axes of a space; the content of an `fcs` element is a schedule of events, which could be declared as follows:

```
<!ELEMENT      evsched      - - (event+)>
<!ATTLIST      evsched
    HyTime     NAME         #FIXED "evsched"
    id         ID           #IMPLIED
    axisord    CDATA        #FIXED "time">
    basegran   CDATA        #FIXED "minute"
    gran2hmu   NUMBERS      #FIXED "1 1">
```

Each event schedule defines its measurement properties for each axis of the space. The `basegran` and `gran2hmu` attributes specify the HMU to be used by all measurements on each axis in the schedule. `Basegran` specifies the name of a known granule, and `gran2hmu` specifies the number of HMUs per granule. For simplicity the ratio in this example is defined so that the FCS, axis, and event schedule all use the same units of measurement. If the value of `gran2hmu` were "`60 1`" the schedule would specify the positions of events in hours rather than minutes.

The ability to define different units for different schedules does not negate the requirement that the MDU of the FCS be a common denominator of them. The **evsched** form also takes the `axisord` attribute, which defines the order in which axis coordinates will be specified.

The final thing that needs to be specified is the form of an event. There is a lot of leeway in how events are defined (the architectural form has a `%HyBrid;` content model), but we use an EMPTY element and a single ENTITY attribute called `data` which names the data to be rendered. Supporting elements and attributes are also required:

```
<!ELEMENT       event          - O EMPTY>
<!ATTLIST       event
    HyTime      NAME           #FIXED "event"
    id          ID             #IMPLIED
    data        ENTITY         #REQUIRED
    exspec      IDREFS         #IMPLIED>

<!ELEMENT       extlist        - - (dimspec+)>
<!ATTLIST       extlist
    HyTime      NAME           #FIXED "extlist"
    id          ID             #IMPLIED>
```

An `event` element specifies a list of extents into which its data should be rendered, by referring to `extlist` elements. A single event can have several extents if it recurs in the schedule. An `extlist` always represents a series of `dimspecs`, one for each dimension of the schedule.

For simplicity, we have not shown the declarations of **dimspec** elements; they are explained in Section 6.3.2. We use minimization here to reduce clutter in the examples. With all these declarations in place, we can construct a simple schedule in a document:

```
...
<time id=time-axis>
<musicfcs>
    <evsched id=pop-concert>
       <event data=velocity-girl     exspec=act1>
       <event data=th-faith-healers exspec=act2>
       <event data=MBV              exspec=act3>
    </evsched>
</musicfcs>

<extlist id=act1><dimspec>  1 45</dimspec></extlist>
<extlist id=act2><dimspec> 61 45</dimspec></extlist>
<extlist id=act3><dimspec>121 60</dimspec></extlist>
```

This schedule places three events in two extents of 45 minutes and one of 60 minutes. The length of time from the start of the earliest event to the end of the last event is three hours total. The schedule has two gaps of 15 minutes. To fill both those gaps with a single data item we could add the following `event` to the schedule, and `extlist` elements to the document:

```
...
    <event data=bar-tape exspec="int1 int2">
...
<extlist id=int1><dimspec> 46 15</dimspec></extlist>
<extlist id=int2><dimspec>106 15</dimspec></extlist>
```

Linking to extents with fcsloc

In Section 8.4.5 we discuss the **fcsloc** form, which can be used to address portions of a data object by imposing a new FCS onto it and then specifying extents within that space. The extents are specified using the techniques just described, but in terms of the axes of the imposed FCS specified by the **fcsloc**, not in terms of the axes of the data object. The specified extent is then the referenced location. A simplified example is also available in Section 4.4.

13.4.2 Dimension references

An obvious inconvenience with schedules as presented so far is that all coordinate positions are scheduled with absolute numerical values even though there are *relative* constraints on the sizes and positions of events in schedules. For example, one event follows after another ends, or two events should always have the same length, or they should end at the same time. HyTime provides a wide range of features to handle such situations, but we examine just one feature in detail: dimension references.

A dimension reference can replace one of the markers (numerical values) in a **dimspec**. The dimension reference extracts one of the markers from another **dimspec** and uses it. This feature, in conjunction with the range of alignment specification methods possible with the different combinations of positive and negative markers, provides a way to express constraints between dimensions (and hence extents) as long as those involve making the endpoints or sizes of dimensions equal.

Dimension references are specified with the **dimref** architectural form, and their use requires that the `dimref` option of the Scheduling module be enabled. A **dimref** selects a value from a **dimspec** and copies the resulting number into the place where it appears. The **dimspec** to which a **dimref** refers is normalized to absolute coordinates. A dimension reference can select one of three different aspects of a dimension:

- Its starting point is always a positive number counting from that start of the axis forward to the point it describes.
- Its ending point is always a negative number counting backwards from the last value on the axis in question (recall from Section 6.3.2 that position –1 refers to the last quantum in a range).
- Its length is a positive number representing the length of the dimension.

This means, for instance, that selecting the second marker of a **dimspec** always yields a negative number because that is the normalized form of the dimspec.

The following example adjusts the schedule from the previous section to impose dependencies between the dimensions (remember that the original schedule simply placed five events so that they occupied three hours):

```
<extlist id=act1>
    <dimspec id=dim1>1 45</dimspec></extlist>

<extlist id=intermission1>
    <dimspec id=int1-dim>
       <dimref elemcomp=dim1 selcomp=last>
       15
    </dimspec></extlist>

<extlist id=act2>
    <dimspec id=dim2>
       <dimref elemcomp=int1-dim selcomp=last>
       45</dimspec></extlist>

<extlist id=intermission2>
    <dimspec id=int2-dim>
       <dimref elemcomp=dim2 selcomp=last>
       15</dimspec></extlist>

<extlist id=act3>
    <dimspec id=dim3>
       <dimref elemcomp=int2-dim selcomp=last>
       60</dimspec></extlist>
```

Attributes of dimref

Each `dimref` element has two critical attributes. The first is `elemcomp`, an IDREF which specifies the `dimspec` from which the marker is to be copied. The second is `selcomp`, which specifies what information from the `dimspec` is needed. The values that `selcomp` can take are:

`first` selects the first marker of the dimension

`last`	selects the last marker of the dimension
`qcnt`	selects the "quantum count," in other words, the length of the dimension

Notice that each first marker of every extent other than the first simply refers back to the last marker of the previous event. These definitions show that all five events are a chain, and once the starting point of the first is fixed all the rest are positioned relative to that, adjusted according to the lengths of their extents. This method of specifying constraints is a consequence of HyTime's fundamental approach to scheduling, which is that a schedule is an idealized representation of how things are *supposed* to be. If an event must be delayed or change its length due to rendering difficulties, a HyTime engine should preserve the constraints on event placement. To allow such rendering strategies, the constraints must be made explicit.

The example schedule above actually misrepresents the constraints of the desired schedule, since in a concert the endpoints of the intermissions are fixed by the adjacent events, not by a desired duration. This can also be expressed by **dimref**, but to do so requires an additional feature that we have not yet examined.

The problem is that the `last` marker of the intermission should get its value from the `first` marker of the following extent, which has a positive value; however, under the rules for **dimspec** a negative value is needed to fix the end of the intermission by position, rather than length.

The flip attribute

HyTime's solution to this problem is an additional attribute of the **dimref** form called `flip`, which can have the values `flip` and `noflip`. The default value is `noflip`; specifying `flip` causes the normalized form of the attribute to be measured from the end of the axis towards the beginning. In accordance with the rules for **dimspec** elements this means that not only are the origins of the markers different, but their signs are interchanged: when measuring from the right end of the axis, the first marker is always negative and the second is always positive. We use `flip` in the following example to fix the previous schedule:

```
<time id=time-axis>
<musicfcs>
     <evsched id=pop-concert>
        <event data=velocity-girl     exspec=act1>
        <event data=th-faith-healers exspec=act2>
        <event data=MBV               exspec=act3>
     </evsched>
</musicfcs>
```

```
<extlist id=act1>
    <dimspec id=dim1>1 45</dimspec></extlist>

<extlist id=intermission1>
    <dimspec id=int1-dim>
       <dimref elemcomp=dim1 selcomp=last>
       <dimref flip=flip elemcomp=dim2 selcomp=first>
    </dimspec></extlist>

<extlist id=act2>
    <dimspec id=dim2>61 45</dimspec></extlist>

<extlist id=intermission2>
    <dimspec id=int2-dim>
       <dimref elemcomp=dim2 selcomp=last>
       <dimref flip=flip elemcomp=dim3 selcomp=first>
       </dimspec></extlist>

extlist id=act3>
    <dimspec id=dim3>106 60</dimspec></extlist>
```

This schedule specifies the start and end of the intermissions as derived from the start and end of the musical events. This allows a rendering engine to handle intermissions properly even if there are irregularities in the scheduling of the events on which they are based.

Limitations of dimref

There is a problem with the example we have just shown. Because **dimref** copies coordinates without modification, it can only schedule an event so that one of its ends occupies the *same* quantum as the first or last quantum of another event's extent. For some applications it may be preferable to schedule events so as not to overlap.

Consider scheduling 45 minutes of performance and 15 minutes of canned applause to form a 60 minute program. If the performance occupies minutes 1 through 45, the applause should occupy minutes 46 through 60. But one cannot use **dimref** to obtain the value 46 from the scheduled extent of the performance: only 45 or –16 (representing the same quantum, but measuring from opposite ends of the space).

Because **dimref** gives no way to increment or decrement coordinates it can schedule events that overlap by a single quantum, but not events that are adjacent. To do that one must use the HyOp or HyFunk features to perform calculations on coordinates. We discuss these features briefly in Section 13.6, and show how to use HyFunk to address this particular problem.

13.5 Representing tables

The notion of a finite coordinate space is very similar to a standard table: a rectangular space is divided into rectangular subunits, with data associated with regions of that space. Representing tables is often problematic because of cells that span several columns or rows. Occasionally even non-rectangular cells are required. The typical SGML method using a hierarchy of rows (or columns) that contains the columns (or rows) of a table is not very satisfactory. Cells that span rows or columns are difficult to represent, and such a representation, by making a hierarchy of rows and columns, implicitly subordinates one to the other, which does not correspond well to the way tables work.

HyTime can avoid many of these problems by declaring a finite coordinate space using generic quanta as measurement domain. The quanta are the smallest units of the table, so that any division between cells anywhere in the table corresponds to a boundary between quanta along the axes of the table. For instance, the following table has a fundamental grid of 4 columns by 5 rows:

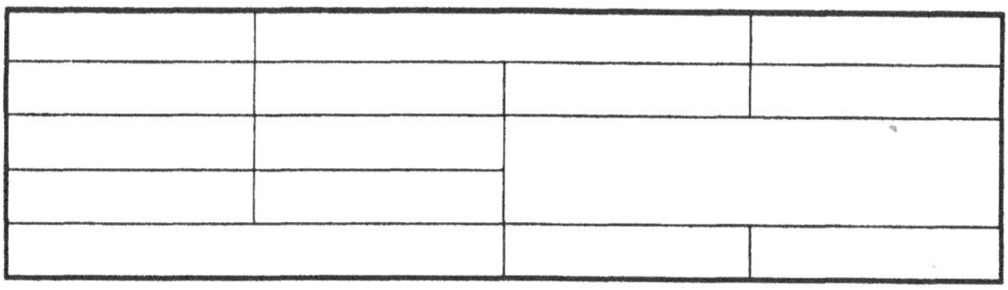

The table itself can be represented by a schedule that associates cell contents with extents in the grid. A cell can be scheduled into several extents to indicate that its content should flow to fill a non-rectangular or even discontiguous area. This approach is conceptually similar to the table markup described in clause 4.11.8 of ISO standard "ISO/IEC TR 9573-11: Techniques for using SGML." Alternatively, such multiple extents can be used to indicate that the cell's content should be fully duplicated into the rectangular area specified by each of the extents. The distinction is a matter of the application's formatting choices (we follow the second strategy in the example below).

Although this is a very powerful technique for representing tables, it also has some problems. Since a HyTime FCS is defined by an element with all of its attributes #FIXED in the DTD, using an FCS of the exact size of each separate table would require a large number of different element declarations: one per table. A better approach is to declare a single FCS with axes long enough for the largest table needed. Each individual table is then represented by a schedule in this generic space. HyTime limits each **fcs** element type to a single instance in a document unless the `splitfcs` option is specified. With this option, each table can be represented by an instance of its `fcs` element containing the schedule representing that table. Without this option, the schedules representing tables would all have to be placed in the single table `fcs` element. When using finite coordinate spaces to represent tables we recommend the `splitfcs` option.

The following example declares a table FCS (using the `cell` unit of the `gquantum` measurement domain):

```
<!ELEMENT       rows          - O EMPTY>
<!ATTLIST       rows
    HyTime      NAME          #FIXED "axis"
    axismeas    CDATA         #FIXED "cell"
    axisdim     CDATA         #FIXED "100000">

<!ELEMENT       cols          - O EMPTY>
<!ATTLIST       cols
    HyTime      NAME          #FIXED "axis"
    axismeas    CDATA         #FIXED "cell"
    axisdim     CDATA         #FIXED "100000">

<!ELEMENT       tablefcs      - - (table+)>
<!ATTLIST       tablefcs
    HyTime      NAME          #FIXED "fcs"
    id          ID            #IMPLIED
    fcsmdu      CDATA         #FIXED "cell 1 1"
    axisdefs    NAMES         #FIXED "rows cols">
```

In this example the `tablefcs` element type refers to the two axes, `rows` and `columns`, and contains a list of `table` elements. The `table` elements are of the **evsched** form and contain the cell data of the table. The remaining declarations follow:

```
<!ELEMENT       table         - - (cell+)>
<!ATTLIST       table
    HyTime      NAME          #FIXED "evsched"
    id          ID            #IMPLIED
    axisord     CDATA         #FIXED "rows cols">
    basegran    CDATA         #FIXED "cell"
    gran2hmu    NUMBERS       #FIXED "1 1">
```

```
<!ELEMENT      cell          - O #PCDATA>
<!ATTLIST      cell
     HyTime    NAME          #FIXED "event"
     id        ID            #IMPLIED
     exspec    IDREFS        #IMPLIED>

<!ELEMENT      extlist       - - (#PCDATA)>
<!ATTLIST      extlist
     HyTime    NAME          #FIXED "extlist"
     id        ID            #IMPLIED>
```

The remaining declarations declare `evsched` elements to represent tables and `event` elements to represent cells. The HMU of a table schedule is a single cell. We have taken advantage of HyTime's abbreviation facilities to put markers directly into the `extlist` element, rather than using explicit `dimspecs`.

To create a table using these declarations, an `fcs` element needs to be created to hold the schedule, which in turn contains the cells. The extent lists that place the cells within the table go outside the FCS but, in well encoded documents, nearby.

Following we show an example of a chart of software quality compared by the major and minor parts of software revision numbers like 1.0:

<table>
<tr><td></td><td colspan="4">Minor Rev.</td></tr>
<tr><td>Major Rev.</td><td>0</td><td>1</td><td>2</td><td>3</td></tr>
<tr><td>1</td><td rowspan="3">buggy</td><td>buggy</td><td>pretty buggy</td><td>pretty stable</td></tr>
<tr><td>2</td><td>pretty buggy</td><td>pretty stable</td><td>stable</td></tr>
<tr><td>3</td><td>pretty stable</td><td colspan="2">N/A</td></tr>
</table>

This table needs a coordinate space with five rows and five columns; (which we will count from top to bottom and left to right). There is one vertical spanning cell, reflecting the proverbial reliability of software with version numbers that end in zero, and two horizontal spanning cells, the column header and the `N/A` cell.

The content of each cell is chosen from a small set of values, some of which repeat in different cells of the table. The table's data could be marked up as follows:

```
<tablefcs><table id=rev-table>
    <cell exspec=major>Major Rev.</cell>
    <cell exspec=minor>Minor Rev.</cell>
    <cell exspec=label0>0</cell>
... <!-- other numerical labels omitted --> ...
    <cell exspec=buggy>buggy</cell>
    <cell exspec=pretty-buggy>pretty buggy</cell>
    <cell exspec=stable>stable</cell>
    <cell exspec=pretty-stable>pretty stable</cell>
    <cell exspec=na>N/A</cell>
</table></tablefcs>
```

Cells in this table point by IDREF to the following extent lists, which associate the cells with the extent(s) they are to occupy in the cell grid. Each extent consists of two **dimspec** specifications, the first for the row number and the second for the column number (in accordance with the `axisord` attribute declared for the `table` element type). The **dimspec** elements themselves are optional, and we leave them out for brevity:

```
<extlist id=major>
    <extent>2 1 1 1</extent></extlist>
<extlist id=minor>
    <extent>1 1 2 4</extent></extlist>
<extlist id=label0>
    <extent>2 1 2 1</extent></extlist>
... <!-- other numerical labels omitted --> ...

<extlist id=buggy>
    <extent>3 3 2 1</extent>
    <extent>3 1 2 1</extent></extlist>
<extlist id=pretty-buggy>
    <extent>4 1 3 1</extent>
    <extent>3 1 4 1</extent></extlist>
<extlist id=pretty-stable>
    <extent>3 1 5 1</extent></extlist>
    <extent>4 1 4 1</extent></extlist>
    <extent>5 1 3 1</extent></extlist>
<extlist id=stable>
    <extent>4 1 5 1</extent></extlist>
<extlist id=na>
    <extent>5 1 4 2</extent></extlist>
```

This rather long example places the captions and the contents of the cells onto a base grid. IDREFs connect each cell to a list of the extents at which that cell's contents should be rendered. For example, the header "`Major Rev.`" has one extent at the coordinates starting at row 2, column 1, that is 1 quantum long along each of the axes. Its marker list is equivalent to the following **dimspec** elements:

```
<extlist id=major>
    <extent>
       <dimspec>2 1</dimspec>
       <dimspec>1 1</dimspec></extent></extlist>
```

The cell content "buggy" is more interesting because it is repeated in two different cells, one of which is a vertical span covering three rows.

Another feature to note is that the headers are explicitly included in this table. A more complex, but more useful solution would define two element types `cell` and `header`, both of the **event** architectural form. With this information an application could search either table cells or table headers at the user's request, as the difference would be clear.

There are also many table formatting issues that a full-fledged solution would have to address, whether with additional elements or attributes — we have not considered such details here. If custom axes were used for each table instance (rather than the generic FCS used in this example) then the axes themselves could record the header information in whatever way is convenient for the program. This method is probably preferable except for the practical problem that each such axis definition requires a new element to be defined. This would make the use of a common DTD impossible, and rule out the technique for many applications and environments.

13.6 Marker functions

Among the most important and powerful of the scheduling features are **marker functions.** These are described in clause 7.4.1.3, and allow far more complex constraints on schedules than are possible with the **dimref** form. Like a **dimref**, a marker function occurs in place of a coordinate for a **dimspec**, but unlike a **dimref** a marker function can execute an arbitrary program to determine its value. HyTime provides two particular languages for creating marker function programs: HyOp and HyFunk. Using either of them requires setting the `markfun` option of the Measurement module.

13.6.1 HyOp

HyOp is defined in clause A.4.1, and allows marker values to be combined by a single arithmetic operator that is expressed by an SGML element of type `HyOp`. Using it requires setting the `HyOp` option.

The HyOp element conforms to the **markfun** form. It takes an opname attribute that specifies what operator should be applied from among the names listed in the next section. The element's content lists the operands as any number of **marklist** elements. These may in turn contain other elements including dimension references).

13.6.2 HyFunk

HyFunk is a language for functional expressions, defined in clause A.4.2. HyFunk includes a lexical type syntax and an element type that can express complex arithmetic functions. HyFunk provides a more palatable syntax for combinations of operations that would require many levels of nested HyOp markers, although the same functions are available. Like HyQ, HyFunk supports macros; like HyOp, it supports basic mathematical operators. It also provides functions that correspond to the various forms of **dimref**. Using it requires setting the HyFunk option.

The mathematical operators of HyFunk (and HyOp) are avg, decr, div, incr, max, min, mod, mult, abs, nabs, rand, subt and sum. These have the behaviors one would expect given their names. Avg rounds the result of averaging its operands; div truncates after dividing its first operand by its second. HyFunk function names are always preceded by "@" to distinguish them from content tokens.

The following example applies HyFunk to address the problem we discussed in Section 13.4.2, of scheduling events next to each other rather than overlapping. We first define a HyFunk macro called onepast that takes an IDREF as its sole argument. It uses the @last() function of HyFunk to resolve that IDREF in the fashion of a dimension reference, obtaining the normalized last coordinate. It then adds one to that value and returns the result (thus pointing to the quantum immediately following the end of the referenced scheduled extent). HyFunk syntax shares some characteristics with HyQ, for example using %n to refer to the nth argument of a macro, as well as using the function attribute list form to define macros:

```
<HyFunk fn=onepast> @sum(@last(%1) 1) </HyFunk>
```

In addition to @last(), HyFunk provides @first() and @qcnt() for the other options of dimension referencing, and functions for the same options assuming flip=flip: @flfirst(), @fllast(), and @flqcnt().

The onepast macro can be used to correct the placement of the first intermission from the example in Section 13.4.2:

```
<extlist id=act1>
    <dimspec id=dim1>1 45</dimspec></extlist>

<extlist id=intermission1>
    <dimspec id=int1-dim>
       <HyFunk usefn=onepast args=act1>
       15
    </dimspec></extlist>
```

The `usefn` attribute of `HyFunk` specifies the macro to execute, and the `args` attribute gives the arguments to pass it, each of which must be either an integer or an IDREF.

13.7 Other features

This section gives an overview of some of the scheduling features that we do not discuss in detail. It is intended to provide a directory of features of the standard that may be worth further investigation for specific applications.

13.7.1 Calendars

A special form of axis, a **calendar**, is available to represent time data that is not relative but tied to a particular historical point on a time scale. The time axis of a calendar is measured from a base point specified using **UTC (Coordinated Universal Time)**. The HMU of a calendar is not restricted by the choice of base date used.

Calendars also require their own versions of the standard dimension and marker references, since axis markers can be specified by dates as well as by numerical quantities.

13.7.2 Extent reconciliation

A number of attributes can be put on events to specify **extent reconciliation**, the degradation strategies a HyTime engine should follow when an event cannot be scheduled as desired. These can specify which alignment constraints are most important, whether the object to be rendered should be replaced with another one (that presumably is a better fit) or whether it should be cropped. For an event that is too small for its extent, they vary from repeating an event to fill the scheduled extent, to inserting a special padding event to fill the excess space.

Several elements can be attached to an event, each representing extent reconciliation policies and giving the application a choice of strategies in a given situation. The order in which the different strategies are tried and the determination of whether a strategy has been successful is an application detail which is not defined by HyTime. While this flexibility is necessary given the flux in this whole area, complete portability will require more detailed standards and conventions to be developed about how these facilities are to be applied.

13.7.3 Event projection

HyTime's **event projection** facility allows the representation of processes that reconfigure, reorder, or otherwise transform extents in an FCS. When the projection facilities are in use, extents within one event schedule are projected into another event schedule according to an application-defined rule. Different rules (called **projectors**) may apply to different regions of the source schedule. The set of all the rules that apply to a particular schedule is called a **baton**, by analogy with an orchestra conductor's baton that controls projection from the graphical space of a score into the temporal space of a musical performance.

Because event projectors are evaluated at rendition time, they can be used to represent situations where a needed extent is not known until rendition. For instance, a projector could be used to represent an extent such as the duration of a button depression. Then, at rendition time, the button would actually be depressed for some period, and the resulting event schedule (which might contain extents related to the duration of the button press) could finally be calculated. Less complex input could be handled without the projection capabilities of the Rendition module by using special marker functions (whose value would be calculated based on user input) to determine the dimensions of relevant extents.

13.7.4 Event modification

Event modification is a catch-all facility for representing effects that apply to the extents in a schedule in order to control how it is rendered for presentation. It differs from the projection facilities in that the transformations affect data objects rather than their extents. Each such effect has a unique name (assigned by the application) and is represented by a **wand**. Wands can be arbitrarily interconnected to create composite effects. The name wand reflects the fact that their effect is magical: it is entirely defined by particular HyTime applications.

14

The HyTime Base Module

14.1 Introduction

The **Base module** of HyTime includes syntactic parts used throughout the rest of HyTime, and is described in clause 6 of the standard. Many parts of it are best understood in relation to the other parts that use them, and these have already been explained. Among the constructs defined in the Base module are these:

- HyTime concepts and terminology (already described)
- the means for identifying a HyTime document and declaring needed options (already explained)
- the particular HyTime options that turn capabilities of the Base module on and off
- many **common attributes** that can apply to any HyTime element — because many of these are specialized features or optimization hints rather than additional capabilities, they require setting a corresponding option
- a small number of architectural forms for elements needed to support the common attributes

Many of the Base module's optional features are likely to be needed only occasionally. The most important exception is also simple: all HyTime elements have an optional ID attribute (also named `id`).

Each common attribute is part of some attribute architectural form, whose name always begins with "`all-`". Many common attributes can only be used if a corresponding option is set. We list all common attribute forms in Appendix A; their definitions in the HyTime standard are in clause 6.5. Some also require the use of closely related architectural forms for elements; we present those element forms along with the related attributes.

14.2 Entity trees

HyTime makes extensive use of the idea of collections of entities. HyTime uses the term **entity tree**, to mean the main document entity with its DTD, all the entities it declares, any entities that those declare and so forth. Technically, this entity "tree" may be a directed acyclic graph (since an entity may be re-used), but the idea is clear. If you collect all of these entities you have everything that is reachable from the starting point.

Since a truly complete entity tree may be very large, HyTime permits a hyperdocument to include all of such a tree, or only a subset, as desired. In either case the collection of entities is called a **bounded object set** or **BOS** (a complete BOS is a **HyTime BOS**; the set of entities that an application accesses is the **application BOS**).

14.3 Base module option summaries

The Base module options are described briefly below (based on clause 6.8). These descriptions are intended to give a brief overview of the module's parts, since it covers a wide variety of options. This section can be thought of as a menu that can help you decide which parts are relevant to your tasks. Descriptions appear in following sections, as referred to from the corresponding summaries.

14.3.1 The context option

Permits using the `context` common attribute, which governs how HyTime tests validity with respect to the meta-content models printed in the standard (as opposed to SGML validation, which applies only to actual SGML content models in a DTD). This option is discussed in clause 6.5.1 and Section 14.4.5 below.

14.3.2 The lextype option

Permits defining and using lexical models and lexical types, for example to validate the form of particular attributes or content, using the `lextype` and `lextypgi` common attributes. HyTime uses lexical types to specify the legal values for many attributes. Thus `lextype` is needed to understand the HyTime standard even if you do not use it to validate your documents. This option is discussed in clause 6.5.2, Chapter 11, and Section 14.5 below.

14.3.3 The HyLex option

Permits using `HyLex`, a particular notation HyTime defines for expressing lexical type models that describe string patterns in a way somewhat similar to regular expressions. HyTime uses `HyLex` to express constraints on attribute values and occasionally content of HyTime elements; applications can also use other lexical modeling languages. This option is discussed in clause A.1 and in Section 11.5.

14.3.4 The lexord option

Permits using lexical ordering definitions to control how character strings are sorted, compared, or otherwise processed. This permits you to ignore case or accent distinctions, to reconcile character sets for comparison or sorting, and so on. Thus `lexord` is especially important for use with lexical type checking, querying and sorting.

Lexical ordering can be used with the **`lexmodel`** architectural form and as a parameter to the HyQ comparison functions. A lexical ordering specification points to an element of form **`lexord`**, which contains a translation table that HyTime applies to operands before any comparison, pattern match, or other testing. This option is discussed in clause 6.5.2.2 and in Section 14.7.

14.3.5 The refctl option

Permits using the `refrange`, `reflevel`, and `reftype` common attributes, which let a HyTime engine do special checking for how IDREF attributes are used (beyond that known to an SGML system). This option is discussed in clause 6.5.3 and in Section 14.8.

14.3.6 The exidrefs option

Permits attributes that are semantically IDREFs to point outside the current document. This requires setting the `refctl` option, and setting the `refrange` common attribute to `X` when external values are used (see below for information on the `refrange` attribute). External reference is normally indirect, as shown in Section 4.3 and elsewhere: one element points to an external document entity and another finds a given ID relative to it.

HyTime options such as `exidrefs` do not affect SGML parsing. Therefore any attribute that is declared *in the DTD* to be of type IDREF must still be a direct reference to some ID in the same document. The `exidrefs` option affects only attributes that are IDREFs for HyTime but not SGML. It thus can affect attributes declared as type NAME or CDATA, or even text content, so long as these have HyTime meaning as IDREFs. This option is discussed in clause 6.5.3 and in Section 14.8.

14.3.7 The dvlist option

Permits overriding SGML's way of assigning default values to attributes, using the `sibdvl` and `subdvl` common attributes. This option is defined in clause 6.5.5 of the HyTime standard. We do not discuss it.

14.3.8 The desctxt option

Permits an element to declare via the `desctxt` attribute that its content is to be taken from some other element. HyTime locates that element indirectly, by treating the value of the `desctxt` attribute as a name in a lookup table. This option is defined in clause 6.5.6 of the HyTime standard. We do not discuss it.

14.3.9 The activity option

Permits an element to use the `activity` common attribute to declare that systems should do something when the element is created, modified, deleted, linked, accessed, or unlinked. The application must define what constitutes one of these events, and how and when the associated activity tracking action is to be executed. This option is discussed in clause 6.5.7 and in Section 14.9.

14.3.10 The dcnatts option

Permits using certain attributes that apply not to elements at all, but to entities. These are called **data attributes**, apply to external entity declarations, and are one of the less well known features of SGML. The syntax of such attributes is defined in the sole amendment to SGML.

The HyTime data attributes appear in two lists, defined in clause 6.6 of the HyTime standard; we do not treat them in any detail:

`sbento` — Attributes for defining granularity for partitioning compound entities into sub-parts, such as by the byte.

`any-dcn` — Attributes for individual entity declarations that permit specifying a wide variety of information about how to parse, interpret, decode and process the entity.

14.3.11 The xpropdef option

Permits using the **propdef** architectural form to define new named properties. The **proploc** form from the Location address module and the `Proploc()` function of HyQ can access such properties. Custom properties must also be implemented in a HyTime engine that uses them. This option is discussed in clause 6.7; we discuss property definition in Section 11.8.

14.3.12 The HyPD option

If the `xpropdef` option is also specified, then the `HyPD` option permits using HyTime's `HyPD` element type, a particular element type conforming to the **propdef** form. HyTime itself uses `HyPD` elements to illustrate declarations for the inherent properties that a HyTime engine calculates and stores with various data objects. This option is discussed in clauses A.2 and 6.7.2 of the HyTime standard; we discuss property definition in Section 11.8.

14.3.13 The unparsed option

Permits certain HyTime operations to refer to the unparsed form of SGML documents. HyTime capabilities such as counting through words or characters of data (see the **dataloc** form in section 8.4.1) normally use the Element Structure Information Set (ESIS) of a document, which is a well formed tree of elements, pseudo-elements, and data entities. The ESIS expresses the essential structure and content of an SGML document, abstracting away from such syntax details as how markup was entered. For many reasons, including the fact that HyTime does not standardize non-ESIS information about documents, we do not recommend using this option. This option is discussed in clause A.2.1.2.3.

We now proceed to a more detailed discussion of the individual attribute list architectural forms defined in the Base module, and invoked through the options just described.

14.4 The all-id attribute form: identification attributes

The identification attributes include not only attributes to identify elements, but also to perform a wide range of globally applicable functions. A more precise description of the attributes in the **`all-id`** attribute list form is that it contains all the common attributes that do not require any HyTime options in order to be used. None of these attributes is optional in the sense that a HyTime engine can ignore them if present. All are optional in the sense that they need not be declared on any HyTime element unless required by the definition of a particular architectural form. The `all-id` attributes are discussed in clause 6.5.1.

14.4.1 The ID attribute

Any HyTime element type may declare and use an SGML ID attribute. This is required in many cases by the definitions of architectural forms. This is by far the most important of the common attributes.

14.4.2 The notation attribute

Any HyTime element type may declare that its content is in a non-SGML notation, such as a bitmap representation, a regular expression or programming language, or anything else. Any such content must, however, avoid strings that an SGML parser would mistakenly recognize as markup. That is, no part of the data content may look like an SGML delimiter that would confuse the SGML parser, such as "</".

The HyTime `notation` attribute uses the standard SGML technique for this purpose except that the attribute *need not* have a declared value of NOTATION. If it does not, only HyTime is aware that the content is in some other notation — SGML is not aware of this. It seems advisable to take advantage of SGML's feature, and so we recommend that if this attribute is used it always have declared value NOTATION even though HyTime does not formally require it.

For example, it is possible to include a bitmap image directly in an SGML file, rather than referring to it using an entity. One trivial way of ensuring that the data does not contain prohibited strings such as "</" is to convert every byte of the image data into two hexadecimal digits. Many interchange formats do this, such as encapsulated PostScript™ bitmaps, RTF graphics, and uuencoded files.

Such data cannot confuse an SGML parser using the reference concrete syntax or most likely variations, because the data contains only digits and the letters A-F, never characters from SGML delimiters such as "<" and "&". The fact that the content is a bitmap, not character content, must then be expressed using the `notation` attribute. This attribute's value must always be a notation name that was declared in the DTD, as shown here:

```
<!NOTATION      bitmap      PUBLIC
    ...>

...
<graphic notation=bitmap>
    0000ffff0000ffff...
</graphic>
```

The SGML or HyTime implementation can pass this data to an appropriate processor when needed. The data can be easily converted back to plain binary form and then displayed in whatever way is appropriate. Many other ways of converting data so as not to conflict with SGML parsing rules also exist, most of them more compact than this simple example.

14.4.3 The delims attribute

The `delims` attribute is meaningful only in conjunction with the preceding `notation` attribute. If some particular notation uses named delimiter strings (similar to SGML), then those delimiter strings can be redefined by specifying a list of names an new values on this attribute. This can be useful to avoid colliding with SGML delimiters such as "<".

As one example, some common notations use "\" to mean that a following character should be taken literally. If data in such a notation appeared within a HyTime element, one could change it to "`!`" in this way (thus causing the "`.`" in the expression to be literal rather than a wildcard):

```
<regex HyTime=HyBrid delims="ESCAPE !">
    ^[TD]!. D[eu]r[oa][sn][ed]
</regex>
```

The `HyLex` element discussed in section 11.5 uses a notation with this kind of delimiters, and we give more complete examples there of how to use the `delims` attribute.

14.4.4 The conloc attribute

HyTime defines an extension to SGML minimization in the `conloc` attribute. When `conloc` is present a HyTime engine examines the element *pointed at* to calculate the content of the element that *specifies* the `conloc` attribute. Syntactically this makes use of SGML's #CONREF attribute default value; however, the restriction that the attribute be an IDREF and the particular meaning that the target of the IDREF should be treated as if it were the content are HyTime extensions.

This HyTime extension of #CONREF attributes permits reusing any HyTime construct (so long as it contains no ID attributes or context-sensitive SGML structures such as #CURRENT, USEMAP, certain minimizations, and so on).

Given these declarations a HyTime engine would treat the two following `warning` elements as the same (although an SGML parser would not):

```
<!ELEMENT       warning        - - (#PCDATA)>
<!ATTLIST       warning
    priority    NUMBER         #REQUIRED
    conloc      IDREF          #CONREF
    HyTime      NAME           #FIXED "HyBrid">

...
<warning priority=1>Beware of Trojans</warning>
...
<warning priority=1 conloc=warn37>
...
<p id=warn37>Beware of Trojans</p>
```

HyTime defines special processing for such referenced elements to ensure that the content conforms to the content model of the referencing element. To that end, HyTime:

a) tests whether the destination *itself* satisfies the content model (if so it is used)

b) tests whether the destination's *content* satisfies the content model (if so it is used)

c) reports an error

In the example above, the `conloc` attribute points to a `p` element, not merely #PCDATA, so (a) is not satisfied. But because the content of the `p` element is only #PCDATA, (b) is satisfied and the content "`Beware of Trojans`" was thus the result. HyTime does not treat the `p` element itself as part of the referenced content for the `warning` element.

This set of conventions can save some space should data be reused many times, yet not be an entity. It can become confusing if overused or used in a non-obvious way:

```
<nameloc id=nl7>tgt1 tgt2</nameloc>

<nameloc id=nl8 conloc=tgt-list.1>
...
<p id=tgt-list.1 conloc=tgt-list.2>
...
<p id=tgt-list.2>tgt1 tgt2</>
```

Both forms mean the same thing to HyTime, but the second is confusing because its content is hard to find, and because the p element cannot be recognized as consisting of IDREFs without knowing about the **nameloc** in advance and working through the interpretation rules. In fact the content of the paragraph could be treated as IDREFs in this case, while the paragraph itself treated it as text information, and a conloc somewhere else treated the same content in another completely different way (perhaps as the name of a property).

Other HyTime methods of indirect reference, such as lexical type names, location ladders, and other #CONREF attributes can be combined with conloc but the results can be subtle.

14.4.5 The context attribute

This attribute applies only when the context option is set. If the context attribute's value is context instead of its default value ncontext, then a validating HyTime engine checks "whether the content of the element (if any) must be valid in the context in which the element occurs, in both the DTD and the meta-DTD." Since SGML itself enforces validity with respect to the DTD, the ncontext value serves to turn off HyTime validation for the element.

Context affects HyTime validation only; it is not an SGML error for any element to violate HyTime meta-content models.

14.4.6 The HyNames attribute

This attribute permits renaming other HyTime attributes. HyTime depends on attribute names to find information, for example, it expects the linkend attribute of a link element which points to the destination of a link. If it is necessary to change this name, the HyNames attribute can inform the HyTime engine by adding an attribute declaration:

```
<!ELEMENT     clink        - - ANY>
<!ATTLIST     clink
    target    IDREF        #REQUIRED
    HyTime    NAME         #FIXED "clink"
    HyNames   CDATA        #FIXED "linkend target">
```

```
...
<xref target=chap12>
```

The HyNames attribute is a list of pairs: the first item in each pair is the HyTime name for the attribute that is to be renamed; the second item is the new name. Given the declaration above, when HyTime sees the xref element it knows to treat it as a subclass of **clink** because of the HyTime attribute, and it knows to look for the linkend value in the target attribute.

It is also possible to declare that some value HyTime would normally expect on an attribute is instead found in content (the reverse is not possible). For example, instead of placing the linkend value in another attribute as just shown, you could put it in content (so long as the content is not used for something else and so long as you do not need SGML validation of the IDREF values):

```
<!ELEMENT clink - - (#PCDATA)>
<!ATTLIST clink
    HyTime   NAME  #FIXED "clink"
    HyNames  CDATA #FIXED "linkend #content">
...
<xref>chap12</xref>
```

The HyNames attribute cannot be used to rename itself, because HyTime must be able to find it. In the unlikely event that the name HyNames is already used, the HyTime architectural form attribute can be renamed by specifying the new name in the SGML declaration as discussed in Sections 5.6.1 and 10.3.2.

14.5 The all-lex attribute form

If the lextype option is set, the lextype and lextypgi attributes can be used to enable a validating HyTime engine to ensure that the attributes and/or content of an element fit defined lexical patterns. In HyTime such restrictions can be specified using lexical model expressions. Many useful lexical models are built in, and can be used by name; you can define new ones using the **lexmodel** element form.

Many examples of lexical type specifications occur throughout the HyTime standard itself, because HyTime uses lexical types to specify the legal values for various attributes. Lexical types are thus needed to understand the HyTime standard; we discuss them in detail in Sections 11.2-11.6. The HyTime standard defines all-lex in clause 6.5.2.

14.6 The lexmodel architectural form

The **lexmodel** element form provides a container within which individual lexical models are defined. Each `lexmodel` element has an `ltn` attribute that gives its name (which must be unique within the set of all `ltn` attribute values defined on instances of the same element type). Its content is the lexical model expression. Optional attributes include `lexord` for managing character-set conversion issues, and `boundary`, which determines whether the expression must account for the entire string being tested, or merely be contained in it.

We discuss lexical models in Sections 11.2-11.4, and the HyLex lexical modeling language in Section 11.5. The HyTime standard defines **lexmodel** in clause 6.5.2.1.

14.7 The lexord architectural form

Lexical orderings control the way in which strings of characters are sorted, compared, or otherwise processed. HyTime's lexical ordering feature allows definition of lexical orderings, and is defined in clause 6.5.2.2. By setting the `lexord` option and then defining orderings using `lexord` elements, you can choose to ignore case and accent distinctions, to reconcile character sets of various languages for comparison and sorting, and so on. This is a very important feature, especially in combination with lexical type checking, querying, and sorting.

A lexical ordering specification points to an element of form **lexord** that contains a translation table that HyTime applies to operands before any comparison, pattern match, or other testing. As an alternative to such a pointer, the forms that use `lexord` can specify the reserved word `#SGMLCASE'`, indicating that the SGML case translation table of the active document is to be used as described in Section 11.4.

Lexical ordering can be used in these ways:

- with the **lexmodel** form (and usually HyLex)
- as a parameter to the HyQ comparison, `Match()`, or `HyLex()` functions

A **lexord** definition element consists of a list of `grapheme` elements Each of these specifies the sort position to be used for a character or significant string from the input.

For example, a lexical ordering definition can "fold" characters to upper-case before comparison. For the widely used ISO 646 character set such a **lexord** would translate the lower-case letters `a-z` (coded as decimal numbers 97-122) into the corresponding upper-case letters `A-Z` (coded as 65-90). The input characters go on the gs attribute and the value to be substituted goes on the gck attribute:

```
<lexord id=upcase>
    <grapheme gs="&#97;" gck=65>
    <grapheme gs=b gck=66>
    <grapheme gs=c gck=67>
    ...
    <grapheme gs=z gck=90>
</lexord>
```

The gs attribute specifies the input character(s) to be translated as what HyTime calls a **grapheme string** (the string as a whole constitutes a single unit for processing). A grapheme string may appear either literally (as shown above for b-z), or as an entity (as shown for a).

The gck attribute specifies the number into which the grapheme string is translated (HyTime calls this result a **grapheme comparison key**). It must be one or more decimal numbers. By definition **lexord** leaves all unmentioned input characters unchanged; thus this example leaves all characters other than lower-case letters unchanged.

For most languages a useful **lexord** table is more complicated. For many European languages accented vowels usefully translate into the corresponding unaccented vowels using the method just shown. Some languages and some sorting conventions are more complex, and a one-to-one mapping is not possible. **Lexord** can handle such cases too.

In Spanish, for instance, the sequence "ll" is treated as a separate letter: it has its own pronunciation and sorts as one letter, not two. Thus, the following strings sort into one order under Spanish rules and another under English rules:

Spanish	English
paloma	pollo
pollo	paloma
pomona	pomona

Lexord achieves this effect by translating not just the letter "l," but the string "ll." "ll" is assigned a code greater than that of "l" but less than that of "m." Since the gck values in the example above leave no room between "l" and "m", all the values higher than that for "l" must increase by one (in both upper and lower case):

```
<lexord id=upcase.spanish>
    <grapheme gs=a  gck=65>
    ...
    <grapheme gs=l  gck=76>
    <grapheme gs=ll gck=77>
    <grapheme gs=m  gck=78>
    <grapheme gs=n  gck=79>
    ...
    <grapheme gs=z  gck=91>
    ...
    <grapheme gs=LL gck=77>
    <grapheme gs=M  gck=78>
    <grapheme gs=N  gck=79>
    ...
    <grapheme gs=Z  gck=91>
</lexord>
```

In all such cases the input data is processed from beginning to end, taking the longest match available starting at each character, without any overlaps. Given the **lexord** above, the string "`lllll`" would be divided into "`ll`" "`ll`" "`l`," and so sort as { 77 77 76 }.

Some other natural languages present the opposite difficulty: a single grapheme should sort as if it were several. For instance, some languages treat vowels so that "`über`" and "`ueber`" are equivalent and sort between "`ud`" and "`uf`". This can be handled with **lexord** by mapping the accented character to a sequence of `gck` numbers:

```
<grapheme gs="&uuml;" gck="85 69">
```

Finally, in some sorting or comparison methods specific characters should be entirely ignored. American telephone books, for example, typically treat plural and possessive forms as equal, ignoring the apostrophe character: thus "`Browns`" and "`Brown's`" are treated the same. A **lexord** with no `gck` value at all is defined to mean that the character (or character sequence) is entirely ignored:

```
<grapheme gs="'" gck="">
```

14.8 The all-ref attribute form: IDREF control attributes

These attributes permit a HyTime engine to do special checking of IDREF attribute use. The **all-ref** form is discussed in clause 6.5.3. It requires setting the `refctl` option. The resultant checking applies not only to SGML IDREF attributes, but also anything HyTime declares to contain values which are to be treated as IDREFs. For non-IDREF attributes, such declarations are accomplished with `lextype` specifications. These may be attribute values or content. For example, the sub-elements used with **`nameloc`** hold IDREF values in their content.

There are three types of control, each expressed by a corresponding controlling attribute:

`refrange`	hints at where the IDREF's corresponding ID is
`reflevel`	places a limit on levels of indirect reference
`reftype`	permits validation that the destination conforms to a particular content model

Each of these controlling attributes takes a value consisting of a list of pairs, each containing the location of an IDREF to constrain and a constraint. This allows a single controlling attribute to constrain several different IDREF attributes and/or element content.

The first item in each pair specifies the IDREF being controlled by giving one of the following values. An attribute name or reserved word should only occur once in a given controlling attribute:

`#ALL`	means that the following constraint affects all associated IDREF values not otherwise specified. `#ALL`, if present, must be the first location in any controlling attribute. Later pairs can override it for specific cases.
`#CONTENT`	affects all IDREF values appearing as contents of the element. No HyTime architectural forms use IDREFS as a lextype constraint on content, although **`nmlist`** uses NAMES, and the content can be IDREFS (or entity names, or IDREFS valid only in external documents).
`name`	any other value must be an attribute name declared for the current element's type. If an attribute contains several IDREFS, there is no way to constrain a particular one.

The second item in each pair specifies the constraint that the IDREFS in question must obey. Its value differs for each of the three controlling attributes `refrange`, `reflevel` and `reftype`, as described below.

14.8.1 The refrange attribute

Short for "ID reference resolution range," this attribute can be used to give optimization hints to a HyTime engine. The second value specified in each pair indicates how far the application may need to look in order to resolve the IDREF in question to its destination. The value must be one of these four:

B *Backward* reference indicates that the destination precedes the reference and is in the same document.

D *Direct* reference indicates that the IDREF points to a destination in the same document. The destination may be either before or after the reference.

I *Indirect* reference indicates that the destination must be in the same document, but may be reached indirectly. Indirection is only possible when using the Location address module.

X *External* reference indicates that the destination may be anywhere in the same or a different document, and may be directly or indirectly reached. If external references are used, the `exidrefs` option must be set.

For example, the following `link` element claims that the element having `id=procedure12` occurs somewhere earlier in the same document:

```
<link linkend=procedure12 refrange="linkend B">
```

The default value of `refrange` is "`#ALL I`", which allows indirect access on any IDREF value used by HyTime unless an overriding specification is made. Although it is not completely clear whether **`nameloc`** forms that use the `docorsub` attribute are affected by `refrange`, it is probably best, if any external references are used, to change the default `refrange` to "`#ALL X`" for all HyTime elements.

14.8.2 The reflevel attribute

This attribute gives a limit to the number of levels of indirect pointers to be followed when seeking the destination of the IDREF. Unless location addresses are in use, this is not possible, so using this attribute requires use of the Location address module. If the attribute is not specified, HyTime resolves pointers fully: any pointer that points to another is treated as if it pointed to the ultimate destination.

For example, consider the following chain of IDs and IDREFs:

```
<section id=sec12>...</section>
...
<nameloc id=c1><nmlist>sec12</nmlist></nameloc>
<nameloc id=c2><nmlist>c1</nmlist></nameloc>
<nameloc id=c3><nmlist>c2</nmlist></nameloc>
<nameloc id=c4><nmlist>c3</nmlist></nameloc>

<clink id=origin1 linkend=c4>
<clink id=origin2 linkend=c4 reflevel="linkend 2">
```

Element `origin1` is a pointer to the `section` with `ID=sec12`, because the `reflevel` default is unlimited. Element `origin2`, however, specifies a resolution level limit of two and so is a pointer to the `nameloc` with `ID=c3`. It is two pointer-resolution actions away from `origin2`. The `reflevel` is the maximum number of steps beyond the original reference that may be taken. If specified, it must be a positive integer.

If more than one element along such a location ladder specifies a `reflevel` limit, each counts from where it is first specified, and the first limit reached ends the ladder. Thus the following elements, when added to the previous example, both point at the element with ID `c1`:

```
<clink id=origin3 linkend=c4 reflevel="linkend 4">
<clink id=origin4 linkend=c3 reflevel="linkend 3">
```

For most applications it is enough either never to specify `reflevel`, or always to specify `reflevel=1`. In the former case no interactions arise, and all references are fully resolved. In the latter case no indirection occurs, so the destination of a link is always immediate.

14.8.3 The reftype attribute

This attribute permits you to constrain the element type to which an IDREF can point. Only one element type may be specified per constrained IDREF. A `reftype` constraint gives the name of an IDREF attribute to constrain and the element type that it must point to:

```
<clink linkend=chap37 reftype="linkend CHAP">
```

Such a constraint can in fact be satisfied in two distinct ways. The most obvious way is when the target element is a `chap` element. The other way in which a `reftype` constraint can be satisfied is if the target does not have the specified GI, but does satisfy the content model specified for that GI in the DTD. The following structure is therefore accepted:

```
<!ELEMENT     book       - - (chap)*  +(footnote)>
...
<!ELEMENT     mylist     - - (item*)  -(footnote)>
<!ELEMENT     thing      - - ANY>
```

```
<book>
    ...
    <thing id=forbin>
       <item id=i1>Portable diagnostic station</>
       <item id=i2>Replacement boards</>
       <footnote id=f1>As many as possible</>
       <item id=i3>Screwdriver</>
    </thing>
    ...
    <clink linkend="i1" reftype="linkend mylist">
    ...
<book>
```

This structure satisfies the `reftype` constraint because the `linkend` of the `clink` points to an `item` element, and a single `item` element does fulfill the content model for `mylist`, namely `(item*)`.

For exactly the same reason, the following multiple location link satisfies the constraint by picking out three `item` elements that together satisfy the content model (see Section 8.7 for more about multiple and span locations):

```
<nameloc id=itemlist>
    <nmlist>i1 i2 i3</nmlist>
</nameloc>
<clink linkend="itemlist" reftype="linkend mylist">
```

The `thing` element would not satisfy the constraint, even though the *content of* the `thing` would. This is because the content model for `mylist` has an exclusion exception ruling out `footnote` elements. Thus, the following is illegal:

```
<clink linkend="forbin" reftype="linkend mylist">
```

One can declare an element type whose purpose is to provide a content model that is the OR of several acceptable types for a `reftype` (see note 104 in the HyTime standard). In that case if the target is of any of the listed types, the constraint is satisfied. For example, given this declaration an element with `reftype=targets` may point to a `list`, to a `thing`, or to a `para`:

```
<!ELEMENT       targets     - - (list | thing | para)>
```

All `reftype` constraints apply to the ultimate endpoint only. Intermediate pointing elements need not satisfy the specified type.

There are other options beyond constraining to a GI's content model. The keyword `#ANY'` can be used to indicate that a particular IDREF is *not* constrained. This is required only if a constraint applied to `#ALL` must be overridden. The following example constrains the `editor` and `approved` attributes to point to elements of type `person-desc`, but imposes no requirements on the `error-loc` attribute (which could point to any portion of the text under review):

```
<mylink editor=sjd approved=dgd error-loc=para12
    reftype="#ALL person-desc error-loc #ANY">
```

A constraint can also be a number (rather than `#ANY` or an element type name). In that case the number indicates a specific number of targets needed to satisfy the constraint.

14.9 The all-act activity tracking attributes

The activity tracking attributes provide a simple way to record and act on operations that affect components of a document over its lifetime. This optional attribute list form is discussed in clause 6.5.7, and is enabled by the `activity` option.

The features provided by this attribute are best viewed as a set of "hooks" — places where full-featured activity tracking applications can connect with HyTime in a standardized way. By itself HyTime activity tracking provides only a starting point for addressing the complexities of these generally application-specific facilities.

14.9.1 The activity attribute

The `activity` attribute specifies that the HyTime system should keep track of how an element that bears it is used. A HyTime engine that supported activity tracking would notice when a "tracked" element undergoes any of several actions. When such an action occurs, the IDREFS specified as the attribute value are followed to find elements of form **`activity`**.

The **`activity`** form holds instructions for what to do when a tracked event occurs. The instructions appear in the element's content, and can take any form needed. They might be in some application defined activity tracking language which is defined as a data content notation and labeled with the `notation` common attribute.

The HyTime engine passes the content of the elements along with the tracked element to whatever activity tracking facility the application provides. Each indicated **`activity`** element is applied only if the activity occurring is listed on its `actypes`. The following distinctions of activity are known to HyTime:

`create` — A tracked object is created. The application could know to apply such tracking if the `activity` attribute has a default or #FIXED value in the DTD (otherwise no pointer to an **`activity`** element could yet exist).

`modify` — A tracked object is modified, for example, if its attributes or content change.

`delete` — A tracked object is completely deleted.

`link` — A hypertext link is created for which a tracked object is an anchor.

`access` — A tracked object is accessed when an application uses its contents. As note 120 in the standard states, applications may define their own varieties of "access."

`unlink` — A link to a tracked object is deleted. This includes the case where a multi-ended link itself continues to exist, but loses a linkend which points to a tracked object).

The meaning of the activity tracking facilities must be specified by the application. For example, the HyTime standard does not state whether activity tracking processing is invoked before or after the action being tracked. Security and copyright control require that activity processing occur prior to an event's completion, so that access privileges can be determined, while tracking element creation for an "audit trail" might not be possible until after an event is complete. It is also an application-dependent decision whether activities are tracked for intermediate locations accessed while processing a location ladder.

14.10 The any-dcn data content notation attributes

These attributes can be used to store several entities in a single entity if HyTime's `dcnatts` option is set. They include a variety of specifications that can be used to pick out sub-parts of the entity, list what to do if the entity can't be rendered as requested, state where to find the same information in alternative notations, and so on. We do not discuss these features.

14.11 The all-qual qualified lexical type and property name attributes

The `qpnpsn` and `qltnlmgi` attributes can be used to specify what named property sets and what lexical model-defining element types are to be used in an element. They apply to any references to qualified property names or qualified lexical type names that do not specify the same information.

14.11.1 The qpnpsn attribute

This attribute specifies a list of NOTATION names, each of which represents a HyTime property set. A property referenced without a property set name is searched for in those property sets, in the order specified. We discuss properties in Sections 11.7-11.9, and **`proploc`** in Section 8.5.1.

14.11.2 The qltnlmgi attribute

This attribute applies to the search for lexical models with particular qualified lexical type names. Lexical models are grouped by the GI of the elements that define them. Thus, the `qltnlmgi` attribute is a list of element types from the document's DTD, whose element instances should conform to the **`lexmodel`** form. If a lexical type is referenced without specifying the GI that defines it, the elements of the first type listed on `qltnlmgi` are checked for the requested lexical type name, then the elements of the second type listed, and so on. See Sections 11.2-11.6 for much more information on lexical types, models, names, and their usage.

Appendix A

HyTime Meta-DTD

This appendix contains the complete set of meta-declarations for HyTime architectural forms for elements and attributes. It contains all corrections agreed to by the HyTime committee as of July, 1993. Note, however, that those corrections (while clearly necessary) have not been formally reviewed and balloted by ISO, and so do not yet constitute a formal amendment to HyTime. When such an amendment appears, readers should consult it for the final details and for any additional corrections that may have been found. We thank Charles F. Goldfarb for kindly providing a machine-readable copy of the updated declarations and permission to integrate them here.

The formal SGML specifications are individually subject to the following copyright notice and license:

We have reformatted the declarations for greater readability. We have deleted discursive comments and those comments that specify the default value for ID attributes (always "none"), but retained other default, constraint, lexical type and reference type comments (see Sections 11.2, 11.3, and 14.8). Attribute default values appear in comments after the symbol "δ" for brevity. Further information about individual architectural forms we discuss can be located via the index and table of contents.

A.1 Base module (clause 6)

HyTime Document (clause 6.4)

```
<!ENTITY % loc
   "bibloc|nameloc|dataloc|treeloc|pathloc|
   listloc|relloc|proploc|notloc|fcsloc">
<!ENTITY % link
   "clink|ilink">
<!ENTITY % resbase
   "activity|dvlist|desctab|lexmodel
   |lexord|propdef|qltn|qpn">
<!ENTITY % resmeas
   "dimspec|extent|extlist|dimref|markfun|measure">
<!ENTITY % resschd
   "axis|exrecon|calspec|mallobj">
<!ENTITY % resrend
"rendrule|batrule|modrule|wandrule|wndpatch|modpatch">
<!ENTITY % resorce
   "(%resbase;)|(%resmeas;)|(%resschd;)|(%resrend;)">
<!ENTITY % HyBrid
   "fcs|HyBrid|sHyTime|#PCDATA">
```

HyTime Document Element

```
<!element       HyDoc          - O (%HyBrid;)*
                               +(%loc;|%link;|%resorce;)>
<!attlist       HyDoc
   HyTime       NAME           HyDoc
   id           ID             #IMPLIED
   boslevel     NUMBER         #IMPLIED    --δappl'n BOS --
   unmspace     (unified|separate)         separate
   -- docmdu attributes -->
```

HyTime/non-HyTime Bridge Element

```
<!element       HyBrid         - O (%HyBrid;)*>
<!attlist       HyBrid
   HyTime       NAME           HyBrid>
```

Suppress HyTime Element

```
<!element       sHyTime        - O ANY>
<!attlist       sHyTime
   HyTime       NAME           sHyTime>
```

Common Attributes (clause 6.5)

Identification

```
<!attlist       all-id
   id           ID            #IMPLIED
   notation     NAME          #IMPLIED     --δnone --
   delims       CDATA         #IMPLIED     --δno change --
   -- lextype( (NAME,s+,char*), (s+,NAME,s+,char*)* ) --
   conloc       IDREFS        #CONREF      --δ content --
   context      (context|ncontext)         ncontext
   HyNames      CDATA         #FIXED ""    --δnone --
   -- lextype(ATTNAME, s+, (NAME|(RNI,"CONTENT")),
         (s+, ATTNAME, s+, (NAME|(RNI,"CONTENT")))*) -->
```

Lexical Types

```
<!attlist       all-lex
   lextype      CDATA         #FIXED ""    --δnone --
   -- lextype(ATTORCON, s+, QLTN,
         (s+, ATTORCON, s+, QLTN)*) --
   lextypgi NAMES             #FIXED in-DTD
   -- lextype(GIL) -->
```

Lexical Model

```
<!element       lexmodel      - O (%HyBrid;)*>
<!attlist       lexmodel
   HyTime       NAME          lexmodel
   ltn          NAME          #REQUIRED
   lexord       CDATA         #IMPLIED     --δchar set --
   -- reftype(lexord) --
   -- lextype(IDREF|(RNI,"SGMLCASE")) --
   boundary  (sodeod|sodiec|isceod|isciec|inmodel)
                sodeod>
```

Lexicographic Ordering Definition

```
<!element       lexord        - O (grapheme+)>
<!attlist       lexord
   HyTime       NAME          lexord
   id           ID            #REQUIRED>

<!element       grapheme      - O (%HyBrid;)*>
<!attlist       grapheme
   HyTime       NAME          grapheme
   gs           CDATA         #REQUIRED
   -- Constraint: must be unique in lexord --
   gck          NUMBERS       #IMPLIED     --δignored -->
```

ID Reference Resolution Control

```
<!attlist      all-ref
   refrange CDATA            #FIXED "#ALL I"
   -- lextype((RNI,"ALL", s+, ("B"|"D"|"I"|"X"))?,
          (s+, ATTORCON, s+, ("B"|"D"|"I"|"X"))* ) --
   -- Constraint: a given ATTNAME or #CONTENT
      can occur only once --
   reflevel CDATA            #IMPLIED    --δunlimited --
   -- lextype( (RNI,"ALL", s+, unzi)?,
           (s+, ATTORCON, s+, unzi)* ) --
   reftype     CDATA         #FIXED "#ALL #ANY"
   -- lextype((RNI,"ALL", s+,
      (((GI|unzi), (s+, RNI,"SEQ")?)|(RNI,"ANY")))?,
      (s+, ATTORCON, s+,
      (((GI|unzi), (s+, RNI,"SEQ")?)|(RNI,"ANY")))*)
   -- Constraint: a given ATTNAME or #CONTENT
      can occur only once -->
```

Bit Combination Skip Count

```
<!attlist      all-bits
   bitskip     NUMBERS       #IMPLIED    --δnot known -->
```

Default Value List Attributes

```
<!attlist      all-dvl
   subdvl      IDREFS        #IMPLIED    --δnone --
   -- reftype(dvlist) --
   sibdvl      IDREFS        #IMPLIED    --δnone --
   -- reftype(dvlist) -->
```

Default Value List

```
<!element      dvlist        - O (#PCDATA)
   -- ulextype(attspec) -->
<!attlist      dvlist
   HyTime      NAME          dvlist
   id          ID            #REQUIRED
   dvgi        NAMES         #IMPLIED    --δall --
   -- lextype(GIL) --
   preatts     NAMES         #IMPLIED    --δnone --
   -- Constraint: must be in dvlist content -->
```

Descriptive Text Attributes

```
<!attlist      all-desc
   desctxt     CDATA         #CONREF     --δnone --
   -- lextype(words) --
   desctab IDREFS            #CURRENT
   -- reftype(desctab) --
   -- Constraint: searched in order listed -->
```

Description Table

```
<!element       desctab       - O (desctxt, descdef)+>
<!attlist       desctab
   HyTime       NAME          desctab
   id           ID            #REQUIRED>
```

Descriptive Text

```
<!element       desctxt  O O      (#PCDATA)
   -- lextype(words) -->
<!attlist       desctxt
   HyTime       NAME          desctxt>
```

Descriptive Text Definition

```
<!element       descdef  O O      (%HyBrid;)*>
<!attlist       descdef
   HyTime       NAME          descdef>
```

Activity Tracking Policy

```
<!entity % actions
   '("CREATE"|"MODIFY"|"LINK"|"ACCESS"|"UNLINK"|"DELETE")'>

<!attlist       all-act
   activity IDREFS            #IMPLIED    --δnone --
   -- reftype(activity) -->

<!element       activity      - O (%HyBrid;)*>
<!attlist       activity
   HyTime       NAME          activity
   id           ID            #REQUIRED
   actypes      NAMES         access
   -- lextype(%actions;,(s+, %actions;)*) -->
```

HyTime Data Attributes (clause 6.6)

Common Data Attributes

```
<!attlist       #NOTATION     sbento
   HyTime       NAME          sbento
   unitsize     NUMBER        8>
```

Referred to by forms: sbento, sHyTime.

```
<!attlist       #NOTATION any-dcn
   HyTime       (data|document|subdoc|text) data
   insbento     CDATA         #IMPLIED    --δnot in sbento --
   -- lextype(ENTITY, (s+, digit+, s+, digit+)+) --
   -- ENTITY: sbento entity in which this occurs.
      Digit+: Offset in sbento units (origin 1).
      Digit+: Size in sbento units.
      Offset/size repeatable for segmentation --
```

```
modgen        NUMBERS       #IMPLIED    --δnot tracked --
-- Constraint: two numbers
   1st: 0 when created; incremented when modified.
   2nd: Set to 1st when validated by application. --
altreps       NAMES         #IMPLIED    --δnone --
-- lextype(ENTITIES) --
superdcn NAME               #IMPLIED    --δnot a derivation--
-- lextype(NOTATION) --
template NAME               #IMPLIED    --δnone --
-- lextype(ENTITY) --
methods       CDATA         #IMPLIED    --δnone --
degrade       CDATA         #IMPLIED    --δnone --
encoding      NUMBERS       "8 12"
-- Constraint: Constraint: bit-combination size and
   "word" size, expressed as permutation of normalized
   word of 2, 4, or 8 bit combinations.
   MSB is leftmost and numbered "1"
   Normalized="8 12", "8 1234", "8 12345678"
   Example: Intel="8 21", "8 2143", "8 21436587" --
HyNames       CDATA         #FIXED ""   --δnone --
-- lextype(ATTNAME, s+, NAME,
      (s+, ATTNAME, s+, NAME)*) -->
```

Property sets (clause 6.7)

Property Definition

```
<!element       propdef        - O (%HyBrid;)*>
<!attlist       propdef
   HyTime       NAME           propdef
   pn           NAME           #REQUIRED
   - Constraint: must be unique in property set --
   psn          NAME           #REQUIRED
   -- lextype(NOTATION) --
   lex          CDATA          #IMPLIED
   -- reftype(qpn|qltn) --
   -- lextype(QPN|QLTN|("Oo",GRPO,IDREF,GRPC)) --
   inherent     NAME           #IMPLIED
   -- lextype(NOTATION) --
   dspec        CDATA          #IMPLIED
   -- reftype(qpn|qltn) --
   -- lextype(QPN|QLTN|("Oo",GRPO,IDREF,GRPC)) --
   deforsyn     (def|syn)      def>
```

Qualified Property Name

```
<!element       qpn            - O (pn, spec?)+>
<!attlist       qpn
   HyTime       NAME           qpn
   id           ID             #REQUIRED>
```

Property Name

```
<!element       pn              - O RCDATA
   -- lextype(PN) --
   - Constraint: must be a valid property name in psn ->
<!attlist       pn
   HyTime       NAME            pn
   psn          NAME            #IMPLIED    --δfrom qpnpsn --
   -- lextype(NOTATION) -->
```

Specifier for Property

```
<!element       spec            - O ((qpn|qltn)+|pval)>
<!attlist       spec
   HyTime       NAME            spec>
```

Qualified Lexical Type Name

```
<!element       qltn            - O RCDATA
   -- lextype(LTN) --
   -- Constraint: must be a valid ltn of lmgi element type ->
<!attlist       qltn
   HyTime       NAME            qltn
   lmgi         NAME            #IMPLIED    --δfrom qltnlmgi --
   -- lextype(GI) -->
```

Property Value

```
<!element       pval            - O RCDATA
   -- Constraint: must satisfy property -->
<!attlist       pval
   HyTime       NAME            pval>
```

Qualifying Name Attributes

```
<!attlist       all-qual
   qpnpsn       NAMES           #IMPLIED    --δstandard sets --
   -- lextype(NOTATION, (s+, NOTATION)*) --
   -- Constraint: searched in order listed --
   qltnlmgi     NAMES           #IMPLIED    --δnone used --
   -- lextype(GIL) --
   -- Constraint: searched in order listed -->
```

A.2 Measurement (clause 7)

Dimension Specification

```
<!element       dimspec         O O   (marklist,marklist?)
   -- Constraint: Content must resolve to a pair of markers
      (unless marker1 omitted for implied dimref) -->
<!attlist       dimspec
   HyTime       NAME            dimspec
   id           ID              #IMPLIED>
```

Overrun Handling

Referred to by forms: evsched, baton, wand, relloc, dataloc, treeloc, pathloc, listloc, fcsloc.

```
<!attlist       overrun
   overrun      (error|wrap|trunc|ignore)error>
```

Axis Marker List

```
<!ENTITY % marker
   "marklist|dimref|markfun|mrkquery|calspec">
<!element       marklist   O O       (%marker;|#PCDATA)*
   -- lextype(snzi*) --
   -- Constraint: nested marklists merge into single list --
   -- Constraint: calspec permitted only in calendars -->
<!attlist       marklist
   HyTime       NAME            marklist>
```

Dimension Specification List

```
<!element       dimlist    O O
                (dimlist|dimspec|%marker;|#PCDATA)*
   -- lextype(snzi*) --
   -- Constraint: derives dimspecs from marker pairs.
      Nested marklist/dimlist merge into single list with
      effect of "((marker1,marker2)|dimspec)*" --
   -- Constraint: calspec permitted only in calendars -->
<!attlist       dimlist
   HyTime       NAME            dimlist>
```

Scheduling and extents (clause 7.2)

Extent Specification

Referred to by forms: event, proscope, modscope.

```
<!attlist       exspec
   exspec       IDREFS          #REQUIRED
   -- reftype(extlist) --
   -- Constraint: multiple references concatenated -->
```

Scheduled Extent

```
<!element       extent     O O       (dimlist+)
   -- Constraint: multiple dimlists concatenated into one list
      which must contain one dimspec per axis -->
<!attlist       extent
   HyTime       NAME            extent
   id           ID              #IMPLIED>
```

Scheduled Extent List

```
 <!element      extlist    O O
   (extlist|extent|dimlist|dimspec|%marker;|#PCDATA)*
   -- lextype(snzi*) --
   -- Constraint: derives dimspecs from marker pairs and
      extents from dimspec sequences (one per axis) and
      interspersed syntactic extents --
   -- Constraint: nested marklist/dimlist/extlist merge into
      single list with effect of
      "(((marker1,marker2)|dimspec)+|extent)+" --
   -- Constraint: calspec permitted only in calendars -->
<!attlist       extlist
   HyTime       NAME          extlist
   id           ID            #IMPLIED>
```

Measurement units (clause 7.3)

Measurement Domain Definition

```
<!element       measure       - O (granule+)>
<!attlist       measure
   HyTime       NAME          measure
   id           ID            #IMPLIED
   smu          NAME          #REQUIRED
   -- Constraint: notation name of an SMU.
      If virtual, it must have a formal public ID
      of "Virtual Measurement Unit" -->

<!element       granule       - O (%HyBrid;)*>
<!attlist       granule
   HyTime       NAME          granule
   gn           CDATA         #REQUIRED
   -- lextype(word) --
   -- Constraint: cannot be same as SMU name
      (with case ignored) --
   gd           CDATA         #REQUIRED
   -- lextype(frac, s+, word) --
   -- Constraint: ratio, and reference granule that
      ratio is multiplied by (or the SMU, for which
      case is ignored) -->
```

Schedule Measurement

Referred to by forms: evsched, baton, wand.

```
<!attlist       schdmeas
   basegran CDATA             #FIXED ""    --δSMU per --
   -- lextype(words) --
   gran2hmu NUMBERS           #FIXED "1 1"
   -- lextype(fracs) --
   -- Constraint: 1 ratio per axis, or 1 for all -->
```

Dimension referencing (clause 7.4)

Dimension Reference

```
<!element       dimref          - O (%HyBrid;)*>
<!attlist       dimref
   HyTime       NAME            dimref
   id           ID              #IMPLIED
   elemref      CDATA           #REQUIRED
   -- reftype(dimspec|axis|extent|evsched|wand|baton
      |evgrp|event|modscope|proscope|calspec) --
   -- lextype(IDREF|(RNI,"SCOPE")) --
   -- Constraint: semantic constraints on references
      across axes (for example, a calspec is only
      permitted in a reference to a calendar event).
      #SCOPE permitted only in a scheduled extent in a
      projectr, meaning dimension of projectr scope,
      or a grpdex, meaning dimension of grpscope. --
   extref       NUMBER          1
   axisref      NAME            #IMPLIED    --δdimspec or 1 axis--
   -- lextype(GI) --
   -- Constraint: must be axis of referenced event --
   projectr IDREF               #IMPLIED    --δnot projected --
   -- reftype(projectr) --
   -- Constraint: in same pevsched as reference --
   selcomp      (first|last|qcnt)           qcnt
   flip         (flip|noflip)               noflip
   calevref     (calevref|normal)           normal>

<!element       markfun         - O (%HyBrid;)*>
<!attlist       markfun
   HyTime       NAME            markfun
   id           ID              #IMPLIED
   -- function attributes -->
```

Referred to by forms: markfun, nmquery, mrkquery, notloc, bibloc.

```
<!attlist       function
   fn           NAME            #IMPLIED    --δnone --
   -- Constraint: unique in element type --
   usefn        NAME            #CONREF     --δnone --
   args         CDATA           #IMPLIED    --δnone -->
```

Document MDU Attributes

Referred to by forms: HyDoc.

```
<!attlist       docmdu
   docmdu       CDATA           #FIXED ""
                                --δ"1 1 for each SMU" --
   -- Constraint: SMU name and ratio for all of the
      measurement domains used in the document. --
   -- lextype((NAME,s+,frac),(s+,NAME,s+,frac)*) -->
```

A.3 Location address (clause 8)

Location module attribute forms (clause 8.2)

Location Source

Referred to by forms: dataloc, treeloc, pathloc, relloc, listloc, proploc, fcsloc.

```
<!attlist       locsrc
   locsrc       IDREFS       #CURRENT     --δprev specified --
   -- Constraint: No HyTime reftype constraints -->
```

Multiple Location

Referred to by forms: nameloc, dataloc, treeloc, pathloc, listloc, relloc, proploc, notloc, fcsloc.

```
<!attlist       multloc
   ordering     (ordered|noorder)         noorder
   set          (set|notset)              notset
   aggloc       (aggloc|agglink|nagg)     nagg>
```

Span Location

Referred to by forms: nameloc, dataloc, treeloc, pathloc, listloc, relloc.

```
<!attlist       spanloc
   spanloc      (spanloc|spanlink|nspan) nspan
   -- Constraint: spanlink requires hyperlinks module --
   limsort      (limsort|nlimsort)        nlimsort>
```

Name Space Locations (clause 8.3)

Named Location Address

```
<!element       nameloc      - O (nmlist|nmquery)*
   -- Constraint: name list derived from content elements. -->
<!attlist       nameloc
   HyTime       NAME         nameloc
   id           ID           #REQUIRED
   -- multloc attributes --
   -- spanloc attributes -->
```

Name List Specification

```
<!element       nmlist       - O (#PCDATA)
   -- lextype(NAMES) -->
<!attlist       nmlist
   HyTime       NAME         nmlist
   nametype     (entity|element|unified) entity
   obnames      (obnames|nobnames)        nobnames
   docorsub     ENTITY       #IMPLIED     --δno change --
   dtdorlpd     NAMES        #IMPLIED     --δunchanged|base --
   -- lextype(DTD|LPD+) -->
```

Coordinate Locations (clause 8.4)

Data Location Address

```
<!element       dataloc       - O (dimlist*)>
<!attlist       dataloc
   HyTime       NAME          dataloc
   id           ID            #REQUIRED
   quantum      (str|norm|word|name|sint|date|time|utc)
                                             str
   catsrc       (catsrc|catsrcsp|nocatsrc) nocatsrc
   catres       (catres|catressp|nocatres) nocatres
   -- overrun attributes --
   -- locsrc attributes --
   -- multloc attributes --
   -- spanloc attributes -->
```

Tree Combination Attributes

Referred to by forms: treeloc, pathloc.

```
<!attlist       treecom
   treecom      (treecom|ntreecom)       ntreecom>
```

Tree Location Address

```
<!element       treeloc       - O (marklist*)
   -- Constraint: marklists are merged into a single list that
      contains 1st markers only; implied marker2 is 1 -->
<!attlist       treeloc
   HyTime       NAME          treeloc
   id           ID            #REQUIRED
   -- overrun attributes --
   -- treecom attributes --
   -- locsrc attributes --
   -- multloc attributes --
   -- spanloc attributes -->
```

Path Location Address

```
<!element       pathloc       - O (dimlist*)
   -- Constraint: dimlists are merged into a single list that
      resolves to pairs of dimspecs -->
<!attlist       pathloc
   HyTime       NAME          pathloc
   id           ID            #REQUIRED
   -- overrun attributes --
   -- treecom attributes --
   -- locsrc attributes --
   -- multloc attributes --
   -- spanloc attributes -->
```

List Location Address

```
<!element       listloc       - O (dimlist*)>
<!attlist       listloc
   HyTime       NAME          listloc
   id           ID            #REQUIRED
   -- overrun attributes --
   -- locsrc attributes --
   -- multloc attributes --
   -- spanloc attributes -->
```

Relative Location Address

```
<!element       relloc        - O (dimlist*)
   -- Constraint: dimlists are merged into a single list that
      resolves to pairs of dimspecs -->
<!attlist       relloc
   HyTime       NAME          relloc
   id           ID            #REQUIRED
   root         IDREFS        #IMPLIED
                              --δdocument root per node --
   -- Constraint: 1 per starting node or 1 for all --
   relation (anc|esib|ysib|des|parent|children)
                              parent
   -- Constraint: des requires "pathloc" option --
   -- overrun attributes --
   -- locsrc attributes --
   -- multloc attributes --
   -- spanloc attributes -->
```

Semantic Locations (clause 8.5)

Property Location Address

```
<!element       proploc       - O (QPN|#PCDATA)
   -- lextype(QPN) -->
<!attlist       proploc
   HyTime       NAME          proploc
   id           ID            #REQUIRED
   joint        (joint|several)            several
   apropsrc     (apropsrc|solesrc)         solesrc
   notprop      (error|empty|ignore)       ignore
   -- locsrc attributes --
   -- multloc attributes -->
```

Notation-specific Location Address

```
<!element       notloc        - O (%HyBrid;)*>
<!attlist       notloc
   HyTime       NAME          notloc
   id           ID            #REQUIRED
   -- query attributes --
   -- function attributes --
   -- multloc attributes -->
```

Bibliographic Location Address

```
<!element       bibloc        - O (%HyBrid;)*>
<!attlist       bibloc
   HyTime       NAME          bibloc
   id           ID            #REQUIRED
   -- query attributes --
   -- function attributes -->
```

Querying (clause 8.7)

Query Attributes

Referred to by forms: nmquery, mrkquery, notloc, bibloc.

```
<!attlist       query
   qdomain      IDREFS        #IMPLIED    --δinherent --
   -- Constraint: No HyTime reftype constraints --
   qcontext     IDREF         #IMPLIED    --δinherent --
   -- reftype(HyBrid) -->
```

Name List Query

```
<!element       nmquery       O O (%HyBrid;)*>
<!attlist       nmquery
   HyTime       NAME          nmquery
   id           ID            #IMPLIED
   -- query attributes --
   -- function attributes -->
```

Axis Marker Query

```
<!element       mrkquery      O O (%HyBrid;)*
   -- Constraint: represents axis markers in form required
      by context: single marker, marker pair, etc. -->
<!attlist       mrkquery
   HyTime       NAME          mrkquery
   id           ID            #IMPLIED
   -- query attributes --
   -- function attributes -->
```

A.4 Hyperlinks (clause 9)

Independent Link

```
<!element      ilink        - O (%HyBrid;)*>
<!attlist      ilink
   HyTime      NAME         ilink
   id          ID           #IMPLIED
   anchrole    CDATA        #FIXED in-DTD
   -- lextype((NAME, s+, (RNI, "AGG")?),
        (s+, NAME, s+, (RNI, "AGG")?)+) --
   -- Constraint: one per anchor --
   linkends    IDREFS       #REQUIRED
   -- Constraint: one anchor per anchor role. If one
      is omitted, ilink element is first anchor. --
   -- Constraint: No HyTime reftype constraints,
      but application designers can constrain
      element types with reftype attribute --
   extra       NAMES        #IMPLIED
                            --δNo HyTime traversal --
   -- lextype(("E"|"I"|"A"|"N"|"P"),
        (s+, ("E"|"I"|"A"|"N"|"P"))*) --
   -- Constraint: one per anchor or one for all --
   intra       NAMES        #IMPLIED
                            --δNo HyTime traversal --
   -- lextype(("E"|"I"|"A"|"N"|"P"),
        (s+, ("E"|"I"|"A"|"N"|"P"))*) --
   -- Constraint: one per anchor or one for all --
   endterms    IDREFS       #IMPLIED    --δnone --
   -- reftype(HyBrid) --
   -- Constraint: one per anchor or one for all --
   aggtrav     NAMES        agg
   -- lextype(("AGG"|"MEM"|"COR"),
        (s+, ("AGG"|"MEM"|"COR"))*) --
   -- Constraint: one per anchor or one for all -->
```

Contextual Link

```
<!element      clink        - O (%HyBrid;)*>
<!attlist      clink
   HyTime      NAME         clink
   id          ID           #IMPLIED
   linkend     IDREF        #REQUIRED
   -- Constraint: No HyTime reftype constraints,
      but application designers can constrain
      element types with reftype attribute -->
```

A.5 Scheduling (clause 10)

Finite Coordinate Space (clause 10.2)

Finite Coordinate Space

```
<!element      fcs            - O (evsched|wand|baton)+>
<!attlist      fcs
   HyTime      NAME           fcs
   id          ID             #IMPLIED
   fcsname     NAME           #IMPLIED    --δunnamed --
   fcsmdu      CDATA          #FIXED ""   --δ=docmdu --
   -- lextype((NAME,s+,frac),(s+,NAME,s+,frac)*) --
   axisdefs    NAMES          #FIXED in-DTD
   -- lextype(GIL) -->
```

Axis Definition

```
<!element      axis           - O (%HyBrid;)*>
<!attlist      axis
   HyTime      NAME           axis
   id          ID             #IMPLIED
   axismeas CDATA             #FIXED in-DTD
   -- lextype(NOTATION) --
   axismdu     CDATA          #FIXED ""   --δ=fcsmdu --
   -- lextype(frac) --
   axisdim     CDATA          #FIXED in-DTD
   -- lextype(number) --
   -- calendar attributes -->
```

Schedules (clause 10.3)

Schedule

Referred to by forms: evsched, baton, wand.

```
<!attlist      sched
   axisord     CDATA          #FIXED "" --daxisdefs in FCS --
   -- lextype(GIL) --
   -- Constraint: GIs of axis element types. Omitted
      GI means all events in schedule fully occupy
      the omitted axis --
   apporder    (order|disorder)        order
   sorted      (sorted|unsorted)       unsorted>
```

Event Schedule (10.4)

Event Schedule

```
<!element      evsched      - O (evgrp|event)*>
<!attlist      evsched
   HyTime      NAME         evsched
   id          ID           #IMPLIED
   -- sched attributes --
   -- schdmeas attributes --
   -- overrun attributes --
   -- pls2gran attributes -->
```

Event Group

```
<!element      evgrp        - O (evgrp|event)+>
<!attlist      evgrp
   HyTime      NAME         evgrp
   id          ID           #IMPLIED
   grpscope    IDREF        #IMPLIED    --δto be calc'd --
   -- reftype(extent) --
   grpdex      IDREFS       #IMPLIED    --δno derivation --
   -- reftype(extlist) --
   -- Constraint: multiple references concatenated --
   -- pls2gran attributes -->
```

Event

```
<!element      event        - O (accanch|%HyBrid;)*>
<!attlist      event
   HyTime      NAME         event
   id          ID           #IMPLIED
   exrecon     IDREF        #IMPLIED    --δnone --
   -- reftype(exrecon) --
   -- exspec attributes --
   -- pls2gran attributes -->
```

Pulses

Referred to by forms: evsched, evgrp, event.

```
<!attlist      pls2gran
   pls2gran    NUMBERS      "1 1"
   -- lextype(fracs) --
   -- Constraint: 1 ratio per axis, or 1 for all -->
```

Objects (10.5)

Malleable Object

```
<!element      mallobj      - O (%HyBrid;)*>
<!attlist      mallobj
   HyTime      NAME         mallobj
   id          ID           #IMPLIED
   effect      (pause|hold|wallpapr)    pause>
```

Accessed Anchor List

```
<!element      accanch       - O (acctype|acclink)*
   -- Constraint: if empty, all anchors and link end terms of
      all links, when accessed, are the object of this event if
      they are not included in another accessed anchor list. -->
<!attlist      accanch
   HyTime      NAME          accanch>
```

Referred to by forms: acctype, acclink.

```
<!attlist      accend
   accrole     NAMES         #IMPLIED    --δall link ends --
   -- Constraint: names of anchor roles --
   accend      (endterm|anchor)          anchor>

<!element      acctype       - O (%HyBrid;)*>
<!attlist      acctype
   HyTime      NAME          acctype
   linktype    NAMES         #REQUIRED
   -- lextype(GI) --
   -- Constraint: GIs of link element types --
   -- accend attributes -->

<!element      acclink       - O (%HyBrid;)*>
<!attlist      acclink
   HyTime      NAME          acclink
   linkid      IDREF         #REQUIRED
   -- reftype(ilink|clink|nameloc|dataloc|treeloc|
      pathloc|listloc|relloc|proploc|notloc|fcsloc)--
   -- Constraint: "locs" must be agglink or spanlink --
   -- accend attributes -->
```

Extent Reconciliation (clause 10.6)

Extent Reconciliation Strategy

```
<!element      exrecon       - O (%HyBrid;)*>
<!attlist      exrecon
   HyTime      NAME          exrecon
   id          ID            #REQUIRED
   altrecon IDREF            #IMPLIED    --δno more to try --
   altcrit     IDREF         #IMPLIED    --δnone --
   replace     IDREF         #IMPLIED    --δdon't replace --
   align       CDATA         C
   -- lextype(("F"|"C"|"L"|(snum, s+, snum))+) --
   -- Constraint: one F|C|L or snum pair per axis,
      or one for all --
   vamp        NAMES         novamp
   -- lextype(("VAMPCROP"|"VAMPFILL"|"NOVAMP"),
         (s+, ("VAMPCROP"|"VAMPFILL"|"NOVAMP"))*) --
   -- Constraint: one keyword per axis or one for all--
   filler      IDREF         #IMPLIED    --δpause --
   -- reftype(mallobj) -->
```

Finite coordinate space location address (clause 10.7)

Finite Coordinate Space Location

```
<!element       fcsloc          - O (extlist*)
   -- Constraint: extlists are concatenated into one list
      of extents, each in impfcs order in MDUs -->
<!attlist       fcsloc
   HyTime       NAME            fcsloc
   id           ID              #REQUIRED
   impfcs       NAME            #REQUIRED
   -- lextype(GI) --
   -- overrun attributes --
   -- locsrc attributes --
   -- multloc attributes --
   -- spanloc attributes -->
```

Calendar (clause 8)

Calendar

Referred to by forms: axis.

```
<!attlist       calendar
   calendar     CDATA           #FIXED "" --δnot a calendar --
   -- reftype(calspec) --
   -- lextype(IDREF, s+, ("GMT"|"UTC")) --
   -- Constraint: only if axismeas is SIsecond -->
```

Calendar Specification

```
<!element       calspec         - O
                (abstime | ((date | juldate), abstime?) )
   -- Constraint: omitted content elements are those of
      previous specified event in this schedule. -->
<!attlist       calspec
   HyTime       NAME            calspec
   id           ID              #IMPLIED>
```

Date and Julian Date

```
<!element       date            - O (#PCDATA)
   -- lextype(char+) --
   -- Constraint: date is valid date in UTC year-month-day
      format, except that "day" and "month-day" are also
      accepted.  Year has 4 digits, month and day have two,
      with high-order zeros used to maintain digit count. -->
<!attlist       date
   HyTime       NAME            date
   era          (bc|bce|bp|ad|ce)         #CURRENT>
```

```
<!element       juldate         - O (#PCDATA)
    -- lextype(snum) -->
<!attlist       juldate
    HyTime      NAME            juldate>
```

Absolute Time

```
<!element       abstime         - O (#PCDATA)
    -- lextype(char+) --
    -- Constraint: time is valid 24-hr time in UTC
       "hour:minute:second.decimal" format, except that
       "minute", "hour:minute", and "hour:minute:second"
       are also accepted.  Component values are: hour=00-23,
       minute and second=00-59, and decimal=any number. -->
<!attlist       abstime
    HyTime      NAME            abstime
    timeoff     IDREFS          #IMPLIED    --δlocal time --
    -- reftype(timeoff) -->

<!element       timeoff         - O (#PCDATA)
    -- lextype(char+) --
    -- Constraint: valid time zone offset in UTC "hour:minute"
       format, preceded by hyphen for negative offset -->
<!attlist       timeoff
    HyTime      NAME            timeoff
    id          ID              #REQUIRED
    effdate     CDATA           #IMPLIED    --δalways --
    -- Constraint: UTC date format -->
```

A.6 Rendition (clause 11)

Object Modification (clause 11.1)

Object Modification

```
<!element       wandrule        - O (%HyBrid;)*>
<!attlist       wandrule
    HyTime      NAME            wandrule
    evscheds    IDREFS          #REQUIRED
    -- reftype(evsched) --
    wand        IDREF           #REQUIRED
    -- reftype(wand|wndpatch) --
    -- Constraint: must be aligned with evscheds -->

<!element       modrule         - O (%HyBrid;)*>
<!attlist       modrule
    HyTime      NAME            modrule
    events      IDREFS          #REQUIRED
    -- reftype(event|evgrp) --
    modpatch    IDREF           #REQUIRED
    -- reftype(HyBrid|modpatch) -->
```

Wand

```
<!element       wand          - O (modscope+)>
<!attlist       wand
   HyTime       NAME          wand
   id           ID            #REQUIRED
   -- sched attributes --
   -- schdmeas attributes --
   -- overrun attributes -->
```

Modifier Scope

```
<!element       modscope      - O (%HyBrid;)*>
<!attlist       modscope
   HyTime       NAME          modscope
   id           ID            #IMPLIED
   -- exspec attributes -->
```

Patches

```
<!element       wndpatch      - O (#PCDATA)
   -- ulextype(char*) --
   -- reftype(wndpatch|wand) --
   -- Constraint: subset of SGML model group with IDREFs as
      names and no occurrence indicators or OR connectors. -->
<!attlist       wndpatch
   HyTime       NAME          wndpatch
   id           ID            #REQUIRED>

<!element       modpatch      - O (#PCDATA)
   -- ulextype(char*) --
   -- reftype(modpatch|HyBrid) --
   -- Constraint: subset of SGML model group with IDREFs as
      names and no occurrence indicators or OR connectors. -->
<!attlist       modpatch
   HyTime       NAME          modpatch
   id           ID            #REQUIRED>
```

Event Projection (clause 11.2)

Baton Rule

```
<!element       batrule       - O (%HyBrid;)*>
<!attlist       batrule
   HyTime       NAME          batrule
   evscheds     IDREFS        #REQUIRED
   -- reftype(evsched) --
   baton        IDREF         #REQUIRED
   -- reftype(baton) --
   -- Constraint: must be aligned with evscheds --
   pevsched IDREFS            #REQUIRED
   -- reftype(evsched) --
   -- Constraint: must be different FCS from baton --
```

Baton

```
<!element       baton          - O (proscope+)>
<!attlist       baton
   HyTime       NAME           baton
   id           ID             #REQUIRED
   -- sched attributes --
   -- schdmeas attributes --
   -- overrun attributes -->
```

Projector Scope

```
<!element       proscope       - O (projectr)>
<!attlist       proscope
   HyTime       NAME           proscope
   id           ID             #IMPLIED
   -- exspec attributes -->
```

Event Projector

```
<!element       projectr       - O (extlist+|profun|scaleref)
   -- Constraint: extlists are concatenated into one list -->
<!attlist       projectr
   HyTime       NAME           projectr
   id           ID             #IMPLIED
   strict       CDATA          #IMPLIED     --δstrict proj'n --
   -- lextype(words) -->
```

Projection Function

```
<!element       profun         - O (%HyBrid;)*>
<!attlist       profun
   HyTime       NAME           profun>
```

Scaling Reference

```
<!element       scaleref       - O (dimref+)
   -- Constraint: one dimref per axis of baton -->
<!attlist       scaleref
   HyTime       NAME           scaleref>
```

Rendition Rule (clause 11.3)

Rendition Rule

```
<!element       rendrule       - O
                (rendrule|batrule|wandrule|modrule)+>
<!attlist       rendrule
   HyTime       NAME           rendrule
   id           ID             #REQUIRED
   apporder     (order|disorder)            order>
```

A.7 Useful types and notations (annex A)

HyTime Lexical model

```
<!NOTATION      HyLex
   PUBLIC       "+//ISO/IEC 10744:1992//NOTATION
                HyTime Lexical Model Notation//EN" >

<!ELEMENT       HyLex        - - (#PCDATA)>
<!ATTLIST       HyLex
   HyTime       NAME         #FIXED lexmodel
   notation     NAME         #FIXED HyLex
   delims       CDATA        #IMPLIED    -- δnot changed --
   -- lextype( (NAME, s+, char*), (s+, NAME, s+, char*)* ) --
   -- Constraint: names are delimiter role names --
   -- Constraint: a given NAME can occur only once --
   ltn          NAME         #REQUIRED
   lexord       CDATA        #IMPLIED    -- δchar set order--
   -- reftype(lexord) --
   -- lextype(IDREF|(RNI,"SGMLCASE")) --
   boundary     (sodeod|sodiec|isceod|isciec|inmodel) sodeod
   qpnpsn       NAMES        #IMPLIED    -- δstandard sets --
   -- lextype(NOTATION, (s+, NOTATION)*) --
   -- Constraint: searched in order listed --
   qltnlmgi     NAMES        #FIXED HyLex
   -- lextype(GIL) --
   -- Constraint: searched in order listed --
   norm         (norm|unorm) norm
   wildmax      NUMBER       512>
```

HyQ element type (clause A3)

```
<!NOTATION      HyQ
   PUBLIC       "+//ISO/IEC 10744:1992//NOTATION
                HyTime Query Notation//EN">
```

```
<!element       HyQ          - O (#PCDATA)>
<!attlist       HyQ
   HyTime       (nmquery|mrkquery)       nmquery
   qdomain      IDREFS       #IMPLIED    --δin query --
   -- Constraint: No HyTime reftype constraints --
   notation NAME             #FIXED HyQ
   delims       CDATA        #IMPLIED    --δnot changed --
   -- lextype( (NAME,s+,char*), (s+,NAME,s+,char*)* ) --
   -- Constraint: names are delimiter role names --
   -- Constraint: a given NAME can occur only once --
   fn           NAME         #IMPLIED
   usefn        NAME         #CONREF
   args         IDREFS       #IMPLIED    --δnone --
   -- Constraint: 1-999 IDREFS --
   -- Constraint: No HyTime reftype constraints --
   qpnpsn       NAMES        #IMPLIED    --δstandard sets --
   -- lextype(NOTATION, (s+, NOTATION)*) --
   -- Constraint: searched in order listed --
   qltnlmgi NAMES            #IMPLIED    --δnone used --
   -- lextype(GIL) --
   -- Constraint: searched in order listed -->
```

Measurement (annex A.5)

```
<!NOTATION      gquantum     -- Generic Quantum --
   PUBLIC       "+//ISO/IEC 10744//NOTATION
                Virtual Measurement Unit//EN">

<!NOTATION      SIsecond     -- Time --
   PUBLIC       "+//ISO/IEC 10744//NOTATION
                Systeme International second//EN">

<!NOTATION      SImeter      -- Length --
   PUBLIC       "+//ISO/IEC 10744//NOTATION
                Systeme International meter//EN">

<!NOTATION      virtime      -- Virtual Time Unit --
   PUBLIC       "+//ISO/IEC 10744//NOTATION
                Virtual Measurement Unit//EN">

<!NOTATION      virspace     -- Virtual Space Unit --
   PUBLIC       "+//ISO/IEC 10744//NOTATION
                Virtual Measurement Unit//EN">

<!NOTATION      udomain
   PUBLIC       "ISO/IEC 10744:1992//TEXT
                Useful Measurement Domain Definitions//EN">
```

```
<measure smu=gquantum>
   <granule    gn=quantum          gd="1 1 GQUANTUM">
   <granule    gn=bit-combination gd="1 1 quantum">
   <granule    gn=token            gd="1 1 quantum">
   <granule    gn=node             gd="1 1 quantum">
   <granule    gn=cell             gd="1 1 quantum">
</measure>
<measure smu=virtime>
   <granule    gn=vtu              gd="1 1 VIRTIME">
   </measure>
<measure smu=virspace>
   <granule    gn=vsu              gd="1 1 VIRSPACE">
</measure>
```

Other standard measurement units

```
<!NOTATION     SIkg          -- Mass --
   PUBLIC      "+//ISO/IEC 10744//NOTATION
               Systeme International kilogram//EN">

<!NOTATION     SIkelvin      -- Thermodynamic Temperature --
   PUBLIC      "+//ISO/IEC 10744//NOTATION
               Systeme International kelvin//EN">

<!NOTATION     SIcd          -- Luminous Intensity --
   PUBLIC      "+//ISO/IEC 10744//NOTATION
               Systeme International candela//EN">

<!NOTATION     SIampere      -- Electric Current --
   PUBLIC      "+//ISO/IEC 10744//NOTATION
               Systeme International ampere//EN">

<!NOTATION     SImole        -- Amount of Substance --
   PUBLIC      "+//ISO/IEC 10744//NOTATION
               Systeme International mole//EN">

<!NOTATION     SIradian      -- Plane Angle --
   PUBLIC      "+//ISO/IEC 10744//NOTATION
               Systeme International radian//EN">

<!NOTATION     SIsr          -- Solid Angle --
   PUBLIC      "+//ISO/IEC 10744//NOTATION
               Systeme International steradian//EN">
```

Appendix B

Graphics Notations

The last few years have seen a great proliferation of formats to represent graphical data. This chapter provides names and registered formal public identifiers for many of these representations, though we make no pretense of completeness. We have included, in the same order, the formats described in Kay and Levine (1992). We recommend that book for further details on all these formats, and for useful and accessible background information on kinds of formats, the advantages and limitations of each, how widely each is supported by software, and so on.

For each notation we provide a formal SGML NOTATION declaration. The declarations constitute a public text entity which also has a formal public identifier. SGML and HyTime documents may freely use these declarations rather than re-inventing them. They can be included in a DTD by a declaration and reference such as this:

```
<!ENTITY        % graphics  PUBLIC
    "+//ISBN 0-7923-9432-1::Graphic Notations//TEXT
    Graphical Notation Names//EN">
%graphics;
```

For each of the formats we provide a data content notation whose name is the short name of the format (usually this is an acronym), and a public identifier mentioning the owner/creator of the standard and a descriptive name. If official FPIs are introduced for these notations at a later time, they should be used. The owner name in the FPIs below identifies us as the owners of these identifiers, not of the notations themselves (see Section 3.6).

```
<!NOTATION      PCX          PUBLIC
    "+//ISBN 0-7923-9432-1::Graphic Notation//NOTATION
    ZSoft PCX bitmap//EN">

<!NOTATION      MacPaint     PUBLIC
    "+//ISBN 0-7923-9432-1::Graphic Notation//NOTATION
    Apple Computer Macintosh Paint//EN">

<!NOTATION      TIFF         PUBLIC
    "+//ISBN 0-7923-9432-1::Graphic Notation//NOTATION
    Aldus/Microsoft
    Tagged Interchange File Format//EN">

<!NOTATION      GIF          PUBLIC
    "+//ISBN 0-7923-9432-1::Graphic Notation//NOTATION
    CompuServe Graphic Interchange Format//EN">

<!NOTATION      GEM          PUBLIC
    "+//ISBN 0-7923-9432-1::Graphic Notation//NOTATION
    Novell GEM Image Format//EN">

<!NOTATION      IFF-ILBM     PUBLIC
    "+//ISBN 0-7923-9432-1::Graphic Notation//NOTATION
    Electronic Arts embedded bitmap//EN">

<!NOTATION      TARGA        PUBLIC
    "+//ISBN 0-7923-9432-1::Graphic Notation//NOTATION
    Truevision Targa Image Format//EN">

<!NOTATION      BMP          PUBLIC
    "+//ISBN 0-7923-9432-1::Graphic Notation//NOTATION
    Microsoft Windows bitmap//EN">

<!NOTATION      SUNRASTER    PUBLIC
    "+//ISBN 0-7923-9432-1::Graphic Notation//NOTATION
    Sun Microsystems raster//EN">

<!NOTATION      PBM          PUBLIC
    "+//ISBN 0-7923-9432-1::Graphic Notation//NOTATION
    Jef Poskanzer Portable Bit Map//EN">
```

```
<!NOTATION      XBM          PUBLIC
    "+//ISBN 0-7923-9432-1::Graphic Notation//NOTATION
    MIT X Consortium bitmap//EN">

<!NOTATION      XWD          PUBLIC
    "+//ISBN 0-7923-9432-1::Graphic Notation//NOTATION
    MIT X Consortium Window Dump//EN">

<!NOTATION      JPEG         PUBLIC
    "+//ISBN 0-7923-9432-1::Graphic Notation//NOTATION
    Joint Photographic Experts Group raster//EN">

<!NOTATION      JFIF         PUBLIC
    "+//ISBN 0-7923-9432-1::Graphic Notation//NOTATION
    JPEG File Interchange Format//EN">

<!NOTATION      JPEG-TIFF    PUBLIC
    "+//ISBN 0-7923-9432-1::Graphic Notation//NOTATION
    JPEG TIFF encapsulation//EN">

<!NOTATION      FITS         PUBLIC
    "+//ISBN 0-7923-9432-1::Graphic Notation//NOTATION
    International Astronomical Union
    Flexible Image Transfer System//EN">

<!NOTATION      DXF          PUBLIC
    "+//ISBN 0-7923-9432-1::Graphic Notation//NOTATION
    AutoDesk Drawing Interchange Format//EN">

<!NOTATION      HP-GL        PUBLIC
    "+//ISBN 0-7923-9432-1::Graphic Notation//NOTATION
    Hewlett Packard Graphics Language//EN">

<!NOTATION      LOTUS-PIC    PUBLIC
    "+//ISBN 0-7923-9432-1::Graphic Notation//NOTATION
    Lotus Development Corporation PIC//EN">

<!NOTATION      UNIX-PLOT    PUBLIC
    "+//ISBN 0-7923-9432-1::Graphic Notation//NOTATION
    UNIX Systems Labs plot//EN">

<!NOTATION      HP-PCL       PUBLIC
    "+//ISBN 0-7923-9432-1::Graphic Notation//NOTATION
    Hewlett Packard Printer Control Language//EN">

<!NOTATION      EPS          PUBLIC
    "+//ISBN 0-7923-9432-1::Graphic Notation//NOTATION
    Adobe Systems Encapsulated PostScript//EN">
```

```
<!NOTATION      WMF          PUBLIC
    "+//ISBN 0-7923-9432-1::Graphic Notation//NOTATION
    Microsoft Windows Metafile//EN">

<!NOTATION      PICT         PUBLIC
    "+//ISBN 0-7923-9432-1::Graphic Notation//NOTATION
    Apple Computer QuickDraw Picture//EN">

<!NOTATION      CGM          PUBLIC
    "+//ISBN 0-7923-9432-1::Graphic Notation//NOTATION
    ANSI/ISO Computer Graphics Metafile//EN">
```

Kay and Levine describe several more formats briefly. For those we give notation names and the individual portion of public identifiers for them here (the remainder of the FPI follows the pattern above). For some of these formats the owner is not known.

FLI	Autodesk Animator FLI
SLIDE	Autodesk slide file
EPSON	Epson printer bitmap
FACESAVER	Lou Katz bitmap
GROUP3	CCITT Group 3 facsimile
GROUP4	CCITT Group 4 facsimile
GRASP-GL	Microtex Ind. Graphical System for Presentation
HP-PAINTJET	Hewlett Packard PaintJet
IGES	NIST Initial Graphic Exchange Standard
PDES	ISO Product Data Exchange Standard
IG-TIFF	Island Graphics TIFF subset
KODAK-ICC	Kodak ICC high resolution printer
MSW-ICON	Microsoft Windows Icon
MSW-PAINT	Microsoft Windows Paint
MPEG	Motion Picture Experts Group video
OFF	Digital Equipment Corp. OFF CAD
PC-PAINT	PC Paint bitmap
PIXAR	Pixar Corp. PIC bitmap
PDS	Jet Propulsion Laboratory(?)
RENDERMAN	Pixar Corp. RIB metafile
RIFF	Microsoft/IBM Reverse IFF
SGI	Silicon Graphics bitmap
SIXEL	Digital Equipment Corp. color bitmap
UTAH-RLE	University of Utah RLE color bitmap

VICAR	Astronomical bitmap
WP-GRAPHICS	WordPerfect graphic file
XPM	MIT X Consortium color bitmap

We list below a few other formats that we have encountered although Kay and Levine do not discuss them. We list them merely to provide a formal name, with contact and owner information when available; *not all this information is certain*.

ACR-NEMA	National Electrical Manufacturers Association medical raster: Standards Publication No 300-1988 from NEMA, 2101 L Street, N.W., Washington, DC 20037 USA
CALS	US DoD CALS group IV raster: a CCITT Group 4 bitmap with a header defined in US Department of Defense standard MIL-M-28002.
CFF2	Common File Format: A format for vector image and text interchange, based on DDES2-IADD.
DDES	ANSI Digital Data Exchange Specifications: IT8.1.
DDES2-IADD	Digital Data Exchange Specification-International Association of Diecutting-Diemaking: ANSI IT8.6.
GKS	ISO Graphical Kernel System: ISO standard 7942.
GKS-3D	ISO Graphical Kernel System 3D extension: ISO standard 8805.
IPI-IIF	ISO Image Processing and Interchange: Image Interchange Facility. Draft standard 12087.
JBIG	ISO/CCITT Joint Bilevel Image Group: Draft standard 11544, and CCITT T.82.
PHIGS	ISO Programmer's Hierarchical Interactive Graphics System: ISO standard 9592.
PHIGS-PLUS	ISO Programmer's Hierarchical Interactive Graphics System, extended.
PHOTO-CD	Kodak Photo CD: Kodak Limited, R & D, Headstone Drive, Harrow, Middlesex HA1 4TY, UK.
QUICKTIME	Apple Computer QuickTime movie: Apple Computer Incorporated, 10201 North de Anza Boulevard MS 23AQ, Cupertino, California 95014 USA.
SET	Standard d'Echange et de Transfert: Association Francaise De Normalisation (AFNOR), Tour Europe, Cedex 7, F-92049 Paris la Defense, France.
VDAFS	VDA Surface Interface: DIN (Germany)

Appendix C

HyTime Reference Material

This appendix describes the organizational modules of HyTime, along with their options and the element and attribute list architectural forms defined in each module. Each group is listed in alphabetical order.

The HyTime standard itself is ISO standard 10744. It can be obtained from the national standards organizations in most countries. In the US, as of this writing it is available from:

American National Standards Institute
11 West 42nd Street, 13th floor
New York, NY 10036 USA
Phone 212-642-4900, fax 212-302-1286

C.1 Module and option list

The HyTime standard is divided into numbered clauses, most of the top-level ones representing modules, each of which defines a related set of constructs. The architectural forms listed in the next section are organized in clause order. The modules and their options, along with where the HyTime standard and this book discuss them, are:

Base

The base module is identified in HyTime Declarations by the keyword `base`.

Clause 6; Chapter 14 and as needed: defines basic terminology, HyTime module and option declarations, and architectural forms that can be used with the constructs in other modules.

Options: `activity`, `context`, `dcnatts`, `lextype`, `HyLex`, `lexord`, `refctl`, `exidrefs`, `dvlist`, `desctxt`, `xpropdef`, `HyPD` and `unparsed`.

Measurement

The Measurement module is identified in HyTime Declarations by the keyword `measure`.

Clause 7; Chapters 6 and 13: provides for defining and expressing units of measurement in time, space and/or other domains. A small portion of this is used by the Location address module and then the Hyperlinks module, for counting and finding locations.

Options: `dimref`, `markfun`, `HyOp`, `HyFunk`, `homogran`, `fcsmdu`, `axismdu`.

Location address

The Location address module is identified in HyTime Declarations by the keyword `locs`.

Clause 8; Chapter 8: uses measurements, formal names and other techniques to indicate locations within data, as for use by the Hyperlinks module to create links to locations within data.

Options: `multloc`, `spanloc`, `anysgml`, `anydtd`, `mixspace`, `coordloc`, `pathloc`, `relloc`, `notsrc`, `query`, `HyQ`, `mixcase`, `bigmatch`, `uassert`.

Hyperlinks

The Hyperlinks module is identified in HyTime Declarations by the keyword `links`.

Clause 9; Chapter 7: facilitates the creation of hypertext links between locations in documents.

Options: only one, `manyanch`, which can take a parameter. The `manyanch` option enables links with multiple linkends; if specified simply as `manyanch` it allows any number of anchors; if specified as `manyanch=n` for some number n, that is the limit.

Scheduling	The Scheduling module is identified in HyTime Declarations by the keyword `sched`. Clause 10; Chapter 13: provides for events to be specified and scheduled in space and time for presentation or analysis. Options: `manyaxes=n`, `splitfcs`, `grpdex`, `accanch`, `exrecon`, `calspec`, `juldate`.
Rendition	The Rendition module is identified in HyTime Declarations by the keyword `rend`. Clause 11; not discussed here: allows certain presentational aspects of HyTime documents to be described. Options: `modify`, `patch`, `project`, `profun`, `scaleref`.

C.2 Architectural form index

For each form in the tables below, we give clause and page references to the section in the HyTime standard that defines the form. The last column also lists important relationships to other forms as appropriate. When individual attributes are mentioned they appear in roman type; attribute forms appear in italic. The forms in **boldface** type are the ones we consider to be most commonly needed. Discussions of particular forms in this book can be located under the form's name in the Index.

Attribute forms usable on all HyTime elements

Name	Clause	Pg	Attributes included
all-act	6.5.6.4	31	activity
all-bits	6.5.4	27	bitskip
all-desc	6.5.6.1	29	desctxt, desctab
all-dvl	6.5.5.1	28	subdvl, sibdvl
all-id	6.5.1	21	id, notation, delims, conloc, context, HyNames
all-lex	6.5.2	22	lextype, lextypgi
all-qual	6.7.2	37	qpnpsn, qltnlmgi
all-ref	6.5.3	26	refrange, reflevel, reftype
any-dcn	6.6.2	33	insbento, modgen, altreps, superdcn, template, methods, degrade, encoding, HyNames (for #NOTATION)
sbento	6.6.1	32	unitsize (for #NOTATION)

Attribute forms used by specific element forms

Name	Clause	Pg	Attributes	Used by
accend	10.5.3	83	accrole, accend	acctype, acclink
calendar	10.8	86	calendar	axis
docmdu	7.4.2.3	49	docmdu	HyDoc
exspec	7.2.2	42	exspec	event, proscope, modscope
function	7.4.1.3	48	fn, usefn, args	markfun, nmquery, mrkquery, notloc, bibloc
locsrc	8.2.1	52	locsrc	dataloc, treeloc, pathloc, relloc, listloc, proploc, fcsloc
multloc	8.2.2	53	ordering, set, aggloc	nameloc, dataloc, treeloc, pathloc, listloc, relloc, proploc, notloc, fcsloc
overrun	7.1.2.1	40	overrun	evsched, baton, wand, relloc
pls2gran	10.4.3	80	pls2gran	evsched, evgrp, event
query	8.7.1	67	qdomain, qcontext	nmquery, mrkquery, notloc, bibloc
schdmeas	7.3.3	44	basegran, gran2hmu	evsched, baton, wand
sched	10.3	77	axisord, sorted, apporder	evsched, baton, wand
spanloc	8.2.3	54	spanloc, limsort	nameloc, dataloc, treeloc, pathloc, listloc, relloc
treecom	8.4.2.3	60	treecom	reeloc, pathloc

Architectural forms for elements

Name	Clause	Pg	Attributes and *attribute forms*
abstime	10.8.1.2	88	timeoff
accanch	10.5.3	82	
acclink	10.5.3	83	linkid, *accend*
acctype	10.5.3	83	linktype, *accend*
activity	6.5.7	31	id, actypes
axis	10.2	76	id, axismeas, axismdu, amisdim, *calendar*
baton	11.2.3	94	id, *sched, schdmeas, overrun*
batrule	11.2.2	94	evscheds, baton, pevsched
bibloc	8.5.3	65	id, *query, function*
calspec	10.8.1	86	id
clink	9.2.2	75	id, linkend
dataloc	8.4.1	58	id, quantum, catsrc, catres, *overrun, locsrc, multloc, spanloc*
date	10.8.1.1	87	era
descdef	6.5.6.4	30	
desctab	6.5.6.2	29	id
desctxt	6.5.6.3	30	
dimlist	7.1.2.3	41	
dimref	7.4.1.2	46	id, elemref, extref, axisref, projectr, selcomp, flip, calevref
dimspec	7.1.2	40	id
dvlist	6.5.5.2	28	id, dvgi, preatts
event	10.4.2	80	id, exrecon, *exspec, pls2gran*
evgrp	10.4.1	79	id, grpscope, grpdex, *pls2gran*
evsched	10.4	78	id, *sched, schdmeas, overrun, pls2gran*
exrecon	10.6	84	id, altrecon, altcrit, replace, align, vamp, filler
extent	7.2.3	42	id
extlist	7.2.4	42	id
fcs	10.2	76	id, fcsmdu, axisdefs
fcsloc	10.7	86	id, impfcs, *overrun, locsrc, multloc, spanloc*
granule	7.3.1	44	gn, gd
grapheme	6.5.2.2	24	gs, gck
HyBrid	6.4.1	20	
HyDoc	6.4	19	id, boslevel, unmspace, *docmdu*
ilink	9.2.1	74	id, anchrole, linkends, extra, intra, endterms, aggtrav
juldate	10.8.1.1	87	

lexmodel	6.5.2.1	23	ltn, lexord, boundary
lexord	6.5.2.2	24	
listloc	8.4.2.6	62	id, *overrun, locsrc, multloc, spanloc*
mallobj	10.5.2	81	id, effect
markfun	7.4.1.3	48	id *function*
marklist	7.1.2.2	41	
measure	7.3.1	43	id, smu
modpatch	11.1.4	92	id
modrule	11.1.1	90	events, modpatch
modscope	11.1.3	91	id, *exspec*
mrkquery	8.7.3	69	id, *query, function*
nameloc	8.3.2.1	55	id, *multloc, spanloc*
sHyTime	6.4.2	20	[this form was previously named nHyTime]
nmlist	8.3.2.2	56	nametype, obnames, docorsub, dtdorlpd
nmquery	8.7.2	68	id, *query, function*
notloc	8.5.2	65	id, *query, function, multloc*
pathloc	8.4.2.5	62	id, *overrun, treecom, locsrc, multloc, spanloc*
pn	6.7.2	37	psn
profun	11.2.3.3	96	
projectr	11.2.3.2	95	id, strict
propdef	6.7.1	36	pn, psn, lex, inherent, dspec, deforsyn
proploc	8.5.1	64	id, joint, apropsrc, notprop *locsrc, multloc*
proscope	11.2.3.1	95	id, *exspec*
pval	6.7.2	37	
qltn	6.7.2	37	lmgi
qpn	6.7.2	37	id
relloc	8.4.2.7	63	id, root, relation, *overrun, locsrc, multloc, spanloc*
rendrule	11.3	97	id, apporder
scaleref	11.2.3.4	96	
spec	6.7.2	37	
timeoff	10.8.1.2	88	id, effdate
treeloc	8.4.2.4	61	id, *overrun, treecom, locsrc, multloc, spanloc*
wand	11.1.2	91	id, *sched, schdmeas, overrun*
wandptch	11.1.4	92	id
wandrule	11.1.1	98	evscheds, wand

Bibliography

Akscyn, Robert, Donald McCracken, and Elise Yoder. 1987. "KMS: A Distributed Hypermedia System for Managing Knowledge in Organizations." In *Proceedings of Hypertext '87, Chapel Hill, NC, November 13-15, 1987*. Baltimore, MD: Association for Computing Machinery Press: 1-20.

André, Jacques, Richard Furuta, and Vincent Quint. 1989. "By Way of an Introduction. Structured documents: What and why?" In *Structured Documents*, ed. Jacques André, Richard Furuta, and Vincent Quint. Cambridge: Cambridge University Press.

Association of American Publishers. 1986. *Reference Manual on Electronic Manuscript Preparation and Markup*. Electronic Manuscript Series. Washington, DC: Association of American Publishers, May, 1986. Available from Electronic Publishing Special Interest Group (EPSIG).

Bornstein, Jeremy and Victor Riley. 1990. "Hypertext Interchange Format." In Moline et al. (1990): 39-47.

Buckland, Michael K. 1992. "Emanuel Goldberg, Electronic Document Retrieval, and Vannevar Bush's Memex." *Journal of the American Society for Information Science* 43 (4): 284-294.

Burkowski, Forbes J. 1991. "An Algebra for Hierarchically Organized Text-Dominated Databases." Waterloo, Ontario, Canada: Department of Computer Science, University of Waterloo. Manuscript. Portions appeared as part of a paper presented at RIAO '91: Intelligent Text and Image Handling, Barcelona, Spain, April 1991.

Bush, Vannevar. 1945. "As We May Think." *Atlantic Monthly* 176 (July): 101-108.

Carmody, Steven, W. Gross, Theodor H. Nelson, David E. Rice, and Andries van Dam. 1969. "A Hypertext Editing System for the /360." In *Pertinent Concepts in Computer Graphics*, M. Faiman and J. Nievergelt (eds.). Chicago: University of Illinois Press: 63-88.

Catano, James V. 1979. "Poetry and Computers: Experimenting with the Communal Text." *Computers and the Humanities* 13 (9): 269-275.

Coombs, James H., Allen H. Renear, and Steven J. DeRose. 1987. "Markup Systems and the Future of Scholarly Text Processing." *Communications of the Association for Computing Machinery* 30 (11): 933-947.

Cover, Robin C., Nicholas Duncan, and David T. Barnard. 1991. *Bibliography on SGML (Standard Generalized Markup Language) and Related Issues*. Technical Report 91-299. Kingston, Ontario: Queen's University, February, 1991. Extract reprinted in *Literary and Linguistic Computing* 6 (3): 200-212.

Cover, Robin. 1992. "SGML: Annotated Bibliography and List of Resources." *<TAG>* 5 (3-5). In three parts.

Cover, Robin. 1993. "Appendix C. SGML Bibliography." In Sandy Ressler, *Perspectives on Electronic Publishing: Standards, Solutions, and More:* 285-320. Englewood Cliffs, NJ: PTR Prentice Hall.

Crane, Gregory. 1987. "From the Old to the New: Integrating Hypertext into Traditional Scholarship." In *Proceedings of Hypertext '87, Chapel Hill, NC, November 13-15, 1987*. Baltimore, MD: Association for Computing Machinery Press: 51-55.

DeRose, Steven J. 1989. "Expanding the Notion of Links." In *Proceedings of Hypertext '89, Pittsburgh, PA, November 5-8, 1989.* Baltimore, MD: Association for Computing Machinery Press: 249-257.

DeRose, Steven J. 1990. "Biblical Studies and Hypertext." In *Hypermedia and Literary Studies*, ed. by George Landow and Paul Delany. Cambridge: MIT Press: 185-204.

DeRose, Steven J. 1993. "Markup Systems in the Present." In *The Digital Word: Text-Based Computing in the Humanities*, ed. by George Landow and Paul Delany. Cambridge: MIT Press: 119-135.

DeRose Steven J. and David G. Durand. 1987. "Applications of Hypertext to Humanistic Analysis." Manuscript, July 22.

DeRose Steven J., David G. Durand, Elli Mylonas, and Allen H. Renear. 1990. "What is Text, Really?" *Journal of Computing in Higher Education* 1 (2): 3-26.

Engelbart, Douglas C. 1963. "A Conceptual Framework for the Augmentation of Man's Intellect." In *Vistas in Information Handling*, Vol. 1 (P. Howerton, ed.). Washington, DC: Spartan Books: 1-29. Reprinted in Greif (1988): 35-65.

Engelbart, Douglas C. and William K. English. 1968. "A Research Center for Augmenting Human intellect." In *Proceedings of the Fall Joint Computer Conference, 1968.* Reprinted in Greif (1988): 81-105.

Engelbart, Douglas C., Richard W. Watson, and James C. Norton. 1973. "The Augmented Knowledge Workshop." In *AFIPS Conference Proceedings, vol. 42*. The National Computer Conference and Exposition, June 4-8, 1973, New York. Montvale, New Jersey: AFIPS Press.

Feiner, Steven, S. Nagy, and Andries van Dam. 1981. "An Integrated System for Creating and Presenting Complex Computer-Based Documents." *Computer Graphics* 15 (August): 181-189.

Feiner, Steven. 1988. "Seeing the Forest for the Trees: Hierarchical Display of Hypertext Structure." In *Conference on Office Information Systems, March 23-25, 1988, Palo Alto, CA.* New York: Association for Computing Machinery Press: 205-212.

Furuta, Richard. 1991. *Important Papers in the History of Document Preparation Systems: Basic Sources.* Technical Report UMIACS-TR-

91-7, January, 1991. College Park: University of Maryland Department of Computer Science.

Furuta, Richard and P. David Stotts. 1991. *Structured Dynamic Behavior in Hypertext.* Technical Report UMIACS-TR-91-14, January, 1991. College Park: University of Maryland Department of Computer Science.

Garret, L. Nancy, Karen E. Smith, and Norman Meyrowitz. 1986. "Intermedia: Issues, Strategies, and Tactics in the Design of a Hypermedia System." In *Proceedings of the Conference on Computer-Supported Cooperative Work.*

Goldberg, Emanuel. 1932. "The Retrieval Problem in Photography." Tr. by Michael K. Buckland. *Journal of the American Society for Information Science* 43 (4): 295-298.

Goldfarb, Charles F. *The SGML Handbook.* Edited and with a foreword by Yuri Rubinsky. Oxford University Press, 1990.

Goldfarb, Charles F., Edward J. Mosher, and Theodore I. Peterson. 1970. "An Online System for Integrated Text Processing." In *Proceedings of the American Society for Information Science* 7: 147-150.

Greif, Irene (ed.). 1988. *Computer-Supported Cooperative Work: A Book of Readings.* San Mateo, California: Morgan Kaufmann Publishers.

Gurwitz, Robert F., Steven K. Feiner, Read T. Fleming, and Andries van Dam. 1979. *Future Technical Documentation Delivery Systems for Naval Maintenance and Repair.* Final Report for Period 1 April 1978 - 30 September 1979, contract N00014-78-C-0396. Prepared for Office of Naval Research.

Halasz, Frank. 1987. "Reflections on NoteCards: Seven Issues for the Next Generation of Hypermedia Systems." Address presented at Hypertext '87, Chapel Hill, NC, November 13-15, 1987. Reprinted in *Communications of the Association for Computing Machinery* 31 (7), July 1988: 836-855.

Halasz, Frank and Mayer Schwartz. 1994. "The Dexter Hypertext Reference Model." In *Communications of the Association for Computing Machinery* 37 (2): 30-39.

Hardman, Lynda, Dick C.A. Bulterman, and Guido van Rossum. 1994. "The Amsterdam Hypermedia Model: Adding Time and Context to the Dexter Model." In *Communications of the Association for Computing Machinery* 37 (2): 50-63.

Hughes, John. 1988. "Studying Ancient Greek Civilization Interactively — The Perseus Project." *Bits and Bytes Review* 2 (1): 1-12.

Institute for Research in Information and Scholarship. 1989. *Hypermedia Bibliography.* Providence: Brown University: IRIS.

International Organization for Standardization. 1986. ISO 8879. *Information Processing — Text and Office Information Systems — Standard Generalized Markup Language.*

International Organization for Standardization. 1988. ISO 639. *Codes for the representation of names of languages.*

International Organization for Standardization. 1988. ISO 9069. *Information Processing — SGML Support Facilities — SGML Document Interchange Format.*

International Organization for Standardization. 1991. ISO 9070. *Information Processing — SGML Support Facilities — Registration procedures for public text owner identifiers.*

International Organization for Standardization. 1992. ISO/IEC TR 9573-11. *Information Processing — SGML Support Facilities — Techniques for using SGML — Part 11: Application at ISO Central Secretariat for International Standards and Technical Reports.*

International Organization for Standardization. 1992. ISO/IEC 10744. *Hypermedia / Time-based Structuring Language: HyTime.*

International Organization for Standardization. 1994. ISO/IEC DIS 10179. *Document Style Semantics Specification Language.*

Kahn, Paul and Norman Meyrowitz. 1988. "Guide, HyperCard, and InterMedia: A Comparison of Hypertext/Hypermedia Systems." *IRIS Technical Report* 88-7. Providence: Brown University: IRIS.

Kay, David C. and John R. Levine. 1992. *Graphics File Formats.* New York: Windcrest/McGraw-Hill.

Kernighan, Brian. 1990. "Issues and tradeoffs in Document Preparation Systems." In *EP90: Proceedings of the International Conference on Electronic Publishing, Document Manipulation & Typography,*

Gaithersburg, Maryland, September. Richard Furuta (ed.). Cambridge: Cambridge University Press.

Killough, Ronnie Lynn. 1990. "Hypertext Interchange with the Dexter Model: InterMedia to KMS." Master's Project. College Station, Texas: Department of Computer Science, Texas A&M University.

Kipp, Neill, and Steven R. Newcomb. 1990. "SMDL: A Language for Music Documents." *Computing in Musicology* 6: 53-56.

Leggett, John J. and John L. Schnase. 1994. "Viewing Dexter with Open Eyes." In *Communications of the Association for Computing Machinery* 37(2), February 1994: 76-86.

Maurer, H. and I. Tomek. 1990. *Hypermedia Bibliography*. Report 286, November. Later reprinted in *Journal of Microcomputer Applications*.

Meyrowitz, Norman and Andries van Dam. 1982. "Interactive Editing Systems." *Computing Surveys* 14 (3). Part I: 321-352; part II: 353-415.

Meyrowitz, Norman. 1986. "Intermedia: the Architecture and Construction of an Object-Oriented Hypermedia system and Applications Framework." In *Proceedings of OOPSLA*. Portland, OR.

Moline, Judi, Dan Denigni, and Jean Baronas (eds.). 1990. *Proceedings of the Hypertext Standardization Workshop, January 16-18, 1990, National Institute of Standards and Technology*. Washington: U.S. Government Printing Office. Available from the National Technical Information Service as Publication PB90215864.

Mylonas, Elli, and Sebastian Heath. 1990. "Hypertext from the data point of view: Paths and Links in the Perseus Project." In *Hypertext: Concepts, Systems and Applications. Proceedings of the European Conference on Hypertext, INRIA, France, November 1990*. A. Rizk, N. Streitz and J. Andre (eds.). Cambridge, UK: Cambridge University Press: 324-336.

Mylonas, Elli, Gregory Crane, Kenneth Morrell, and D. Neel Smith. 1993. "The Perseus Project: Data in the Electronic Age." *In Accessing Antiquity: The Computerization of Classical Databases*, J. Solomon and T. Worthen (eds.). University of Arizona Press.

Nelson, Theodor H. 1987. *Computer Lib*. Redmond, Washington: Tempus Books of Microsoft Press.

Nelson, Theodor H. 1987. *Literary Machines*. Edition 87.1. South Bend, Indiana: The Distributors.

Newcomb, Steven R. (ed.). 1991. *SGML SIGhyper Newsletter* 1 (1). Tallahassee, Florida: TechnoTeacher, Inc.

Nyce, James M. and Paul Kahn (eds.). 1991. *From Memex to Hypertext: Vannevar Bush and the Mind's Machine*. San Diego: Academic Press.

Nyce, James M. and Paul Kahn. 1991. "A Machine for the Mind: Vannevar Bush's Memex." In Nyce and Kahn (1991): 39-66.

Okerson, Ann (ed.). 1993. *Scholarly Publishing on the Electronic Networks: The New Generation: Visions and Opportunities in Not-for-profit Publishing*. Proceedings of the Second Symposium, December 5-8, 1992, Washington DC. Association of Research Libraries, Office of Scientific and Academic Publishing.

Oren, Tim. 1990. "Toward Open Hypertext: Requirements for Distributed Hypermedia Standards." In Moline et al. (1990): 189-196.

Prusky, John. 1978. *FRESS Resource Manual*. Providence: Brown University Division of Applied Mathematics.

Reid, Brian. 1981. *Scribe: A Document Specification Language and its Compiler*. Ph.D. thesis, Carnegie-Mellon University, Pittsburgh, PA. Also available as Technical Report CMU-CS-81-100.

Reynolds, Louis R. and Steven J. DeRose. 1992. "Electronic Books." *Byte* June 1992: 263-268.

Rubinsky, Yuri. 1990. "Standards for Hypertext Interchange." *SGML Users' Group Newsletter* 15, January, 1990: 14-15.

Salton, G. and M. J. McGill. 1983. *Introduction to Modern Information Retrieval*. New York: McGraw Hill Book Co.

Sloan, Donald. 1992. "HyTime/Standard Music Description Language and Computer-Aided Music Research," *Computing in Musicology* 8: 127-30.

Smith, Joan M. and Robert Stutely. 1988. *SGML: The User's Guide to ISO 8879*. Chichester, West Sussex, England: Ellis Horwood Limited.

Sperberg-McQueen, C. Michael and Lou Burnard (eds.). 1990. *Guidelines for the Encoding of Machine-readable Texts*. Also known as Text

Encoding Initiative document P1. Chicago: Text Encoding Initiative. First revision forthcoming.

Tompa, Frank W. 1989. "What is (tagged) text?" In *Dictionaries in the Electronic Age: Proceedings of the Fifth Annual Conference of the UW Centre for the New Oxford English Dictionary:* 81-93.

Trigg, Randall H. 1991. "From Trailblazing to Guided Tours: The Legacy of Vannevar Bush's Vision of Hypertext Use." In Nyce and Kahn (eds.) 1991: 353-367.

van Dam, Andries and Carol L. Chomsky. 1971. *FRESS Reference Manual: Structure and Commands.* Providence: Brown University.

van Dam, Andries and David E. Rice. 1971. "On-line Text Editing: A Survey." *Computing Surveys* 3(3): 93-114.

van Herwijnen, Eric. 1990. *Practical SGML.* The Netherlands: Kluwer Academic Publishing Group.

van Herwijnen, Eric. 1993. *SGML Tutorial.* Providence: Electronic Book Technologies.

van Herwijnen, Eric. 1994. *Practical SGML: Second Edition.* The Netherlands: Kluwer Academic Publishing Group.

Yankelovich, Nicole, Norman Meyrowitz, and Andries van Dam. 1985. "Reading and Writing the Electronic Book." *IEEE Computer* 18 (October): 16-30.

Zellweger, Polle. 1989. "Scripted Documents: A Hypermedia Path Mechanism" in *Proceedings of Hypertext '89, Pittsburgh, PA, November 5-8, 1989.* Baltimore, MD: Association for Computing Machinery Press: 1-14.

Glossary

Activity tracking
An optional feature of HyTime by which user actions such as accessing, creating, linking, or deleting HyTime elements can be tracked by the application program. This could be used to invoke security or validity checking or to keep audit trails or logs.

Aggregate location
A location, typically specified by Location address module facilities, that includes several potentially discontiguous members but is considered as a single component. For example, the set of all document components found by a query. See also "multiple location."

Alternate property source (or apropsrc)
The place where HyTime looks for a property if the property does not exist for the object of which it is requested. For example, text content portions in SGML do not have attributes, but may be treated as if they had the attributes of their immediately containing element.

Alternative single-character pattern (or ASCP)
A feature of the HyLex lexical modeling language, by which a bracket-enclosed list of characters matches against any character from that list (much like the same syntax in regular expression languages).

Ambiguous content model
An SGML content model that permits documents to be constructed whose structure could not be unambiguously interpreted. Such content models are prohibited. For example, a long series of elements of type `item` could satisfy the model below in several ways (it would be unclear how many were part of the first `item+` requirement, and how many were part of the second):

```
<!ELEMENT ambiguous-list - - (item+, item+)>
```

Anchor
The actual data at one end of a hypertext link. It is pointed to (directly or indirectly) by a linkend of a link. A single anchor can be pointed to by link ends in many different links.

Anchor role
Each linkend of a HyTime hypertext link assigns a named anchor role to the corresponding anchor. That role is a declared name that can be used to communicate the meaning or significance of the anchor (in relation to the other anchors pointed to by the link). For example, reviewers commenting on a document draft might create three-ended links with the following anchor roles: text being commented on; text of comment; suggested replacement text.

Architectural form
A template for a class of SGML element or set of attributes, such as those defined by HyTime. Specific DTDs may declare element types to be subclasses of such a class by giving them a #FIXED attribute with a special name, whose value is the architectural form name. In HyTime, the special attribute is called `HyTime`.

Attributes
Data on some or all instances of an SGML element type, typically giving specific information about the properties or significance of the instance. Unique identifiers are also specified on elements via attributes.

Axis
A direction along which distances may be measured, such as each dimension of a graphical image, the frame sequence of a video, or the list of subelements of an SGML element.

Basic hyperlinking HyTime document
A kind of HyTime hyperdocument that uses the basic features of HyTime needed for hyperlinking, bringing in few other optional features.

Basic SGML document
A Basic SGML document uses those SGML features most commonly considered useful and thus is quite portable. It uses only the SHORTTAG and OMITTAG features, and only a few predetermined short references.

Bounded object set (or BOS)
A collection of data units (entities) of interest for some purpose, for example, all the interconnected documents and multimedia objects to be browsed by some user.

Callout
See "hot spot."

CDATA
"Character data:" an SGML element or entity of type CDATA contains no markup (characters that would normally signify markup are treated as literal data within such an object). Related to, but not the same as, PCDATA and RCDATA.

Chunky hypertext
A model of hypertext structure in which all information is divided into small chunks with little internal structure, and is connected by links between entire chunks. As opposed to "creamy hypertext."

Common attribute
An attribute defined in the HyTime Base Module (see Section 14.5) that may apply to any HyTime element at all. The most important is `id`.

Connector
Any of the delimiters used between two element type names in an SGML content model or HyTime lexical model, to indicate their co-occurrence restrictions. Connectors include "|" meaning that either may occur but not both, and "," meaning that both may occur, in order. SGML content models, but not HyTime lexical models, also include "&", meaning that both may occur in either order. See also "occurrence indicator."

CONREF attribute
An SGML attribute that has been assigned the default value #CONREF. This means that if the attribute is specified on an instance of the element, that instance can have no content or subelements. A CONREF attribute may be of type CDATA, ID, IDREF, or any other type supported by SGML.

Content model
An expression in an element declaration in an SGML DTD that specifies what kinds of subelements can be directly contained in the element being declared. A content model appears as a parenthesized expression containing element names, occurrence indicators, and connectors. See also "declared content."

Contextual link (or clink)
A HyTime architectural form used to represent a hypertext link that is marked up at the location of its source linkend and points to one other location, its destination. This is the kind of hypertext link traditionally encoded in SGML using IDs and IDREFs (although many other kinds have also been used).

Coordinate
An integer position along any HyTime axis, used for referring to parts of data by counting along the axis.

Coordinate addressing
A method used by HyTime's Location address module for referring to parts of data by counting along an axis such as the list of subelements of a particular element, or a particular distance along axes of height, width, time, and so on.

Creamy hypertext
The original model of hypertext and hypermedia structure in which documents of arbitrary size can be represented, along with potentially complex internal structure and pointers between and among documents and their sub-components at all levels. Compare "chunky hypertext."

Data content notation
A representation for data, for which a name is declared in an SGML DTD. Entities can then specify that their data is in the notation, so that an SGML or HyTime processor can direct them to an appropriate processing program (whether or not that program is fully integrated with the SGML or HyTime system).

Declared content
The alternative to a content model in an element declaration; used when the element being declared cannot contain subelements but has some special, restricted kind of content (or no possible content).

Delimiter
Any of the 30-odd strings used in SGML to demarcate structural portions of a document. For example, the start-tag open delimiter has abstract name "STAGO" and its value in the "reference concrete syntax" is "<". Delimiters also exist in many other notations, including HyLex.

Delimiter-in-context
An SGML delimiter string (such as "<") that occurs in a structural context where it will be recognized (such as in content and followed by certain characters). When not recognized, an SGML delimiter is treated as literal data. For example, "<" followed by a space cannot represent start-tag open, because space is not a name-start character; therefore it is a literal less-than sign.

Descriptive markup
The principle of marking parts of document by names directly related to their purpose, significance, or function, rather than with names directly related to their formatting or other specific processing. Also known as "content," "generalized" or "generic" markup.

Dimension
A location along a given axis, normally specified as a starting point and length. Locations can instead be counted backward from the end of an axis, which requires that HyTime know the axis length as well.

Document instance
An individual SGML document.

Document tree
A direct hierarchical representation of document structure, built by a HyTime engine from an SGML document and associated entities in various data content notations for graphics, video, sound and other special data types.

Document type
A kind or class of document as defined by a particular SGML DTD. See also "document type declaration."

Document type declaration (or DTD)
A required part of an SGML document that formally specifies what elements, attributes, entities, and notations can occur in it, and where. Typically, academic, industry, or other groups with a common interest define a DTD that describes the typical structure of documents of interest, and encourage people to use that DTD to encode such document, enhancing portability and consistency.

Electronic publishing
The act of publishing documents in online form rather than on paper. This term can also refer to paper publication using computer tools at any point in the production process.

Element content
The content of an SGML element that contains no character data, but only subelements. See also “mixed content.”

Element instance
An occurrence of an element of a particular type within an SGML document instance. The element extends from its start-tag to its end-tag (even if either or both is left implicit by minimization).

Element structure information set (or ESIS)
The information that an SGML parser passes back to typical applications. This includes structural information about where elements start and end, their attributes and content, etc. However, it does not include information about what syntax was used to express the structures (such as whether a tag or attribute was implicit, or in what order attributes were specified), about the declared values of attributes, about embedded comments, etc.

Element type
A defined class for components of a document, such as `chapter`, `title`, `link`, etc. Each type must be defined in the document's DTD. Processing is usually similar for all instances of an element type, and different for instances of different element types.

EMPTY element
An SGML element whose declaration specifies that it cannot have content, any subelements or an end-tag.

End-tag
A marker indicating the end of an element instance in an SGML document.

Entity
A unit of storage declared and given a name in an SGML DTD. An entity can be a literal string or an external data object such as a file, and may be in SGML or any other notation (so long as the notation name is declared and specified). Entities can be referred to in a document instance, for instance to assemble documents out of component parts.

Entity reference
An invocation of an entity within an SGML document instance.

Event
A placement of a data object into a HyTime finite coordinate space. An event associates the data object with a "scheduled extent" that determines how it is processed in relation to other events.

Event schedule
A sequence of events placed in space and/or time.

Exclusion exception
A list of tag names in parentheses after a content model in an element declaration, prefixed by "–". This specifies elements that cannot occur *anywhere* within any instance of the element being declared or any subelements of such instances. This overrides any applicable "inclusion exceptions."

Extent
A HyTime concept (and architectural form) used to specify where in a finite coordinate space a given event occurs.

Finite coordinate space (or FCS)
A sequence of one or more axes, each having a domain consisting of a contiguous range of positive integers (such as 1 to 100). Events (data objects) are placed into an FCS by "scheduling" them, giving them positions and sizes along the axes.

Formal public identifier (or FPI)
A unique name by which users can refer to some piece of data. A format for such identifiers is defined in ISO 9070 and used by SGML and HyTime.

Fully qualified generic identifier (or FQGI)
The list of all the element types in the line of descent between the root of the document tree and some particular element. For example, a paragraph might have a FQGI of:

```
BOOK, CHAPTER, SECTION, PARA, FOOTNOTE, PARA
```

An FQGI does *not* uniquely identify an element instance, so cannot constitute a location for use in linking. However, it incorporates much of the contextual information required to process an element correctly for some purposes.

General entity
An SGML entity defined for use within a document instance, not within a DTD. Such entities are referenced via the ERO delimiter ("&"), not the PERO delimiter ("%"), which is used for "parameter entities."

Generalized markup (or generic markup)
Synonyms for descriptive markup.

Generic identifier (or GI
The formal name for an SGML element type. Commonly called the "tag name."

Granule
A unit of measurement defined for some HyTime measurement domain, such as the inch for the SImeter domain.

Hierarchical structure
The division of documents into successive layers of structure, such as chapter, sections, lists with items, multimedia objects and their portions, on down to significant phrases, frames, or other components. HyTime makes use of hierarchical structure and provides a way to overlay hypermedia links onto it, thus retaining the benefits of both organizational structure and unrestricted linking.

Hot spot
A portion of a graphical image that serves as a link to some associated information. On paper hot spots are represented by "callouts," usually containing an arrow and letter, number, or name that also appears in a caption. In electronic form the same methods may be used, or the user might simply click on the image to have the explanation appear.

Hub document
A HyTime document that can serve as the starting point for exploring and navigating through a hyperdocument. There may be any number of hub documents; they must be in SGML and use HyTime conventions, but all other data in HyTime hyperdocuments can be in any notation at all.

HyBrid element
An element of the **`HyBrid`** architectural form. This can be used for any element needing general HyTime processing (such as interpretation of common attributes), but is not a special HyTime semantic form such as a **`clink`**, **`event`**, etc. See also "non-HyTime element" and "suppress HyTime element."

Hyperlinks, Hypertext links, Hypermedia links, Links
A connection between discontiguous components in a collection of documents, typically intended to express a meaningful relationship between the connected data. Some systems restrict hyperlinks to be from or to only point locations, only to entire documents, or only to components at a single level such as paragraphs; HyTime imposes no such restrictions. See also "chunky hypertext" and "creamy hypertext."

Hypermedia
See "hypertext."

Hypertext
The practice of connecting portions of documents and other data objects together, such as by cross-references, quotations, annotations, and the like. Used especially when such connections are automated through the application of computers. This term uses "text" in the sense of "document," not in the sense of opposing letters to other media.

HyTime
ISO/IEC 10744, the international standard for hypermedia and time-based systems. HyTime defines a language for representing hypertext linking, temporal and spatial event scheduling, and synchronization, all using SGML as a representation language.

HyTime application
A DTD with elements conforming to HyTime architectural forms and that is expected to be processed by a HyTime implementation.

HyTime element
An SGML element that conforms to a HyTime architectural form (and declares that it does by virtue of a `HyTime` attribute).

HyTime engine or HyTime implementation
A program that can operate on HyTime hyperdocuments and apply some particular processing to them. For example, a program that accepts HyTime input, displays it to the user, and responds to requests for scrolling, link traversal, queries, and so on.

HyTime traversal
Particular types of hyperlink traversal that are subject to HyTime-defined rules for user accessibility. See also "traversal."

ID and IDREF
Special declared values for SGML attributes. An attribute defined as an ID takes a value that must be a unique identifier for the element instance it appears on; the value may then be used to specify links to the element. An attribute defined as an IDREF takes the IDs of other elements in the same document as values, and so may serve as a link origin.

Inclusion exception
An option in SGML element declarations used to specify elements that can occur *anywhere* within any instance of the element being declared or their direct and indirect subelements. See also "exclusion exception."

Independent link (or ilink)
A HyTime architectural form that represents a hypertext link without having to be located at any of its endpoints. See also "contextual link."

ISO
The International Organization for Standardization, which undertakes to develop and promulgate standards in a wide variety of technical areas. ISO worked with the International Electrotechnical Commission to develop HyTime.

Lexical model or Lexical type
A named syntactic description that can be used to constrain the legal values of attributes, content, search hits, or other data. Regular expressions can be lexical models, as can be HyLex or other expressions.

Lexical ordering
A specification of how to treat various characters or character strings for lexical operations such as searching, sorting, and comparing. Supported by HyTime's **`lexord`** architectural form.

Link
See "hypertext link." The word "link" can also refer to an optional feature of SGML unrelated to hypertext, but it is seldom used in that sense in this book.

Linkend
A part of a hypertext link that points to some data object or portion of one. HyTime links may have any number of linkends.

Link end term
Part of a HyTime **`ilink`**, expressed by the `endterms` attribute, that points to a specification intended to control how the link is to be shown to the user (say, by a particular icon, text style modification, etc.). An **`ilink`** may specify one end term for all its linkends or one for each.

Link process definition (or LPD)
An option of SGML, unrelated to hypertext linking.

Location ladder
A sequence of HyTime locators chained together via the `locsrc` attribute so that each serves as a point of reference from which the next one locates another place.

Locator
Any of the HyTime architectural forms whose purpose is to pick out a location within data. These are defined in the Location address module.

Marker
A numeric indicator used to pick out a certain location along some measurement axis such as used in the Location address and Scheduling modules.

Markup
Information included in a document that is not properly part of the linguistic, graphical, or other content, but instead gives information *about* the content. SGML provides a standard syntax for including certain kinds of markup in documents.

Minimal SGML document
An SGML document instance that uses no minimization or other optional SGML features and uses the default syntactic settings.

Minimization
A blanket term for SGML methods for omitting or abbreviating markup when it can be inferred from context. A document that uses minimization is by definition *not* a "minimal SGML document."

Mixed content
An SGML model group in which both subelements and PCDATA portions can co-occur. Proficient DTD writers avoid mixed content models except those that permit #PCDATA everywhere. See also "element content."

Model group
Almost synonymous in SGML with "content model," however, the reserved word ANY is considered a content model, whereas only a parenthesized expression including generic identifiers is a true "model group."

Module
A major division of the HyTime standard. Most of the modules deal with particular functional areas, such as hypertext linking; the Base module describes other HyTime features.

Multiple location
A location, typically specified by Location address module facilities, that includes several potentially discontiguous members considered as a group. See also "aggregate location" and "span location."

Name space addressing
A method of referring to data objects having unique names, such as information units that have been declared as SGML entities, or elements in a document that have IDs.

NDATA
"Notation data:" refers to SGML entities in representations or "data content notations" other than SGML. For example, graphic and multimedia objects are not typically represented in SGML, but may be referred to after identifying them and their notation in an ENTITY declaration.

Node
Any of the locations in the tree HyTime makes to represent a hyperdocument. They include SGML elements, pseudo-elements, and data entities.

Non-HyTime element
Any element in a HyTime document that lacks a HyTime architectural form attribute, and so receives no special HyTime processing. This is distinct from the **nHyTime** architectural form defined in the standard, for which see "suppress HyTime element." See also "HyBrid element."

Notation
See "data content notation."

Occurrence indicator
Any of the characters used to indicate how many times the preceding structure can be repeated. These appear in SGML content models and in HyTime lexical type specifications. Occurrence indicators include "?" when the structure is optional, "*" when zero or more instances of the structure may occur, and "+" when at least one instance must occur. See also "connector."

Ordered hierarchy of content-based objects (or OHCO)
A name for the abstract document model used by SGML and some other representations. This model views documents as nested structures of components, each of which has a specified type that specifies the significance of its content for various kinds of processing.

Parameter entity
An SGML entity defined for use within a DTD, not within a document instance. Such entities are referenced via the PERO delimiter ("%"), not the ERO delimiter ("&"), which is used for "general entities." The HyTime standard uses these to provide more compact presentations of structures it defines.

PCDATA
"Parsed character data:" the name used in SGML element declarations (prefixed by "#") to specify where within an element text content may occur. See also "CDATA" and "RCDATA."

Preorder traversal
A way of listing all the nodes in a tree so that every parent is listed before any of its children, and the children are listed in order. This is also the order in which start-tags occur in an SGML document's unparsed form.

Procedural markup
A way of marking up texts, in which portions are labeled by how they are to be processed (typically for formatting), rather than what they are (as in "descriptive markup").

Processing instruction (or PI)
A syntactic feature of SGML that permits inserting application-specific commands into a document. Processing instructions compromise portability of documents, and are not needed for HyTime except for a few special HyTime setup declarations.

Proper subelement
An SGML element that is permitted in its containing element by virtue of the content model of its containing element, rather than because of any applicable inclusion exception.

Property
A piece of information that HyTime associates with data in its trees. For example, an SGML element has attributes associated with it via the `attval` property. The **`proploc`** architectural form and the HyQ Proploc() function are used to gain access to property values, given their names.

Pseudo-element (or pelement)
A portion of an SGML document that is not properly an element, but constitutes a node in the document tree because it is a portion of character data with no internal markup. See also "PCDATA."

Qualified lexical type name (or QLTN)
The name of a defined lexical type used for validation or pattern matching in HyTime, possibly made unique by specifying the particular set of lexical types from which it comes.

Qualified property name (or QPN)
The name of a property that a HyTime engine calculates and associates with data objects, to obtain information about the context or properties of the object. A property can be "qualified" by adding the name of the property set of which it is part, a specifier for a particular instance of the property (such as a particular attribute name to pick out an instance of the `attval` property), or other information.

Quantum
A unit of measurement along any axis. HyTime provides ways of measuring along both physical axes, such as length and voltage, and conceptual axes, such as the number of words or characters in an element.

RCDATA
"Replaceable character data:" the name used in element declarations to specify that an element can contain text content and entity references, but no subelements. See also "CDATA" and "PCDATA."

Reference concrete syntax
The "least common denominator" settings for SGML. When none of the SGML delimiters strings (such as "<" for start-tag open, etc.) are changed from their normal values, and none of the default size limits are changed, a document is said to use the reference concrete syntax and the reference quantity set.

Reserved name indicator (or RNI)
A special delimiter string (normally "#") prefixed to some SGML and HyTime reserved words to distinguish them from other tokens that could also occur in the same context. For example, the `HyNames` attribute gives new names to HyTime attributes by specifying the standard and corresponding local attribute names. However, `HyNames` would specify the token #CONTENT to indicate that a given HyTime attribute's value appears as the element's content. The RNI prevents conflict should there be an attribute named `content`.

Schedule
A list of events and their locations within a finite coordinate space, for example to arrange their presentation within space and time.

Scheduled extent
The position assigned to an event within a schedule.

SDATA
"Specific character data:" a type of SGML entity most commonly used to represent special characters or other data that must be handled differently on different computer hardware, operating systems, or software applications.

SDIF
"SGML Document Interchange Format:" a standard method of collecting a DTD, a document instance, and any related SGML entities into a single bundle for transmission, for example across a wide-area network. SDIF is one way to transmit a HyTime Bounded Object Set between systems. SDIF is defined by international standard ISO 9069 (ISO 8824 "Abstract Syntax Notation 1" is a prerequisite).

Semantic addressing
A way of referring to locations in data based on particular characteristics they have, such as a HyTime property. HyTime also considers non-HyTime locator methods used via the **`notloc`** and **`bibloc`** forms to be semantic addresses.

SGML
The Standard Generalized Markup Language, ISO 8879. HyTime uses SGML to represent hypertext links and related information; both SGML and HyTime documents can include information in an unbounded range of multimedia data formats.

SGML application
An SGML DTD, along with rules and documentation for the use of that DTD for processing documents appropriately for a given purpose. See also "SGML implementation."

SGML declaration
The first major component of an SGML document. It specifies the character set for the following document, any changes to the SGML delimiters and other syntactic settings, changes to name length limits, and so on.

SGML implementation
A computer program that can read SGML documents, find the boundaries of all their parts, and process them for some useful purpose. A single SGML implementation can typically support a wide range of SGML applications.

SMDL
"Standard Music Description Language:" an ongoing project to develop a notation to represent written and performed music. The HyTime standard had its origins in SMDL.

Span location
A portion of a document that is specified not as a component of inherent hierarchical structure, but as all data between given starting and ending points. For example, the last word of one paragraph, the end-tag for the paragraph, the start-tag for the following paragraph, and the first word of that paragraph. The HyTime Location address module provides mechanisms for linking to and from such spans when needed. See also "aggregate location" and "multiple location."

Start-tag
A marker that indicates the start of an SGML document element, its type, and any attributes specific to the element instance.

Style sheet
A specification of how to process various types of objects in a document on the basis of their types. Style sheets are most commonly used to specify formatting, but the same idea is used in other kinds of processing such as information retrieval, sorting, searching, linking and navigation.

SUBDOC
A kind of SGML entity that represents an entire SGML document when it must be embedded in the midst of another SGML document (possibly with a different DTD).

Subelement
An element directly contained within another element (see clause 4.309 of the SGML standard). Outside of the SGML and HyTime standards themselves, the term also refers to indirectly contained elements (such as a paragraph that is directly inside a section but only indirectly inside a chapter).

Suppress HyTime element
An element in a HyTime document within which HyTime processing is suppressed for all direct and indirect subelements. The "nHyTime" element type defined in the standard, being renamed "sHyTime," has this effect. See also "HyBrid element" and "non-HyTime element."

Tag
A marker for the start or end of an SGML element. See also "start-tag" and "end-tag."

Text Encoding Initiative (or TEI)

The Text Encoding Initiative is a major international effort that has established guidelines for the encoding and interchange of electronic texts. It includes representatives from many learned societies in the humanities and social sciences and the resulting DTDs and methods have been applied to a wide variety of major text collections.

Traversal

The user's act of following a hyperlink from one of its anchors to another. The HyTime standard defines certain particular kinds of traversal as HyTime traversals, but implementations are permitted to support other kinds of navigation as well.

Validation

The process of checking an SGML or HyTime document so that all formal errors are reported.

Web

A collection of hyperlinks, typically having some common purpose or application.

Wildcard

A reserved character or string used in a pattern matching language (such as HyLex) to match anything at all at a certain point in the pattern.

Index

SPRINGER NATURE

GPSR Compliance

The European Union's (EU) General Product Safety Regulation (GPSR) is a set of rules that requires consumer products to be safe and our obligations to ensure this.

If you have any concerns about our products, you can contact us on ProductSafety@springernature.com

In case Publisher is established outside the EU, the EU authorized representative is:

Springer Nature Customer Service Center GmbH
Europaplatz 3
69115 Heidelberg, Germany

FSC
www.fsc.org
MIX
Papier | Fördert
gute Waldnutzung
FSC® C083411

Kolibri 360 GmbH
Ferdinand-Jühlke-Straße 7
99095 Erfurt, Deutschland
produktsicherheit@kolibri360.de